CLAUS WESTERMANN

ISAIAH 40–66

THE OLD TESTAMENT LIBRARY

CLAUS WESTERMANN

ISAIAH 40-66

A Commentary

The Westminster Press

Philadelphia

© SCM Press Ltd 1969
Translated by David M. G. Stalker from the German
Das Buch Jesaia, 40–66
(Das Alte Testament Deutsch 19)
first edition 1966
published by Vandenhoeck & Ruprecht,
Göttingen

Standard Book No. 664-20851-7

Library of Congress Catalog Card No. 69-18647

Published by The Westminster Press®
Philadelphia, Pennsylvania

PRINTED IN THE UNITED STATES OF AMERICA

Dedicated to Professor D. Gerhard von Rad, DD
my honoured teacher and colleague
on his sixty-fifth birthday
with gratefulness and admiration

CONTENTS

viii CONTENTS

PART TWO

TRITO-ISAIAH
Chapters 56–66

ABBREVIATIONS

ANET	J. B. Pritchard, *Ancient Near Eastern Texts*, 2nd ed., 1955
AO	*Archiv für Orientforschung*
BH	*Biblia Hebraica*, ed. Rudolf Kittel, 3rd ed., 1952
Bibl	*Biblica*
Bibl Stud	*Biblische Studien*
BJRL	*Bulletin of the John Rylands Library*
BWANT	Beiträge zur Wissenschaft vom Alten und Neuen Testament
BZ	*Biblische Zeitschrift*
BZAW	Beihefte zur *Zeitschrift für die alttestamentliche Wissenschaft*
CBQ	*Catholic Biblical Quarterly*
EKL	*Evangelisches Kirchenlexikon. Kirchlichtheologisches Handwörterbuch*, 1955–
EvTh	*Evangelische Theologie*
HAT	Handbuch zum Alten Testament, ed., O. Eissfeldt
HUCA	*Hebrew Union College Annual*
IB	*Interpreter's Bible*
JAOS	*Journal of the American Oriental Society*
JBL	*Journal of Biblical Literature*
JNES	*Journal of Near Eastern Studies*
JPOS	*Journal of the Palestine Oriental Society*
JSS	*Journal of Semitic Studies*
KuD	*Kerygma and Dogma*, 1955–
LXX	Greek translation of the Old Testament (Septuagint)
MT	Massoretic text
RGG	*Die Religion in Geschichte und Gegenwart*
RSV	The Revised Standard Version of the Bible
SBT	Studies in Biblical Theology
TB	*Theologische Bücherei*

ThR	*Theologische Rundschau*
TLZ	*Theologische Literaturzeitung*
TSK	*Theologische Studien und Kritiken*
TWNT	*Theologisches Wörterbuch zum Neuen Testament*
V	Latin translation of the Bible by Jerome (Vulgate)
VT	*Vetus Testamentum*
ZAW	*Zeitschrift für die alttestamentliche Wissenschaft*
ZDPV	*Zeitschrift des Deutschen Palästinavereins*

BIBLIOGRAPHY

COMMENTARIES

BENTZEN, A., *Jesaja fortolket, Bind II, Jes. 40–66*, Copenhagen, 1943.
BUDDE, K., *Das Buch Jesaja, Kap. 40–66* (Kautzsch), Tübingen, 1922.
CASPARI, W., *Lieder und Gottessprüche der Rückwanderer (Jes. 40–55)*, BZAW, 65, 1934.
DUHM, B., *Das Buch Jesaja*, Göttingen, 1892, 4th ed. 1922.
FELDMANN, F., *Das Buch Isaias*, Münster, 1925/26.
HALLER, M., *Deuterojesaja*, Göttingen, 1925.
KISSANE, E. J., *The Book of Isaiah*, Dublin, 1943.
GLAHN, L., und KÖHLER, L., *Der Prophet der Heimkehr*, Giessen, 1934.
KÖNIG, E., *Das Buch Jesaja*, Gütersloh, 1926.
MUILENBURG, J., 'The Book of Isaiah, Ch. 40–66', *IB*, V, New York, 1956, pp. 381–773.
NORTH, C. R., *The Second Isaiah*, Oxford, 1964.
SKINNER, J., *The Book of the Prophet Isaiah*, Cambridge, 1915.
SMART, J. D., *History and Theology in Second Isaiah, A Commentary on Isaiah 35; 40–66*, Philadelphia, n.d.
TORREY, C. C. , *The Second Isaiah*, New York, 1922.
VOLZ, P., *Jesaja II*, Leipzig, 1932.
ZIEGLER, J., *Isaias*, Regensburg, 1948.

SURVEYS

FOHRER, G., 'Neuere Literatur zur alttestamentlichen Prophetie', *ThR*, 1951, 1952, 1962.
MOWINCKEL, S., 'Neuere Forschungen zu Deuterojesaja', *AO*, XVI, Leiden, 1938, pp. 1–40.
NORTH, C. R., 'The Interpretation of Deutero-Isaiah', *Festschrift for Mowinckel*, Oslo, 1955, pp. 133–45.
WESTERMANN, C., 'Sprache und Struktur der Prophetie Deuterojesajas', *Forschung am Alten Testament, TB*, Munich, 1964, Erster Teil: Der Stand der Diskussion, pp. 92–117.

OTHER WORKS

BEGRICH, J., *Studien zu Deuterojesaja*, 1938, new impression, *TB*, 20, Munich, 1963.

BLANK, S. H., 'Studies in Deutero-Isaiah', *HUCA*, 15, 1940, pp. 1–46.

BOER, P. A. H. DE, *Second Isaiah's Message*, Leiden, 1956.

ELLIGER, K., *Deuterojesaja in seinem Verhältnis zu Tritojesaja*, BWANT, IV, 11, 1933.

GRESSMANN, H., 'Die literarische Analyse Deuterojesajas', *ZAW*, 34, 1914, pp. 254–97.

KÖHLER, L., *Deuterojesaja, stilkritisch untersucht*, Giessen, 1923.

MOWINCKEL, S., 'Die Komposition des deuterojesajanischen Buches', *ZAW*, 49, 1931, pp. 87–112; 242–60.

NORTH, C. R., 'The "Former Things" and the "New Things" in Deutero-Isaiah', *Studies in Old Testament Prophecy*, Edinburgh, 1950, pp. 111–26.

PORTEOUS, N. W., 'Jerusalem-Zion, The Growth of a Symbol', *Festschrift for W. Rudolph*, Tübingen, 1961, pp. 235–52.

RAD, G. VON, *Old Testament Theology*, II, Edinburgh 1965, pp. 238–62, Deutero-Isaiah.

RIGNELL, L., *A Study of Isaiah, Ch. 40–55*, Lund, 1956.

ROBERTS, B. J., 'The Second Isaiah Scroll from Qumran', *BJRL*, 42, 1959, pp. 132–44.

SCHARBERT, J., *Heilsmittler in Alten Testament*. Freiburg, 1964. pp. 178–212, Mittler in Is. 40–66.

SMITH, S., *Isaiah, Ch. XL–LV, Literary Criticism and History*, Schweich Lectures, London, 1944.

STEINMANN, J., *Le livre de la consolation d'Israel*, Paris, 1960.

WALDOW, H. C. VON, 'Anlass und Hintergrund der Verkündigung des Deuterojesaja', Dissertation, Bonn, 1955.

WESTERMANN, C., 'Sprache und Struktur der Prophetie Deuterojesajas', *Forschung am Alten Testament*, *TB*, 24, Munich, 1964, pp. 92–170.

SURVEYS ON THE SERVANT SONGS

HAAG, H., 'Ebed-Jahwe-Forschung 1948–58', *BZ*, 1959, pp. 174–204.

MOWINCKEL, S., *He that Cometh*, Oxford, 1959, pp. 187–260.

NORTH, C. R., *The Suffering Servant in Deutero-Isaiah*, 2nd. ed., Oxford, 1956.

ROWLEY, H. H., *The Servant of the Lord and other Essays on the Old Testament*, London, 1952.
Also the survey given by O. EISSFELDT (see his *The Old Testament, an Introduction*, Oxford, 1965) and G. Fohrer (see above.)

BIBLIOGRAPHY ON TRITO-ISAIAH

ABRAMOWSKI, R., 'Zum literarischen Problem von Jes. 56–66', *TSK*, 96/97, 1925, pp. 90–143.
ELLIGER, K., *Die Einheit Tritojesajas*, BWANT, 45, Stuttgart, 1928.
'Der Prophet Tritojesaja', *ZAW*, n.s. 8, 1931, pp. 112–40.
GLAHN, L. and KÖHLER, L., *Der Prophet der Heimkehr (Jesaja 40–66)*, Giessen, 1934.
KESSLER, W., 'Studie zur religiosen Situation im ersten nachexilischen Jahrhundert und zur Auslegung von Jesaja 56–66', *Wissenschaftliche Zeitschrift der Martin Luther-Universitat Halle-Wittenberg*, 1956/57, 1, pp. 41–74.
'Zur Auslegung von Jes. 56–66', *TLZ*, 1956, cols. 335–8.
ODEBERG, H., *Trito-Isaiah (56–66)*, Uppsala, 1931.
ZIMMERLI, W. ,'Zur Sprache Tritojesajas', Schw. Th. Umschau 3/4, 1950, pp. 1–13.

PART ONE

DEUTERO-ISAIAH

Chapters 40–55

INTRODUCTION

THE PERIOD

THE TIME OF Deutero-Isaiah's activity lay for certain between the destruction of Jerusalem in 587 and the downfall of the Babylonian empire in 539. All the evidence points to a date towards the end of this period, probably some time after 550, the year which saw the beginning of the victorious campaign of Cyrus. An attempt has been made to mark off different stages in the prophet's work (Begrich), but this remains very doubtful. The content of chs. 40–55, does, however, show that Deutero-Isaiah was active for some considerable length of time, perhaps several years. The general outline of the political events of the period is known.[a]

1. The Babylonian empire remained at the height of its power under Nebuchadnezzar (604–562), the greatest ruler it ever had. After destroying Jerusalem, he undertook a further series of campaigns in the west. In 585 he began the siege of Tyre, but, in spite of a thirteen years' investment of the city, failed to take it. According to Jer. 52.30, he made a further campaign against Judah, leading to yet another deportation; this, however, is all we know of it. In 586 he marched against Egypt.

Nebuchadnezzar's death was followed by the first signs of the decline of Babylon. Within the seven years leading up to the accession of Nabonidus, the last king of Babylon (556–539), there were three changes in the throne; Nabonidus, who was of priestly descent, was particularly devoted to the moon-god Sin, and restored her temple in Haran, thereby antagonizing the powerful priesthood of Marduk in Babylon, a factor which played no small part in the fall of Babylon. Nabonidus made Tema, in the Arabian desert, his new capital,

[a] For what follows, cf. the history of Israel as given in the works of Martin Noth and John Bright, the articles on the history of Israel and on Babylonian and Persian history in *RGG* and *EKL* and the literature given there. The most thorough treatment of this period of history is contained in Sidney Smith, *Isaiah Ch. XL–LV*, Schweich Lectures, British Academy, 1944, Part II, History of the years 556–539.

remaining there for eight years, during which he left the government in Babylon in the hands of his son Sheshbazzar.

2. By now the kingdom of Media had become Babylon's chief rival. Cyaxares of Media had been her ally in the overthrow of Assyria. Thereafter he enlarged the scope of his sway, and made Ecbatana his capital. In the west his kingdom extended as far as the Halys, the frontier of Lydia. His successor was his son Astyages (585–550), whose vassal Cyrus, king of Anshan in southern Iran (formerly Elam), rose against him. In this, Cyrus had the support of Nabonidus, who hoped that the power of Media would thereby be diminished. However, by 550 Cyrus had captured Ecbatana and made himself master of the kingdom. At this point the Lydian king Croesus, feeling that he himself was now in danger, took the field against Cyrus, but there was no decisive engagement. Once Croesus disbanded his forces, Cyrus made forced marches during the winter on Sardis, and the city fell in 546. (Deutero-Isaiah appears to allude to this in 41.2–3 and 45.1–3.) Some time before this, Babylon had entered into a defensive pact with Egypt and Lydia, but after the latter's fall, she found that she herself was face to face with the menace of Cyrus, who, in the three years following 546, still further extended the limits of his territory, although the details are not known. This at last brought Nabonidus back to Babylon. But it was too late. The forces arrayed against him there, in his own country, in particular the priesthood of Marduk, were too strong, and put any marshalling of the empire's total resources out of the question. Not a few of the Babylonians actually hailed the coming of Cyrus, for they looked on him as their liberator (the Cyrus cylinder). The northern parts of the empire broke away. One of Nabonidus' generals, Gobryas (Gubaru), deserted to Cyrus and, appearing at the Tigris, inflicted a crushing defeat on his fellow-countrymen at Opis. Nabonidus fled to Borsippa. Led by Gobryas, Cyrus' troops entered the city of Babylon without striking a blow (539). The mighty world-empire had fallen, as Deutero-Isaiah (particularly Isa. 47) and other prophets (particularly Jer. 50–51) had proclaimed it would. Babylon's entire empire came under the sovereignty of Cyrus.

Surveying the course of world-history from the height of the Babylonian empire's power down to the time when the swift rise to greatness of the Persian empire in turn spelt its downfall, one can only stand back in amazement at the closeness with which Deutero-Isaiah's utterances on the subject are answered by the mighty sweep of events themselves, with their strongly marked rhythm of rise and fall. The very fact that the prophet neither expected nor proclaimed that his own people had any active role to play in the events allowed him to discern God's hand in history on the grandiose scale that matched the events of his day:

> Behold, nations are like a drop in the bucket . . .
> Who brings the princes to naught . . .
> Scarcely are they planted, scarcely sown . . .
> Then he blows upon them, and they wither,
> The tempest carries them off like stubble.

3. Israel during the exile. While the large-scale world events of Deutero-Isaiah's time are well-known and attested, our knowledge of Judah during the period of the exile, and of the fortunes of those taken to Babylon, is both scanty and uncertain. Among the uncertainties are the numbers of those deported in 597, 587 and 582. Jer. 52.28–30 puts the sum-total at 4,600: we do not, however, know whether this includes women and children. If it does not, the figure comes to between 12,000 and 15,000. We do know that a considerable part of the population was not, in fact, deported; and this also implies the persistence of no small measure of intellectual and religious life. Our main source of information here is the collection called 'Lamentations', which originated in Judah after the fall of Jerusalem. Probably the Deuteronomic histories, too, originated in the homeland during the exile. Even prophecy did not completely cease in Judah with the exile; witness, among other evidence, the oracles against Babylon collected in Jer. 50–51, which in all likelihood were composed there at the same time as Deutero-Isaiah, and which display some striking parallels to him.

Nevertheless, the most important written evidence of continuance of Israel's traditions after the fall of Jerusalem came into being outside Judah, among the exiles in Babylon: it consists in the prophecies of Ezekiel and Deutero-Isaiah. Those taken to Babylon were the leading sections of the community. As we know, even after the first deportation in 597 it was possible for the Israelites to build houses, engage in farming and other means of livelihood, and continue to live in families (Jer. 29.5f.), while notices in the Book of Ezekiel leave no doubt that they were settled in communties of their own, and could therefore continue to enjoy some measure of communal life (Ezek. 3.15; 8.1; 14.1; 33.30f.). This also implies the possibility of coming together for worship. Thus, the national traditions of worship were not completely broken off even among the exiles. Neither in Ezekiel nor in Deutero-Isaiah is there the slightest evidence that they were forced to worship the gods of Babylon. Rather—as has been made clear, particularly by von Waldow in his *Anlass und Hintergrund der Verkündigung Deuterojesajas*—the very close affinities between the preaching of Deutero-Isaiah and the communal lamentation as made in public worship prove in themselves that worship persisted in one form or another. Since there could be no sacrifices, the main emphasis was necessarily put on the oral element in worship: we have every reason for believing that one, at least, of the roots of the synagogue service is to be found in the exile. At the same time, however, several of Deutero-Isaiah's utterances suggest, as was only to be expected, that the downfall of the state, the destruction of the temple, and the end of the Davidic dynasty also meant, in many people's eyes, the end of Yahweh's action on behalf of his people. Victory had gone to the gods of Babylon, and the pomp of the worship offered to them must have made a tremendous impression. For many, therefore, the old faith lost its fervour, and not a few turned to the gods who now had the mastery.

This situation finds its echo in Deutero-Isaiah, in a special feature of his diction. His language is from first to last evocative, arousing, even insistent—witness the way in which he piles imperative on imperative. This accords well with the situation just outlined. It was the way he adopted to speak to men whose faith was flagging, and who were at the point of letting themselves drift. At the same time, he used it to address men who kept clinging to the past, even when their observance of traditional usage had no power to lead them to expect any new thing from their God.

THE PROPHET HIMSELF

We know practically nothing about Deutero-Isaiah himself, not even his name. Only once, and even then only for a moment, does he let himself be seen. This is in the prologue, in 40.6–7, which gives his call. The prophet hears a voice summoning him to preach, and counters it with the question 'What shall I cry?', lamenting, as his reason for asking it, that all things are transient: 'All flesh is grass.' Although the answer he receives begins by endorsing his plaintive description of the situation, it nevertheless goes on to add, 'but the word of our God stands for ever'. No intimation of a call could be briefer: yet it does supply us with some reliable information about the prophet.

1. Deutero-Isaiah regarded himself as the lineal descendant of the pre-exilic prophets. This is shown, first, by the fact that, in substantiation of his message he adduces a call, and, second, that like Isaiah and Jeremiah, his first reaction is to shrink from it. The thesis just stated is frequently confirmed throughout the book, particularly in 43.22–28, where the way in which Deutero-Isaiah ranks himself alongside the pre-exilic prophets of doom is left in no doubt whatsoever.

2. Deutero-Isaiah completely identified himself with his fellow-countrymen. For when he demurred at the summons to preach, his reluctance was not the expression of his own personal lament, but of that of his fellow-exiles (as the gloss, 'surely the people is grass', rightly understood it). He was at one with them in believing that the downfall of the nation was the result of divine judgment ('for the breath of Yahweh blows upon it'), and that all that remained for the survivors was to acknowledge the justice of the sentence, the line also taken by the psalms of lamentation composed during the period. Deutero-Isaiah's insistence on his solidarity with his people is supremely important for our understanding of him. One of its implications is that he had not been made a prophet because he had some clearer insight into the existing situation than they, or because he kept hoping and trusting that this situation would change, or because of the strength of his faith. The thoughts of his fellow-exiles were his thoughts, too, and he had been every bit as flagging and weary as they. It was a word from outside himself, a command, that made him a prophet, as it had done his predecessors. This was the source of all that he was to say, as well as its substantiation. It was 'the word of our God', and it alone, as God guaranteed, would not become void (Isa. 55.6–11). Since God still spoke it, Deutero-Isaiah was able to preach.

3. This is why Deutero-Isaiah's preaching is throughout simply the putting forth of this word that was now being spoken. It is also the reason for his complete concealment of himself in its shadow. It was essential that there should be a spokesman for the new word which God was now speaking. But he is merely the voice. And the word itself has one theme: 'Cry to her that her time of service is ended' (40.2). This is the one motif on which all the forms used by Deutero-Isaiah

turn; hence the situation to which he addressed himself was also uniform and unchanging. No special occasions were required to move him to speech, nor had he any need, like the pre-exilic prophets, to adopt special modes of address for different sets of people or for representatives of different interests. Deutero-Isaiah's whole proclamation is summed up in its opening and closing statements (40.8 and 56.6–11), concerning the word of God.

4. The cry, 'the grass withers, the flower fades', in 40.7 is taken from the Psalter (e.g., Ps. 90). A leading characteristic of Deutero-Isaiah's prophecy lies in its affinities with the diction of this book. The prophet's familiarity with the psalms must have been quite exceptional. It is, of course, true that they played a leading part in the exiles' services of worship, and that everyone, therefore, who joined in these might have been as well versed as he. Remarkably enough, however, there is absolutely no trace of this in Ezekiel; instead, what runs through his proclamation is a wide range of forms taken from the usage of the priesthood (Zimmerli). Perhaps, then, Deutero-Isaiah was in some way connected with the temple singers, who were the people principally in charge of the Psalter and its transmission. If so, his writing would yield excellent support to the contention that the *Sitz im Leben* of the Psalms was not the isolation of a cultic milieu, but rather the heart of the chosen people's life whence it radiated into every area. Since Deutero-Isaiah's gospel embraced the whole of his people's life, only on such conditions could he clothe it so largely in the diction of the Psalter.

Leaving aside for the moment the interpretation of the servant songs, apart from 40.6ff. there is absolutely nothing in the nature of a direct allusion to the prophet, and no further information about him. If we wish to know more about him, we must listen to his message.

THE MESSAGE OF DEUTERO-ISAIAH

It is here assumed that chs. 40–55 of the book of Isaiah are independent of the rest of it, and represent the prophecy of someone who lived during the exile in Babylon, and worked among the exiles there. That he and the prophet Isaiah, the author of chs. 1–39, whose date is in the eighth century, are two quite different people, no longer needs proof. The first person to differentiate between them was Döderlein, in 1775; his thesis was accepted by Eichhorn (1780–83);

and since then, it has steadily won its way to universal recognition in Old Testament scholarship.

In his commentary on Isaiah (1892), Duhm suggested that Deutero-Isaiah's own proclamation ended with ch. 55, and that chs. 56–66 belonged to the post-exilic period. He also separated out the so-called servant songs (42.1-4; 49.1-6; 50.4-9; 52.13-53.12). To the author of chs. 56-66 he gave the name of Trito-Isaiah. Duhm's thesis in regard to these last chapters has also been largely accepted, although considerable difference of opinion still remains as to their relationship with chs. 40–55, and in particular, as to their own unity and proper order.

I have stated the reasons for my own view of the origin and composition of the Book of Deutero-Isaiah in my article 'Sprache und Struktur der Prophetie Deuterojesajas', *TB*, 24 (1964), pp. 92–170,[a] the first part of which gives a survey of criticism up to that date, as far as it concerns the structure and composition of Isa. 40–55.

The unique feature of the prophecy of Deutero-Isaiah is this, the hour summoned him to the task of proclaiming salvation, and nothing but salvation, to his people; at the same time, however, he wears the mantle of the pre-exilic prophets of doom. He is a prophet of salvation standing in the ranks of the prophets of doom. The explanation is quite simple. The fall of Jerusalem meant that the judgment predicted by the eighth- and seventh-century prophets had been fulfilled. Any possibility, therefore, of prophecy's continuing now depended on its being prophecy of salvation. Another instance of the same change of front within the ranks of the prophets of doom is to be found in Ezekiel. Up to the fall of Jerusalem, his sole theme was the impending judgment. But once the city actually fell, he turned into a prophet of salvation.

This characteristic mark of Deutero-Isaiah's prophecy draws attention to a basic feature of Israelite prophecy in general. Prophecy is not merely foretelling the future. The prophets of doom in their day were commissioned to speak God's word of judgment to a particular situation for which this was *the* word of God. In just the same way, Deutero-Isaiah in his day had to speak the word appropriate to a different situation. It is quite impossible to dissociate the prophetic word from the time at which it was uttered. Although the God whose words the prophets proclaimed to his chosen people remained the

[a] Henceforth cited as 'Sprache und Struktur'.

same, this was not always so of his words. Thus, God's word can never be of the nature of general teaching—perennially valid without reference to its original context. It is a living word, changing with the changing years.

What means did the prophet use to proclaim this exceptional message of salvation which he was commissioned to deliver? The first thing to be realized is that he made a very restricted selection from the various available modes of expression and forms of specifically prophetic diction. Not only is there no prophetic proclamation of judgment—this formed no part of his task; there is also a complete absence of accounts of specific events. Absent, too, are words addressed to individuals, to particular sets of people, and to officials (in the exile these last no longer existed). Nor are there accounts of visions or anything else touching the prophet himself. Yet, although we find practically nothing but the one narrow field of oracles of salvation, the number of variations which he devised on this one theme allotted to him, is little short of amazing. Central to his message is the oracle of salvation, or the promise of this, with its cry, 'Fear not', which forms the basis of the divine promise of grace given in answer to an individual's lament. We also find the proclamation of salvation: this runs through the whole of the prophecy, and is sometimes found in association with the promise of salvation, though it may also stand alone. In addition, from time to time, Deutero-Isaiah clothed his message of salvation in the language of the psalms of praise. Again, the oracle concerning Cyrus, which is the pivot on which all that is said in the book turns, is integrally related to the message of salvation. The disputations with Israel and the trial speeches against her are also, if less directly, words of salvation, for they join issue with the mental attitude of weariness or despair that set itself against the message of salvation. The relationship of the sentence passed on the gods of the foreign nations to the message of salvation is this: there Yahweh is shown to be the one and only God who, in spite of the disaster of 586, continues to have dealings with his chosen people. The oracle against Babylon in ch. 47 (and also in 46.1f., the tidings of the fall of the gods of Babylon because of the victory of Cyrus), as well as the hymns of praise which run right through the book and the commands to exult at Israel's redemption as a thing already accomplished—these, too, are all indirect proclamations of salvation.

Up to ch. 45 (the Cyrus oracle) these direct or indirect proclamations of salvation are generally found in pure form: thereafter they usually occur in poems of some considerable length in which several different forms are combined.

The variety of forms which Deutero-Isaiah used to express the gospel of salvation makes him unique in the Old Testament. Neither before nor after him did anyone devise so many different ways of expressing it.

1. The most characteristic form of Deutero-Isaiah's words of salvation is the promise, or oracle, of salvation.[a]

The word of salvation receives its peculiar stamp from its origin in the cult. As Begrich was the first to show, here Deutero-Isaiah starts from the priestly oracle of salvation, the answer communicated by the priest to an individual lament, as we see it in I Sam. 1. It is introduced by the call 'Do not fear' (so Lam. 3.57), and the promise of salvation is substantiated by means of a clause with the verb in the perfect tense (and/or a noun clause). Strictly, the answer is the promise that a prayer is to be granted: the priest thereby promises that God has hearkened to the supplication. It rests on the assumption that God has already decided how he means to act: this is why it is couched in the perfect tense. As long as the exile lasted, there could be no oracles of salvation. Deutero-Isaiah, however, detached the form from its original cultic setting, and changed it into a promise of salvation decided upon by God for the nation.

To Deutero-Isaiah's appropriation of the oracle of salvation are due three basic characteristics of his preaching. His differs from all other Old Testament preaching of salvation in that its essence is the proclamation of an event regarded as having already come about; Deutero-Isaiah proclaimed that the great change from judgment to salvation was already accomplished fact. This holds true beyond the passages whose literary form shows them to be promises of salvation. The prologue itself starts with this accomplished fact, 'Cry to her that her time of service is ended, that her iniquity is pardoned.' The same standpoint is also taken in the psalms of praise. Their structure, a simple one, is a summons, in the imperative mood, to give praise or to exult, substantiated by a past tense: 'For the Lord has redeemed Israel . . .' (44.23). The reason for the exultation for which these hymns appeal is that something has already been brought about.

[a] It stands alone in 41.8–13, 14–16; 43.1–4, 5–7; 44.1–5 and is frequently combined with other forms. There are also echoes of it in other oracles. Cf. 'Sprache und Struktur', pp. 117–20, and, at greater length, 'Das Heilswort bei Deuterojesaja', *EvTh*, 7 (1964), pp. 355–73.

The hymns just mentioned also reveal the second leading characteristic of Deutero-Isaiah's gospel, joy. His gospel spontaneously evokes
joy. The moment the exiles arrive back home, Zion-Jerusalem
becomes a herald of joy (40.9; 52.8); from then on, page after page,
there are commands to exult and rejoice. They reach out far beyond
the little band directly affected by the saving event (41.16; 51.11;
52.9; 54.1; 55.1), for they are addressed to the inhabitants round
about (42.11f.), to the ends of the earth (42.10), to the sea and the
islands, the desert and its inhabitants (42.10f.), to the wild beasts of
the desert (43.20), to heaven and earth, mountains and trees (44.23;
49.13; 55.12). But there is more to it than expressing commands to
rejoice: since by its very nature Deutero-Isaiah's message was bound
to evoke joy as its inevitable response, it is itself everywhere irradiated
with joy.

The way in which this second basic characteristic of Deutero-
Isaiah's preaching follows from the first may be illustrated by the
story of Hannah in I Sam. 1. Verse 10 runs, 'She was deeply distressed
and prayed to the Lord, and wept bitterly.' Immediately, however,
she received the assurance that her prayer was granted, 'then the
woman went her way and ate, and her countenance was no longer
sad' (v. 18). God heard her supplication, and this turned her mourning into joy. A simple proclamation of salvation produces expectancy,
it cheers and makes the spirit new; it does not, however, awaken the
joy that there and then finds expression in exultation. Hebrew has no
word for the anticipation of joy; there is no verb in the 'being joyous'
category with which to render our concept of 'looking forward to
something'. 'Rejoicing' (in both verb and noun forms) always
denotes reaction to something that has already taken place. Thus, the
second characteristic of Deutero-Isaiah's preaching, the distinctive
note of joy, stems from the element of what has already been accomplished, inherent in the assurance of salvation. (This is paralleled in
the saving message of the New Testament: it, too, is rooted in a past
event. This is why it evokes joy in those who accept it, as is seen in
Luke or the Epistle to the Philippians: 'Behold, I bring you good
news of great joy . . . to you is born this day the Saviour.')

A third distinctive note owes its origin to the fact that Deutero-
Isaiah's assurance of salvation is based on an oracle of salvation
addressed to an individual. This is what makes possible the amazingly
personal language which he uses in his gospel. Throughout, the
dominant note is of personal address. This is struck right at the very

beginning: 'Comfort, comfort my people.' Never before had a prophet addressed Israel in such terms. Here, at the very start, the words which serve to summarize the prophet's whole proclamation are taken from the personal sphere. Deutero-Isaiah's message is certainly always addressed to the nation taken all together; nevertheless, the personal stamp of address to individuals is so marked as to leave its impress on every page. By their very nature as answers to individual laments, assurances of salvation employ the diction customary here. The address, 'You worm Jacob' (41.14), goes back to the words of an individual lament, 'But I am a worm, and no man' (Ps. 22.7[6]); the command, 'Do not fear', was originally made to an individual, as were also the phrases 'I am with you', 'I am your God', 'I have called you by name', etc. This same context is also responsible for the personifications so frequent in Deutero-Isaiah, and for Israel's being addressed as God's creature (43.1). A whole series of other passages containing this personal element will be indicated in the commentary. The audience addressed by the prophet is the entire nation taken as a unit; nevertheless, the word of God given him to proclaim is meant to affect every individual member at the most personal and existential level.

2. As well as the assurance of salvation, Deutero-Isaiah also employs the usual proclamation of salvation found in prophecy of salvation. One difference between the two is that the latter speaks of events which still lie in the future. Although the proclamation may be combined with the assurance (as, for example, in 41.8–13; vv. 11f.), it stands by itself alone in 41.17–20; 42.14–17; 43.16–21; 49.7–12. A further distinction is that the proclamation is connected not with the individual lament, but with that of the community. It generally begins by citing (41.17) or alluding to (42.14) words of a lament. Further, whereas the assurance, tied as it is to the individual lament, makes its promise in general and, for the most part, very personal terms, the proclamation, tied in turn to the community lament, speaks concretely—of the exiles' liberation, of the return, of the journey through the wilderness, and of the transformation of this into a garden. Again, as well as in the passages mentioned above, the proclamation is often found in the poems which follow on ch. 45, variously combined with other forms. In the three poems comprising 46.1–13, 48.1–11 and 12–17, a cluster set round the glad tidings of the fall of the gods of Babylon (46.1f.) and the oracle concerning Babylon (ch. 47), what was said to the nations in the trial speeches and

the Cyrus oracle is converted into a word to Israel: all this has been done for your sake. The substantiation of this proclamation of salvation is the act which God is accomplishing by means of Cyrus (46.11; 48.7; 48.14).

The proclamation may also be combined with a disputation. In 49.14–26 Zion's lament is called in question, and countered by the proclamation of the rebuilding of the city (vv. 16f.), the return of the exiles (18, 21ff.), the extension of her territory (v. 19), and the breaking of the power of those who held Israel captive. In 51.9–52.3 a proclamation is combined with a community lament. And to take a final example, it plays quite a large role in chs. 54–55. Here, however, the emphasis is no longer upon the act of liberation itself, but upon the new state of salvation which results from it—this is the reason why here (and only here) what is proclaimed is a new covenant, described in 54.9 as the covenant with Noah and in 55.3b–5 as the covenant with David. This is followed by a series of further proclamations concerning the age of salvation. The chapters end with the simple proclamation of the departure from Babylon and the journey home (55.12f.).

3. One of the reasons for the note of exultation that rings through Deutero-Isaiah's preaching is the fact that he dresses his gospel in the language used in praise of God. An excellent example of this is 40.12–31, its diction and poetic rapture being exceptionally fine. In the descriptive psalms of praise (hymns), God is extolled for his majesty and goodness. In ch. 40, praise of the divine majesty is the theme of the first three sections (vv. 12–17, 18–24, 25f.), and they contrast God's glory with the poverty of Israel's faith; the fourth section (vv. 27–31) comforts the nation in its despair by extolling the goodness of God who 'gives power to the faint'.

The category of the praise of God also includes the titles used by God to describe himself, particularly the self-predications found in the trial speeches and the Cyrus oracle (41.4; 43.10–13, 15; 44.6, 8; 44.24–28; 45.3b, 5; 45.12; 45.18f., 21ff.; 46.4, 9ff.; 48.12f., 15); these contain the praises of the creator and lord of history in the guise of self-predications. What Deutero-Isaiah is seeking to do by this means is, in the time of his people's deep affliction, to make them recapture the vision of God as great and majestic; for only such a God can be imagined powerful enough to bring about the new miraculous deliverance. This is particularly apparent in the introduction to the Cyrus oracle (44.24–28), where the series of appositions begins with 'your Redeemer' (v. 24a), and then proceeds to extol this redeemer as also the creator (v. 24) and the lord of history (v. 25); as such he can establish the truth of the prophecies of old (v. 26a) and rebuild the ruins of Jerusalem (v. 26b). This resuscitation of the praises of God and their fusion with the proclamation of salvation is particularly characteristic of Deutero-Isaiah.

4. Deutero-Isaiah's preaching also includes polemic, which, while conscripted in the service of the message of salvation, is nevertheless thoroughly aggressive. The objects of its attack are two, the foreign nations and their gods, and the prophet's own nation. In the trial speeches (41.1–5, 21–29; 43.8–15; 44.6ff.; 45.20–25 and [?] 45.11ff.) Yahweh and the gods of the nations confront one another in a legal process, the purpose of which is to decide who is truly God. The prophet's adoption of this particular form is due to the actual situation of the exiles. Since Israel had ceased to be an independent state, her God could not now prove his superiority to the gods of Babylon by means of victory over her foes. So Deutero-Isaiah shifts the arena of decision from the battlefield to the law court. This was a complete innovation on the prophet's part and it represents the first move in human history towards the dissolution of the link between 'religion' and politics. It does not, however, in any way imply a severance of the link between God's action and history; it only means that the hitherto accepted proof of a god's divinity, his power to win military victory for his own people, was replaced by another, the dependable and unremitting continuity between what a god says and what he does. The argument that decides the issue in the legal contest between Yahweh and the gods is this: the statement made about the word of God for Israel's consolation, that it does not return to him void (55.6–11)—in other words, the continuity in any divine activity between the announcement of an event in advance and its realization in actual fact—is made the criterion of true divinity *vis-à-vis* the foreign gods. In this way Deutero-Isaiah magnificently sums up the pre-exilic prophets' proclamation of doom. There Yahweh proved himself to be God by announcing the doom of his chosen people in advance and then giving effect to this by destroying them as a nation. That a god should prove his divinity by letting his own people be defeated was something the ancient world had never even dreamt of! This, however, alone afforded any possibility of renewed historical action on God's part after his people's downfall, and this is the very thing that Deutero-Isaiah proclaims: by giving effect to his sentence

of doom, God proved himself to be God: therefore, Israel may now place utter confidence in his word of salvation. It is this continuity between word and act that constitutes lordship over history and, consequently, the truth of a claim to divinity.

These are the theological presuppositions upon which Deutero-Isaiah introduces Cyrus into his message. In all five references to him, we find that Yahweh 'stirs him up'. This prepares the way for the oracle about him (44.24–45.7). Even before Deutero-Isaiah's time, the pre-exilic prophets had maintained that the continuity between God's word and act applied to more than matters within Israel herself. For Isaiah, the king of Assyria, and for Jeremiah, the king of Babylon, had their parts to play in God's designs for his chosen people; similarly, for Deutero-Isaiah, the king of Persia. The only novel element in our prophet is that the design which Cyrus is to serve is God's purpose of salvation for his people. This strikes a completely new note; God is about to save his chosen people from the destruction of their national life without the deliverance being bound up with military victory on their part. In order that liberty may be won for the people of the true God, the victory is to go to the foreign king who serves other gods. The severance of the link which tied God's salvation of his chosen people to their independence also explains why the one who is now to bring deliverance is a 'servant'. In Deutero-Isaiah's trial speeches the idea of the relationship between God's action and political events is absolutely different from what it had ever been previously; when it was actually spoken, their polemic against the gods of the great powers may have sounded ridiculously bold, even almost the product of a fevered imagination. None the less, the course which events took vindicated it. The time of Cyrus and of the establishment of the Persian empire marks the point at which the close link which till then had obtained between a god's lordship and the political power possessed by his sphere of influence began gradually to be severed, until finally it broke altogether. The political power wielded by the Christian Church in the Middle Ages represents a serious decline from this insight of Deutero-Isaiah.

The polemic against the foreign gods in the trial speeches includes a series of statements that God is one: 'I am the first and I am the last, and beside me there is no God' (44.6, 8; 45.5, 6, 21; 41.4; 43.15; 46.4; 48.12). These are not to be taken in terms of our present-day concept of monotheism, but can only be understood against the background of Deutero-Isaiah's theology of history. Their origin is the argument used in the trial speeches, that there should be a dependable and unremitting continuity between a god's word and his acts. They do not mean uniqueness as regards existence, but that God is unique in the sense that he is the only God who acts in history seen as a whole. The fact that Marduk acquired a vast empire for Babylon did not prove him to be lord of history. For him to be so would have required an announcement in advance that Babylon would fall, and a subsequent deliverance of his people after the downfall. Yet it was this that the God of Israel had done (46.1–4). And why? Because as creator he was the lord of history, and as both, the deliverer of his people. The fusion of these three spheres of divine action—creation, control of world-history, and deliverance—excluded any other possibility than that God was one. A god closely tied to the political power within his sphere of influence implies polytheism, for we can never conceive of only one political power in the world. Deutero-Isaiah's severance of a god's action from the political power possessed by his sphere of influence signified the breakthrough to the proclamation of the one God. As he did so, however, and just because he did so, Deutero-Isaiah took the other gods seriously, more so, indeed, than any other previous prophet. This is seen in the literary form which he used, the trial speech, in which the foreign gods are summoned to judgment. Had Deutero-Isaiah's intention been to prove that these had no real existence, such a procedure would have been pointless. What he here demonstrates is that their pretentions to divinity were baseless—a very different thing. This is so because the prophet opened up a new dimension as regards lordship over events. With him, God ceased to be the one who showed himself as powerful merely because his chosen people were also powerful. Rather, he is a God who evinces himself as lord through the continuity of his word and his act, which is able to bridge the gulfs that history tears open (46.1–4).

5. Deutero-Isaiah's polemic against his own nation is found in the trial speeches in which Yahweh confronts Israel (43.22–28; 50.1f.; 42.18–25) and in the disputations. Polemic also occurs in vv. 12–31 of the one great poem in ch. 40 and in vv. 14–26 of the other in ch. 49, as well as in reminiscences of these in 45.11ff.; 45.18f.; in chs. 46 and 48, and 55.8.[a]

The trial speeches against Israel are chiefly concerned with her past sins. They reveal Deutero-Isaiah as following the tradition of the

[a] Cf. 'Sprache und Struktur', pp. 141–4, 124–34.

pre-exilic prophets of doom, affirming and reiterating the message which they also declared. His hearers were still unable to realize that the origin of the doom which had overtaken God's chosen people lay in God himself. They were bringing charges against him (hence the form of the trial speech) accusing him of having cast his people off (43.28; 42.24a, 25; 50.1), one of their arguments being that for many years they had loyally served him by coming to him with their sacrifices (43.22ff.). In answer to this, Deutero-Isaiah said that there was no other way in which God could have acted (43.28); for Israel sinned against him (43.24b, 27; 50.1b) and the sacrifices she offered to him had not really given her national life its direction, and in consequence had never been accepted (43.23f.). The charges which she was still bringing against him even today were therefore baseless. Now, however, comes the amazing transformation of the situation. The trial speeches which the prophet addressed to his fellow-countrymen were not designed to move Israel to repentance, now that she saw the true state of things, and to make her beg God for mercy; no, with a certitude which admitted of no doubt Deutero-Isaiah now tells them that the situation has been completely transformed. God has forgiven his people (43.25). And he now looks for one thing and one only from men who could not understand him, and who accused him—their acceptance of the change to salvation which accompanied forgiveness, and their joyous affirmation of the opening words of the prologue, 'cry to her that her iniquity is pardoned'.

Whereas the trial speeches emphasize Israel's past guilt, and seek to prove that God was bound thus to chastise her, the disputations, on the other hand, look to the future and inveigh against the weariness and despair of the survivors of the year 586; all of them are finally words of salvation. In each case, the utterances which the prophet disputes are not private utterances taken from conversations with other exiles; they are without exception liturgical, words used by the community in its worship; they are all excerpts from laments such as are found in the psalms of lamentation. During the exile this genre of psalm had acquired the status of the vehicle best adapted to express the worshipping community's circumstances. But continual lamentation could also lead to a fixed mood of always looking backwards, with no expectation of fresh action on the part of God. This mood the disputations shatter, jerking the mourners out of their depression and sadness and turning their gaze to a new action on God's part. In this respect, too, Deutero-Isaiah shows himself the successor of the pre-exilic prophets; they, too, when faced with a lifeless cult, told their hearers to look to a different quarter. In the disputations, the number of motifs taken from the psalms of lamentation is quite amazing. In the one represented by 49.14–26, which falls into three parts, vv. 14–18, 19–23, 24ff., we should pay special attention to the fact that these answer to the three component parts of a lament, showing how deliberately the words of salvation were modelled on the elements that go to make up a lament. In 40.12–31 the disputation is levelled against that with which God is charged in 40.27, 'My right is disregarded by my God'. The words are taken straight from a lament, and imply the question, has God still the power and the will to help his chosen people? To allay this doubt Deutero-Isaiah strikes up afresh the praise of God's majesty and goodness that had fallen silent (see above). Several other passages suggest a disputation, and we find it joined with other motifs. In each case what is disputed is an attitude or utterance on Israel's part which declines to close with the proffered message of salvation. The antithesis in vv. 12f., within 51.9ff., an adaptation of a lament, is a striking instance of this: 'I, I am he that comforts you—who are you that you are afraid . . . and have forgotten the Lord your Maker . . .?' Israel does not take God's majesty seriously if in fear she draws back and refuses to accept the word of salvation.

6. The songs of praise or cries of exultation (42.10–13; 44.23; 45.8; 48.20f.; 49.13; 51.3 [? fragment]; 52.9f.; 54.1f.).[a] A further resemblance of Deutero-Isaiah's message to that of the pre-exilic prophets of doom is that both call for decision. Its very nature as a gospel of salvation rules out any idea of avoiding commitment. In the disputations the prophet attacked all shrinking from it in fear and lack of faith (see above). Now, from such as do accept, he expects more than intellectual or spiritual assent: he looks for acceptance in the existential plane. This is what the summons to render praise or to exult found in the songs of praise, generally the end-piece of a section, are designed to elicit. All of them have substantiations with verbs in the past tense (see above); this implies that the event the prophet proclaims has already come to pass. Existential acceptance of his message consists in the immediate raising of shouts of jubilation; jubilation indicates a response in faith. Deutero-Isaiah's songs of praise show that in the Old Testament praise may take the place of what the New calls faith. They also let us see a particularly interesting

[a] Cf. *ibid.*, pp. 157–63.

and profound connection between Deutero-Isaiah and Isaiah of Jerusalem. The concept of faith bulks large in the latter; in the former's hymns of praise, faith in his message is expressed by raising of cries of exultation at God's act of deliverance, conceived as already accomplished, even although there is no visible evidence to prove it (Heb. 11.1).

7. The 'servant songs'. The songs contained in the group just considered are genuine songs, i.e., psalms. With the so-called 'servant songs', however, the position is not nearly so clear; and if the traditional name is to be retained, this must be borne in mind. The songs are found in 42.1–4; 49.1–6; 50.4–9; 52.13–53.12. Duhm was the first to see that the four of them form a group, and constitute a separate strand in the book of Deutero-Isaiah. All attempts to account for them by reference to their immediate context fail; Duhm's view is therefore still the most acceptable. Adopting it, the question of authorship is of only secondary importance. Deutero-Isaiah himself may well have composed the first three—this seems probable to the present writer. In any case, as most scholars have always believed, the four of them together form a separate strand different from the rest of the material in the book.

The four servant songs do not have one and the same literary category, and none of them has a form used elsewhere in Deutero-Isaiah. The song found in 42.1–4 gives God's designation of the Servant, a designation similar to that of a king. In 49.1–6 a prophetic report of the Servant about himself is continued with motifs taken from the psalms (with echoes of declarative praise). In structure, 50.4–9 resembles a psalm of confidence. The last of these songs (52.13–53.12) is a report (53.11b–13) preceded and concluded by a divine utterance (52.13–15 and 53.11b–13), and spoken by those for whom the Servant's fate had spelled change. The songs thus differ completely in kind, their link being a subject in common, God's Servant. One thing at least is obvious; their language at once reveals and conceals the Servant. He is not described in the terms used elsewhere in the Old Testament of a king, a prophet, Israel, or an individual righteous man, although there are reminiscences of each of these. This is clear from the forms employed, the statements made, and the general designation 'Servant'. Any interpretation, therefore, of the Servant along any single one of the above lines, king, prophet, the nation, or a righteous man, may be ruled out on principle. The veiled allusions, now to one now to another of these, forbid the adoption of any one to the exclusion of the rest. This much, however, is certain: the Servant has a task imposed on him by God and it embraces the Gentiles as well as Israel. It is also certain that his function is that of proclaiming God's word, and to this extent it very closely approximates to a prophet's. This, however, is not all; for the way in which he is designated in 42.1–4 recalls that of a king, while his office as depicted in 50.4–9 and chs. 52f. involves him in suffering, which ch. 53 explains as vicarious, for 'the many'. So far, but no further, are we on firm ground. The Servant has a place in the history of the office of mediator, which begins with Moses, who is also designated as servant of God. The terms used of the servant have direct links with that stage in the history of prophecy which immediately preceded Deutero-Isaiah; these are clear echoes of the complaints of Jeremiah, the last prophet before the exile. At the same time, however, both because of the positive value attributed to the servant's vicarious suffering, and since in his hands the office of mediator was expanded to take in the Gentiles—the Servant is destined to be a light to the nations—the songs point forward to a new era in the history of that office.

Further knowledge of the servant can only be derived from the detailed exegesis of the songs.

TRADITIONS IN THE PROPHECY OF DEUTERO-ISAIAH

1. *Historical traditions.* For Deutero-Isaiah the most important event in Israel's history was the Exodus. The great prominence which he gives it is due to the fact that he himself was involved in a situation similar to it. At the same time, however, this well accords with the place which it occupies in the old historical *credo*, of which it forms the heart (von Rad). Deutero-Isaiah proclaimed the release from Babylon as a second Exodus. Many of the passages which herald it or describe the return contain reminiscences of the deliverance from Egypt. It is recalled in vv. 16f. of 43.16–21, a proclamation of salvation, and also in v. 10 of 51.9–52.3, an adapted lament, where, as in certain of the Psalms, it is equated with the struggle against the powers of chaos (v. 9). There are obvious reminiscences of the Exodus from Egypt in the summons to depart from Babylon in 52.11f. ('you shall not go out in haste'), while the proclamations which announce the return through a wilderness miraculously transformed recall the

earlier wanderings in the wilderness (43.19f.; 55.12f.; 51.11; 49.9f.) under the leadership of Yahweh (42.16f.; 48.20f.).

The place which Deutero-Isaiah gives to the Exodus is so conspicuous that all the other events in Israel's history recede into the background. An arch which spans the nation's entire history has as its one pillar the release from Egypt and as its other the new, imminent release from Babylon. If Deutero-Isaiah had been asked what was the most important event between these two, he would unhesitatingly have replied, the complete breakdown of Israel's national life due to the fall of Jerusalem and the exile. This, however, he does not speak of as an historical event, but as a judgment wrought upon Israel by the hand of God (43.28). Her wickedness made such treatment of her inevitable. The events of 586 also form the background of a large number of other passages, including the beginning of the prologue itself (40.2); but in these cases they are no more than suggested or alluded to, and are, in general, only reflected in the laments to which they gave rise.

As regards the remainder of Israel's history, Deutero-Isaiah does no more than occasionally mention a name or speak summarily of what God has done in it (he was her helper and redeemer, he bore her, etc.). He takes up the Zion tradition to the extent that, in the second part of the book, he frequently calls Israel by that name, while the prophecies concerning the city of Jerusalem (particularly 54.11–17) are based on the praises rendered to her in the songs of Zion. He must therefore also have known of the historical events which formed the background of the Zion tradition, even if he never mentions them. The name of David is mentioned only once, in the promise of 'the sure mercies of David' (55.3). The background here is the Nathan prophecy in II Sam. 7, as well, of course, as the events which gave rise to it. Deutero-Isaiah also recalls the covenants with Noah (54.9), the patriarchs (43.27), and Abraham (41.8), but in each case only because they bear directly on the particular prophecy he is uttering. We may therefore conclude that Deutero-Isaiah was familiar with his nation's history in all its phases, and that he assumed a similar knowledge on the part of his hearers, although he only made direct reference to it when it bore on the message which he was commissioned to deliver.

2. *Prophetic traditions.* While Deutero-Isaiah was a prophet of salvation, his affinities with the pre-exilic prophets of doom are in many respects closer than with the prophets of salvation. In 43.22–28 he expressly refers to earlier prophecy of doom, declaring that God

spoke by means of it. There, the charge of unreality in sacrificial worship was particularly important and frequent among the many made by the pre-exilic prophets of doom: this Deutero-Isaiah takes up, and endorses in retrospect. While this is his clearest link with pre-exilic prophecy of doom, his most important reference to it is the argument which he employs in the trial speeches against the gods of the foreign nations, the trustworthy and unremitting continuity which should exist between what a god says and what he does, i.e. with earlier predictions. Here Deutero-Isaiah relates himself to former prophecy. 'Have I not told you beforehand?' recurs constantly. Although he had prophecies of salvation in mind as much as prophecies of doom, his clinching argument was connected with the latter, that Yawheh had announced in advance the judgment coming upon his own people. The threat was fulfilled, and now, after the national life has broken down, the datum of the word of God that outlasts it, remains (40.8 and 55.10f.). What enabled Deutero-Isaiah to use such language about the word of God was the course of earlier prophecy.

In one matter Deutero-Isaiah simply continues the tradition of earlier prophecy—the oracle against Babylon in ch. 47, which falls into the literary category of oracles against foreign nations. In this respect Deutero-Isaiah is only one of numerous prophets who predicted the fall of Babylon.

3. *The traditions found in the Psalter.* Almost every page in Deutero-Isaiah reveals affinities between his proclamation and the language of the Psalter. The form of the oracle of salvation as constituting the answer to a lament is not native to the prophetic tradition, but to that of the Psalms. The Psalter survived the loss of the temple and became an important component part of the exiles' worship. Although later in date, the book of Tobit bears striking witness to the significance which could attach to the Psalms for a Jew living outside Palestine. One can well understand why Deutero-Isaiah's proclamation links up with them. Because of the circumstances in which the exiles found themselves, the psalms which the prophet most frequently echoes are inevitably the psalms of lamentation; however, since the Psalter shows that lament and praise are essentially co-related, we may logically expect to find Deutero-Isaiah's diction influenced by the psalms of praise as well. The influence is, in actual fact, much stronger than has hitherto been realized.

Deutero-Isaiah is very often designated as the prophet who was at the same time a poet, or as the poet-prophet. At bottom, this is due to the linguistic affinities between himself and the Psalter. When we speak, however, of 'poet' and 'poetry', these terms are not identical with those that have arisen in the course of literary history, in which art is regarded as autonomous; instead, words in rhythm, designed for invocation, and swept along by its ardour, are as such poetry, and this is the kind of poetry we find in Deutero-Isaiah.

There are numerous links between Deutero-Isaiah's proclamation and the psalms of lamentation, and they vary in kind. The prologue itself suggests Israel's laments in exile as, in vv. 6–8, it deplores the evanescence of all things (Pss. 39; 49; 90, and frequently in Job), a lament which describes the plight in which the nation then found itself. Verse 27 of 40.12–31 quotes words taken from a community lament: the accusation it brings against God forms the subject of the disputation in the passage. In the three sections of 49.14–26, another disputation, the subject is again a lament on the part of Israel. The proclamation of salvation is related to the community lament in the same way as the promise of salvation to the individual lament. The place where a community lament can be most clearly discerned is in 51.9–52.3: the verses are full of phrases, motifs and vocabulary taken from laments.

Of equal importance, however, for Deutero-Isaiah is the Psalter's praise. Its strongest and most direct influence is found in the poem contained in 40.12–31. The poem bears the stamp of that polarity which marks Israel's praise of God throughout: God is praised both in his majesty, and as the one who, from majesty, stoops down to enter into the depths of the sufferers' plight. Nowhere in the Old Testament is this basic motif of praise so powerfully and artistically elaborated as in this poem. Looking at it, it is not hard to see why the prophet wove these motifs taken from divine praise into his proclamation. As is in the Psalter, he usually develops praise of the divine majesty in two directions: God is creator, and God is lord of history. He weaves these two motifs, the purpose of which is to 'magnify God' (Heb. *giddēl* = Lat. *magnificare*), into the texture of his proclamation now in one way and now in another. In the Cyrus oracle (44.24–45.7) the first is more particularly developed. The whole is placed in a setting of the glory given to the creator (44.24 and 45.7); the creator is the lord of history (44.25f.). This is repeated in vv. 27f., where the two motifs are significantly brought together. The fact that the part of the oracle addressed to Cyrus himself is introduced by and concluded with glorification of Yahweh as creator and lord of history shows what was in Deutero-Isaiah's mind: he wished to make God once more mighty in the eyes of his fellow-countrymen, in order that they should believe that, in his majesty, he could choose whatever tool he wanted for the purpose of effecting his chosen people's redemption.

In 44.24 God is designated in one and the same breath as Israel's creator and her redeemer. As has often been noticed, the collocation is frequent in Deutero-Isaiah, and it can be understood only in the light of Israel's praise; it echoes the polarity described above: Israel's redeemer is the God of majesty who created the world and who directs the entire course of its history. God's work in creation and his work in redemption are here looked on as very closely connected: however, this must never be taken as meaning that, in whole or in part, the two merge, for that would be a misconception of what the prophet had in mind. He used this polarity to make his hearers remember that God's saving action upon his chosen people as proclaimed by himself was, at it were, an island within the mighty universe of God's work as creator. It is therefore no accident that the combination, Israel's creator and her redeemer, most of all occurs in the promises of salvation (43.1, 15; 44. 2; 44.21, 24; 54.5; also 45.11; 51.13). Correspondingly, it is natural that the second aspect of the divine majesty, God's lordship of history, is given its fullest development in the trial speeches in which God confronts the foreign nations or their gods.

One part of the Psalter's praise of the majesty attaching to God's acts states that he is the one who never changes, who casts down the mighty and exalts the lowly in the realm of history, and, in the realm of creation, has the power to change the desert into fertile country and vice versa. Deutero-Isaiah showed great ingenuity in incorporating the last of these motifs into his gospel: for his chosen people's journey back home, God is to transform the desert into fertile country (40.3f.; 41.18f.; 42.16b; 43.19f.; 44.3; 49.9ff.; 55.12f.). Here again the motif is couched in a particular form, that of the proclamation of salvation. But, to answer to the motif as found in the Psalter, there must also be mention of the other aspect of the creator's activity, its destructive side. God can also turn fertile country into a desert (42.15; 44.27; 45.7; the two last refer to the destruction wrought by the campaigns of Cyrus, 50.2f.; 51.9f.).

In the case of certain of the passages already cited, and of many others, their origin in praise is not altogether easy to see, since they are drafted as words spoken by God himself in the first person. This formulation is primarily due to the nature of prophetic discourse itself, in which God speaks in the first person. Another reason for it, however, is to be found in the emphatic 'I am' form used in many religions, and particularly frequently in Babylon, for divine self-predication. We must nevertheless notice that Deutero-Isaiah combines two different types of 'I am' declarations which have different origins. One of them always has a word of salvation attached to it—in Deutero-Isaiah it occurs in the oracle of salvation (41.10, 13, 14b; 43.3), or in other words of salvation (41.17b; 43.25; 46.4; 48.17; 49.23; 51.12). This type has a clearly discernible pre-history in Israel herself (Gen. 15.1, 7; 26.24; 28.13; 46.3; 17.1ff.; 35.11ff.; Ex. 3.6ff.; 6.2ff.). Deutero-Isaiah took it over from the tradition of the oracle of salvation. As its pre-history makes clear, this type of 'I am' saying was used when a god made himself known (Zimmerli calls it *Selbstvorstellungsformel*). The other type is a self-predication (that is, the proclamation of attributes or properties) or a self-glorification on the part of a god, and as such it is a modification of praise. To the best of our knowledge, Deutero-Isaiah was the first in Israel to show God glorifying himself in this way. He took over this non-Israelite, and obviously Babylonian, form with the deliberate polemical purpose of contrasting Israel's God as the one God with the foreign gods who vaunted their power and might against each other. This is made clear from such statements as 'I am the first and the last' (41.4; 43.13; 44.6; 48.12), 'besides me there is no God' (43.11; 44.6b; 45.5; 45.18, 21, 22; 46.9), 'who is like me?' (44.7). Now, the fact that these two different types of 'I am' sayings, called by Elliger 'expressions of majesty' and 'expressions of grace', are found confronting one another shows, once more, a relationship with the twin poles in the Psalter's praise of God. In these 'I am' sayings God declares what he is for his chosen people and for the world in the two basic ways in which the Psalter sings his praise.

All the passages and motifs connected with praise which have been considered in the present section fall into one of the two categories of Israel's praise, namely, descriptive praise (hymns). The other category found in the Psalter is declarative praise (psalms of thanksgiving). In Deutero-Isaiah there is nothing that directly corresponds to this, although there is an important indirect equivalent, the songs of praise already considered, which, with their substantiations in the past tense, do correspond to it. In their case there is one remarkable correspondence. Deutero-Isaiah very often calls the new deliverance he proclaims a new Exodus (see above). The song of Miriam (Ex. 15.21) shows how the earliest song of praise, the first example of descriptive praise, was inspired by the miraculous deliverance at the beginning of Israel's history. God's new act of deliverance has as its accompaniment the 'new song' (42.10), which responds to it with jubilation. Since it strikes up jubilation for the deliverance before this has yet taken place, it becomes a song of faith. Thus, the songs of praise which accompany the preaching of Deutero-Isaiah stand midway between the descriptive praise sung by God's people of old and the song of faith of his new chosen people, who sing of the victory of the king and lord of the world before it is revealed as such.

THE ORIGIN AND GROWTH OF THE BOOK

None of the prophetic writings was composed *en bloc*. All of them came into being as the result of a long and gradual process, which started with oral tradition. This primary stage of transmission does not, however, suddenly disappear when written collections of traditions begin. For long both may co-exist side by side. The preservation and collection of prophets' oracles was generally the work of their disciples, as is stated expressly in the cases of Isaiah and Jeremiah. But such custodians of traditions were never themselves cut off from the world around them; their whole concern was to get a hearing for the prophets' words from the nation or the community assembled for worship. As a result, many of the prophetic writings show traces of continuing use in worship, as is shown by the doxologies in Amos or the psalm in Isa. 12 that rounds off the oracles collected in chs. 1–11.

As we saw above, there is an inter-relationship in principle between Deutero-Isaiah's proclamation and the exiles' services of worship. From the beginning there must also have been a very close inter-relationship between these services and the collection and transmission of his oracles. As we know, however, Deutero-Isaiah, too, had, if not a band of disciples, at least a single one, Trito-Isaiah. The primary element in chs. 56–66 is so obviously dependent on Deutero-Isaiah that the hypothesis of discipleship alone explains it. It was therefore Trito-Isaiah, helped perhaps by others, who collected and preserved his master's oracles, and saw to it that they were brought to Judah from Babylon, the scene of Deutero-Isaiah's own labours. The fact that Trito-Isaiah quotes from or alludes to Deutero-

Isaiah is proof positive that the latter's message continued its work in Judah after the exile had ended, and this fresh life and the formation and transmission of the book are closely inter-related. No attempt is made here to discover the extent to which Trito-Isaiah (or the group who formed about him) made changes in his master's message, reshaping and expanding it. Elliger[a] assumes that considerable parts of chs. 40–55, e.g., the whole of chs. 54–55, come not from Deutero-Isaiah, but from Trito-Isaiah. My own view is that, in all essentials, chs. 40–55 go back in their entirety to Deutero-Isaiah himself, and that their contents represent what he himself preached.

Further, chs. 40–55 show such clear signs of a deliberate, orderly arrangement as to lead me to believe that the form in which we have them goes back basically to Deutero-Isaiah himself. The following considerations suggest a deliberate, orderly arrangement: (a) the whole is set within the framework of a prologue (40.1–11) and epilogue (55.6–11), which are in turn related in content; (b) the position of the songs of praise or cries of exultation, which form the conclusions of various divisions of the book; (c) the position of the Cyrus oracle, at the very centre of the book, the place appropriate to the importance of its content; (d) the position of the two poems arising from disputations (40.12–31 and 49.14–26): each opens one of the two sections of the book; (e) the exceptional nature of chs. 54 and 55 at the end of the book, in which the subject of the proclamation of salvation is not the actual liberation itself, but the conditions that are to obtain in the new state of salvation after it. These indications of deliberate, orderly arrangement are best understood as the work of the prophet himself, the result of his desire to transmit his message as a balanced whole.

What is less intelligible is the division into two different kinds of discourse. With few exceptions, chs. 40–45 are composed of short oracles, each belonging to one single literary category, but after ch. 45 the major place is taken by poems of considerable length which combine several literary categories. I myself am quite sure that the oracles were originally spoken, but the longer poems like 49.14–26 or 51.9–52.3 may have been literary productions from the beginning. Presumably these two different kinds of discourse represent two different kinds of activity on the prophet's part, an idea supported by the fact that they were transmitted in different complexes (before and after ch. 45).

[a] *Deuterojesaja in seinem Verhältnis zu Tritojesaja*, BWANT, IV, 13, Stuttgart, 1933.

Thus far the origin and growth of the book is to be attributed to Deutero-Isaiah himself, just as the main body of the book of Jeremiah comes from that prophet himself. In contrast, the four servant songs represent a separate strand, and form a subsequent addition to the book, even if, as I assume, the author of the first three was Deutero-Isaiah himself. The fourth, which pre-supposes the Servant's death, is later than the others, although it was added to the book along with them. It is easy to see why the fourth song was placed after 52.7–12, for these verses conclude the main section of the book, but the reason why the others were inserted where they are is obscure.

Another piece of evidence that the first three songs are a later addition comes from the fact that, in each case, the verses which follow them are unusually difficult. 42.5–8 (9) are a later expansion and development of the song in 42.1–4, although they do have affinities with Deutero-Isaiah. 49.7–12 represents a proclamation of salvation composed by the prophet himself, but by redaction made to refer to the Servant. 50.10f., along with 51.1–8, comprises a poem in three parts, added to 50.4–9 by means of the words in 50.10, 'who among you fears the Lord and obeys the voice of his servant?'. The three additions have a common factor: they take up the figure of the Servant and interpret and develop it in the light of the songs. Nevertheless, and even although here and there they repeat one another verbally, they are quite different in kind.

The Cyrus oracle (44.24–45.7), too, had a similar addition made to it, in vv. 9–13. This was quite certainly deliberate. The two verses beginning with 'woe to', vv. 9 and 10, made vv. 9–13 (vv. 11ff. had a different frame of reference) into a disputation directed against those who took umbrage at the Cyrus oracle. As with the servant songs, the oracle continued in use and gathered these additions to it.

The polemic against the manufacture of idols in 40.19f. and 41.6f.; 42.17; 44.9–20; 45.16f., 20b, and 46.5–8, forms a group of homogeneous additions. My reasons for regarding these passages as homogeneous, and distinct from the rest of the prophecy, are given in the commentary on 44.9–20. They, too, quite obviously are inspired by Deutero-Isaiah: for example, 49.19f. links on to his question, 'To whom then will you liken God . . .?'. These additions show how Deutero-Isaiah's impassioned proclamation that there can only be one God continued to be effective; the long insertion comprising 44.9–20 links directly on to this sentiment (44.8b). Israel may perhaps have possessed a special literary category comprised of verses or songs in mockery of idols, of which these additions are examples.[a]

A less closely knit group of additions to Deutero-Isaiah is made up of occasional admonitions and accusations. Examples are the admonition to return to Yahweh in 44.21, 22b, the expansion in ch. 48 (1c, 4, 5b, 7b, 8ff., 18f.), which are parallel to Ps. 81; also the two verses beginning 'Woe to', 45.9f., the poem of three stanzas in 50.10f. and 51.1–8, and the addition 48.21b. This group is very reminiscent of Trito-Isaiah. The primary element in chs. 56–66 represents a revival of the prophecy of Deutero-Isaiah, but it is accompanied by admonitions and accusations, the same feature as appears in this group of additions to Deutero-Isaiah. We also find that a verse of Trito-Isaiah's, originally a part of 60.3–14, became displaced and was incorporated into Deutero-Isaiah (45.14), or that small fragments (in this case originally Deutero-Isaiah's), such as 42.9; 48.16b or 51.16b, appear in other contexts.

Finally, I gather together a little group of additions which I call 'Amen glosses'. These occur throughout the whole Bible and constitute a valuable and often touching witness to the way in which, in the generations after the biblical writings came into being, these were hearkened to and read by the circles by whom they were preserved and transmitted. One of them is the brief note added in the prologue (40.7), 'Surely the people are grass', another the words in 45.15 which have no relation at all to their context, 'Truly, thou art a God who hidest thyself', words which reverently say 'Amen' to God's incomprehensible way of working through the instrumentality of the heathen king (45.1ff.). We may also include here 42.21, 24b, additions at the beginning and the end of an oracle which use the language of Torah piety and say 'Amen' to the fate of those who, although aware of God's direction, turn aside from it. Last of all, there is an observation made in 52.4ff. which links on to the words 'for nothing': the liberation from Babylon ought to make Israel recognize that God is at work for the honour of his name.

To summarize: as it now stands, by far the greatest part of the book of Deutero-Isaiah derives from the prophet himself. One or two passages which are independent of one another, as well as some which are grouped about the same subject-matter, furnish us with a vivid picture of the way in which the generations after Deutero-Isaiah took up his message, thought it through anew, and evoked a response to it.

[a] J. C. Kim, *Jahwe und die Götter bei Deuterojesaja*, Heidelberg Dissertation, 1964.

CHAPTER 40.1–11

Comfort my people

1 Comfort, comfort my people,   says your God;
2 Speak tenderly to Jerusalem   and cry to her,
   that her time of service is ended,   that her iniquity is pardoned,
   that she has received from Yahweh's hand
   double for all her sins.

3 A voice cries:
   'In the wilderness prepare   the way for Yahweh,
   make straight in the desert   a highway for our God.
4 Let every valley be lifted up   and every mountain and hill be made low,
   Let the uneven ground become level   and the rough places a plain,
5 and the glory of Yahweh shall be revealed,
   and all flesh shall see it together,
   for the mouth of Yahweh has spoken.'

6 A voice says, 'Cry!'
   And [I][a] say, 'What shall I cry?'
   All flesh is grass   and its beauty like the flower of the field.
7 The grass withers   the flower fades
   when the breath of Yahweh   blows upon it.
     Surely, the people is grass!
8 The grass withers   the flower fades,
   but the word of our God stands for ever.

9 Get you up into a high mountain,   O Zion, herald of good tidings!
   Lift up your voice with strength,   O Jerusalem, herald of good tidings!
   Lift it up, fear not,   say to the cities of Judah,
10 'Behold your God!   Behold Yahweh the Lord!'
   He comes with might   and his arm rules for him.

[a] Read, along with LXX, V and DSS Isa., *wā'ōmar* instead of *wᵉ'āmar*.

11   Like a shepherd who tends his flock,
      he gathers the lambs in his arms
      and carries them in his bosom,
      and leads those that are with young.

Bibliography: L. J. Kuyper, 'The meaning of ḤSD in Isa. XL 6', *VT*, 13 (1963), pp. 489–92; H. J. Stoebe, 'Zu Jes. 40.6', *Wort und Dienst,* Jahrbuch der theologischen Schule Bethel, n.s. 2, 1950; J. Hempel, 'Wort Gottes und Schicksal' (on 40.7f.), *Festschrift für Bertholet,* 1950.

Unlike the majority of the prophetic books, Deutero-Isaiah is without any superscription or literary introduction. It may at one time have had the former, this being dropped when the chapters were combined with Isaiah. However, taking the book all in all and viewing it as a whole, more probably there never was a superscription to 'Deutero-Isaiah'. If this is so, it well accords with the prophet's way of withdrawing entirely into the background of his message. Again, 40.1–11 seem so much like a beginning, an overture, a prologue, as to suggest that they come from the prophet himself, and were intended by him as the introduction to his message.

Several of the prophetic books start with an account of the prophet's call. Most critics regard vv. 6–8 as the equivalent of this. Nevertheless, these verses form part of a larger unit whose subject is not the messenger, but the message. The really important thing is that the message should be introduced: the introduction of the messenger is peripheral and forms only a part of the larger whole, a part, moreover, couched in veiled terms. The two passages which precede and follow vv. 6ff. (3ff. and 9ff.) are two cries which form a framework for the prophet's call: the one an order given to unspecified listeners to prepare a way in the wilderness (3ff.), the other a summons to Zion to get up into a high mountain and proclaim to the cities of Judah, 'Behold, your God!' (9ff.). All three sections together are in turn introduced by the cry, 'Comfort my people', (1f.). The whole makes up one cry, and the context is to be understood as an interlinked series, in which the first 'Comfort' has obvious priority not only of place but also of importance. 'Comfort my people'—this cry determines, and sets the pattern for, all that is to follow: the starting-point of the series, it resembles the general's order that gets stationary troops on the move by being taken up and passed on in the form of 'operation orders', until finally every single man is on the move. In order that God's people may be comforted, a way has to be prepared in the wilderness, a herald's voice heard telling the people that, ruined as the nation is, the word of God still stands unchanged; exultant proclamation has to be made to the cities of Judah that God's coming is at hand. It is astonishing to see how the form employed for the message answers to its substance. Of itself, the series of imperatives in 40.1–11 suggests a moment when men are starting out, getting on the move. What is pictured here is the very moment at which the prophet proclaims his message of God's *new* act; and with its delivery the new event, the exiles' release and the new exodus, is already under way. This is the new thing which, from this point on, is to be the constant burden of Deutero-Isaiah's message.

Since, however, the linked series of cries in 40.1–11 forms the prelude to the return from the exile, one would naturally expect it to issue in the express command to depart, move out from Babylon. This does in fact occur, but not at the end of the prologue; it comes only just before the final servant song, at 52.11, 'Depart, depart, go out thence'. As we shall see later, these verses represent a temporary break in the book. The cry, 'Comfort my people', leads ultimately to the cry, 'Go out'; between these lies the proclamation of Deutero-Isaiah, whose task it was to conduct his people from the first cry to the second.

Regarded in this way, Deutero-Isaiah's message, already present *in nuce* in the prologue, is from the very start securely linked with the Exodus tradition which forms the heart of the historical *credo*. The first Exodus, too, began with a cry to depart from bondage; then, too, there was the voice of one crying, with the function of proclaiming the release on which God had resolved; then, too, the decisive move towards this was the making of the way through the wilderness,

[1–2] As was made clear in the introduction just given, the cry, 'Comfort my people', is meant to lay down the lines of the whole prologue. The series of linked cries, beginning with 'Comfort' and leading on to 'Depart', can only properly be understood in the light of a difference in meaning between the Hebrew and the German words for 'to comfort'. In a number of passages where the one who comforts is a human being, the *piel* of the root *nhm* has exactly the same meaning, and occurs in the same contexts, as '*trösten*' (comfort); so, for example, when in Gen. 37.35 all the sons and daughters of Jacob wished to comfort him for the supposed death of his son Joseph, or when Job's friends came to comfort him (2.11). Not in every case, however, does the German word have the same meaning as the Hebrew one. When 'comfort' is used with a negative, 'there is none to comfort', particularly in Lam. 1.2, 9, 16f., 21, the context or the parallelism make clear that here comforter means helper. So too in Lam. 2.13 and the Psalms, e.g. 86.17, 'Because thou, Lord, hast helped me and comforted me'; similarly Isa. 12.1; Jer. 31.13; Zech. 1.17. The most marked examples of this usage in Deutero-Isaiah come in 49.13; 51.3, 12; 52.9. All these passages have the following features in common: (a) the one who comforts is God, and the one comforted Israel; (b) comforting signifies God's intervention to help and restore; (c) the comforting is spoken of in the past tense (in 51.12 the participle is used). Presumably, therefore, this particular use of the *piel* of *nḥm* was coined by Deutero-Isaiah himself, perhaps on the basis of the lament common in Lamentations, 'There is no helper.' The cry which introduces our book thus points away from the lament implied in the vanquished nation's question, 'Who helps you and comforts you?' (Lam. 2.13 and Isa. 51.19), to the exultant cry, the anticipated answer of those delivered, 'for Yahweh has comforted his people' (Isa. 49.13). What comforts Israel is the word of the messenger now sent to her with the proclamation that God has forgiven his people and resolved upon their deliverance. This word of comfort is spoken with authority, because the cry 'Comfort' proceeds to the cry 'Prepare'; the messenger's word that turns lamentation into joy has as its counterpart the intervention in history of the God who is lord of history, who exalts the humble and casts down the mighty.

The duplication of the cry at the beginning, 'Comfort, comfort my people', is an example of an important stylistic feature in Deutero-Isaiah's preaching, duplication as the expression of urgency. It occurs similarly with imperatives in 51.9, 'Awake, awake', and 51.17, 'Rouse yourself, rouse yourself', cf. 52.1, and in a different way in 48.15, 'I even I, have spoken', and in 43.11; 48.11 and frequently. This urgency in crying and speaking to Israel is found time and again throughout the book, and forms a leading characteristic of the prophet's proclamation. For, taken in its entirety, the latter is a cry uttered at a time when men were gradually turning away from God, gradually closing their minds to him, and gradually letting their faith grow cold. These are the circumstances which lent urgency to the cry. Israel must be aroused. A moment, and it may be too late. And the book's opening words attribute the urgency to God himself, who in his cry insists in bringing comfort to his people.

Verses 2b and c give the tersest possible summary of the message to God's people; all that we shall find later throughout the many facets of Deutero-Isaiah's proclamation derives from this one fact which signifies the turning-point in Israel's fortunes, 'her time of service is ended, her iniquity is pardoned.' Upon this turning-point all else depends. The two clauses form a synonymous parallelism; they are rhythmed expressions of the same situation. Nevertheless, they clearly show the two aspects of the situation. The first is the change wrought on the ever-present harsh realities of Israel's existence as a nation: its time of service is ended, over and done with. The particular nuances of the term 'service' are elucidated by reference to Job 7.1 and 10.17.ª The echo of the glad tidings that Israel's physical hardships in enforced exile are now at an end is to recur on every page of the chapters that follow. But the tidings are not understood unless the parallel clause, too, which gives the second aspect, is taken into account, 'her iniquity is pardoned'. The change in Israel's fortunes is based on the divine forgiveness. This at the same time means that, in Deutero-Isaiah's view, the fundamental and determining factor in that period of Israel's history which led to the 'service' was iniquity or involvement in guilt. This carries two implications. First, it shows that, over Deutero-Isaiah's entire proclamation, there is still no radical divorce of religion from politics; a non-religious understanding of history (history, that is, not determined by God or gods) was still quite impossible for him. Were God to be deprived of his activity in history, i.e. in politics, were he to be conceived 'completely religiously', then he would no longer exist. For Deutero-Isaiah, God and history are linked inseparably, a fact which makes iniquity and forgiveness apply not only to the individual, but to the nation as well. The second implication is that the words with which Deutero-Isaiah headed his message of comfort set him in line with the pre-exilic prophets of doom, whose chief task was to make Israel aware of the ever-increasing accumulation of her iniquity, which ultimately led to the 'service'. It is therefore not sufficient to say that, in distinction to these prophets of doom, or even as opposed to them, Deutero-Isaiah is a prophet of salvation. Rather, he is a continuation of their line; he concurs in the message which they proclaimed, and could never have constructed his own one of salvation had he not been able to build on theirs of doom. The opening words of the prologue themselves make this clear.

ª In 10.17 RSV keeps the Hebrew root ṣbʾh and translates 'hosts'.

The parallelism in the two clauses of v. 2b is an impressive example, both for Deutero-Isaiah and the whole of the Old Testament, of how closely deliverance and forgiveness are bound together. The fact that God turns once again to his chosen people in forgiveness puts *everything* right. This, and this alone, is the cause of the change in their fortunes, the end of service to alien masters. And, to view it from the other angle, God's turning again to his people, his forgiveness, has consequences far transcending his relationship to them: it projects into world-history itself—the theme taken up in the very next verses, the preparation of the way. Thus, concerns belonging to the realm of the personal, such as failure and forgiveness, are here made the basis of changes in world-history. So great is God in Deutero-Isaiah's eyes!

In the Hebrew, v. 2c is introduced by the same conjunction (*ki*) as 2b. With the rendering, 'for she has received', one has to remember that the clause is in fact co-ordinate with the one preceding, and therefore strictly cannot substantiate it. Israel's having received from Yahweh's hand double—double punishment, that is—for all her sins is not to be taken as implying calculation. Deutero-Isaiah is thinking of the actual condition of the victims of the punishment. The people he addresses are no longer able to sustain the burden of their grievous fate. The prophet says to them, 'now is enough, now it is over and done with'. But his words make them once more aware that what is now over and done with was the consequence of Israel's iniquities. And only recognition of this fact made any continuance of her history possible.

[3–5] Verse 3, vague and cryptic, introduces a new factor, 'A voice cries'. Whose the voice is, is deliberately left unsaid. The prophet obviously intended to make the speaker hard to recognize, and this must be given due weight in exegesis. We may say that 'the one who calls and those to whom he calls are invisible powers' (Volz), or we may discover an allusion to the heavenly court (de Boer). All that matters, however, is that the subject of vv. 3ff. is the carrying out of the order given by Yahweh in vv. 1f. God's summons, 'Comfort, speak, cry', has been heard. The person of the hearer is of no importance, and is to remain in the dark. The voice that cries the words of vv. 3ff. introduces the fulfilment of the divine order by giving a new one, an operation order, 'Prepare the way'.

The manner in which vv. 3ff. follow upon vv. 1f. is the first instance of the truth expressed at the end of the book: 'My word shall not return to me empty, but it shall accomplish . . .' Once Yahweh cried, 'Comfort my people', something was bound to happen. The cry could not return to him empty.

The surprising thing, however, is that the fulfilment of the call to 'comfort' is the order that a way is to be prepared. Comfort is to start with the preparation of a way!—and this is the only possible meaning. But it at once becomes comprehensible when we remember the meaning given above of the Hebrew word for 'comfort': a turning away of suffering, which in certain circumstances means helping, and so, an active intervention to turn the suffering away. This is precisely the sense here. Israel's comforting begins with the preparation of a way, for the way spoken of is the one which brings her through the desert back home.

In regard to the construction of v. 3, it must first be noted that the more precise determinative 'in the wilderness' is to be taken along with the verb 'to prepare', and not with the preceding clause, 'a voice cries'—this in spite of the tradition represented in LXX and the citations of the passage in the New Testament in Matt. 3.3 (and par.) and John 1.23. A reading of v. 3 in the original leaves hardly any doubt as to the proper connection of the clauses. Accentuation, parallelism and rhythm alike establish it. Precisely at this point in v. 3 there is a clear sequence of four lines each with two accents and preceded by the introduction, 'a voice cries':

| In the wi'lderness prep'are | the w'ay for Yahw'eh |
| make stra'ight in the de'sert | a hi'ghway for our G'od. |

In addition, there are proofs from the subject-matter. The train of thought demands, not the ringing out of the voice in the wilderness, but that in the wilderness—which, of course, separates the people of Israel from their homeland—the way should be prepared. Nothing at all in the whole of Deutero-Isaiah answers to or picks up a 'voice in the wilderness', whereas the book is full of the proclamation of the way through the wilderness.

Although we must therefore resign ourselves to the fact that 'the voice of one crying in the wilderness' as applied to John the Baptist does not exactly correspond to the Old Testament text which it cites, the quotation, with its differences from the original, has nevertheless something to tell us. It shows that, as a general rule, in dealing with citations of the Old Testament in the New, we must never set the New Testament version, its precise wording and meaning, directly over against the Old Testament original, but must take account of the whole road over which, through translation and other processes in tradition, the words of the Old Testament had travelled up to the point where they took on the meaning given them in the New.

As for the idea of preparing a way, we have here the first instance of a special feature which constantly recurs in what Deutero-Isaiah has to say. His proclamation gives signs of encounter with the world in which the prophet lived, the sphere of influence of the Babylonian empire and its capital city. 'The highway' has its own peculiar place in the Babylonian hymns; the layout of the city of Babylon is itself proof of the importance of the great processional highway.[a] The highways of the gods and the highways of kings meet.

> From hostile Elam he entered upon a road of jubilation,
> a path of rejoicing . . . of success to Su-an-na.
> The people of the land saw his towering figure,
> the ruler in (his) splendour.[b]
> Hasten to go out, (Nabu), son of Bel,
> you who know the ways and the customs.
> Make his way good, renew his road,
> make his path straight, hew him out a trail.[c]

Thus, triumphal highways, ways prepared and made level for the triumphal entry of the god or the king, were also well-known in Babylon, and, thanks to archaeological discoveries, we can have a first-hand idea of their magnificence and importance. They are the background both of the present passage and of many others in our prophet's proclamation. For the exiled Israelites in Babylon, these imposing highways were symbols of Babylon's might, the might that had brought about Israel's own downfall. These are the circumstances in which they heard the cry to make straight in the desert a highway, a highway 'for Yahweh . . . our God'. Although this is not said until the motif is further developed, the highway of which the prophet thinks is the one that is to enable Israel to make her way homeward through the desert. It is, however, designated a highway 'for Yahweh our God', just as the magnificent highways of Babylon were strictly highways for her gods. Its designation as the highway for Yahweh is more precisely explained in v. 5, 'And the glory of Yahweh shall be

[a] Stummer, 'Einige keilschriftliche Parallelen zu Jes. 40–66', *JBL*, XLV (1926), pp. 171–89; H. Schmökel, *Ur, Assur und Babylon*, 4th ed., Stuttgart, 1958, ch. XII and figs. 115f.

[b] Stummer, *op. cit.*, p. 172.

[c] Quoted in Volz, Commentary *ad loc.*, p. 4, following Ebeling.

revealed'. This, too, is to be read against the Babylonian background: there, the primary function of the processional highways was to allow the great processions to display the power and majesty of the gods in visible form. But this very background highlights the difference in the being of Yahweh: his 'glory', his *kābōd*, cannot possibly be manifested in the same way as that of the gods of Babylon; for what created the impression of majesty in the Babylonian processions—the images of the gods—is absent here. What reveals Yahweh's glory is his action in history. Therefore, the highway which is to be made through the desert is the way on which Yahweh now gives proof of himself, in a new and quite unlooked-for historical act: the way for leading his people home.

This restoration demands a divine intervention in history: the way through the desert presumes the release from Babylon. As the prologue suggests, this intervention is what the construction of the way to freedom in vv. 3ff. properly signifies. Thus, the language in 40.3ff. about making straight the way in the desert is figurative rather than literal. As we shall see later, this part of the prologue is expanded in those sections or complexes of Deutero-Isaiah's proclamation which gave a picture of the divine intervention in history, in particular in the commission to Cyrus to carry out the work which makes it possible for Israel to go free.

Verse 4 continues, in the jussive, the imperatives of v. 3; it makes still more clear that, in the matter of the preparation of the way, there are obstacles which block it or make it difficult, and which must be removed. This development of the theme itself points to the historical reality of what is here proclaimed: a great deal is therefore to be said later on about obstacles in the path of the chosen people's return.

Verse 5b: 'And all flesh sees it together.' When the glory of Yahweh is revealed, it is for the whole world to see. Not, of course, in the direct way in which, as Israel might see, 'all the world' were spectators of the processions of the gods or of the king in Babylon, and joined in the jubilation and were moved by this impressive demonstration; rather, it was indirectly, in a more profound way which had also a broader field: when Yahweh's glory was revealed, the contemporary world could not but realize that the vanquished god of a vanquished nation was fulfilling his word and restoring his chosen people to live in the land of their ancestors. This motif, too, is often taken up again in the rest of the book.

Verse 5c: Here the divine origin of the cry is once more stressed: 'for the mouth of Yahweh has spoken it.' The words cannot be connected with 'a voice cries' in 3a, for, whoever may be the speaker there, it is certainly not Yahweh. Verse 5c can only refer back to v. 1, 'Says your God.' This justifies the exegesis given above, that vv. 3ff. are meant as the 'operation order' of v. 1f. The order that Israel was now to be comforted had been issued by Yahweh. Since this was what his mouth spoke, intervention in history followed inevitably, and in vv. 3ff. this is represented as the preparation of a way. Yahweh's intervention is thus grounded in his word. This sets the stage for the section which follows.

[6–8] A fresh cry, a fresh command rings out: 'A voice says, "Cry!"' The introduction is similar to that of vv. 3ff.; this is very clear proof that the sections of the prologue are the skilfully dove-tailed parts of a single unit. The speaker is again unspecified. The important thing lies in what he says: the execution of what was commanded in vv. 1f. is carried a further step forward. The voice in v. 6 has the same function as that in v. 3: the 'crying' commanded in vv. 6ff. and the preparation of the way commanded in vv. 3ff. serve the same end—the comforting of Israel. This, however, only under-lines the contrast between the process described in vv. 3ff. and the sequel in vv. 6ff. In the former we found only the operation order answering the call to comfort, an order whose execution is taken for granted. Here, in vv. 6ff., however, the singularly brief command, 'Cry', is as abruptly followed by a word that reacts against it; the series of commands starting with v. 1 is interrupted by a question which offers resistance to the command—'what shall I cry?' (Luther's rendering here, 'preach', very well expresses the meaning, which is different from that of 'cry' in v. 3.) Here Deutero-Isaiah's language is terse in the extreme. The command consists of one word, the question which resists it (in the Hebrew) of two. With an artistry as incompar-able as, of course, it is unpremeditated, the collision of two differently directed wills is expressed at its most succinct. Because of the call 'preach' interposed into the stream of imperatives originating from 'comfort', a human voice with the question, 'What (shall I) preach?', resists this mighty downward pouring of God's gracious will, and with its words, so brief and so charged with emotion, perfectly gathers up all the vanquished nation's lamentation and sheer despair. The person addressed is he who was commanded to cry, the unknown prophet to whom we give the name of Deutero-Isaiah. Verses 6ff.

present his call with the minimum of detail. When he demurs with his counter-cry, 'What shall I preach?', he is only 'one of the people', and he speaks as one whose own thoughts are those of the vanquished nation that no longer believes in the possibility of any new beginning.

The counter-cry is given its particular shade of meaning and precise nuance in the words which follow it and form its substantiation. These, the substantiation of the objection, continue to the end of v. 7. Verse 8, on the other hand, gives the answer to the objection; the speaker is therefore identical with the one who uttered the command, 'Cry', at the beginning in v. 6. (Many regard the answer to the question in 6a as beginning immediately with 6b. This is very unlikely, because in that case we should have to take the main theme of Deutero-Isaiah's proclamation to be the evanescence of all things, which it is not.) How, then, are we to understand vv. 6b–7? The words sound familiar; indeed, they almost look as if they were meant to be a quotation. Our familiarity with them is due to such psalms as Pss. 39, 49 and 90, and similar passages in the book of Job. They represent a well-defined form often found in the Psalter—lament because of the evanescence of all things. The form represents the lament in the first person singular or plural expanded from personal into general, universal terms. Its finest example is the book of Job, where Job repeatedly widens the compass of his own suffering so that it applies to the suffering which characterizes the human lot in general.

If, however, the prophet's counter-cry was due to a particular set of circumstances, how can he substantiate it by means of such general sentiments? The answer is that the exiles' greatest temptation—and the prophet speaks as one of their number—was precisely to be resigned to thinking of themselves as caught up in the general transience of all things, to believing that nothing could be done to halt the extinction of their national existence, and to saying, 'just like the countless other nations destroyed before our time, in our time and after our time, we are a nation that perishes: all flesh is as grass!'

Here we encounter a further basic feature of what Deutero-Isaiah has to say: much of the book is steeped in the diction of the Psalter. That the verses before us are not—as might have been expected—a community lament, but the most universal form of lament, is due to the character of the prologue, which raises a particular into a universal. As a result, this particular formulation of the lament, designed to substantiate the prophet's objection, suggests that from which there is absolutely no appeal, that which cannot be averted. Only the last stage of utter resignation or despair employs language such as this (cf. Job); and resignation and despair constitute the spiritual state of the Israel to which the prophet is called to preach! He, the prophet, declares that he agrees with such thoughts; therefore even for him there can be no point in further preaching.

Here, between the prophet's objection and its answer, the text as we have it contains an addition: 'Surely the people is grass.' It is not someone's attempt to elucidate, but the comment of a reader who was deeply moved. He took the prophet to mean what we ourselves also read into him, namely, that the lament gathered up in this lament at the evanescence of all things is Israel's. And by means of this marginal note, he expressed this in such a way that even today we can still mark how Deutero-Isaiah's words came home to the mind and experience of one of his readers; he said 'Amen' to them and understood them. This is one of the numerous examples of additions or glosses which constitute valuable witnesses as to what happened to the biblical text as it was read by or to the congregation of the faithful.

Verse 8 contains the answer given to the prophet when he objected. The first part (8a) takes up the substantiation of the objection word for word and thus admits its truth. The voice that now speaks does not therefore intend to deny that Israel's circumstances are what the prophet, as 'one of the nation', takes them to be. From the human point of view there is nothing more to be done: crying or preaching to the dying remnant is pointless. In 8b, however, the sheer hopelessness of the situation is confronted with the reality of the word of God. The 'word of our God' spoken to Israel in her past history is not part and parcel of the inevitable decay: it stands, it persists, it abides. The reference is primarily, but not solely, to the promises which Israel once received. The prophet's objection thus falls to the ground. The word which he was required to cry (6a) does not belong to the realm of transitory things, but to that which abides. Nothing in existence has the power to make it void, not even the desperate plight which was Israel's.

The words 'But the word of our God stands for ever' form the point of focus in the prologue (in the prologue to the Fourth Gospel, too, 'the word' is determinant). They express what is basic to, and crucial for, the proclamation of Deutero-Isaiah. One thing itself proves this—the remarkable fact that in the final verses of the book (55.10f.) words occur which closely correspond to 'the word of our

God stands for ever' and develop its thought. The two of them, the word of God which abides, and the word of God which does not return to him void, but accomplishes the purpose for which he sends it, form the frame within which Deutero-Isaiah's proclamation is set and mounted. Israel had lost not only her land and her statehood, but also her temple and its worship, the fountain-head of life for land and nation. But she was still left with the word of God committed to her keeping, which at once took on a significance never hitherto seen, or even dreamed of. This is the starting-point of Deutero-Isaiah's proclamation.

Verses 6ff. remind us of the accounts of calls of other prophets (Isa. 6; Jer. 1; Ezek. 1–3). These all have one common factor: the man given the duty of proclaiming objects to it. As a man of unclean lips, Isaiah was afraid when face to face with the holiness of God; Jeremiah shrank from the task with the words, 'I am too young'; Deutero-Isaiah felt the plight of the remnant to be so hopeless as to make proclamation vain. The words in which he objected to his call are the only ones in the whole book where we hear the man himself. Elsewhere, he stands so completely in the shadow of his message that of him himself we hear and learn nothing more. It is touching that, in the one place where we do catch a glimpse of him, he proclaims his solidarity with his fellow-countrymen in their suffering and despair.

[9–11] In the third of the three cries which carry out the command to 'comfort', a completely different, a new, note is heard. The cry is directed to Jerusalem, but is given no specific introduction; the voice which utters it may possibly be the same as that in v. 6. This apart, however, vv. 9ff. perfectly correspond, both in form and structure, to the two preceding sections, vv. 3ff. and 6ff. Here, too, a duty is assigned by means of an imperative which links on to the preceding imperatives. In this case, however, the recipient is addressed by name. Zion is called upon to bring to the (other) cities of Judah the glad tidings, 'Behold, here is (comes) your God!'

Verses 9ff. go along with vv. 3–8; this is an important pointer to the way in which they are to be taken; each section within the series of imperatives contains a summons to a means of carrying out the command to comfort. The duty imposed upon the powers who are called on in vv. 3ff. is clear: they are to prepare the way. The same is true of the duty laid on the prophet in vv. 6ff. But how does the task to which Jerusalem is summoned fit in with these? Here, as often,

Zion, or Jerusalem, stands by synecdoche for Israel. But is not Israel entirely the one acted upon in the event described in vv. 1–11? Is it not Zion herself who is to be comforted? What then can it mean if she herself is allotted a task, and obviously an important one, in the execution of the work of comfort?

The Zion here spoken to is called herald of good tidings, *m^ebasseret*. The verb is used of the bringing of good news, e.g., I Sam. 31.9 (news of the victory of the Philistines), II Sam. 18.19 (Ahimaaz wishes to bring David the good news), and Jer. 20.15 (news of the birth of a child). In these passages, the event which the glad tidings announce has already taken place. Now, what clearly differentiates the task imposed upon Zion from that of the herald, the one who cries on God's behalf in vv. 6ff., is that, whereas the latter is to announce that God intends to deliver his chosen people, Zion as messenger of good tidings is joyfully to announce to the others (the cities of Judah) that this has already taken place. Does this mean, then, that the order here given is not to be carried out until the first caravans have already made the journey home and arrived in Jerusalem? Not at all. Rather, the 'herald of good tidings, Zion', is to proclaim the advent of Yahweh *now*, and to proclaim it 'without fear', even if it still lies in the future. She is to call for praise of the one who comes to help his people, *as if the help were already given*. There is now added to the task of proclamation, which concerns one single person (vv. 6ff.), an essentially different one, and it falls to the choir which responds to the herald, and is even now striking up praise of the future miraculous act of God. These verses of the prologue (9–11) are the basis of the literary category of 'eschatological psalm of praise' peculiar to Deutero-Isaiah and found throughout his preaching. Here the call to praise is always substantiated by a verb in the perfect tense: God has already acted.[a] For the comfort to become effective, Zion (that is, the people of Israel) must herself accept and assent to the message (vv. 6ff.) of the coming salvation (vv. 3ff.). If now, while still in exile, she is bold enough to break into jubilation at it, then she has accepted it. In this respect the song of praise which Zion is summoned to raise in vv. 9ff. corresponds to that literary category which bulks largest in Deutero-Isaiah's proclamation, the oracle of salvation in which the deliverance promised to Israel is proclaimed in the perfect tense—that is, which says that in the counsel of God, the change in her fortunes has already

[a] Westermann, *The Praise of God in the Psalms*, trs. K. R. Crim, Richmond, Virginia, 1966, pp. 142–5.

taken place (40.1f.). The connection of the two literary categories is also suggested by the words 'fear not' at the end of v. 9; they are taken from the oracle.

Verse 9: Just as the watchman who has to announce the coming of the king mounts the tower, Jerusalem is to 'get up to (the) high mountain', in order to see the exiles approaching while they are still far off, so to be able to announce this to many and far-scattered cities. Such a high degree of personification of Zion shows that the prophet's way of speaking is extremely figurative and indirect: the thing would be fantastic as actual fact. Then in vv. 9b–11, too, what is described is not properly and directly the return of the exiles. Rather, the one who comes is Yahweh himself: he 'just' brings Israel in his train. So little prominence is here given to the nation that it can be de-scribed as brought by God along with himself as a booty he has won! This is a particularly fine and impressive example of Deutero-Isaiah's ability to express theological concepts as event. (We shall find recurrences of the same trait in the passages where Yahweh confronts the foreign gods.) His description of Israel's return as divine advent or epiphany is his way of implying that this is solely and entirely the work of Yahweh. At the same time, he links up with the ancient tradition of the 'divine epiphany',[a] the earliest 'form' in which Israel sung the praises of the God who made haste to help his people in their direst need. These old epiphanies always depict Yahweh's advent as a bi-polar event: he comes as the mighty, the majestic one, his advent convulsing the cosmos and overthrowing the foe; but also as he who condescends to his people in their need, and graciously has compassion on them. Both motifs are taken up here: 'He comes with might, and his arm rules for him'; the nation's restoration needs his antecedent victorious intervention. But there-after how different is Deutero-Isaiah's picture of Yahweh's mighty intervention from that of the old songs of victory! The second motif is profoundly changed, as we see it in the event which Deutero-Isaiah had to proclaim. While it chiefly appears in the complex whose subject is the work which Yahweh makes Cyrus accomplish for him, there is a suggestion of it even here—at the end the light falls on the picture of the shepherd (v. 11), a fitting simile for the condescension of the God of majesty, and for his gracious compassion with the afflicted. Israel had thus made supplication to her Lord in community laments: 'Give ear, O Shepherd of Israel!' (Ps. 80); now the very

[a] *Ibid.*, pp. 93–101.

thing for which these suppliants looked from Israel's shepherd becomes actual fact. The details given in v. 11b emphasize the fact that the shepherd does not lead an undifferentiated multitude, but individuals: each one receives the care he needs from him, all are to share in the joy of the return (cf. John 10.14); and the shepherd knows how to make the way easy for every single one.

The reason for the importance attaching to the simile of the shepherd at the end of the prologue, and particularly as it is developed in v. 11b, is that in Deutero-Isaiah's proclamation the object of God's saving work is always the nation *en bloc*. We never find God acting with individuals or with sections of the nation. Deutero-Isaiah is concerned with 'the whole and nothing but the whole', in the truest sense of the words. (The same holds good for Exodus.) The conclusion of the prologue speaks for the whole of Deutero-Isaiah's proclamation, saying that, while in the acts of God which the prophet is to describe, the object of the shepherd's loving care is the whole nation, this is only so in the form of his leading, directing and carrying of individuals, in order that the promise made to the whole should be shared in by every single one of them.

Chapter 40.12–31

The Creator is the Saviour

12 Who measures the waters in the hollow of his hand
and measures off the heavens with a span,
and encloses the dust of the earth in a measure
and weighs the mountains in scales, and the hills in a balance?
13 Who judges the Spirit of Yahweh,
who is his counsellor who instructs him?
14 Whom does he consult for his enlightenment
that he may instruct him in the right way
and teach him knowledge[a] and show him the path of understanding?

15 Behold, nations are like a drop in the bucket,
they are accounted as the dust on the scales.
Behold, islands weigh as a grain.

[a] 'And teach him knowledge' is perhaps an addition.

16   Lebanon does not suffice for fuel,
     nor are its beasts enough for a burnt offering.
17   All the nations are as nothing before him,
     they are accounted by him as nothing and emptiness.

18   And to whom will you liken God,
     or what likeness compare with him?[a]
21   Do you know? Do you not hear?
     Has it not been told you from the beginning?
     Have you not understood [from the] foundation of the earth?[b]
22   He who is enthroned above the circle of the earth,
     and its inhabitants are like grasshoppers;
     who stretches out the heavens like a curtain,
     and spreads them like a tent to dwell in;
23   who brings the princes to nought,
     and makes the rulers of the earth as nothing;
24   scarcely are they planted, scarcely sown,
     scarcely has their stem taken root in the earth,
     when he blows upon them, and they wither,
     the tempest carries them off like stubble.

25   To whom then will you compare me,
     that I should be like him? says the Holy One.
26   Lift up your eyes on high
     and see: who created these?
     He who brings out their host by number,
     calling them all by name;
     for him who is great in might and strong in power,
     not one is missing.

27   Why do you say, O Jacob, and speak, O Israel,
     'My way is hid from Yahweh,
     and my right is disregarded by my God'?
28   Have you not known? Have you not heard?
     Yahweh is an everlasting God, Creator of the ends of the earth.
     He does not faint or grow weary,
     his understanding is unsearchable.
29   He gives power to the faint,
     and strength in plenty to him who has no might.
30   Youths shall faint and be weary,
     and young men shall stumble and fall;
31   but they who wait on Yahweh renew their strength,
     they mount up with wings like eagles,

[a] Vv. 19f. are an addition, see below.
[b] Read *mīsudat.*

they run and do not faint,
they walk and are not weary.

Bibliography: H. A. Brongers, *De scheppingstradities bij de profeten*, Amsterdam and Paris, 1945; J. Guillet, 'La polémique contre les idoles et le Serviteur de Jahvé', *Biblica*, 40 (1959), pp. 428–34; J. Begrich, *Studien zu Deuterojesaja*, 1938, n.e., *TB*, 20 (1963), pp. 48–53; 'Sprache und Struktur', pp. 124–34.

[12–31] 40.12–31 is a unity; the sections (vv. 12–17; 18–24; 25f.; 27–31) all fall into the one literary category of disputation. The chief proof that the passage is in fact a unity is the mutual relationship of the sections. Looking closely at the questions by which each is introduced, we find that in vv. 12 ('Who measures the waters . . . the heavens?'), 13f., 18 and 25, they are really rhetorical; only the final section, vv. 27–31, is introduced by a true disputation: v. 27, 'Why do you say, O Jacob . . . my right is disregarded by my God?'. Here the prophet quotes the assertion being made by Jacob-Israel, that God had abandoned his people, and in vv. 28ff. he challenges it: 'Do you not know? Have you not heard?' These are the words in which the poem contained in vv. 12–31 reaches its objective: the three preceding sections headed by rhetorical questions simply prepare the way for the disputation proper in vv. 27–31, and only in the light of the fourth does their point and function become clear. The people whose words of accusation are quoted in v. 27 began to be addressed in v. 12, while the accusation itself, first explicitly stated there (v. 27), is implicitly challenged from v. 22 onwards. One basis of the lament 'My way is hid from Yahweh' (v. 27) could be that Yahweh does not have the power to help his people; this the first three sections challenge. Or else it could be that Yahweh no longer has the will to help; this the fourth challenges. Only vv. 27–31 make the sections in vv. 12–26 into significant component parts of a whole: only there are we given the precise conclusion of all four sections. The background of vv. 12–26 is the unspoken question—inevitable in view of the situation into which Isaiah's defeat had brought her—'Can our God still really help us?' The answer given to this first question depends on the answer to the other, 'Does our God still want to have anything more to do with us?' Both are then in fact gathered up in vv. 28–31. The one is given in v. 28, which gathers up what God said in vv. 12–26. The other comes in vv. 29–31. The correspondence between the two answers, 'He does not faint or grow weary' (v. 28c) and 'He gives power to the faint' (v. 29a), is perfectly deliberate.

The structure of vv. 12–26 is such that each of the three sections relates to a specific challenge confronting Israel in her present plight:

I.   (12–17)   the nations and isles
II. (18–24)   the princes and rulers
III. (25–26)   the heavenly host

To counter the challenges offered by the foreign nations in their might, the princes in their power, and the apparently victorious star-gods, Deutero-Isaiah proclaims to the weary and despondent the majesty of the creator and lord of history, who in his compassion towards the weary (IV: 27–31) comes to meet his people. At the same time, the prophet's answer, his proclamation designed to counter this challenge, also has an inner consistency, for he reminds his people of the God whose praises they themselves had sung in the past in their hymns; he revives their forgotten praise. The passage taken altogether is modelled on the structure found in descriptive praise;[a] in this God is extolled in respect of his majesty and of his goodness. Clearly, it is this twofold division that makes the relationship between vv. 12–26 and 27–31. Praise of God's majesty is frequently developed along the two lines (e.g. Ps. 33), that he is the creator and lord of his creation (so here vv. 12–17), and that he is the lord of history (so here vv. 18–24). Part III (vv. 25–26) is a deliberate addition of Deutero-Isaiah's own, to counter the challenge offered by the astral gods of Babylon: the creator is also the lord of the stars, for he made them.

Thus, 40.12–31 not only contain features deriving from hymnody and display the style proper to it; the model for the verses is manifestly the structure found in descriptive praise, which Deutero-Isaiah wants to revive for his people to counter their laments. (For this reason it is associated with the disputation.)

It is certainly not by chance that this poem forms the opening of Deutero-Isaiah's proclamation; there is good reason for it. All that is to follow depends upon God's becoming once more great in his chosen people's eyes. For Israel in her existing circumstances solemnly to aver that God was lord of creation and of history is far from being an obvious thing to do, and it raises basic questions which are hard to answer. These are to be dealt with later. But to ask in what way God could now still be, or again be, to his people what he had been in the

[a] Westermann, *The Praise of God* . . ., pp. 116ff.

old psalms with their joyous confidence of victory, is only possible, indeed only has meaning, on the basis of countering lamentation by means of a new, free affirmation of him. This is why, in 40.12–31, Deutero-Isaiah sets out to revive praise.

[12–17] I. The questions introduced by the word 'who' lay down the lines of vv. 12ff. The link between them is their subject-matter: v. 12 'Who measures the waters with . . .?', vv. 13f. 'Who measures the Spirit of Yahweh . . .?'. They are quite clearly rhetorical; the answer (nobody) is so obvious as not to need stating. The relationship between the two parts may be taken as a comparison resolved into two questions: one can no more measure the Spirit of God than one can measure the sea in the hollow of one's hand. It may also be meant in the sense of a conclusion from the lesser to the greater . . . how much less can a man measure the Spirit of God! The difference is immaterial.

The verbs in v. 12—measure, enclose, weigh—are all different ways of describing the same process, ascertaining the total amount of something by measuring or weighing it.[a] The prophet ranges over the sea (or the waters), the heavens, the earth, and the mountains. These stand, as in Job. 38, Ps. 90 and elsewhere, for the basic magnitudes of the created universe, the magnitudes which constitute it in its totality. The verbs in the rhetorical questions make the heavens, the earth, the sea and the mountains stand for that which is absolutely immeasurable.[b]

Verses 13f. appear to continue in just the same style: to how much greater a degree does this immeasurability pertain to God! Verse 13a, however, puts the question, 'Who measures the *Spirit* of Yahweh . . .?', while v. 13b takes the line, 'Who is his counsellor who instructs him?'. The 'Spirit of Yahweh' does not mean either 'the all-encompassing and spiritual nature of Yahweh' (Volz) or the 'organ of the divine intelligence' (Duhm), but the power of God which works miracles. The same thing is said in v. 14a and b. The slight difference just noticed reveals something of importance for Deutero-Isaiah's theology. If v. 13b is to be understood as parallel to v. 13a, this must signify that Yahweh's 'measuring' or 'weighing'

---

[a] Sidney Smith *ad loc.*: 'The verbs and the objects are carefully balanced to cover the measurable forms of matter, i.e. liquid, air, powder, solid, and all the types of measurement' (*op. cit.*, pp. 12f. and 97, n. 85).

[b] In a hymn, Marduk is called 'the one who traverses the heavens, heaps up the earth, and measures the waters of the sea' (Stummer, *op. cit.*, p. 174).

could only be the act of a person ('Who is his counsellor?'). There could be no idea of thinking of him as a reality of a kind corresponding to the heavens or the sea. If God is spoken of as immeasurable, this can only mean the immeasurability of a planning, active person. The measure here would be the word that 'measures up' to him, that would be in a position to have an equally strong voice in God's plan. The divine incomparability and immeasurability consist in the fact that nobody possesses the measures for pronouncing judgment on the divine planning and acting; as a result, nobody can give him advice, or say to him that in this or in that he ought to have acted rather differently (exactly as in 45.9ff.). This suggests, however, that although these words come right at the beginning of the book, they relate to the whole of it, and therefore to Deutero-Isaiah's proclamation in his own particular situation. That no one can measure the Spirit of Yahweh, or arrive at the divine plan in his thoughts, is not here said as a general statement; as we shall see later, even in these verses Deutero-Isaiah is already at grips with his own particular task.

[15–17] Only now are we told what had been meant by the divine plan on the one hand, and the 'measuring' or understanding of it on the other. When water is drawn, the drop that falls from the bucket does not matter, nor, when things are weighed, does the dust on the scales. In the divine plan, whole nations may matter as little! Admittedly, this relationship is not brought out until the very end of the passage, v. 17: 'All the nations are as nothing before him.' But the prophet can only be thinking of the divine plan or historical design spoken of in vv. 13f. Verses 15 and 17 then say that in it, in the divine planning and acting, the nations are not a factor to be seriously reckoned with, the empires and powers of this world are as nothing before him. Verse 16 does not fit into this context. Its subject is not God's plans and actions with the nations, but his greatness as such. God is so mighty, the verse says, that even a sacrifice raised to the nth degree could not give his greatness the honour it deserves. Since v. 16 does not perfectly harmonize with vv. 15 and 17, it may be a later addition. But this is not necessarily so, since the extravagant metaphor very well accords with Deutero-Isaiah's style. In this case, it is to be thought of as a parenthetical outburst between vv. 15 and 17. Such is the divine majesty that only a sacrifice so great as to be immeasurable would be commensurate with it. Read thus as a parenthesis, it is important for Deutero-Isaiah's conception of sacrifice. Taken along with 48.23ff., it shows that, when Deutero-

Isaiah does mention sacrifice at all, his words have a critical or, at least, not markedly affirmative, tone.

Concluding remarks on 40.12–17: Since vv. 12–31 form a single unit, it follows that vv. 12–17 are themselves part of a conversation. We have to remember that Deutero-Isaiah is speaking throughout to someone actually *vis-à-vis* himself. The questions are of the nature of a challenge, and the two 'Behold's' are clearly addressed to someone who first needs to be made to behold. The possibility of comfort for the nation, whose plight is expressed in the laments contained in 40.6f. and 40.27, depends on the prior removal of a stumbling-block in its path, the mood of resignation which had grown up because of the view which they themselves took of the way in which God acted in history. This was based on the facts as they appeared to be. There was no gainsaying that Israel had been vanquished, and that, to all intents and purposes, the bottom had been knocked out of her worship. This is the ground for the view of the situation given in 40.6f. and 40.27. Deutero-Isaiah counters it with the extravagant and exaggerated assertion made in 40.12–17, that the nations are as nothing before God, drops in the bucket, dust on the scales. The purpose of the exaggerations, which in fact are only seeming, is the removal of the stumbling-block caused by a sceptical view of the situation. Israel needed to be brought hard up against this, in order that she might once again see what she had known for a long while, that, as the creator, God is the lord of history. The verses are intended to destroy a false premise.

In this respect, Deutero-Isaiah is clearly the successor of the pre-exilic prophets, for part of their function was to warn their fellow-countrymen against either placing too great reliance on one of the world-empires or being too greatly in fear of them. We need only refer to Isa. 2.7ff. and Isa. 31.1ff. In both places the criteria of judgment were the reverse of what they should have been; the manifest expansion of foreign nations' power had meant the lessening or weakening of the power of God in history, and of his lordship over it.

Deutero-Isaiah is not quite the same, due to a change which had come over the situation. The subject of the pre-exilic prophets' words was always one specific nation, a power close at hand for anyone to see. Differently situated, Deutero-Isaiah boldly sets the foreign nations *en bloc* over against God, and says that, as compared with him, they are all nothing. These all-inclusive concepts are characteristic of the prophet; in the trial speeches where he deals with

Yahweh's relationship to the foreign gods, he speaks in exactly the same way. Deutero-Isaiah is the prophet who made 'all' and 'nothing' into determinative concepts. We today can hardly appreciate how momentous they then were, since they had never previously been thus used. According to Gesenius-Buhl, *Lexikon*, 'nothing' used absolutely and as a noun occurs only in Deutero-Isaiah (40.17, 23; 41.11, 12, 24) and in passages that are certainly later than him (Hag. 2.3; Pss. 39.6 (5); 73.2?). Deutero-Isaiah was probably the first to use the term in this way.

Immediately after the prologue, the proclamation itself begins with a reference to God as the lord of universal history, a theme upon which Deutero-Isaiah plays variations down to the last chapter of the book. Reference to the majesty of the lord of history forms an essential part of the Bible's doctrine of God. When men close their eyes to it, or cease to accept it, when what God says and does has lost its universal reference and is applied only to men in their individual existence, this spells the loss of a most important element in the Bible's message.

[18–24] II. There is no agreement as to the way the sections which now follow ought to be divided. The division is, however, clear from the way in which they are made up:

18–24		25–26	
18	To whom . . .?	25	To whom . . . ?
19–20	(with 41.6–7)		lacking
21	the question designed to stir the people up	26a	the cry with the same purpose
22	the creator	26b	the creator
23–24	the lord of history	26c	the lord of history

At the same time, comparison of the two parts shows that vv. 19f. (along with 41.6f.), to which nothing corresponds in vv. 25f., stand outside the schema, and should be considered as an expansion which, whether or not the author is Deutero-Isaiah, is to be read as a parenthesis.

In vv. 12–17, the attention of Deutero-Isaiah's hearers was drawn to the divine immeasurability. In vv. 18ff. the subject is the divine incomparability. Verse 18 is a rhetorical question, just like those in vv. 12ff. It also expects the same answer: there is nobody with whom God can be compared.[a] The second half of the verse, 'or to what

---

[a] It should be translated 'to whom': *contra* de Boer, who because of v. 18b translates 'to what'.

likeness will you compare him? looks for the answer that it is impossible to make a likeness of Yahweh, for he is the creator of all that is. This is said in v. 21, which follows directly on v. 18 as the substantiation of the divine incomparability.

In contrast, vv. 19f., for all that they make a good continuation of v. 18b, refer not to images of Yahweh, but to those of other gods. We are left to supply the logical connection: it is impossible to make an image of God—in the way you have come to know how the images of other gods are manufactured here in Babylon. For, since these words occur in an address, the realism and vividness in the description in vv. 19f. and 41.6f. (as Duhm saw, this second set of verses is to be taken along with 40.19f.) is based on personal observation. We may well suppose that observation of the manufacture of images made a profound impression on the Israelites exiled in Babylon, and this is directly reflected in the interpolation before us (see on 41.6f.).

The description is textually uncertain in several places (the rendering given for v. 20a is no more than a conjecture), and the same is true of the order of the verses; Köhler and many others take 41.6f. between 40.19a and b. However, these difficulties have little effect on the understanding of the verses. The surprising thing in this description of the manufacture of an idol is that its author is content to reproduce the process with an almost photographic exactitude, and adds not even a single word of criticism or direct mockery. The description, he obviously thought, spoke for itself. There was nothing to add to it. Nevertheless, the way in which he stresses the idol's solidity and stability (that does not move) hints at a delicate indirect mockery. This impression is confirmed by the liturgy of the Babylonian New Year Festival, where we find as part of the sacred rite a similar description of the manufacture of statues of the gods; it, too, names the materials and the various craftsmen (*ANET*, p. 331):

> When it is three hours after sunrise,
> [he shall call] a metalworker and give
> him precious stones and gold [from]
> the treasury of the god Marduk to make
> two images (for the ceremonies of) the
> sixth day (of Nisannu). He shall call
> a woodworker and give him (some) cedar
> and tamarisk (pieces). He shall call a
> goldsmith and give him (some) gold . . .

It is very significant that, at the time when Israel's ancestors left the lands where the gods were worshipped by means of images, she was given, along with her election, the commandment forbidding the making of any images of Yahweh. It is equally significant that, when the Israelites again had to leave their own land for a foreign one in which they saw images and their manufacture, they understood the great consequences of the fact that it was impossible to make an image of their God. Just as in the Decalogue there is the closest possible connection between the first and the second commandments,[a] so there is here, in the two questions in v. 18, between the incomparability of Yahweh and the impossibility of representing him by an image.

[21–24] The verses are to be read as the direct continuation of the questions in v. 18. The four questions in v. 21 exemplify a leading characteristic of Deutero-Isaiah's style, intensification by means of putting sentences with the same meaning one after the other, the first often being the shortest and the last the longest. The device justifies the emendation made to the text in the last part of v. 21.[b] It appears again a little later in v. 27.

This time, the questions in v. 21, as well as those in v. 27, are not in any sense simply rhetorical ones. They are true questions expecting an answer. The two pairs of verbs exactly represent the two processes found in tradition. In the word's original meaning, handing something on implies a giving and a taking, an offering and a receiving. The first two verbs 'Have you not known?, Have you not heard?' describe the one aspect, the third, 'Has it not been told you from the beginning?', the other. Now, the way in which the idea of tradition was understood by previous scholars is extremely significant. Duhm's comment on our passage is as follows: 'So far as Deutero-Isaiah derives his knowledge from books, his source is the Yahwist . . . But, for the Yahwist, what stands in his writings is tradition, which therefore goes back to Noah and Adam . . .' For Duhm, tradition is by definition a literary process. His sole interest is in the way in which Deutero-Isaiah himself learned of it, and he never asks how tradition reached the prophet's hearers, how it was handed on to *them*, as the text expressly says it was. This, however, is made quite plain as we read further. The words which follow the questions in

[a] So W. Zimmerli, 'Das zweite Gebot', *Gottes Offenbarung, Gesammelte Aufsätze*, Munich 1963, pp. 234–48.

[b] *Contra* de Boer, who renders, 'have you not understood the solid construction of the earth?' a rendering already rejected (rightly) by Duhm.

v. 21, '. . . who sits above the circle of the earth . . . who stretches out the heavens as a curtain . . .', are, quite obviously, taken from a psalm. Similarly, in vv. 27–31, the same questions are followed by other words also taken from psalms: 'Yahweh is God everlasting, the Creator of the ends of the earth . . .' Therefore, when Deutero-Isaiah put these questions, he was thinking of his people's liturgical traditions, of the psalms in which the praises of the creator were handed on. This is where it had been told them from the beginning, where they heard and knew. These urgent questions running through the different sections of 40.12–31 introduce us to an important element in the prophecy of Deutero-Isaiah. In order to prepare the ground for his message of comfort, he revived among the remnant of his people a particular component of pre-exilic worship. When Israel was no longer able to offer sacrifice, she lost the firmest basis of her community life, the element which in fact held it together. The destruction of the temple spelt the end of one of the two factors essential to worship, the rites performed. But the spoken element in worship was not irrevocably tied to the holy place and the established rites. Naturally, of course, the old hymns of praise and joy became largely muted after 586 (Ps. 137). Naturally, too, it was lamentation that now chiefly lived on, as we see from the Book of Lamentations. This is the situation in which Deutero-Isaiah had the task of reviving the songs of praise. This is the point of the urgent questions in 40.12–31, designed to rouse Israel from her torpor. The last of them, 'Have you not understood from the foundation of the earth?', is taken by some (Volz, Duhm) as meaning the direct revelation through the creation. This is perhaps possible. More probably, however, the words are only meant to continue and intensify the previous question.

Verse 22 contains some very rare words. The word for 'circle' (*ḥūg*) occurs only once or twice and always in the context of the creator and creation (Prov. 8.27; Job 26.10 [conjecturally]; 22.14). The word for 'curtain' (*doq*), and also for 'stretches out' (*mth*), are only found here. This suggests well-defined, distinctive traditions. We may take it that Deutero-Isaiah used the words to call to his hearers' minds a version of the praises of the creator which was still well-known to them. Even if we cannot find every word of it in the psalms (v. 22a is similar to Job 34.13b, and 22b corresponds to Ps. 104.2b), this is quite natural, since what the Psalter hands on to us is only a selection of Israel's praise. One thing, however, we can detect here is the structure of this praise. Verse 22a speaks of God's majesty, of his being enthroned high above the circle of the earth, so high that, in this perspective, men appear as puny and tiny. In praise as found in the Psalms, the theme of the divine majesty is developed along two lines. First, God is creator and lord of history. The calling of the world into being is the subject of the latter part of the verse here, 'who stretches out the heavens like a curtain'. After the questions designed to revive praise, all four sections in vv. 12–31 in one way or another strike up praise of the creator. Praise of the Lord of history is added in v. 23: 'who brings princes to nought. . . .' Something closely resembling this is found in Job 34.19f., cf. also Job 12.13–25. In the picture of the divine lordship over history, Israel recedes into the background, and the emphasis is laid on God's intervention against the mighty ones of the earth, as for example also in Ps. 33.10 and 16f. At this point the correspondence between the two sections, vv. 12–17 and 18–24, is perfectly clear. In vv. 12–17, reference after reference to the creator and lord shows the nothingness of the nations in Yahweh's sight, and in vv. 18–24 the nothingness of the princes. Both passages deal with the situation in which Israel then found herself, and with the challenge to which she was exposed. What the prophet's hearers are to take out of his words is not, as Duhm says, that 'it was Yahweh who created the world', but that Yahweh, who created the world, is absolute lord of the nations and powers.

[25–26] III. In both parts of v. 25, the question is the same as that which introduced the preceding section, vv. 18–24. This is again a characteristic of Deutero-Isaiah's style. Sections in a unit of some length may often be recognized as such because they have clearly marked introductions. In some cases, as here, these are very much alike. In others, they appear to be so because they use the same form, e.g., a series of questions (40.12, 18, 25, 27) or of double imperatives (51.9, 17; 52.1). This remarkable and unique stylistic feature is itself a sure sign that the book is not simply composed of short, unconnected passages strung together: there are also units of considerable length.

The question is followed by the earnest appeal, 'Lift up your eyes on high and see', which corresponds to the question in v. 21 designed to arouse Israel from her torpor ('Do you not know? Do you not hear?') In both cases there is emotion in the references to the creator: 'Who created these?'. And, as in the previous section, the point of the reference is emphasis of the creator's lordship. Here, instead of the divine intervention in history (vv. 15ff., 23f.), we have the direction and control of the stars. The theme of God's majesty ('he who is great in might and strong in power') is developed by speaking of him as the commander of an innumerable host. He it is who sets their myriads in motion. Yet, while thus controlling their great number, he maintains an individual relationship with every single one of them, for every single star is his creation: 'he calls them all by name.'

As we have seen, what was said about the lordship of God, the creator, in the first two sections bears, though not directly, on the situation in which Israel was placed; the same presumably applies to the present section as well. In (I) it is the nations, in (II) the princes, who are as nothing in comparison with the majesty and might of God. Then the words, 'who created these?', refer to the astral bodies which were the chief gods in Babylon, all-dominant, and its virtual rulers. There can be no doubt whatever that they are, as it were, the troops against whom the prophet here deploys his polemic, and his words, spoken of all places in Babylon, are an attack all along the line! Marduk is the sun-god, the king is his priest and representative on earth: the part played by astral cults was immense. To this, Deutero-Isaiah says that the astral bodies, who are lords in Babylon in being the principal deities there, are created things, created things and nothing more.[a] They are all subject to Yahweh, the God of Israel, their creator and lord. Not a single one of them but must obey his commands. 'Who created these?', asks Deutero-Isaiah, and in so doing rejects their claim to divinity and puts them where they belong, under the word of command of their creator and lord. The incongruity of the two statements made in v. 26b may be set in still clearer relief. The names of the stars in Babylon, the objects of praise, worship, and constant invocation, are no more than names which let the real ruler show each star its course and keep it within its proper limits. Spoken in a region where the Babylonian astral cult held sovereign sway, the boldness of the oracle is quite amazing.

[27–31] IV. Here at last the audience which has been addressed from v. 12 onwards is mentioned by name, 'you, Jacob . . . you, Israel', and here it itself is also heard speaking, 'Why do you say? . . .'. In sections I–III the position which the disputation sought to controvert had not as yet been made clear. The questions which introduced them were rhetorical. Here, however, the real feelings of the prophet's hearers, feelings of despondency, and doubt concerning Yahweh's action on their behalf, are brought out into the open. The

---

[a] The mere createdness of the astral bodies is expressed in similar terms in Gen. I.

questions of vv. 21 and 26 designed to arouse Israel from her torpor are now repeated word for word in v. 28a in order to counter the lament that complained of the divine action (v. 21): 'Have you not known? Have you not heard?'. Then, after a summary repetition of the answers of the previous sections (vv. 28b and c), they are given their final answer, in v. 29.

In the three sections which make up vv. 12–26, the prophet in each case draws attention to God's sovereign dignity as displayed in his work as creator and lord. This lord's majesty he sets against the despondency of Israel, who, because of this and its doubting, had ceased to see God as the immeasurable and incomparable. In the fourth section, vv. 27–31, the prophet counters Israel's despondency, now openly expressed in the lament in v. 27, by proclamation of the God who condescends and stoops to help his people in their need. This shows that the whole poem conforms to the structure of descriptive praise.[a] What enabled the prophet to use the Psalter's descriptive praise is that its structure dovetails with the earnest discourse against the nation's weariness and despondency expressed in the four disputations.

Verse 27: Here Deutero-Isaiah obviously quotes words of a community lament, using them to express Israel's complaint and protest against the way in which God acted; and his quotation is, in fact, the central part in a lament, the 'charge brought against the deity'. The 'why' with which he begins combats the 'why' that introduced the charge which the nation made against God, which would have run:

> O Lord, why is our way hid from thee?
> our right disregarded by thee?

Both lines are similar to laments which we know from the Psalter and the Book of Lamentations. The words which set their tone are often found in the two books. 'Hid', e.g. Pss. 13.2 (1); 22.25 (24); 27.9; 30.8 (7); 44.25 (24); 69.18 (17); 88.15 (14); 102.3 (2); 104.29; 143.7; Job 13.24. 'Right', e.g. Pss. 26.1; 35.23; 37.6; 140.13 (12); 146.7. Their parallelism is matched in Ps. 44.25 (24), again a community lament:

> Why dost thou hide thy face?
> forget our affliction and oppression?

[a] Westermann, *The Praise of God* . . ., pp. 116–25.

We may therefore take it for granted that here in v. 27 Deutero-Isaiah cites words from a lament in actual use by the exiles at the time. They imply, as we might also infer from the so-called Lamentations of Jeremiah, that the remnant of the nation held services of lament, and that they connect with these.[a] The prophet counters this lament with the question which disputes its truth: 'Why do you say, O Jacob?' The words whose truth he disputes originated in the liturgy, and people were familiar with them because of their use in worship! Deutero-Isaiah thus here exercises a function very similar to one which the pre-exilic prophets also exercised. They had to raise their voice against a sacrificial worship which had become unreal. With Deutero-Isaiah, the context was the exiles' services of lamentation which were losing their force. His words are designed to shake them out of their torpor.

[28] As he once more takes up the questions of v. 21 and gathers the preceding sections together, the prophet again refers to the majesty of the creator, and here the language is even more clearly that of the psalms of praise:

> Yahweh is an everlasting God,
> he sees unto the ends of the earth.

One of the creator's properties is his limitless extension in time (everlasting) and in space (the ends of the earth). The creator's unrestrained vastness is set over against the narrow lot of Israel and the challenges which faced her. Verse 28c states the significance of this vastness for those who have Yahweh as their God: his understanding is illimitable, and therefore unsearchable; his designs infinitely outstrip those possibilities for the future which Israel herself can see.

[29–31] Here the chapter, a well-constructed unity, reaches its goal, comfort for Israel. The faint, the one who has no might, is the Israel of the day. All that had been said from v. 12 onwards was intended as preparation for the statement made here, to which Israel can freely listen now that stumbling blocks have been removed. (The words are to be regarded as address.) We should not be misled by their being put in general terms applicable at any time; the reason for this is the style used in descriptive praise, which Deutero-Isaiah adopts here. How much this is the case may be seen by comparison with Ps. 33, which these verses resemble very closely:

---

[a] 'Sprache und Struktur', p. 118.

Isa. 40	Ps. 33
Even youths faint and are weary	The king is not saved by his great army;
and young men fall exhausted,	the warrior is not delivered by his great strength.
but they who wait on Yahweh	But the eye of Yahweh is on those who fear him,
renew their strength.	On those who hope in his steadfast love.

In such language, familiar to his hearers from the hymns they had sung at worship in earlier days, the prophet speaks to the nation's heart (40.2). The faint, and those who have no might, are standing before him. In the situation described in the lament in v. 27, the words lose their general reference and applicability to all time, and the paradox in v. 29 is direct address.

Verses 30–31 develop the two sides of the paradox. The strong and stalwart fall exhausted; but the faint and 'spent' complete their journey. While v. 31 equates the 'faint' with those who wait for Yahweh, there is no thought of such waiting being praised as a possibility open to human initiative: the only praise is of the transforming divine act which makes the paradox possible. Here again we find clear echoes of a motif belonging to descriptive praise: the exalting of the humble in vv. 29–31 contrasts with the humbling of the exalted in vv. 15ff. and 23f., and this is the way in which God is praised in the Psalter: 'he casts the mighty from their seats and exalts the humble.' This is the mode of action of him whose power is without limits and whose understanding is unsearchable.

The development of v. 29 strictly ends with v. 31a. Verse 31b introduces fresh matter, to the extent that there is now a clear allusion to the way leading to the homeland. This is the way which was spoken of in the prologue (40.10f.). Thus, the conclusion of vv. 12–31 reminds one of that of vv. 1–11; both point to the destination to which the cry, 'Comfort my people', is designed to lead.

Summary

The section, 40.12–31, is a compilation of four disputations, only the last of which, however, vv. 27–31, contains the real disputation (v. 27); the first three are preparatory in character. In the first three sections, Deutero-Isaiah draws his fellow-countrymen's attention to the incomprehensibility (vv. 12–17) and the incomparability (vv. 18–24 and 25f.) of God, the creator and lord of history, *vis-à-vis* the nations (I), the princes (II), and the astral bodies (astral gods) (III). In the fourth he points his people to the gracious God who gives renewed strength to the faint and to those who have no might. The whole is constructed on the model of the descriptive psalms of praise. In the first three sections Deutero-Isaiah proclaims to the faint and the despondent the majesty of the creator and lord of history (*vis-à-vis* the challenges offered by the nations in their greatness, the princes in their might, and the seemingly victorious astral gods), in the fourth he proclaims the mercy of the God who, in his people's hour of need, condescends to them.

CHAPTER 41.1–5

Who performs and does this?

1 Listen to me in silence, ye islands!
   Nations, [wait before me]!ᵃ
   Let them approach, then speak,
   together let us draw near for judgment.

2 Who stirred (him) up from the east
   whom victory meets at every step,
   who gave up nations before him,
   and kings [he trampled underfoot]?ᵇ
   His sword makes [them]ᶜ like dust,
   his bow like driven stubble.

3 He pursues them and passes on safely,
   not touching the path with his feet.

4 Who performs and does this?
   He who calls the generations from the beginning.
   I, Yahweh, am the first,
   and with the last I am still he.

ᵃ The words *yaḥᵃlīpu kōaḥ* are a dittography of 40.31. In their place *yaḥᵃlu nikḥī* 'wait before me' has been conjectured (*BH, app. cr.*), but this is quite uncertain. Perhaps the last two words of v. 5 stood here in a different form: 'draw near and come!'

ᵇ Instead of *yarᵉd* read *yārōd*.

ᶜ Read *yittᵉnēm*.

5   The islands see this and are afraid,
    the ends of the earth tremble.[a] [   ].

Bibliography: N. Walker, 'Concerning *hū*' and *'ani hū*", *ZAW* 74, 2(1962), pp. 205f.

The section, 41.1–5, opens the series of trial speeches in which Yahweh, the God of Israel, calls the 'islands and nations',[b] and along with the latter their gods, to appear in court. His own people have been vanquished and scattered, and the great powers have written them off. Nevertheless, he summons the nations into court. The point here at issue is the claim to divinity made both by the gods of the foreign nations and by Yahweh, the God of Israel, a claim which of course could only be validly made by one of them. Deutero-Isaiah here avails himself of the form used in pleadings. This allows him to say two things; first, that the foreign gods' claim to divinity, and therefore to worship—as will appear later, he was thinking primarily of the gods of Babylon—can be declared invalid by judicial means, that is, by means of impartial arguments which both sides are bound to accept; and secondly, that it is perfectly possible for such a legal contest or lawsuit to be held, which means that Yahweh recognizes the foreign gods as a body corporate, and that they can perfectly well be summoned and speak. Thus, the background of this literary form is not the criminal case which has to do with an offence and its punishment, but the civil which turns on a claim and its admission or dismissal. Deutero-Isaiah has thus created a new literary form, and by means of it he says to his people what they had never previously heard put in this way. The form came into being because of the position in which the exiles were placed in Babylon. For their daily life, the Babylonian empire was an imposing and undeniable reality, and they knew that its nerve-centre was its cult, with its invocation of the gods, its sacrifices and processions. In such a situation the question of which claim to divinity was true and who was in fact God was inevitable.

[a] On the last two words see n. a on p. 62.
[b] 41.1–5, 21–29; 43.8–15; 44.6–8; 45.20–25; as well as reminiscences of them in other passages. Here cf. J. Begrich, *Studien zu Deuterojesaja*, n.e. *TB* 20, Munich 1963, pp. 26–48; 'Sprache und Struktur', pp. 134–44. The reader is recommended always to compare each particular trial speech with the commentary on the others, for this is a fixed form which in itself makes a connection in subject-matter.

41.1–5 are simple in structure. In v. 1 the islands and nations are summoned to appear in court. The sequel plunges right into the pleadings. The speaker is Yahweh, the one party in the suit, and he proceeds to put a question to his opponent: 'Who stirred (him) up from the east?' (v. 2a expanded in 2b and 3). This is taken up again in v. 4a: 'Who performs and does this?' Since his opponent is unable to reply, he himself gives the answer, 'I, Yahweh' (v. 4b). This decides the case. Verse 5 only goes on to state the effects of the decision, 'the ends of the earth tremble'.

[1] Foreign nations and certain parts of the world are summoned to appear in court and at the same time bidden to be silent (in Hebrew it is possible to express both orders in one single verb: lit., 'coming to me be silent'). These are the formalities necessary and customary at all times throughout the world when pleadings are opened, but here, the two parties in the summons being what they are, they are very much more than empty preliminaries. There may be yet another background, the age-old concept, widespread in the ancient east, of a heavenly court—the classical example is in the Babylonian epic *Enuma Elish*—which, under the presidency of the god-king, deliberated on the destinies of gods and men, and also served as a court of law. If, however, Deutero-Isaiah did have this concept in mind, he demytholgized it, since the gods summoned by Yahweh are replaced by the nations and certain parts of the world, and the aim is the declaration that these gods' claim to divinity is baseless.

[2–3] As the one party in the suit, Yahweh puts the question: 'Who stirred (him) up from the east?' In the Hebrew the sentence is without an object, this being the clause which follows, '(him) whom victory meets at every step', a peculiar form of supplementary parallelism. The wording is due to the fact that Cyrus is not mentioned by name. That Deutero-Isaiah generally does no more than hint at Cyrus—he calls him by name only in 44.28–45.7—is quite in keeping with his style of writing. There can be no doubt, however, that Cyrus is the person meant here, for the next verses manifestly describe his appearance on the scene. They do not announce it in advance. They look back on it, and reflect the stir which it caused throughout the whole world at the time. Poetic both in its freedom and its inspiration, the description pin-points the incredible speed and apparent ease of Cyrus' first conquests. Note how the subject changes: he (Yahweh) gave up nations before him . . . he (Cyrus) pursues them. The same change is found in other descriptions of the divine activity in history (e.g. Ps. 80), and expresses the way in which the divine and the human action are here conjoined.

Deutero-Isaiah makes an assertion which his hearers found both incredible and highly obnoxious, namely that in the rise of the king of Persia, which had never before come within the sphere of Yahweh's action, he saw the hand of the God of Israel. The present passage gives no reason for this belief, and it only emerges from the further trial speeches. This first one merely lays down that such a course of action on God's part is possible.

[4] 'I, Yahweh, the first—and with the last, I, the same.' (This translation attempts to reproduce the fact that the clauses are noun clauses. A verbal sentence can never have the force of such a noun clause, where the predicate is a substantive. Nominal sentences are in general untranslatable.) Properly to understand this 'divine self-prediction', we should remember the opening lines of Ps. 90. There, God's eternity is made a ground for putting absolute trust in him in face of man's appointed end. Here, when God says of himself 'the first . . . the last', this indicates the ground which makes possible an activity of his that embraces the totality of universal history. Because his activity preceded all the movements of history, and will also terminate them all, he is the one 'who calls the generations from the beginning' (v. 4a). These words are only comprehensible if it is realized that v. 4b is not to be taken as it would be in present-day thought, as denoting essence. What is expressed here is not the permanence of an always existent divine being, but the contrast between God and history in its totality ('and with the last I am still he'). It is the expression of a divine eternity related to history, and not of one philosophically contrasted with it. In the context of 41.1–5, the message which the divine eternity is to convey is this: 'our God, who was there at the beginning and will be so at the end, is the one who calls the generations from the beginning (so also in a different context, Ps. 90). In our day this God has the power to commission Cyrus to do his bidding.'

[5] This opening trial speech is confined to the simple fact of the stirring up of Cyrus. Its place in the prophecy as a whole and its significance have to wait till later for their explanation. The simple fact, however, is itself sufficient to cause shuddering and dismay throughout continents, even to the ends of the earth. The consternation implies that men realize what the trial speeches are to prove:

here God is present, here men may see the divine activity in all its grandeur.

Chapters 40.19–20 and 41.6–7

The Manufacture of Idols

19 The idol, the workman casts it,
   and the goldsmith overlays it with gold,
   and [attaches it] with silver chains.[a]
20 He who is too poor for such a work of art
   chooses a tree that does not rot,
   seeks out a skilful craftsman,
   to set up an image that does not move.[b]
41.6 One man helps his neighbour,
   and says to his companion, 'Take courage!'
   The craftsman encourages the goldsmith,
7 and he who smooths with the hammer him who strikes the anvil,
   saying of the soldering, 'It is good,'
   and fastening it with nails that it cannot move.

Compare here the introduction, pp. 29f., and the commentary on 44.9–20. These four verses [40.19–20; 41.6–7] are only a fugitive piece. 44.9–20 shows their context. They describe the several stages in the manufacture of idols, and their revealing, realistic picture of the technicalities of the various processes tells its own story. The contrast is perfectly glaring. This is the way in which the gods whose works are so mightily extolled come into being! The quotation on p. 150 shows that such mockery of the manufacture of idols was not confined to Israel. At the same time we are shown the profound influence of the second commandment on Israel's thinking from the very beginning. It was quite impossible for her to make an image of God. This did not square with his being. In addition, however, as evidenced by the numerous genealogies of the gods in the religions with which she was surrounded, the idea of a god's coming into being

---

[a] In place of $w^e \dot{s} \bar{o} r \bar{e} p$ read $yi \dot{s} r \bar{o} p$.
[b] The translation of the first words of v. 20 is Budde's. The order of the verses is not certain.

was nothing strange. But for her such a thing was excluded *a priori*, cf. Ps. 90.

CHAPTER 41.8–13

Fear not!

8 But you, Israel, my servant,
   you, Jacob, whom I have chosen,
   the offspring of Abraham, whom I loved,
9 whom I took from the ends of the earth,
   you whom I called from its farthest corners,
   and said to you, 'You are my servant,
   I have chosen you and not cast you off':

10 Fear not,   for I am with you,
    be not dismayed,   for I am your God.
    I strengthen you, and I help you,
    I uphold you with my saving right hand.

11 Behold, all who are incensed against you
   shall be put to shame and confounded;
   the men who strive against you
   shall be as nothing and shall perish.
12 You shall seek them, and not find them,
   those who contend with you;
   they shall all be as nothing at all,
   the men who war against you.

13 For I am Yahweh, your God,
   who holds your right hand,
   saying to you, 'Fear not,
   I have helped you.'

Bibliography: G. Fohrer, 'Zum Text von Jes. 41.8–13', *VT*, V (1955), pp. 239–49; on vv. 10 and 13, see Z. W. Falk, 'Gestures expressing Affirmation', *JSS*, 4 (1959), pp. 269f.

The second unit in ch. 41 brings us to the second main literary form of Deutero-Isaiah's proclamation, the oracle, or assurance, of salvation.[a] It is the most characteristic form in which he clothes his message and is central to his proclamation. To begin with, it was not a specifically prophetic form. Its birthplace was Israel's worship. Begrich[b] found that in many of the psalms in the category of 'individual laments' there was a clearly marked sudden transition from lamentation to expressions of the suppliant's conviction that his prayer had been granted, which indicated that someone else, a priest (or cult prophet), speaking in the name of God, had given him assurance. To this assurance Begrich gave the name 'the priestly oracle of salvation', and in it he discovered the prototype of a group of utterances on the subject of salvation found in Deutero-Isaiah, a particularly valuable and fruitful discovery for Old Testament scholarship. Several reasons made it possible for Deutero-Isaiah to take over this form for his proclamation and reshape it for his purpose, the most important being similarity of situation: because of the fate which had overtaken the scattered remnant of Israel, the only thing left for them was to lift up their hands in supplication to God and wait for a word of grace and consolation—precisely like an individual Israelite (such as Hannah in I Sam. 1) coming into the presence of God with his personal trouble and asking the granting of his prayer. Two things show that this oracle assuring the granting of a prayer, an oracle familiar to Israel for centuries, does in fact form the basis of a group of Deutero-Isaiah's utterances on the subject of salvation. The first is the clear echo of a lament in numerous phrases and words in these passages in Deutero-Isaiah (see the commentary). The second, and more direct, proof comes from a few passages in psalms of lamentation which hint at an oracle of salvation which has in no case been transmitted along with them, and here words which we find in Deutero-Isaiah occur:

> Lam. 3.57   Thou didst come near me when I called on thee;
> thou didst say, 'Do not fear.'

and

> Ps. 35. 1ff.   Contend with those that contend against me;
> Say to me, 'I am your help.'
> Let them be put to shame.

[a] 41.8–13, 14–16; 43.1–4, 5–7; 44.1–5; there is an indication of it in 54.4–6 and several other passages. On it see Begrich, *op. cit.*, pp. 6–19; H. E. von Waldow, *Anlass und Hintergrund der Verkündigung Deuterojesajas*, Bonn Dissertation, 1953, especially pp. 11–27; 'Sprache und Struktur', pp. 117–20.

[b] 'Das priesterliche Heilsorakel', *ZAW*, 52 (1934), pp. 81–92.

By clothing his message of salvation in this liturgical form, the oracle of salvation, Deutero-Isaiah achieved a very significant combination of the prophetic proclamation and the cultic declaration of salvation. This was possible because both were words uttered in God's name, and because Deutero-Isaiah's mission was to proclaim to people in trouble the granting of their prayer, which was also the purpose of the oracle of salvation. In respect of the proclamation of salvation in answer to a community lament, the prophetic and the cultic word had parted company, as is shown by the visions of Amos, and also by Jer. 14, where the prophet was forbidden to procure the word of salvation from God for the nation. But in Deutero-Isaiah's oracle of salvation the two lines once again unite.

Construction: Verses 8f. are an address with appositions, giving a résumé of God's dealings with Israel to date. Verse 10 contains the cry, 'Fear not,' substantiated by means of a noun clause and clauses with verbs in the perfect (the assurance of salvation proper). Verses 10f. are a proclamation linked with this assurance, stating that the outcome of God's intervention on Israel's behalf is to be the destruction of her enemies. Verse 13 rounds the section off, repeating the assurance; the cry 'Fear not' is also repeated, with substantiations as in v. 10.

[8–9] The words 'But you', with which the address to Israel begins, are explained by the form taken by the oracle of salvation. They correspond to the *waw* adversative (= but)[a] which in a number of psalms of lamentation indicates the change from distress to salvation in accordance with the oracle of salvation, or presupposing it. Here in ch. 41, this 'but' introduces the word of consolation addressed to Israel as against the pronouncements of judgment on the nations who are dismayed at the evidence of God's power in history. The address is given a series of appositions, all centring on Yahweh's saving acts towards Israel in the past. God addresses Israel as 'you, my servant'. This is the first occurrence of a word which is of tremendous significance in our prophet's proclamation. To understand its particular nuance, the total occurrences of the root in the Old Testament must be studied.[b] Its intrinsic distinctiveness consists in the fact that the Hebrew word for 'servant' (*'ebed*) expresses something

---

[a] Westermann, *The Praise of God . . .*, pp. 70–75.
[b] Attention is drawn particularly to the article '*pais theou*' in *TWNT* and the section on the Old Testament by W. Zimmerli (ET: *The Servant of God*, SBT 20, London, 1957, pp. 15–44).

like a balance between the idea of belonging to someone who protects and gives security and that of standing under someone, being subordinate to him. In the present passage, God's address to Israel, the element of belonging obviously preponderates; in this respect, being a *'ebed* means trust, honour and protection, as for Abraham's servant in the story in Gen. 24. For Israel to be God's servant means primarily that she has a master with whom she feels secure, whom she can trust, and who cares for her. If this is the lord whom she serves, the manner of her service follows as a consequence.

The series of appositions to the address contains another term which is both frequent in Deutero-Isaiah and important for his thought: 'You, Jacob, whom I have chosen' (41.8f.; 43.10, 20; 44.1f.; 45.4). It conveys the same ideas as the appellation 'my servant' (so again in v. 9b, 'you are my servant, I have chosen you'). As applied to Israel, the verb takes its particular shade of meaning in the Old Testament primarily from Deuteronomy. For the one thus addressed, the word signifies that 'out of many other peoples whom God might have chosen, he chose us. In so doing, he gave our life a significance which no person or thing other than himself can ever take away from it. For as long as it remains true that he chose us, we have a future.' The particular stamp which the election bears in Deutero-Isaiah is due to the fact that he makes it stand out in relief from all the rest of God's acts in the whole of history (41.4) and creation.

Israel's election is carried back to the patriarchs: 'the offspring of Abraham, my friend'. The words are proof positive that the historical traditions of his nation were the source of Deutero-Isaiah's inspiration, and that, in particular, he knew the Yahwist, in whose work election goes right back to Abraham, for the pre-exilic prophets never mention him. 'Abraham, my friend': in the Hebrew there is an active verb in the perfect with a suffix, i.e., 'who loves, or loved, me'. The background is perhaps Gen. 18.17, which expresses the exceptional character of Abraham's relationship to God, cf. II Chron. 20.7 and James 2.23, both of which come from the present passage in Deutero-Isaiah. At the same time, we must remember that in Hebrew there is a certain difference in meaning between the participle and the noun 'friend', because the former expresses the element of activity in the relationship. Verse 9 says that the election was an actual event. God intervened in history. He called from the ends of the earth and its farthest corners. (Note the connection between what he says and what he does.) This may represent an amalgamation of the call of Abraham

and the deliverance from Egypt. At the same time, the words bear
on the position in which Israel was then placed. The final words,
'not cast you off', are certainly not, as Duhm supposed, 'a superfluous
filling-out'. Instead, they are the express statement of the bearing of
the apposition's historical retrospect on the present. When the assurance of salvation which follows them came to Israel, her great fear
was just that God had cast her off and disowned her (40.27). To
enable her to accept the assurance, she is reminded of the experience
which she has had, throughout a long history, of the God who elected
her and has never once cast her off.

[10] The central point of the whole oracle is the cry, 'Fear not!'
It is not, contrary to the view of many editors, merely an 'exhortation not to be afraid'. It is the cry which banishes the fear. As such,
it has a long tradition, both in time and in different parts of the
world. But the following should be noticed. The cry, 'Fear not!', as
the word of a god to a human being, may be found in two entirely
different situations and with a different significance in each. First,
it may be connected with a theophany, and spoken in this context.
Here the fear on man's part is due to the manifestation of the deity as
such, and the cry, 'Fear not!', takes this away. Distinct from this is
the individual lament, where the cry comes as the answer to the
lament. In this case, what evokes the fear is the threat or danger
that inspired the lament. The clearest and most detailed instance of
fear evoked simply by the manifestation of the divine being comes in
Dan. 10.8ff. (similarly Judg. 6.23; Ex. 20.18–21). In Gen. 15.1 and
26.24, the thing with which the fear is connected is not certain. In the
great majority of the references, however, it is any kind of danger
into which the one addressed may have come. Deutero-Isaiah is the
same. With him, the cry has very close affinities with those passages
in which, in the context of Yahweh as the man of war (the holy war),
the same cry is spoken to an Israel threatened by enemies (Josh. 8.1;
10.8; Num. 21.34; Deut. 1.21; Ex. 14.13f.). Similarly, a prayer of
Assurbanipal to Nabu, an instance from the world outside Israel,
clearly sets forth the circumstances of an oracle of salvation and its
basic structure.[a]

---

[a] A. Falkenstein and W. von Soden, *Sumerische und Akkadische Hymnen und Gebete*,
Zurich and Stuttgart, 1953, pp. 292–4:
Kneeling, Assurbanipal squats back on his haunches,
bows again and again to his lord Nabu: . . .
I love you, strong and mighty Nabu,

The cry's first substantiation is given in two noun clauses, 'I am with you', 'I am your God'. These two assurances either come into operation at the moment the pledge is made, or else the pledge gives them effect. The first, 'I am with you', has a very long prehistory, outside Israel as well as within it;[a] we find it mainly in the Joseph stories. In Deut. 20.1; 31.8; Jer. 42.11; 1.7ff.; 30.10f. = 46.27 it is united with the cry, 'Fear not!' The second substantiation, 'I am your God', is particularly characteristic of Deutero-Isaiah. To meet the needs of the time, it summarizes what the appositions in the address (vv. 8f.) had said about God's dealings in the past with his people. Deutero-Isaiah's choice of it was probably quite deliberate. He wanted to counter a god's self-predication occurring in the same way in the Babylonian cult. For example:[b]

> I am Ishtar, the goddess of the evening,
> I am Ishtar, the goddess of the morning,
> Ishtar, who opens the shutters of the resplendent heavens,
> this is my glory,
> I make the heavens grow dark, I convulse the earth,
> this is my glory.

This form is also found along with the cry, 'Fear not!':

> I am Ishtar of Arbela . . .
> Fear me not, extol me.[c]

This may be described as an explicit self-glorification on the gods' part which is given its point by the background of polytheism—the glorification of one god rises above that of others. Deutero-Isaiah therefore adopted the form deliberately for purposes of polemic. By putting self-glorification into the mouth of the God who alone is God, he reduces the self-glorification found in the Babylonian pantheon to

---

do not abandon me in the midst of my longings.
A 'breath of wind' replied from his god Nabu:
Fear not, Assurbanipal;
I will give you a long life . . .
The goodness of my mouth
continually blesses you in the assembly of the great gods.
The cry 'Fear not' also occurs, in a collection of replies from oracles received by Esarhaddon (*ANET*, pp. 449f.).

[a] S. N. Kramer, *History begins at Sumer*, London and New York, 1957, p. 177.
[b] F. Norden, *Agnostos Theos*, Leipzig, 1923, n.e., 1956, p. 207.
[c] Norden, *op. cit.*, p. 208.

absurdity. Thus, God's 'self-exaltation' serves only to exalt his being God for Israel: I am your God.

In v. 10b the noun clause substantiation of v. 10a is united with another in the shape of verbal clauses. The verbs are all in the perfect, and this must be kept in mind if they are translated as presents ('I strengthen you . . .'). These, too, are not strictly proclamation of something that is to take place later on. Instead, they express the assurance of salvation which is effective the moment the comfort is given. The three verbs in v. 10b all speak in different ways of intervention on God's part to help, while the substantiating noun clauses in v. 10a express his turning towards those addressed. These two divisions of the oracle of salvation reflect the corresponding two divisions of the prayer in a psalm of lamentation begging God to turn toward the suppliant and intervene.[a] This is clear proof that the oracle of salvation represents the answer to the suppliant's prayer and bears upon this.

[11–12] The part referring to the future (imperfect tense in Hebrew) now follows. In contrast to the assurance of salvation proper, this part alone is proclamation of something that is to take place later on. The four half-verses in vv. 11f. have one single theme— your foes shall be destroyed! The structure is as follows. In the first line of all four the verbs are all variants of 'to perish', while in the second the nouns are all variants of 'your foes'. The verses correspond to a particular part of a psalm of lamentation, the double wish or the one aspect of the 'wish . . . that simultaneously is expressed in two directions',[b] which is often to be found at the end of a psalm of lamentation, e.g., Ps. 35.26; 40.15f. (14f.); 56.10 (9); 58.7–10 (6–9); 63.10f. (9f.). Notice in the first four half-verses the frequency of the terms 'not', 'nothing'. The concept is characteristic of Deutero-Isaiah (see above, the final part of the commentary on 40.12–27, pp. 53ff.).

[13] The final verse repeats the assurance of salvation. Its four half-verses take up words found in v. 10. This again shows quite clearly that the assurance of salvation, the cry 'Fear not' with twofold substantiation, is the central thing in the entire passage, as it is also central to Deutero-Isaiah's proclamation throughout. By means of it he executes the commission God gave him, of comforting his chosen people with the assurance, 'God has espoused your cause.'

a Westermann, *The Praise of God* . . ., p. 64.
b The translation is taken from Westermann, *The Praise of God* . . ., p. 52, n. 1.

CHAPTER 41.14–16

Fear not!

14   Fear not, you worm Jacob,
     [be not dismayed],[a] you worm Israel!
     I, even I, help you, says Yahweh,
     your Redeemer is the Holy One of Israel.

15   Behold, I make of you a[ ]threshing sledge,[b]
     new, sharp, and having teeth.
     You shall thresh mountains and crush them
     and make hills into chaff.

16   You shall winnow them, the wind carries them away,
     and tempest scatters them.
     But you shall rejoice in Yahweh,
     glory in the Holy One of Israel.

Bibliography: E. J. Hamlin, 'The Meaning of "Mountains and Hills" in Isa. 41.14–16', *JNES*, XIII, 3 (1957), pp. 185–90.

These verses form an independent unit. It is an oracle of salvation like 41.8–13, as is shown not only by the cry with which it begins, but also by the similarity in structure, despite several divergencies. Here the address is brief, and follows the cry 'Fear not!' contained in both halves of v. 14a. Verse 14b gives the substantiation which, although shorter than in 41.8–13, consists of the noun clause and the verbal clause, the latter in the perfect tense. This is followed, in vv. 15–16a, by the part referring to the future. (This holds good even though the first verb in v. 15a, which makes the transition from the first part to the second, is in the perfect.) This part expands the corresponding part of 41.8–13 (vv. 11f.), and its subject is Israel herself. The oracle finishes with v. 16b, the vow of praise of the psalms of lamentation being changed into a prophecy.

The juxtaposition of these two oracles of salvation, 41.8–13 and

a Add *'al tište'ī.*
b Both words mean threshing sledge. Perhaps an explanatory addition.

14ff., is no accident. Nor are they without mutual relationship. While both are independent units (v. 13 clearly marks an end), each bears on the other and loosely supplements it. Whereas in vv. 8–13 the main emphasis falls on the introduction—address with appositions—vv. 14ff. alone have a conclusion in the strict sense of the term. Of the parts referring to the future, vv. 8–13 speak of Israel's foes, vv. 14ff. of Israel herself, corresponding to the two aspects of the double wish. Such a collocation of independent units loosely supplementing one another is often found in Deutero-Isaiah.

[14] The text as printed above follows numerous editors in inserting 'be not dismayed' as parallel to 'fear not'. (This brings the verse into line with v. 10.) The cry, which is designed to remove the fear, addresses its hearers as 'you worm Jacob', 'you worm Israel'. Begrich[a] has shown that the words point directly back to a lament, e.g., Ps. 22.7 (6), 'I am a worm, and no man'. Cf. also Ps. 119.141. The same figure is also found in Babylonian psalms.[b]

The substantiation in the noun clause uses the terms, 'your Redeemer', and 'the Holy One of Israel'. Both are characteristic of Deutero-Isaiah, and important to him. 'The Holy One of Israel' is the subject of the clause, 'your Redeemer' the predicate. Deutero-Isaiah very often designates God as 'the Holy One of Israel' (thirteen times: 41.14, 16, 20; 43.3, 14, 15; 45.11; 47.4; 48.17; 49.7 *bis*; 54.5; 55.5). Half of these passages have the same combination as in 41.14, 'the Holy One of Israel', 'your Redeemer' (41.14; 43.14; 47.4; 48.17; 49.7; 54.5; further, in conjunction with 'your Saviour', 43.3; with 'who has chosen you', 49.7; and with 'glorifies', 55.5). The designation is a regular one in Deutero-Isaiah, and must express something important to his proclamation. It also embodies part of the history of prophecy. The creation of the phrase, 'the Holy One of Israel', derives from Isaiah in the eighth century. He uses it to express the truth, of which there is no better expression than the account of his call, Isa. 6, that God's numinous holiness is holiness turned towards Israel. It is the holiness of God the judge (Isa. 1.4: 'they despise the Holy One of Israel'), but the very fact that he does judge Israel makes him her God. Deutero-Isaiah took over this concept of his master's and gave it a special place in his proclamation, clear proof of a line of tradition stretching from Isaiah of Jerusalem to the Isaiah of the

a 'Das priesterliche Heilsorakel', *ZAW*, 52 (1934), p. 87.

b Westermann, 'Struktur und Geschichte der Klage im Alten Testament', *Forschung am Alten Testament*, Munich, 1964, p. 284.

exile. As other passages, too, show, the latter was well acquainted with First Isaiah's prophecy, and deliberately took over some of its elements.

Certain passages where Deutero-Isaiah adds 'your Redeemer' either in apposition to or as predicate of Isaiah's 'the Holy One of Israel' express his own personal proclamation—this holy God who in her past was known to Israel as the God of wrath, the judge, is now solely and simply her redeemer. 'Redeemer' is a term taken from the realm of family and tribal law. The *go'ēl* is the next of kin who has the duty of redeeming or buying back.[a] In Ex. 6.6 the word is used of the redemption from Egypt.

As regards content, the combination of the two designations corresponds to the central statement made in the descriptive psalms of praise (hymns), as expressed, for example, in Ps. 113.5f.: 'Who is seated on high—who looks far down'. Deutero-Isaiah's echoing of this *leitmotif* 'God's majesty—God's turning in grace', 'the Holy One of Israel—your Redeemer', shows the influence of the diction of the Psalms.

[15–16a] This is the part of the oracle referring to the future. The first words (in the perfect tense), 'Behold, I make of you . . .,' form the transition from past to future. Since in 41.8–13 the part which refers to the future proclaimed the destruction of Israel's foes (see above), here one naturally expects a proclamation affecting Israel herself, corresponding to the words of transition, 'Behold, I make of you', and also to the form assumed by the double wish, which is the model here. And this is in fact what vv. 15–16a intend to convey, although the wording does not clearly bring it out. What is actually said looks much more like a supplement to 41.11f., to the effect that the destruction of Israel's foes there proclaimed is to be accomplished by Israel herself. This sense is, however, doubtful, if for no other reason than that in vv. 15f. no name is given to the foes, whereas in 41.11ff. they are four times expressly designated as *Israel's* foes.

---

[a] This comes up in the Book of Ruth. Cf. Haller, *Die Megilloth*, HAT 18, pp. 16f. 'The term "redeemer" combines . . . two different things. First, levirate marriage, which legally obliges the next of kin to marry the widow of a brother who has died without issue . . . But the duty of redemption applies secondly in the laws relating to atonement. The Holiness Code (Lev. 25.25) enacts: "If your brother becomes poor, and has to sell part of his property, then his next of kin shall come to him and redeem what his brother has in mind to sell." '

The metaphor of threshing in v. 15a fits in with the grain and chaff of v. 16a, but not with the object 'mountains and hills' in 15b. On the other hand, the metaphor of the verbs in vv. 15b and 16a, 'threshing . . . crushing . . . making into chaff . . . winnowing' is uniformly carried through. Obviously then, in introducing the odd and incongruous object 'mountains and hills' into the old and common metaphor for the destruction of a foe, Deutero-Isaiah had something particular in mind to emphasize. There can be no doubt that the phrase alludes to these same words in the prologue (40.4: 'every mountain and hill shall be made low'). There they represent the obstacles blocking Israel's return. It is prophesied that they are to be levelled to make a smooth road on which the nation can make its journey home. However, in the prologue it is not Israel herself who removes these obstacles. We have to take it that by inserting 'mountains and hills' into the traditional metaphor for the destruction of foes—threshing and crushing corn—Deutero-Isaiah's real intention was to say, in a deliberately cryptic way, that God is proclaiming to Israel, 'Behold, I make of you an instrument capable of overcoming the obstacles set up by your foes, which separate you from your homeland.' The way in which this is to come about is not specified here, but at all events there is no idea of God's raising Israel afresh to power in the realm of politics that will enable her to destroy her foes with her own arms. The prophet's cryptic way of speaking, using traditional forms and metaphors to express a meaning different from their original one, is characteristic of him. But it has given rise to much false exegesis.

[16b] 'But you shall rejoice in Yahweh, glory in the Holy One of Israel.' The model for this verse is quite obviously the vow of praise, the final part of an individual psalm of lamentation, although here the reference is collective. This is further corroboration that the oracle of salvation corresponds to the individual lament and is co-ordinated to it. Even the direct link with the double wish by means of 'But you (I)' is frequently found there. To take one example of the way in which the psalm of lamentation is reflected in the oracle of salvation:

Ps. 71	Isa. 41.14–16
12 O God, be not far from me; O God, make haste to help me.	14 Fear not . . . I help you.
13 May they be put to shame that hate me . . .	15f. Behold . . . the wind carries them away . . .

Ps. 71	Isa. 41.14–16
14 But I will praise thee yet more and more,	16b But you shall rejoice in Yahweh,
15 My mouth shall tell of thy righteous acts.	Glory in the Holy One of Israel.

That for which the suppliant praised God in the lament (cf. Ps. 71.14), is here proclaimed to the person addressed in the assurance of salvation: 'You shall rejoice in Yahweh'. The fact that Yahweh, who is the real speaker, is put in the third person, is due to the stereotyped diction of the vow of praise in a psalm. The influence on Deutero-Isaiah's proclamation of the language of the Psalter is absolutely obvious at this point. But the final verse of his oracle of salvation here not only assumes the form taken by the vow of praise in the psalms. It also has the same content. God's compassionate condescension and his intervention to help inaugurate an event that does not end with the deliverance and recovery of the one in trouble. Instead, its goal is the joyous praise of God in which his glorious deed is proclaimed.

CHAPTER 41.17–20

I open rivers on the heights

17 The poor[   ]ᵃ seek water, and there is none,
their tongue is parched with thirst.
I, Yahweh, answer them,
I, the God of Israel, forsake them not.

18 I open rivers on the bare heights,
and fountains in the midst of the valleys;
I make the wilderness a pool of water,
the dry land springs of water.

19 In the wilderness I plant cedars,
acacias, myrtles, and olives.
In the steppe I set junipers,
planes and box treesᵇ as well,

ᵃ Delete 'and needy'.
ᵇ The last two kinds of trees are not known, and the translations are only conjectural.

20   that they may see and know,
      may also consider and understand,
      that the hand of Yahweh has done this,
      the Holy One of Israel has created it.

This is a different kind of salvation utterance, and is essentially distinct from the two oracles of salvation which precede it (vv. 8–13, 14ff.). In the latter, the whole emphasis falls on the fact that the assurance bears upon the present. This proclamation of salvation relates to the future. Another difference is that there is no direct address here, and therefore no 'Fear not' either. Again, while 41.17–20, too, are connected with the lament, the connection is different. Properly speaking, the oracle of salvation is the answer to an individual lament; the proclamation, on the other hand, has its affinities with the community lament. Further, the oracle only hints at a lament, whereas the proclamation quotes it, either directly or, as here in 41.17, by allusion to it. The two do approximate at the point where both proclaim God's turning towards Israel and his intervention. Nevertheless, in the proclamation these are both put in the imperfect (future) tense, and God's intervention is not, as in the oracle, a substantiation of the assurance. The structure of the present proclamation is as follows: (I) An allusion to the lament (v. 17a); (II) The proclamation of salvation: (1) God's turning towards Israel (v. 17b), (2) His intervention (vv. 18f.); (III) The end in view (v. 20). Further texts where the structure is similar are 42.14–17; 43.16–21; 45.14–17; 49.17–20. The proclamation is much more frequently found in combination with other forms and motifs, e.g., in 49.14ff.; 51.9–52.6; and in chs. 54 and 55. It occurs throughout Deutero-Isaiah. The difference between the assurance (or oracle) of salvation and the proclamation of it is probably due to the fact that in pre-exilic Israel the divine answer to a community lament and that of an individual were given in a different way, the former by a prophet, the latter by a priest. Both forms were used by Deutero-Isaiah for his message of salvation.[a]

[17] Without the slightest warning, v. 17a introduces an entirely new event. The two half-verses of 17a present a unique thumbnail sketch of an all too familiar occurrence, drought and all its dire consequences. From the patriarchal narratives down to the latest period in the Old Testament, and from its vivid depiction in the

---

[a] For the proclamation of salvation, cf. 'Sprache und Struktur', pp. 120–2.

prophets and the psalms, drought is easily seen to be one of the most grievous calamities that could fall on ancient Israel. To fill out the picture conjured up here in v. 17a one has only to re-read Jer. 14.2–6. These verses are followed by the community lament, begging God for mercy and for the turning of the nation's fortunes. The same is implied here in v. 17b: the cries would be, 'Forsake us not. O Lord, hear us.' God answers, 'I, Yahweh, hear you (or, will hear you; the verb is in the imperfect), (I) the God of Israel do not (or, will not) forsake you!' The two lines of v. 17 are therefore an extremely concise and forceful summary of a thing that was widespread and took many forms, a community lament in time of drought and God's proclamation that he has answered its prayer. The key to the understanding of this summary allusion is the exiles' situation. It reminded them—and the allusion was all that was necessary—of what used to take place in the past, when they experienced their God's most characteristic activity in a very special way, an experience repeated time and again through the centuries of their history: in extremity they cried to him, and he heard them and had the power to change their fortunes.

[18–19] But what does this mean for them at the present? Was it simply a memory? The second part of God's answer proclaiming his intervention as the granting of their prayer completely parts company with the circumstances which led to the old community laments in time of drought, and points to the present and to a future soon to come. 'I open rivers on the bare heights. . . . In the desert I plant cedars.' The scene is changed, and through this the poet is able to add to the topic alluded to in vv. 17a and b, history, a new one telling of the chosen people's future, and opening up a new possibility for this. It is the way through the desert which, as in the prologue, signifies the return. The desert becomes viable, it is given water (v. 18) and trees (v. 19). It thus ceases to be the pitiless, unsurmountable barrier between the exiles and their homeland. It becomes the highway. The same power of miraculous transformation which Israel had time and again experienced in the past, when, with death from drought staring her in the face, she prayed to her God—this same transforming power can turn the desert into fertile country and thus there prepare the way that leads to the homeland.

[20a] What is the end in view? In this event Israel encounters this God and the power that he has, and acknowledges them. The four verbs in the final clauses of v. 20a underline the personal, or rather the dialogical, character of what is here proclaimed as Israel's

future. The final result is not the return itself, but its echo in Israel's joyous, amazed acknowledgement; not what is done, but praise of God's mighty acts. Here the term 'see' has the wider meaning of experience, and 'recognize' that of acknowledging and saying Amen, as in Ps. 46.11 (10): 'Be still, and know that I am God.' The two verbs which follow, 'lay to heart' and 'understand', simply further underline and reinforce. Recognition and acknowledgement thus emphasized are to be directed towards the fact that what is proclaimed in vv. 17b–18 has actually taken place. As Yahweh's act it has already come about. The first half-verse of [20b], 'the hand of Yahweh has done this', recalls the language of the old songs of victory. 'Hand' betokens power, and the retention of this anthropomorphic designation down to a late date is intended to characterize God's power as personal power. The second half of the verse says the same thing in concentrated theological terms. 'The Holy One of Israel' is the designation of God which Deutero-Isaiah took over from the Isaiah tradition, and it includes the two concepts of majesty and of grace as shown in the covenant. The working of this God is gathered up in the specifically theological term for creation ($b\bar{a}r\bar{a}'$); here the verb has the overtone, inherent from the beginning, of miraculous new creation.

CHAPTER 41.21–29

The Former and the Latter Things

21 Set forth your case,   says Yahweh,
    bring forth your proofs,[a]   says the King of Jacob.
22 Let them bring them and tell us
    what is to happen.
    Tell us the former things, what they were,
    we would consider them;
    or let us hear what is to come,
    that we may know when it comes about.[b]
23 Declare to us the things to come,
    that we may know that you are gods.

[a] $^{ca}s\bar{u}m\bar{o}t$ = the strong things, in the sense of strong words, arguments (Köhler).
[b] The last two lines of the verse should be transposed.

Do something, good or evil,
that we may all see it and be dismayed.[a]

24   Behold, you are nothing, and your work is [nothing],[b]
he who chooses you chooses an abomination.

25   I stirred up one from the north, and he came,
from the rising of the sun [I][c] called him by name.
He [trampled][d] rulers as mortar,
as the potter tramples clay.

26   Who declared this from the beginning, that we might know,
and beforetime, that we might say, 'it is right'?

There is none who declares it, none who proclaims,
none hears a sound from you.

27   I first [declared] it to Zion[e]
and gave Jerusalem the herald of good tidings.

28   I look—but no one is there (any more);
[I would speak],[f] but there is none to speak with me,
that I might ask them, and they give me an answer.

29   Behold, they are all [nothing],[g]   their works are vain,
their images are empty wind.

This is the second trial speech (the commentary on the previous
one [41.1–5] is presupposed here). There are two stages in the pro-
ceedings (so also Volz), ending at vv. 24 and 28f. respectively. Both
endings have the same meaning. The structure of the two parts is as
follows: In vv. 21 and 22a Yahweh challenges his opponents, the
gods, to advance their arguments, arguments in support of their claim
to be gods (23a); these must consist of words and deeds. Verse 24
presupposes that the other party in the case is silent. That is, the gods
are unable to produce the required arguments in support of their

[a] Both qĕre and kethib ('that we may be dismayed') make good sense.
[b] Instead of 'āpaʿ (meaning unknown) read 'ēpes, deleting mē in both cases. On
the verse see H. L. Ginsberg, 'Some Emendations in Isaiah', *JBL* 69 (1950),
pp. 51–50.
[c] Read 'eqrā bišmō as 45.3. See the commentary.
[d] Read wayyābos = he trod down. sᵉgānīm is a loan word from Akkadian.
[e] Read higgadtihā. C. E. Whitley, 'A Note on Isa. XLI, 27', *JSS* 2, 1957, pp.
327f.
[f] Instead of ūmē'ēlle' read wa'ᵃmallal (Begrich).
[g] Instead of 'āwen read 'ayin.

claim. Thereupon their claims are declared to be nothing (v. 24). In the second stage (vv. 25–28), Yahweh advances his arguments, something done (v. 25) and something said (v. 27). In between, in v. 26, he turns to his opponents with the question, 'Who declared this beforetime?' (v. 26a), and states that he is given no answer (v. 26b[a]). Yahweh on the other hand, as v. 27 says most emphatically—and this is clearly what the whole oracle stresses—declared it in advance to Zion. His opponents have nothing to say to this. Their claim is then declared to be nothing (v. 29).

The procedure is clear and straightforward. In vv. 21–24 Yahweh's opponents are challenged to produce their arguments, but they have nothing to say. In vv. 25–29 Yahweh brings forward his arguments, and thereby, as before, reduces his opponents to silence. Their claim is therefore nothing (vv. 24 and 29). This claim—'we are gods'—is cited in so many words in v. 23a ('and we see that you are gods'). Opposed to it is Yahweh's claim to be the sole God, the claim which runs through the whole of Deutero-Isaiah's proclamation. It should be noticed right away here that the two claims are not absolutely on the same footing. On the one side, the claim to divinity is made for a plurality of gods, on the other for the one God. Nevertheless, to regard the passage as a confrontation of polytheism with monotheism (the suggestion in Volz's superscription to vv. 21–29, 'the proof of monotheism') would be to misconstrue it. The point at issue is not an idea or concept of deity, but 'what comes about', as the beginning of the oracle states expressly (v. 22), what happens. The issue therefore is not divinity *per se*, but Godhead giving evidence of itself in history, divinity that becomes effective as lordship over history.

[21–22a] Legal terms are used here, clear proof that the prophet wishes to describe something in the nature of a trial. 'To set forth the case' (*rīb* is a technical term for a process), 'bring forth proofs' (properly 'the strong things', which, according to Köhler, may be taken in the sense of 'proofs'), 'let them tell us' correspond to terms which we ourselves use in the law-court. Of the object of the process no more than a hint is given, in the words 'what happens' (which may also be translated 'what will happen'). While the normal legal process can only deal with facts in discussion, this one is concerned with

---

[a] In an oracle to Esarhaddon 'the god who gives it maintains that he does exactly what is demanded of the heathen gods in Isa. 41.22ff.: "I, even I, declare the future as the past" (the speaker is Nebo)'. Stummer, *op. cit.*, p. 179.

'what happens'. Hence, what is introduced as a process is also introduced as a divine oracle, 'says Yahweh', 'says the King of Jacob'. This odd combination of a prophetic form of discourse with one of an entirely different kind is characteristic of Deutero-Isaiah, and is a clear indication that in his hands forms have ceased to be simple and original, and are now modified by being combined in various ways. This is in keeping with the prophet's own particular situation. As for the remnants of his nation, so for him the ties with the original established order and its institutions had come undone.

[22b–23a] The proofs or arguments which Yahweh's opponents are challenged to produce are to be attested by an historical act done by them of which they had spoken in advance. Here the greater importance clearly attaches to the spoken element (vv. 22b–23a, then v. 26). This represents an extension of the first trial speech, 41.1– 5. What there came in question was only an act, an activity in history. Here it is now said that this must not be viewed in isolation: the primary requisite is proclamation that may be relied upon. 'Declare to us the things to come, and we will acknowledge that you are gods' (v. 23a). In two parallel clauses, vv. 22b and 23a, 'the future' is signified by means of the participles of two verbs for 'to come'. The one of them (hā'otiyyōt) reappears in 44.7 with the same meaning and in the same literary category. Köhler (Lexikon) translates it as 'the things that are to come', 'the future events'. These are the only two occurrences of this form (feminine plural participle) of this verb 'to come' in the Old Testament. This shows us a bold experiment in the use of words, an attempt to express what we call 'the future' in conceptual terms. We must bear in mind that, for the stage at which language then was, the expression was an allegory in short, and was doubtless still felt to be such, for, strictly speaking, events cannot 'come'. The process imagined in the verb is only conceivable in space, as movement there. It needs violent and drastic abstraction to transfer it to time and the temporal. The fact that Deutero-Isiaah is the person with whom this concept of the future first emerges is no accident. This abstract, comprehensive term had now become necessary. When the pre-exilic prophets proclaimed a future event, it was a future narrowly limited both in space and time. Now, however, in the situation reflected in the trial speeches, Israel's future and the future as it affected other nations and gods had to be reduced to a common denominator. The conclusion of v. 22c, 'that we may know when it comes about', probably means that when the coming events actually take place, they will be seen to tally with their proclamation. It means the same thing, then, as v. 26a, 'that we might say, "It is right"'. If this is the sole criterion by which the gods can be known as such, the implication is that a god's mere intervention, demonstrable as such, is not enough to prove his divinity, his being a god. One must go further back. There must be a historical continuum, in which word and act have equal importance. The proof of deity is not a god's ability to meet with men, or to reveal himself, as *tremendum*, *fascinosum*, *numinosum* (Otto). Rather, divinity is demonstrated by what may be termed the operational arc connecting his word and its effects at a far remove. The trial speeches in Deutero-Isaiah give the first conceptual expression to what was factually in existence as early as the Exodus—God's deity is shown to be such by the continuity of his action in history.

This trial speech—and it alone—gives the complement of the proclamation of a future event. It adds the other aspect of this proof of divinity, 'Tell us the former things, what they were, we would consider them.' *Mā hēnnā*, 'what they were', means the *interpretation* of the former things. 'Yahweh and his followers understand history' (Volz). Prediction of an event is thus complemented by the event's interpretation in retrospect. Deutero-Isaiah is drawing attention to that element in the interpretation of the past in the light of God's word which was so important for the entire history of the chosen people down to the fall of Jerusalem, and which they worked out in such detail. It may be seen in the prophetic word (the motif of contrast, review of God's former acts in salvation and judgment) and in what is said in the psalms (the motif of review as found in community laments and in praise). It is also given particularly full development in the introductory and final discourses of Deuteronomy, and it led to the production, perhaps contemporaneously with Deutero-Isaiah, of the great Deuteronomic history. Prospect and retrospect, the word that proclaimed and the word that interpreted— both had to be there if the single points at which God intervened were to be made into an unbroken historical continuum.

[23b] This is the sole key to the meaning of the second part of the complement, 'Do something, good or evil, so that we bow down and feel dread.' These final words of the verse have the same meaning as v. 23a: to recognize them as gods signifies, 'bow down and feel dread'. Volz's explanation is excellent—'the gods should give some sign of life, to make us able to feel dismay.' 'Amid all the splendour of

the Babylonian pantheon,' he goes on, 'what a superiority complex grips the exiled prophet!' But the words cannot merely refer to the superiority of the mighty Yahweh to the powerless gods of Babylon. What goes before them suggests instead the superiority of the Yahweh who by his historical word throws a span over events and thereby holds sway over them.

[24] The declaration that the gods are nothing is related to their action ('your work is nothing'; v. 29, 'their works are vain'), just as their claim, here declared to be nothing, is also related to activity. In a legal process, to be designated as non-existent in the sense of having no reality would be meaningless, and would make the whole passage impossible. If the foreign gods do not exist, they cannot make any claim or be summoned into court. Here the ontological question whether these gods exist, whether 'there are such', is entirely wide of the mark and has to be left out of account if the trial speeches are to be properly understood. Consider the situation in which the words were spoken. When Israel was confronted with the claim of the Babylonian gods, she had just been vanquished and in every aspect of her life incorporated within the Babylonian empire. These were facts from which there was no escaping. As the exile went on, this claim bit still more deeply, and by the simple fact of the overwhelming reality of Babylon's supremacy, tried to deprive the survivors, the families and individuals incorporated with her, even of hope itself. It was this overwhelming reality of the gods that surrounded the Israelites as, in their sore straits, in which hope was gradually fading and withering away, they made lamentation (40.27). If in face of this Deutero-Isaiah had proclaimed that these gods were non-existent, he would have been talking at cross purposes with the situation in which his compatriots found themselves. In such a state of affairs, to teach monotheism *per se* would have been empty words. For the men and women living in this epoch, the question whether these gods did or did not exist was of no interest. The declaration that they are nothing is to be taken in the sense of 40.15, 17, 23 and 24. That is to say, quite the only way of taking it is as the other side of the exaltation of Yahweh. It only arises when Yahweh's hidden way of acting in history is again accepted. In this situation, the gods lose their power and become nothing.

[25–29] This, and this alone, gives the background for understanding what Deutero-Isaiah now says of Yahweh's action by means of the Persian king, Cyrus. The latter's being 'stirred up' (v. 25) is not thought of as something unique in history. It can only be under-stood in the context of vv. 26 and 27. Although the words 'I stir up from the north' are followed by 'who declared this from the begin-ning?', this does not imply a proclamation of this event to the whole world. It is simply the message of release as applying to his chosen people (v. 27). Thus, the stirring up of Cyrus does not mean that there was anything exceptional in Yahweh's relationship to the history of Persia. As a matter of fact, the words are entirely in line with those of Isaiah when he called Assyria 'the rod of God's anger', and with what Jeremiah said of the 'foe from the north' in Jer. 4–6. This is the same language as in v. 25b, 'He trod down rulers as mortar, as the potter tramples clay', and it is language already given in trad-ition. Here Deutero-Isaiah says nothing that oversteps the bounds of what had been said by his predecessors, the prophets before the exile. The only difference lies in the fact that our prophet sees the advent of the foreign conqueror whom Yahweh stirs up within the context not of judgment, but of salvation. The one difficulty comes in the second half of v. 25a. The Masoretic Text reads: 'from the rising of the sun he called me by name.' This would mean that Cyrus responded to Yahweh's 'stirring him up' by calling upon him, Yahweh, in the sense of honouring him with worship. Duhm (see above) suggested changing the suffixes and reading, 'and I (Yahweh) called him (Cyrus) by his name'. Today, the majority of com-mentators regard the emendation, unsupported as it is by manuscript evidence or versions, as over-bold. None the less, we now find a variant reading in DSS Isa. I, 'and he called him by his name.' While this is not, of course, the change which Duhm proposed, it does show that what originally stood in the text is not clear. And the occurrence of the same words in 45.3, 'who call you by your name', is a further weighty argument in Duhm's favour, as is also the paral-lelism. I adopt the emendation. Taken thus, the words are an ex-planation in different terms of the first half of the verse, 'I stirred him up from the north, and he has come.' (If Masoretic Text is retained, so much doubt attaches to it as to make it, in my view, no possible basis for the idea that Deutero-Isaiah expected Cyrus to become a worshipper of Yahweh—so Volz and many present-day editors, including Muilenburg).

The words, 'I stirred up from the north, and he has come', represent Deutero-Isaiah's resumption of a very old tradition with deep roots in Israel's history. He wants to set Yahweh's action through

Cyrus in the context of God's acts as Israel had known them from of old.

Excursus on v. 25a

'I stirred up from the north, and he has come.' There are two other places where Deutero-Isaiah uses the same verb in the same context:

41.2   Who stirred him up (Cyrus) from the east . . .
45.13 I stirred him up (Cyrus) . . . and make straight . . .

The tradition with which Deutero-Isaiah here links up can be seen in a group of similar passages:

Isa. 13.17   Behold, I am stirring up the Medes against them . . .
Jer. 50.9   Behold, I am stirring up and bringing against
           Babylon a company of great nations . . .
51.1   Behold, I am stirring up the spirit of a destroyer against
           Babylon . . .
11   Yahweh has stirred up the spirit of the king of the Medes,
           because his purpose against Babylon is to destroy it . . .

In all these passages the meaning is practically the same: Yahweh rouses or stirs up a nation or a king destined to destroy Babylon. In three of the four the proclamation is put in the mouth of Yahweh himself. All are exilic prophecies of unknown origin. During the exile, then, either in Palestine or among sections of the exiles, there were proclamations against Babylon in God's name with the recurring catchword, 'I stir up so and so against Babylon'. They have certainly to be regarded as a continuation of the pre-exilic prophecy of salvation surviving the downfall of 586 in such sayings as these. This, however, implies that such proclamation of the 'stirring up' of a conqueror must be older than 586. 'I will stir up' is in fact found in prophecy of doom, although in this case it is the stirring up of an enemy against Israel, as for example in Ezek. 23.22, and in narratives as well (I Chron. 5.26; II Chron. 21.16). In such instances the verb denotes an action on Yahweh's part that causes the approach of a foreign nation or a foreign king. The movement that can be seen, the approach of the army, has lying behind it an unseen one—God rouses, God stirs up, God sets in motion. Obviously, then, these are very old technical terms for this particular mode of the divine activity in history. They always represent an influence brought to bear on foreign kings or powers. But this is always with reference to Israel. It is an indirect action on Israel. Never once is there any idea that the power or king in question stands in a direct relationship to Yahweh, that is to say, that they worship him, or the like. This cannot, then, be what is meant in the original text of 41.25, either.

The basic meaning in the *qal* is most likely to be literal stirring up, shaking awake, setting in motion. So Zech. 4.1; Job 14.12, etc. It relates in particular to stirring up for battle:

Joel 3.14 (9): Prepare war, stir up the mighty men.

The sword can also be addressed in similar terms:

Zech. 13.7: Awake, O sword, against my shepherd.

Stirring up for battle forms the background of the prayer, often found in the Psalter, that God should intervene:

Ps. 7.7 (6): Arise, O Lord,
in thine anger lift thyself against the fury of my enemies.

Similarly Pss. 35.23; 44.24 (23); 59.5 (4). With Deutero-Isaiah, this form is also found in 51.9–52.5, a passage where he takes over a community lament:

51.9: Awake, put on strength, O arm of the Lord.

Cf. 51.17 and 52.1. The presumption is that this imperative of the *qal* is both the verb's oldest form and the one most likely to be used. It is found in calls to sing (Pss. 57.9 [8]; 108.3 [2], as well as in summons to do battle. Both stand side by side in v. 12 of the song of Deborah (Judg. 5). In this, its oldest form, it can be an appeal both to human beings and to God, and the Psalter continues this down to a late date. The form in the first person, 'I will arise', is related to the *qal* as its answer (so perhaps the conjectured reading in Ps. 60.9 (7), in an oracle of salvation in answer to such a prayer). 'I will stir up', the starting-point of the present excursus, represents a further development.

Isaiah 41.2; 41.25 and 45.13 thus form part of an old strand of tradition going right back to Israel's earliest days. In times of national distress, prayer is made to God to bestir himself, awaken, and intervene. He answers with the proclamation 'I will stir up' in the form of an oracle of salvation to his chosen people. Thus, as Yahweh here confronts the foreign gods, his argument, the stirring up of Cyrus, is a mode of his action of which Israel had had experience during the entire course of her history. Even if, from another angle, his release

of her by the Persian king is proclaimed as something new and unprecedented, the novelty is solely due to the unprecedentedness of
the situation. The method itself, 'stirring up' a foreign power in order
to change history on Israel's behalf, had been known to her for
generations.

In this connection it is particularly important to remember that,
even before Deutero-Isaiah, 'stirring up' is found in proclamations
put into the mouth of Yahweh—in the context of proclamation and
its fulfilment, which is the very thing on which Deutero-Isaiah always
makes the trial speeches turn.

[26–27] In v. 26 Yahweh's opponents are challenged with the
question, 'Who declared this beforehand, that we might know?', and
the second part of the half-verse runs in similar terms. Here the
proclamation is presented in retrospect as a total process. The verbal
element in a proclamation is incomplete until the thing it proclaims
has come to pass and the people who heard it made and experienced
its fulfilment can now say, 'It is right'. It is this total event that
forms the subject of Yahweh's question to his opponents in v. 26, and
this is the very thing that they are unable to advance as argument,
v. 26b. Yahweh, however, is (v. 27). He proclaimed it in advance to
Zion, to his people, and sends the messenger of good tidings, who
announces the fulfilment. If this exegesis of v. 26 is correct, the point
at issue is not whether the two parties in court have, say, proclamation, foretelling and prophecy to show. It is the connection, visible at
a glance, between proclamation and its fulfilment.

There is an obvious objection. When Deutero-Isaiah makes the
gods of the foreign nations have no answer to give to the question of
proclamation in advance on their part, is this true to the facts? He
cannot seriously mean to maintain that Israel is the one place where
this occurs and has occurred. The question is put by Duhm, who
continues: 'any adherent of another faith would have given him the
lie, if not actually held him in derision, if he maintained that there
was no foretelling outside the religion of Israel. . . But our prophet
obviously finds this quite inconceivable. For him the mere utterance
of his conviction is proof enough: there is not the slightest element of
self-criticism in his make up. . . Deutero-Isaiah thinks that he speaks
as a prophet. He speaks, however, as a poet. Enthusiasm deludes
itself.'

At a first glance this judgment is true. In the world in which the prophet lived there most certainly was proclamation in advance of future events spoken either by a god or in a god's name. There is evidence of it. Documents containing such oracles are extant. Nor can we take Volz's way out of the difficulty. In his opinion, they are mantic, ends in themselves of human device, and therefore not strictly religious. Deutero-Isaiah certainly does not say that these other gods' words have nothing to do with religion. His assertion is that they show no comprehension of what really makes up history. His criterion is not their religious character, but their lack of this historical comprehension. But how can the prophet maintain that they had absolutely nothing to show? Any assertion that he was unaware of such oracles is just as much to be rejected as is Duhm's view that poetic rapture led him to ignore them. He takes the Babylonian cult so seriously, and there is so much evidence of his close knowledge of it, that we are bound to believe that he was fully *au fait* with the Babylonian oracular techniques.

The point at issue in the trial speeches is not just proclamation in itself, the giving of oracles. It is the reliable connection between a god's word and his deed. In one of the later trial speeches, Israel is called upon to bear witness to this. She can attest that 'it is right.' We have to remember that, ever since the time of Amos, which means for more than a century, Israel's history had had the dark cloud of a proclamation of doom lowering over it. The fate which overtook the exiles was its fulfilment. But it is to be just the same with the proclamation of salvation beginning with Deutero-Isaiah's message of comfort. This it is which in fact entirely determines the fate of the present generation and of those to come. The unique thing that the God of Israel can adduce as against the foreign nations' gods is his faithfulness as shown in this message of comfort spoken on the other side of the gulf torn open by the year 586, and now made known to his chosen people by his word, upon which they can rely. It has to be stated as a fact that the comparative study of religion shows that, even from the purely phenomenological point of view, neither the religion of Babylon nor that of Egypt has anything even remotely comparable to set alongside this.

CHAPTER 42.1–4

Behold, my Servant

1 Behold my servant, whom I uphold,
   my chosen, in whom I have delight.
   I bestow my spirit upon him,
   he is to bring forth justice to the nations.
2 He does not cry or lift up his voice,
   or make it heard in the street.
3 The broken reed he does not break,
   and the dimly burning wick he does not quench.
   He brings forth righteousness as truth.

4 He does not burn dimly, nor is he broken,
   till he establishes justice in the earth,

   and the islands wait for his teaching.

Bibliography: For a survey of the literature on the Servant Songs, cf. G. Fohrer, *ThR*, NF 28, 1962, pp. 234–9 and C. R. North, *The Suffering Servant of Deutero-Isaiah*, 2nd ed., Oxford, 1956; H. Haag, 'Die Ebed-Jahwe-Forschung 1948–58', *BZ*, 3 (1959), pp. 174–204.

42.1–4 give the first so-called servant song (this generally accepted designation is retained here, although the poems are not properly songs). While the passages concerned (42.1–4 and 5–9; 49.1–6 and 7–13; 50.4–9 and 1off.; and 52.13–53.12) would be better taken and commented on as forming a group by themselves, they will here be treated as they occur in the text. One of the results of exegesis needs to be anticipated. The songs represent a special strand within the book of Deutero-Isaiah, and therefore they did not come into being at the same time as their contexts. Nevertheless, they owe their origin to Deutero-Isaiah, the last being probably the work of a disciple.

The structure of this first song is very clear and concise. The keynote of it all is given in the first two words, 'Behold, my Servant', or 'This is my Servant'. These in themselves epitomize the event described throughout—God points to someone and designates him as his servant. The song is thus the designation of God's Servant. The two clauses in v. 1a that follow the words have the same significance, and underline God's turning towards this servant. Then, in v. 1b, come the way in which the chosen servant is equipped, and the task for whose sake this is done. The task is again stated in v. 3b, the intervening lines giving the way in which he is to accomplish it. This is done in four negative clauses, which in fact say how he is not to accomplish it. He is not to perform it by making clamour when he appears (v. 2) and by destroying what is already at the point of extinction (v. 3a). Verse 4 adds a promise for the servant, again put in negative terms. He is not to burn dimly and be broken before he has accomplished his task. This is the third mention of his task. The song ends by saying that the 'isles' are awaiting it.

Clear and concise though the song is, its interpretation is very difficult. On three matters we are left in the dark. Who is the servant here designated by God for a task? What is the nature of the task? And in what context is the designation made? Exegesis must never ignore the limits thus put upon it. The cryptic, veiled language used is deliberate. This is true of every one of the servant songs alike. From the very outset there must be no idea that exegesis can clear up all their problems. The veiled manner of speaking is intentional, and to our knowledge much in them was meant to remain hidden even from their original hearers. Exegesis must then be conscious of the limit thus imposed, and be careful to call a halt at those places where the distinctive nature of the songs demands this. One thing in particular will need to be heeded—and here the present writer disagrees with the majority of the innumerable commentaries on the songs. On principle, their exegesis must not be controlled by the question, 'Who is this servant of God?' Instead, we must do them justice by recognizing that precisely this is what they neither tell nor intend to tell us. The questions which should control exegesis are: 'What do the texts make known about what transpires, or is to transpire, between God, the servant, and those to whom his task pertains?'

[1] The first words plainly describe a designation. This means that someone with the right so to do designates or appoints someone else to perform a task or to hold an office. It was chiefly in connection with the charismatic leaders of her early days that Israel knew of such designations. Gideon is a case in point: God's emissary designated him as the one through whom God intended to deliver his people (Judg. 6). They are much in evidence during the transition from charismatic leadership to the monarchy, although here designation by God is

accompanied by acclamation on the part of Israel.[a] In I Sam. 9.15–
17, we are told of the designation of Saul: 'And Samuel saw Saul.
And Yahweh told him, "Here is the man (*hinnē hā'iš*, exactly corresponding to the first words of the passage before us, *hēn 'abdī*), of
whom I spoke to you. He it is who shall rule over my people." ' The
designation of David (I Sam. 16) adds equipment with the spirit. The
parallel with 42.1–4 is so striking that the latter's wording was
probably intended to suggest a royal designation. One feature makes
a clear distinction between the designation of the Servant here and
that of a prophet—the very nature of the latter means that there can
be no witnesses to it. All the passages which describe a prophet's call
leave this in no doubt. On the other hand, as evidenced also in I
Sam. 9.15–17, at a king's designation the presence of witnesses to
whom it is said, 'Behold this is . . .' is essential. Confirmation of this
is given by the account of Jesus' baptism, Mark 1.11 par., where Isa.
42.2 is combined with Ps. 2.7.

'Whom I uphold': The one who upholds gives his own strength to
the one upheld (cf. Ex. 17.12). 'My chosen' here preserves its original
meaning: out of many who might have performed the task, this is the
one whom God chooses for it, and the designation makes the choice
public and known. The reason for the choice of this man, and no
other, rests with God alone. God has pleasure in him. That is all that
is needed. Such things as special qualities in the one chosen are un-
essential. The verse from Mark just mentioned (1.11), 'and a voice
came from heaven, "thou art my beloved Son; with thee I am well
pleased" ', brings this out quite clearly. As in Isa. 42.1, the words
represent the public designation of the one chosen by God to perform
the task which he wishes carried out. The parallel passage in Mat-
thew (3.13–17) follows Isa. 42.1 in adding that he is equipped with
the spirit. This is the first indication of a curious parallel between the
servant songs of Deutero-Isaiah and the writers of the New Testament
gospels. Both begin with God's designation of the man concerned for
a specific task. And in both, the work of the one thus chosen ends with
his death for those on whose behalf his work is to be done.

Analogies thus allow us to have perfect confidence about one aspect
of what is described in 42.1. Someone is appointed and equipped by
God for a task whose nature is no more than suggested in the description which follows. And this is a public act. His designation is
differentiated from the call of a prophet by the fact that the latter is

[a] A. Alt, *Kleine Schriften II*, Munich, 1953, p. 23.

ı between God and the prophet alone. But the
equires the presence of others who witness it,
˷ ˷ ˷˷˷ ˷˷˷˷˷ ˷˷˷ stamp of an accrediting. These features link it
with a royal designation: its importance and historical significance are
the same.

The Servant's task:

1c: he is to bring forth justice to the nations.
3c: he brings forth justice in truth.
4b: till he establishes justice in the earth.

These few words give three descriptions of the Servant's task. All three
lines contain the word *mišpāt*. In two of them, too, the same verb is
also used—the Servant is to 'bring forth' *mišpāt*. Thus 'establish' in
v. 4b is also to be taken in the same sense: making *mišpāt* prevail
abroad, 'in the earth'. This is itself an important clue for the meaning
of *mišpāt*. It must eventually have reference to the Gentiles. Taking
49.6, 'I will give you as a light to the Gentiles', into consideration as
well, this is certain.

But what is *mišpāt*? The basic meaning of the word is 'justice' or
'judgment', and this is the sense which it very frequently has. The
rendering 'truth' (so Volz, with the meaning of 'true religion', cf.
also the Zurich Bible and many other commentators) is conjecture
rather than certainty, and need only be assumed if the usual and
generally accepted meaning makes no sense at all. Now, if we examine
Deutero-Isaiah for instances of *mišpāt* with reference to the Gentiles,
we shall at once find them in the 'trial speeches' (see above on 41.1–5
and 21–29) which present a legal process between Yahweh and the
gentile nations. They all turn upon justice, *mišpāt*, and result in the
Gentiles' gods' claim to divinity being declared to be nothing:
Yahweh alone is God. This can perfectly well be the meaning of
mišpāt in 42.1–4. It gives excellent sense. And the probability is
increased by taking the final trial speech (45.20–25) into account as
well. In it the 'survivors of the nations' are invited to participate in
Yahweh's salvation (cf. 49.6). This being so, the Servant's task,
according to 42.1–4, would be to bring this judgment to the Gentiles.
About his way of doing this, vv. 2–4 give only a veiled hint. And this
is certainly only one aspect of his task: a wider one is to be indicated
in the servant songs that follow. We must anticipate here and say
that these lend no support to the idea that the servant was to go as a
missionary to the Gentiles. (The chief representative of this view is

Volz, and he made a strong case for it.) Instead, they suggest the other possibility, that because of his *via dolorosa* among his own nation, the servant was to bring God's *mišpāṭ* to the Gentiles in an indirect way, so becoming their light.

[2] As the servant promulgates judgment, he is not to follow custom and cry aloud in public. Here we may remember that in oriental law, when a new king succeeds to the throne, he re-enacts the laws and has them publicly proclaimed. The way in which the servant was to bring forth justice and establish it is to be the opposite of this. So far, the actual method is not stated.

[3a] Verse 3 is to be taken as pointing in the same direction. Begrich may possibly be right in thinking that the metaphors have an old legal usage as their background. But if so, their wording preserves no more than a faint echo of it. For those concerned, bringing forth the divine justice is not to mean death for those already under sentence of death. The servant makes God's justice prevail in such a way that his action contradicts the harsh law of the world, which says that what is broken and burns dimly inevitably perishes. This may be regarded as to a certain extent parallel to 40.6–8. There the prophet's word of comfort brought life to Israel as she was pining away. The Servant's work has a similar effect on the rest of the world. This is emphasized in the final words of v. 3, 'he is to bring forth justice in truth' (strictly, 'to be truth', i.e. that it becomes the truth, is made to prevail).

[4a b] The lines allude to the verbs in v. 3a and promise the Servant himself that he will not burn dim or be broken before he has completed his task. This is the only place in the song which suggests that the Servant's task is to involve him in grievous suffering—this is to be taken up in the other songs. Thus, here alone is there any hint of that aspect of his work which is reminiscent of the call of a prophet (Jer. 1.19).

[4c] 'And the isles wait for his teaching.' Compare 51.4, where the same thing is said not of the Servant, but of God: 'for teaching will go forth from me, and my truth for a light to the Gentiles.' Also 51.5b, 'the furthest climes wait for me, and for my arm they wait.' The Gentiles are already waiting and looking for the divine justice which the Servant is to bring forth. This does not involve our idea of 'seeking after the one God, and yearning for him' (Volz). The verb implies intent expectancy of deliverance or help. The sense is therefore that among the Gentiles the Servant's gospel finds an expectancy

similar to that which greeted Deutero-Isaiah's message to Israel, e.g. in the exile.

Finally, all that can here be said about 42.1–4 is that the echo of the royal designation, as well as the proclamation of justice and the sparing of those already under sentence of death, point in the direction of a mediator who discharges his office by way of action, like the judges (charismatic leaders) and kings in the past. On the other hand, the Servant's task as set forth in vv. 2–4 points rather to one who mediates by word of mouth (this comes out clearly later, in 50.4f.). The suggestion is possibly that the two lines of mediation which had parted company during the course of Israel's history are reunited in the servant. Perhaps this is also implied in the designation 'servant', for the Old Testament very often uses it of Moses, in whose person the two lines were still one.[a]

CHAPTER 42.5-9

I call you in righteousness

5 Thus says Yahweh, the Lord,
who created the heavens and stretched them out,
who founded the earth and what comes from it,
who gives breath to the people upon it
and the breath of life to those who walk in it;

6 I, Yahweh, call you in righteousness
and take you by the hand.
I form and make of you
the covenant[b] of the people, the light of the heathen,

7 to open eyes that are blind,
to bring out prisoners from the dungeon,
from the prison those who dwell in darkness.

[a] See the article by Zimmerli in *TWNT* (ET in *The Servant of God*, London, 1957, pp. 11–44).
[b] H. Torczyner (Tur-Sinai), Presidential address, *JPOS*, 16 (1936), pp. 1–8, derives *berit* from a root brr = *bāran* = 'shine out', and translates: brilliance of the people—light of the heathen.

8　I, Yahweh, that is my name,
　　and my glory I give to no other
　　nor my praise to graven images.
9　Behold, the former things have come to pass
　　and new things I now declare.
　　Before they spring forth, I tell you of them.

There is general agreement today that 42.5–9 form a unit (cf. Volz on the subject). But critics are still extremely divided as to the meaning of the passage; it is one of the pericopes in the book which so far no one has succeeded in really explaining. What constitutes the difficulty is the fact that the connections are not clear. Only this much is plain—the speaker is Yahweh, in v. 6 he utters what seems like a call, and v. 7 states the purpose which this is to serve. But who it is that Yahweh calls, on whom the person called is to act, and the nature of his task, are obscure. Commentators differ as to whether the oracle is addressed to the servant (who, however, is not mentioned in vv. 5–9, and there is not sufficient evidence for assuming, as is often done, that the 'servant' of 42.1–4 is the same person as is addressed in v. 6), or to Israel, or to Cyrus. Accordingly, there is disagreement in determining the task given to the one called here. Exegesis has therefore to distinguish carefully between firm ground and what is open to question.

The introductory messenger-formula is followed by a series of clauses in apposition to 'the God Yahweh' (the only occurrence of the term in Deutero-Isaiah): he is the creator of heaven and earth and mankind, phraseology often used by the prophet. This forms the introduction to the oracle proper, which comes in vv. 6 and 7 and speaks of someone who is given neither name nor designation, but whom God intends to make the 'covenant of the people' and the 'light of the nations' (v. 6), in order to open blind eyes and bring out prisoners from the dungeon (v. 7). The conclusion takes the form of one of Deutero-Isaiah's frequent self-predications on the part of Yahweh: it insists that he alone is God (v. 8). The remaining verse (9) has no connection with what precedes: its subject is the former things and the new things, and it occurs elsewhere in the book in a different context.

[5] The call. The call is introduced by praise of God's power and wisdom as shown in creation, the diction being that of those Psalms which extol God as creator. The combination 'heaven and earth', of common occurrence in Deutero-Isaiah (40.22; 42.5; 44.23f.; 45.8,

12, 18; 48.13; 49.13; 51.6 *bis*), is a very old one. It appears in many passages in the Old Testament, as, for example, in the superscription to the creation story in P (Gen. 1.1), and continued in use to be taken up into the Apostles' Creed. It is very much older than the Bible and is also found in Babylonian and Canaanite texts. The purpose underlying the combination is that of describing the whole range of creation by means of the two parts, heaven and earth. The verbs unite concepts of the work of creation which differ both in date and content. One of them is theological, and takes in the whole of creation, the other, the older, conceives God as actually working with his hands—he stretches out and beats out (the two verbs recur together in 44.24, while 'stretch out' also appears in Deutero-Isaiah in 40.22 and 45.12, cf. Ps. 136.5f.). Here, quite obviously, there is no sense of the profound difference between the two concepts. No more is mentioned of the creation of man than the one act of the bestowal of (the breath of) life upon him. It is interesting to note that the older concept of the creation of man, the forming of one man (as in Gen. 1 and 2), no longer appears here, being replaced by that of the creation of, or bestowal of life upon, mankind, the human race (similarly in 45.12 and suggested in 45.18, also 57.16). One of the clauses here expresses this as 'he gives breath to the people upon it (the earth)'. The word for people, whose most frequent usage is as a designation of the people Israel, is here expanded to designate all peoples, the human race.

[6] In 41.9 the same verbs as used here, 'call' and 'take by the hand', denote an action on the part of Yahweh with Israel, the reference there being to the start of his activity in her history. The next words in 41.9 run: 'I said to you, "You are my servant." ' This exact parallel suggests that 42.6 also refers to Israel's election. This also supplies the best explanation of the linkage with 42.1-4—the man who added vv. 5-9 to vv. 1-4 supposed that the person addressed in v. 6 was the servant, but in his view the servant was Israel. It also adds significance to the relationship of v. 6 to v. 5—he who elected Israel is the creator of heaven and earth and the creator of mankind. If the servant in v. 6 is taken as an individual, it would be difficult to see why such an interpretation should be substantiated by reference to God's work of creation: elsewhere in Deutero-Isaiah this substantiates or underpins both God's historical action with Israel and the stirring up of Cyrus (with which, of course, the former is most closely connected), but never the call and mission of the servant.

While, like 41.9, v. 6a refers, or at least may refer, to the first

election of Israel, v. 6b specifies a new function for her, a fresh
charge laid upon her. Its first clause constitutes an equation with two
unknown quantities: we do not know what is meant by *berīt ʿam*,
'covenant of the people', and the expression, 'give as a *berīt*', occurs
nowhere else. Thus, until now the interpretation of the clause has
been no more than conjecture. One thing is certain: the words, 'I
make you as', mean that the person addressed is destined to become a
tool or means whereby God effects something on others. This is
shown by the second part of the verse. 'I make you the light to the
nations', which means, 'through you the nations are to experience
light, illumination and salvation'.[a] Then, taking the two phrases as
parallel, *berīt ʿam* supposedly means, 'I make you the covenant-
salvation (that is, the salvation given in the covenant) for all mankind.' If it is the people Israel that is addressed in v. 6, then the *ʿam*
in v. 6b (*berīt ʿam*) cannot possibly also refer to it. Since, however, as
all editors agree, in v. 5 the same word *ʿam* designates the human
race, it should be presumed to have the same, or at least a similar,
comprehensive sense in v. 6 as well (so also Marti, Kittel, Köhler,
Volz and Muilenburg).

[7] As many editors have pointed out, the subject of the infinitives
in v. 7 could equally be Yahweh or the one addressed in v. 6 (the
servant or Israel). This indetermination is characteristic of the
author of 42.5–9. Exactly the same thing is found in Trito-Isaiah, in
61.1ff.; in a context similar to the present, the subject of the infinitives shifts over without warning from the one whom Yahweh calls
(v. 1) to Yahweh himself (v. 3). Here, too, the infinitives relate to a
proclamation of salvation, and there is also release from prison.

Having regard to the character of the passage, we are to suppose
that in the description of the salvation to be brought to mankind by
the servant (v. 6b), the thing envisaged in the three clauses of v. 7
is the removal of suffering in general (as in 61.1ff.); the opening of
the eyes of the blind and the freeing of prisoners are intended to
typify human suffering, the first representing the suffering due to
man's creaturely status, the second that at the hands of other men. At
all events, the reference is not specifically to the blindness of Israel, a
subject treated by Deutero-Isaiah in another context, nor is it to the
fact of exile, which the words used here could have meant. The sense
is that God has designated Israel to be a light to the world and to

---

[a] De Boer's interpretation, *op. cit.*, p. 93, 'a light respected by the nations',
seems to me very forced.

mediate salvation to it; she is to bring enlightenment and liberation to others.[a]

[8] In this saving work, God is to prove himself to be truly God; his name carries the overtone that he is the lord and saviour of the world. His glory and his praise, which he gives to no other, consist in his being recognized in his saving work. Verse 8 is clearly a conclusion and corresponds to the beginning of the oracle (v. 5).

[9] This saying about the former things and the new things gives the impression of being a fragment out of its proper context, the 'you' in the last clause having nothing to which it relates. In the Deutero-Isaianic oracle which underlies vv. 5–9, vv 5, 8 and 9 could be the introduction to a trial speech addressed to the gods of the nations.

A note on 42.5–8 (9) taken as a whole: The commentary has shown it to be quite certain that vv. 5–9 did not come into being at the same time as the servant song contained in vv. 1–4. Although they follow it immediately, their manner of speaking about the 'servant', whom they regard as Israel, is quite different. Their description of the salvation which Israel is to bring to the nations is similar to that of Trito-Isaiah. The verses are therefore a later expansion and continuation of the *ʿebed* song contained in 42.1–4. The other songs, too, were expanded at a later date. We may assume that the basis of the verses is an oracle of Deutero-Isaiah which was only altered in vv. 6 and 7. 42.5–9 thus furnish proof that the servant songs were taken up into a tradition which emanated from Deutero-Isaiah and expanded.

CHAPTER 42.10–13

A New Song

10 Sing to Yahweh a new song,
     his praise from the end of the earth!
     Let the sea [roar][b] and what fills it,
     the islands and their inhabitants.

a In a hymn to Marduk: 'Make him who is cast into prison see light'; in a hymn to Shamash: 'Shamash, it lies in your power to revive the dead, to deliver him that is in fetters' (Stummer, *op. cit.*, p. 180).

b Read *yirʿam* as Pss. 96.11; 98.7.

11 Let the desert and its cities [rejoice],[a]
   the villages that Kedar inhabits.
   The inhabitants of the rocks (are) to sing for joy,
   to shout from the top of the mountain.
12 Let them give glory to Yahweh,
   declare his praise in the islands.

13 Yahweh goes forth like a mighty man,
   like a man of war he stirs up fury.
   He raises the war-cry, the shout of battle,
   shows himself victor over his foes.

This is the first occurrence of the form called the 'eschatological' hymn of praise: it is particularly characteristic of Deutero-Isaiah's proclamation ([40.9ff.]; 42.10–13; 44.23; 45.8; 48.20f.; 49.13; 52.7–10).[b] It represents a new type of psalm, contrived by the prophet because of the specific situation in which his proclamation was delivered. It resembles the descriptive psalm of praise (the hymn) in the introduction (vv. 10ff.), the call to praise in the imperative, which is often extended by means of jussives. However, whereas in the psalms this call is followed by a description of God's majesty and goodness, with Deutero-Isaiah it always introduces an act, a deed done by God, it being the same in the case of all the texts mentioned above. The prophet thus took a form well-known to his people from their worship and so altered it as to give the call to praise its substantiation in a unique act of God which, however, had not as yet taken place, namely, the act of release, which he proclaims in his message of comfort. In this specific hymn-form, Deutero-Isaiah summons his audience, his fellow-countrymen in exile, even now to strike up jubilation at the event which, while it lies ahead of them all, is already a settled fact in the mind of God, the return which he himself brings about. For the prophet's proclamation the hymns of praise express the requirement that those who hear it make a response to it: in the hymns they give it faith's 'Amen'.

[10–12] The same words as here open Pss. 96 and 98, and there are also several reminiscences particularly of the former psalm in 42.10–13. This should first make it clear that 42.10–13 are a genuine psalm; the question whether Deutero-Isaiah is dependent on the above mentioned psalms, or *vice versa*, cannot be taken up at the

[a] Read *yāsīsu*.
[b] Cf. 'Sprache und Struktur', pp. 157–63.

moment. The reason for striking up the 'new song' is a new act on God's part, which completely corresponds to Deutero-Isaiah's proclamation, 'I make a new thing known to you.' The second half of v. 10 more narrowly defines the song as a song of praise. In Israel, dialogue determines the divine-human relationship from beginning to end. When God acts towards men, a response must come from them. The joyous answering rendered in praise is so essential that lack of it would be tantamount to contempt of the divine act. It is as we realize the great significance attaching to praise in Israel's relationship with God that we can appreciate Deutero-Isaiah's daring in here summoning the oppressed, the stricken, and the despairing to sing a hymn in praise of an act of God of which not the faintest trace is discernible in their present situation.

The words, 'from the end of the earth', could allude to the place of exile, but may also have the more general sense of 'from everywhere afar'.

Verse 10b: The imperative of v. 10a is carried on in vv. 10b–12 by four lines in the jussive, exactly as, for example, in Ps. 113. Every one of these clauses is found in identical, or almost identical, terms in psalms. This makes the emendations of the two verbs at the beginning of vv. 10b and 11a particularly certain; they are based on parallels in the psalms.

Those summoned to 'sing' in v. 10a are human beings, the men who listened to Deutero-Isaiah's proclamation. In the expansion in the jussive in the four clauses which follow, this little group, the community summoned to sing the hymn of praise, is enormously extended: the whole of creation is to join in the hymn, and to assume the role of the 'instrumental' accompaniment to the small and feeble choir; only so does the song of praise match the deed which is to be celebrated in it. The summons goes forth to the sea and the coastlands (islands), to the desert and the towns in the oases, and to those who inhabit the mountains: the sea is to roar, the wilderness to exult, and the inhabitants of the rocks to sing for joy; they are to give glory to Yahweh and declare his praise. The conception is no doubt fanciful and extravagant, yet it is magnificent; and it rests on the matter-of-fact premiss which is the determining factor in Deutero-Isaiah's proclamation—that the one whose action towards his people is to be thus re-echoed is the creator of heaven and earth and the lord of everything that happens. This is certainly put in the language of poetry, the poetry of the Psalter. But to say no more than that the words are fanciful and extravagant would be to put a wrong construction on them. The proposition that God is the creator and the lord of history has a very objective significance for Deutero-Isaiah, and is far from being merely a theological idea. This summons to join in the praise of God was not, of course, actually complied with at the time; as an 'eschatological' hymn of praise, the summons points to very much more than the event of the return. Nevertheless, as often elsewhere in the book, the prophet here proclaims as binding that God's final saving act towards his people is to take place in full view of the entire world of men and of nature, and that it looks for the response not merely of the faithful, but of all men and of nature.

[13] The event itself is described in veiled terms, being clad in an ancient form extant in tradition, the diction used for epiphanies. The old descriptions of these (e.g., Judg. 5.4f.; Pss. 18.8–16 (7–15); 114, etc.) depict Yahweh's 'advent', his coming from afar to his chosen people's aid in their need. The motif is most of all at home in the old 'wars of Yahweh', in which he draws near as warrior and smites Israel's foes; Deutero-Isaiah here takes up the tradition exactly. It is quite characteristic of the Psalms that, when they depict the divine action, in particular Yahweh's intervention on behalf of his chosen people, they use extremely ancient delineations and concepts, some of them even derived from myth. In the light of this, v. 13 here is to be taken as cryptic language which at the same time points in a certain direction. The purpose of the simile is to say to those who heard it that God is intervening *now*—and that things are to be as they were in days of old, when God came to his chosen people's aid in its extremity. Without actually saying so, the simile also suggests that 'the God, of whose miraculous acts our ancestors sang the praises, is as much alive as he was then: is as zealous for his people as he was then: acts with deeds as overwhelmingly mighty as then!' In the prologue (40.10), the return from exile is spoken of as Yahweh's coming with power. In the same way, here in 42.13, his marching forth to victory is the first step in the event which is to result in Israel's going forth from Babylon.

CHAPTER 42.14–17

I lead the blind in the way

14　For a long time I have held my peace,
　　I have been dumb, and restrained myself.

　　I cry out like a woman in travail, I groan,
　　my breath comes in gasps.

15　I dry up mountains and hills,
　　and I make all their herbage wither;
　　I turn rivers into dry land,
　　and I dry up swamps.

16　And I lead the blind in the way [　],ᵃ
　　in paths they know not I guide them;
　　I turn the darkness before them into light,
　　and the rough places into level ground.

　　These are the things I do,
　　and I forsake them not.

17　They must be turned back,　　　　utterly put to shame,
　　who trust in graven images;
　　who say to molten images,
　　'You are our gods.'

　　While the passage is obviously an independent unit, the form of the oracle and its meaning are very far from clear. To the latter the best clue is v. 16, which is a proclamation of the chosen people's return home. This suggests that the oracle is a proclamation of salvation (like 41.17–20). There we found one of the marks of the proclamation of salvation to be its relationship to the community lament, which is cited by an allusion at the start. This suggests a line of approach to the meaning of the opening words of [14], which are difficult. The two verbs, 'to restrain oneself' and 'to control oneself', occur in Isa. 63f., a community lament, in a context similar to the present one and, as here, with God as subject. 'Wilt thou restrain thyself at

ᵃ Omit one *lō' yādā'ū*.

these things, O Lord? Wilt thou keep silent, and afflict us beyond measure?' (Cf. also Pss. 79.5; 85.6 (5); 89.47 (46); 74.1, all community laments.) The parallels show that v. 14a alludes to a community lament, and, in fact, to that part of it called 'the allegation made against the deity'. Here, however, Deutero-Isaiah alters this in such a way that, in the introduction to the proclamation of salvation, God admits the truth of the complaint made in the lament, that 'for a long time I held my peace, I was dumb, I restrained myself'. Verse 14a is in the sharpest contrast: it proclaims, 'Now I cry out like a woman in travail.' What is in mind, then, is not the pain of the woman in travail, but the change from long silence to crying out, to loud groaning and panting. The actual change in God's attitude proclaimed in the oracle before us is already given effect to in vv.14a and b; verses 15f. tell of his intervention which is the result of it, while v. 17 states the consequence of this for Israel's foes.

[15] Comparison with the first proclamation of salvation, 41.17–20, helps towards the elucidation of these verses:

  14a   ‖ 41.17a   allusion to the lament
  14b   ‖ 41.17b   the change in God's attitude
  15–16 ‖ 41.18–19   God's intervention
  17   ‖ 41.20   its consequence

Further, comparison of 42.15–16 with its parallel section, 41.18–19, reveals a curious correspondence:

41.18

I open rivers on the bare heights and fountains in the midst of the valleys
I make the wilderness a pool of water
the dry land springs of water.

19

In the wilderness I plant cedars, acacias, myrtles and olives.

In the steppe I set cypresses,

planes and box trees as well.

20

That they may see and know, may also consider and understand, that the hand of Yahweh has done this,

42.15

I dry up mountains and hills and I make all their herbage wither
and I turn the rivers into dry land
and I dry up swamps.

16a

And I lead the blind in the way, on a path they know not I guide them,
I turn the darkness before them into light,
and the rough places into level ground.

16b

These are the things I do, and I do not forsake them.

the Holy One of Israel has created
it.

17
 They must be turned back,
 utterly put to shame,
 who trust in graven images,
 who say to molten images,
 'You are our gods'.

In 41.18 God's intervention consists in the turning of the desert into
fertile country, in 42.15 it is the very reverse: good land is turned into
desert. Now, a glance at Ps. 107, vv. 33–37, shows that these are the
two sides of the selfsame divine act, his intervention that effects
change, corresponding to the humbling and exaltation of human
beings (Ps. 107.40f.). The motif, the two sides of which Deutero-
Isaiah picked up in the two proclamations of salvation, is the same as
that found in the descriptive psalms of praise (hymns). In both contexts, the transformation wrought by God's act serves to prepare the
way for his chosen people to return home; in 41.17–20 this is only
hinted at, but in 42.16 it is explicit. In accord with the two sides of
the divine act of transformation, the end envisaged in 41.17–20 (the
turning of the desert into fertile land) concerns Israel, that in
42.14–17 (the turning of the fertile land into desert), Israel's foes,
the idolaters.

[16] Blindness and darkness describe the Golah's present condition, as in Isa. 9.1. The principal reason why the exiles were now
blind and saw nothing but darkness ahead of them was that they
themselves no longer believed in any future and imagined themselves
to be forsaken by God. This is why the end of the verse insists that
God's work is to continue—the word *debārim*, which we cannot
translate, takes in working and speaking—God has not forsaken Israel.

[17] The result of this new work on God's part is that Israel's foes
turn back (the movement opposed to the mighty rise and advance
of the neo-Babylonian power) and are put to shame: then is seen
what idolatry with its might, splendour and impressiveness, come to
in the end.

CHAPTER 42.18–25

Hear, you deaf!

18 Hear, you deaf!
and look, you blind, that you may see!
19 Who is blind but my servant[a]
and deaf like my messenger whom I send?
(or, but he to whom I sent my messengers)
Who is blind like *mešullām*,
and blind (or, deaf) like the servant of Yahweh?[b]
20 You have seen much, and not observed,
your ears were open, but you did not hear.[c]
21 Yahweh was pleased, for his righteousness' sake,
he magnified the teaching and made it glorious.
22 Yet this is (now) a people robbed and plundered,
they are all of them bound in holes
and they are hidden in prisons.
They became a prey, there was none to rescue,
a spoil, and none said, 'Restore!'

23 Who among you will give ear to this,
attend and listen for the time to come?
24 Who gave up Jacob to be spoiled,
and Israel to the robbers?
Is it not Yahweh, he against whom we sinned?
But they walked not in his ways,
and did not hearken to his teaching.
25 He poured upon them the heat of his anger
and the might of battle.
He sets him on fire round about, but he does not understand,
He burns him, but he does not take it to heart.

With this difficult oracle we must start from what is clearly verifiable and textually certain; too sweeping conclusions based on parts of the text which are not certain have been responsible for

[a] Instead of 'my servant', the versions read the plural. Both are possible. The Vulgate has '*nisi ad quem nuncios meos misi*'.
[b] *mešullām* is left untranslated. In the same verse we should perhaps follow several Mss. and read *hērēš* for the second *ʿiwwēr*.
[c] Read both verbs as second person.

much false exegesis. Further, the character of the oracle has been largely unrecognized. The first thing that strikes the eye is the question put throughout to those addressed (vv. 19a, b; 23.24a): 'Who is?', 'Who will be?', 'Who has?'; after the introductory command to hear in v. 18 it in fact dominates the whole oracle. Muilenburg draws attention to this, and points to the similar use of this question in 40.12ff. This suggests that the oracle is a disputation. Its subject, however, is not easy to see. In the case of the long disputation in 40.12ff., this is clearly stated in v. 27: it is the charge brought by Israel that God has forsaken his chosen people. The same charge may lie behind 42.18–25, namely, that God is blind and deaf to Israel's present burden of suffering. Gross and improbable as this may sound to begin with, it is after all not so very different from what is said in 40.27: 'My way is hid from Yahweh and my right is disregarded by my God.' The first clause there could be exactly rendered as, 'God is blind (or deaf) to Israel's lot.' This interpretation has the support of vv. 24a and 25; a community lament is undoubtedly the source of the words, 'you gave up Jacob to be spoiled, and Israel to the robbers (cf. Ps. 44.12f.). You poured upon them the heat of your anger.' If this is so, the import of the disputation is: I am not the one who is blind and deaf to your lot, who for that reason have brought all these evils upon you; rather, it is *you* who are blind and deaf in that you fail to see and observe and understand what came about here, and why it came about.

This interpretation of 42.18–25 receives corroboration from the oracle contained in 43.22–28. The latter falls into the category of a trial speech between Yahweh and Israel, but also has affinities with a disputation. Here the charge made by Israel runs: 'We rendered you such true service, but you, on your part, what did you do?' God's answer is: 'You were not my servants; on the contrary, you gave me trouble.' Here, too, then, the disputation consists in a reversal of the charge brought by Israel.

[18] This summons to the deaf and the blind to see and hear is not just the summons to hear which Deutero-Isaiah frequently gives; rather, the two lines receive their meaning from the sharp paradox contained in them. The dominant note in these imperatives is not, then, as many commentators think, that of censure or accusation, but of a hidden promise. Muilenburg's comment on the verse, that for Second Isaiah blindness is the cardinal sin of Israel, is difficult to understand. Blindness is not a sin, but an affliction. Even in cases

where blindness and deafness are spoken of metaphorically and do
have the implication of reproach, the original meaning of having
been smitten with blindness always remains the basic note. To take
the summons here as simply or substantially an accusation is a mis-
understanding of the entire oracle. In the main, Duhm's view of it is
apposite.

[19] The explanation of the general character of the oracle given
above is the only one that makes the question, 'Who is blind but . . .',
intelligible. Yahweh argues against his being the one who is 'blind',
who does not regard his chosen people's fate, and asks instead, 'Who
is the one who is blind here?', and himself supplies the answer. Israel
is designated Yahweh's servant (the versions read 'my servants', but
the meaning is the same). Yahweh elected Israel in order that she
might serve him. The first requisite of service is to pay careful attention to the sayings and directions, the words and actions of the master,
so that blindness and deafness preclude the possibility of service.

If the text is correct, the next clause, 'and deaf as my messenger
whom I send', mentions a particular form of such service, that of a
messenger. This throws the paradox into even sharper relief—a deaf
messenger! It is unnecessary to think of any definite service which
Israel is to render as messenger; Volz goes too far when he speaks of
the 'servant's mission to be a witness for Yahweh in the world'. One
reason for proceeding with caution before interpreting the clause in
such a way is its textual uncertainty. The Vulgate translates '*nisi ad
quem nuncios meos misi*'. This would suit the general thought of the
passage admirably—'Who is deaf but the one to whom I sent my
messengers?' We shall have to let both readings stand as equally
possible.

On v. 19b, Elliger says that 'the need to eliminate v. 19b as a
variant is almost universally recognized', and, if less forthrightly,
the *apparatus criticus* in Kittel says the same. The fact that the word
'blind' appears in both halves itself shows that the verse has not been
preserved in its integrity. Verse 19b is merely a repetition of 19a,
except for the one word *me͑šullām*, the meaning of which is still not
certain. In accordance with the *pu͑al* form as met with elsewhere, it
could mean 'to whom recompense is made'; but the sense is quite
uncertain. The numerous translations and emendations which have
been proposed (some of which are collected in Muilenburg) only
show that, so far, we are unable to explain the word.

[20] Verse 20 then links on to v. 19a. Once again, the text is not

in order. The whole verse can only be read in the second person or in the third throughout; because of v. 18, the second person is the better reading. Verse 20 carries on the paradox of v. 18. In his answer to his chosen people Yahweh says that, just because their history was exceptional, they could have seen many things, and their ears been open to know of mighty things: Israel's historical experience should have empowered her not to be deaf and dumb in her most important crisis, but to observe and hear what God was doing to her in his judgment upon her. This verse can best explain the terms 'blind' and 'dumb' with which Israel is addressed. In her history she had seen God's mighty acts and heard his words of promise and instruction; however, she failed to measure up to what she saw and heard, and acted as if she had not seen and heard, that is, as if she were blind and deaf.

[21] This verse is no part of the prophecy of Deutero-Isaiah. It is an extremely typical addition, a gloss. And it allows us to see the definite value of such additions as aids to exegesis. Moved by the prophet's statement in the second half of v. 20, 'their ears (were) open, and (they did) not hear', a reader expanded it in the sense of 'and this in face of the faithfulness of God who nevertheless made his great and glorious words known to his people'. We may regard the man who made this addition as someone like the writer of Ps. 119, a member of a group which cultivated a legal piety that was absorbed in admiring and abiding by God's word, the *tōrāh*. The addition tells us that the group had read and studied the prophet Deutero-Isaiah, and that, because of what he said about the *tōrāh*, God's word of instruction, they deemed him as having an exceptional importance.

[22] In order to understand v. 22, it is important to remember that originally it followed directly on v. 20. The word 'but' (*waw* adversative) makes a contrast with v. 20. The latter certainly contains a charge against Israel, but it is one limited to the past. As far as the present is concerned, her lot stands under different auspices: 'but (now) this is a people robbed and plundered'. Her punishment for slighting God's acts and words (v. 20) has now been inflicted, and Israel is now suffering its effects. In the matter of the rest of the verse, a vivid and realistic description of these effects, exegesis has often been led astray. Certain commentators have felt that each of the statements made, such as 'trapped in holes', 'hidden in prisons', etc., ought to be taken literally, and have therefore concluded that the

expressions cannot refer to the exile in Babylon, since, to the best of our knowledge, this would not be true of conditions there. Others take what is said metaphorically, but are unable to explain why the prophet put his description of Israel's present situation in such a remarkably concrete way if he meant it to be taken only figuratively. The explanation is simple. All the clauses in v. 22 are in the third person, that is, they are taken from a lament, with a change of person to adapt them to the prophet's purpose. They need only to be turned back into the first person to be seen to be taken from a community lament, and from one specific genre in this category, the lament in the first person plural. We know that, in the case of psalms of lamentation, certain terms and metaphors continued in use for centuries, as for example, in individual laments, the metaphor of setting a snare and falling into it. The statements made in v. 22 are to be understood in precisely the same way: they are long-established technical terms and metaphors used by Israel to describe her plight as she made lamentation in the presence of God. To take this language of the psalms of lamentation as applying literally in every term to Israel's situation in Deutero-Isaiah's time would be misconceiving it. The fact that such words of lamentation as Israel had used for generations in bringing her sufferings to God's notice were still found adequate to express even the crowning blow of the year 587 and its effects is something which we, too, today can very well understand. This lets us once more see how Deutero-Isaiah has links directly, and even verbally, with the lamentations used by his fellow-countrymen in exile.

[23] However—and this is a basic motif in Deutero-Isaiah's proclamation—the prophet does not allow those who thus lament to leave it at lamentation. Rather, since their circumstances are now changed, he summons the 'deaf' to cease to be so, and right away to attend anew, and look forward to the time to come. Verse 23 directly picks up the cry in v. 18 with which the poem began, 'Hear, you deaf'. In the lament, and particularly in that part of it which charged God with being deaf and blind to his chosen people's fate, Israel was clinging to the past; and, as long as she continued so to do, she would remain deaf and blind. But everything depends on her opening her ear to the time to come, directing her gaze to the future. The word 'this' in v. 23a (literally ,'who among you will give ear to *this*') does not connect with v. 22, that is, with the nation's present conditions, but with the entire circumstances as described in vv. 18–

22, namely, that Israel herself was blind and deaf, and that this was the reason why God had been obliged to bring judgment upon her. In view of this, she must now direct her gaze to the things to come.

[24] In order to help his hearers to look to the future, as he suggested, and to listen carefully for something new, the prophet puts a further question (the question in v. 24 corresponds to that in v. 19)— who is the God, and what manner of God is he, who brought this judgment upon you? ('Spoiling' and 'robbers' answer the lament of v.22).

The twofold change in the persons makes the rest of the verse difficult. Although still couched as a question, the words 'Is it not Yahweh, against whom we sinned?' represent the correct answer which Deutero-Isaiah desired. It is perfectly in keeping with the general character of the poem, the only surprise being the transition to the first person, making it into a confession of sin, which might have been expected on the people's lips rather than the prophet's. It is not impossible that the prophet took this way of demonstrating his solidarity with his fellow-countrymen, confessing his own sin along with theirs. Yet, there is nothing similar elsewhere in his writings. We must therefore reckon with the other possibility, that here again we have a later addition—a reader supplied the answer which the prophet wanted, but in so doing described himself as one of the people who were bound to utter this confession of sin. No decision between the two possibilities can be advocated here. On the other hand, the rest of the verse is most certainly an addition, as is shown by the mere fact that it is in prose. Since it reverts to the third person, it can have nothing to do with what precedes it, 'Is it not Yahweh, against whom we sinned?' As far as meaning goes, it certainly suits what follows it (v. 25); yet, since it begins with 'and' (or 'but'), it must link up with words which preceded it. It is best taken as a continuation of the addition made in v. 21 and misplaced in the text. The addition (vv. 21, 24c) would then have read as follows:

> Yahweh was pleased for his righteousness' sake:
> He magnified the teaching (*tōrāh*) and made it glorious;
> but they did not walk in his ways,
> and hearkened not to his teaching (*tōrāh*).

[25] Originally, then, v. 25 directly followed v. 24a: 'Who gave up . . . Jacob . . .? He poured upon them . . .' Once again Deutero-Isaiah models his words on a community lament: 'Thou

pourest out upon us the heat of thy anger.' What the prophet wants to say is this: 'Yes, this is indeed the condition of God's chosen people. It is actually quite as terrible as the forceful, pain-charged words of the lament represent it. Thus it is, and yet you do not see what really happened; you do not lay to heart what God wants this chain of events to tell you!'

This is not, however, the prophet's last word on the situation. There is an extremely close connection between 42.18–25 and what follows in 43.1–7. The attention and hearing for which he calls are to be directed towards the future, yes (42.23); but that future is already at the door.

Chapter 43.1–7

Fear not!

1   But now: thus says Yahweh,
who created you, Jacob, and formed you, Israel:

Fear not, for I have redeemed you,
I have called you by name,
you are mine.

2   When you pass through waters, I am with you,
and streams[a] will not overwhelm you.
when you walk through fire, you are not burnt,
and the flame does not scorch you.

3   For I, Yahweh, am your God,
the Holy One of Israel, your Saviour.

I give Egypt as your ransom,
Ethiopia and Seba in exchange for you,
4   because you are precious in my eyes,
and honoured, and I love you.
And I give [countries][b] in return for you,
and nations for your life.

a Read *un^{e}hārōt*.
b Read *'^{a}dāmot* instead of *'ādām*.

5 Fear not, for I am with you.
   I bring your offspring from the east,
   and from the west I gather you;

6 I say to the north, Give up,
   and to the south, Do not withhold.
   Bring home my sons from afar,
   and my daughters from the end of the earth.
7 Everyone who is called by my name;
   for my glory I created them and made them.[a]

Bibliography: H. E. von Waldow, '. . . *denn ich erlöse dich'. Eine Auslegung von Jes. 43*, Bibl. Stud. 29, Neukirchen, 1960.

Words like these take us to the very heart of Deutero-Isaiah's proclamation. Here we can most easily feel the assurance with which he was able to proclaim to his fellow-captives that the decisive change in their lot had already taken place. Even today an oracle like this can still show us how much this man's proclamation meant to those who first heard it, and why it was preserved and incorporated in the Bible.

The oracle falls into the category of an oracle of salvation, the general introduction to which has been given in the commentary on 41.8–13, 14ff. 'But now', it begins, to contrast with 42.18–25, a new hour has struck. It comes along with the new word of God, which cancels (40.2) the old guilt (42.18–25), and thus proclaims the dawn of the day of release. The oracle is constructed in two parts, vv. 1–4 and 5ff., which are parallels. Verse 1 begins with the assurance of salvation, 'Fear not', which is substantiated in the perfect tense ('I have set you free') and by means of a noun clause ('you are mine', also v. 3a, 'I am'), and is carried on in the proclamation of imminent salvation couched in the future tense (vv. 2ff.). The oracle is rounded off in v.4a by the repetition of the substantiation in the perfect.

The same structure is preserved in the much shorter second part. It begins with 'Fear not', which is substantiated by means of a noun clause ('I am with you') and carried on in the proclamation of imminent salvation couched in the future tense (vv. 5b–6). Verse 7 rounds off both parts: 'for the divine glory'.

[a] One of the three verbs is to be omitted.

[1] The note of sheer exultation which rings through this prophetic word is partly due to the fact that the oracle of salvation upon
which it is based is properly one addressed to an individual. This
means that it had been spoken—probably for centuries—to meet a
private need and therefore came as a word of release and redemption.
Similarly, the two verbs—in the perfect tense—of the substantiation are also properly individual in their reference. 'I have redeemed you': the verb *gā'al* signifies the redeeming, or the liberating
by a payment, of a relative imprisoned for debt, and was originally
a technical term of family law. In the same way, the words 'I have
called you by name' can properly relate only to a transaction involving two persons, and has been transferred from this use—between two
human beings—to the realm of the dealings of God with his chosen
people.

This element in Deutero-Isaiah marks the appearance of something new in the relationship between God and his people. The
subject to which Deutero-Isaiah's entire proclamation is addressed is
the nation as a unit; in no case has he anything to say to an individual
or to a section of the nation. In the exile, however, it was individuals
whom the prophet was obliged to address, and individuals who had
to be won to accept his message. As a result, his message to the
chosen people takes on this new note of personal appeal, a note which
could never afterwards be omitted when the relationship between
God and man was under discussion. In Deutero-Isaiah, and particularly in an oracle such as this, we may see one breakthrough to this
new factor.

What made this personal note possible was the prophet's boldness
in adapting the oracle of salvation intended for an individual so as to
make it relate to the nation and its fate. This he would not have been
able to do had there not been a time in the history of God's dealing
with Israel that was completely under the aegis of a personal relationship to him—the patriarchal age. Just as it was once said to Abraham,
'Fear not, Abraham' (Gen. 15.1), so now again, in the hour of her
deepest humiliation, it can be said to Israel, 'Fear not, Jacob'. And
the significance of the words, 'I have called you by name', is made
perfectly clear in the story of the offering up of Isaac, in which, at its
most terrible moment, Abraham hears a voice calling to him,
'Abraham, Abraham'.

This lays down the line of interpretation for the appositional clause
at the beginning, 'he who created you, Jacob, and who formed you,

Israel.' Referred strictly to Israel the nation, the words can only mean, 'who created you as a nation, that is, by delivering you from Egypt and leading you through the wilderness and bringing you into the promised land'. The creating and forming would then refer to an actual historical act of God, the saving act by which he brought Israel into being. Since, however, as we have just seen, the note struck by the oracle of salvation is so very personal, this opening appositional clause, too, will also carry tones of the other sense: the individual Israelite here addressed is told and reminded that he is God's creature, as, for example, in Ps. 139.

[3] The substantiation in the perfect which has just been discussed is accompanied by three others in the form of noun clauses, 'You are mine' (v. 1b), 'I Yahweh, am your God' (v. 3a), and 'I am with you' (v. 5a). These are all time-hallowed formulae known to everyone in Israel. Between them and the substantiation in the perfect there is a difference. The latter refers to a single act ('I have redeemed you'). These, on the other hand, express something which continues, an intrinsic relationship between Yahweh and Israel. This juxtaposition exemplifies a basic feature of Old Testament theology—all along the line the determining factor in the relationship between God and man is the conjunction, and sometimes even the opposition, of an act and a relationship. Each has its necessary place in the history of God's dealings with his chosen people, and the one never completely merges into the other. The declaration, 'you are mine', is originally a legal formula, the form in which a person declares himself to be the owner of something. The noun clause, 'I, Yahweh, your God', is the same as that which introduces the first commandment (Ex. 20.2).[a] On the term, 'the Holy One of Israel', see the commentary on 41.14. Luther's rendering of the Hebrew word mōšiaʿ as 'thy saviour' gives the exact sense of the Hebrew. Volz remarks, 'In Deutero-Isaiah the word mōšiaʿ becomes almost a proper noun.' The formula, 'I am with you', with which we are best acquainted in the Joseph stories, dates back to Israel's very earliest days, and is even found in Sumerian texts. In these a god who is lord of a particular region uses the formula to declare that he will protect someone who intends to travel there.

[2] The assurance with its substantiations in the perfect tense and in noun clauses is now followed by the proclamation, which contains specific promises (vv. 2 and 3b–4b). In v. 2, the speaker is the creator

[a] See M. Noth, *Exodus*, London, 1962, *ad loc.*

and lord of the elements, in vv. 3b–4b, the lord of history. Verse 2 promises Israel safe conduct on her journey. No force of nature, no hostile element, is to be able to do her any harm as she travels. Here, as often, Deutero-Isaiah merely alludes to the journey and does not specify it. The whole oracle, however, shows that he means the journey home from exile. Water and fire stand for dangers from any element, as in Ps. 66.12. Although quite clearly referring to Israel, this promise, too, has a personal note: it is reminiscent of the personal assurance of blessing in Pss. 91 and 121.

[3b–4b] Israel's saviour is the lord of all nations. Israel's situation being what it is, Yahweh can only deliver her from exile if he has the power to intervene in sovereign fashion in the affairs of the nations; and this, the verse says, he has. While v. 4 uses general terms, lands and peoples, v. 3b is specific as to those of them which God is to give in Israel's stead or as her ransom—Egypt, Ethiopia and Seba. We can no longer ascertain whether or not Deutero-Isaiah envisaged a definite change of sovereignty. However, what is most important for the understanding of the verses is that it is here taken for granted that God, the God of vanquished Israel, is at work in the great political changes afoot in the world of the day, changes which revolved round the liberation of Israel.

The middle part of the two verses is occupied by the substantiation, 'Because you are precious in my sight, and honoured, and I love you'. These words, placed as they are between the two descriptions of the way in which God was to intervene in world-history, are a very good illustration of the character of Deutero-Isaiah's proclamation. Here we also have one of the most beautiful and profound statements of what the Bible means by 'election'. A tiny, miserable and insignificant band of uprooted men and women are assured that they—precisely they— are the people to whom God has turned in love; they, just as they are, are dear and precious in his sight. And think who says this—the lord of all powers and authorities, of the whole of history and of all crea- tion! This incomprehensible turning towards Israel is the basis on which the prophet's proclamations rests (cf. 40.1), and if Israel hearkens to, and accepts, the assurance of salvation which flows from it, nothing can be too miraculous in the way by which her redemption is brought about. When the time comes, she will positively be able to pass through rivers and walk through fire, and to discern *this* God at work in the mightly political movements which lead to her return.

[5–7] The second part, while much briefer than the first, is parallel to it in structure and content. The assurance of salvation, substantiated by means of a noun clause, is followed by a proclamation (vv. 5b–6), this time a perfectly clear promise of the return of the diaspora from exile. The activity of the creator and that of the lord of history are here set together: just as the creator commands the winds, since they are his servants (Ps. 104.4), so God commands the four quarters of the heavens to give up and bring back, the quarters being the political powers which prevent the dispersed of Israel from returning home. Deutero-Isaiah's language is often sweeping and extravagant, and we would do him an injustice if we attempted to specify the four quarters geographically or politically. Verse 7, which rounds off the two parts, shows the end which the work of redemption has in view—'for my glory'. However important it may be for Israel that God should thus turn to her (v. 4a) and, as a result, effect her redemption, *her* exaltation is not the final goal of the event: it is the glory of God. All this is done 'that the Father might be glorified', to use the terms of the Fourth Gospel. which has many features in common with Deutero-Isaiah. In v. 7 this indication of the final goal has two reminiscences of the beginning of the oracle united with it, and these round off the poem. In the two clauses in apposition to the address in v. 1, Israel had been reminded of her creator, and here, at the end, she is told the ultimate implication of her having been created: 'for my glory I created you'. Again, at the beginning of the poem, the assurance of salvation was substantiated with the words, 'I have called you by your name': now, at the end, comes a reminiscence of them, where the many exiles dispersed in all the far places of the earth are told that they are all without exception embraced in God's saving work, for 'every one is called by my name'.

CHAPTER 43.8–15

Trial Speech: You are my witness

8   [Bring forth]ᵃ the people who is blind, who yet has eyes,
     and the deaf, who yet have ears.
9   For all the peoples are gathered together
     and nations have assembled.

     ᵃ Read *hōṣī'ū* with DSS, Isa.¹.

Who among them declares this
and tells us the former things?
Let them bring their witnesses, that they may be justified,
that we may hear and say, It is true.

10   'You are my witnesses,' says Yahweh,
    'and my servant, whom I have chosen,
    that you may know and believe me
    and understand that I am he.
    Before me no god was formed,
    nor shall there be any after me.

11   I, I, Yahweh,
    and beside me there is no saviour.

12   I declared [   ]ᵃ and proclaimed
    and am no stranger in your midst.
                 And you are my witnesses, says Yahweh.ᵇ
    I am God [from old],ᶜ
    [today]ᵈ also I am the same.
    And there is none who snatches from my hand,
    I work, and who will alter it.

14   Thus says Yahweh, your Redeemer, the Holy One of
             Israel.ᵉ
    For your sake I send to Babylon,
    and bring them all as fugitives
    and the Chaldeans . . .ᶠ

15   I, Yahweh, your Holy One,
    The Creator of Israel, your King.'

The passage falls into the same literary category as 41.1–5 and
41.21–29: it is a trial speech. On this form see the commentary there.
Here a new element in the trial speeches between Yahweh and the
nations or their gods comes on the scene. Witnesses are adduced, and
the one who is to appear on Yahweh's behalf is Israel. But the other
party is also summoned to produce its witnesses (v. 9c). The subject
of the process is identical with that of the previous trial speeches, the
claim to divinity. As there, it is based on activity in history (v. 13),
allied with a spoken message, a proclamation, which requires to be

ᵃ Delete wᵉhōšaʿtī.

ᵇ V. 12b repeats v. 10a.

ᶜ Insert mēʿōlām after 'ēl.

ᵈ Read miyyōn instead of hayyōm.

ᵉ V. 14a is a mistaken fresh introduction.

ᶠ Vv. 14b and c cannot be read as they stand. For bārīhīm (? bars) LXX reads
bōrᵉhīm = fugitives.

demonstrated as reliable (v. 12). It is to do this that Israel is to appear as witness; and do it she can, because 'God is no stranger in her midst' (v. 12). At this point the legal process becomes very much of a convention: the other party is not given any chance to speak. It is said that they are to bring their witnesses (v. 9c); but all that follows is a further speech by Yahweh (vv. 10–13 or 15). The presumption is that now the other side's claim cannot be other than completely silenced, and that it is also unable to produce any witnesses who might possibly substantiate its claim. In this passage, therefore, what in particular tips the scales in favour of Yahweh's claim is the appearance of witnesses. And this in spite of the fact that at the beginning these are designated as blind and deaf! How is this to be explained?

[8] The paradoxical statement made about the witnesses, that, although possessed of eyes and ears, they are blind and deaf, is explained by reference to 42.18–21, where the same paradox is developed more fully, The witnesses stand for the Israel which, in the course of its long relationship with Yahweh in history, had had the opportunity of learning the way in which its God acted, that is, of hearing and seeing, and thereby becoming qualified to testify as witness. However, their attitude, during the course of this history, showed that they had not seen and heard, which means that by their attitude they had shown themselves to be blind and deaf. Yet in spite of this God can use them as witnesses.

[9] He uses them in the great legal process being enacted at the present moment in history. When the prophet speaks of all the nations coming together for a judical assembly, he is not thinking of an historical event. The figure he uses, that of a legal process, is intended to suggest that the present hour in history is the time for the final decision of the claim to divinity as between the God of Israel on the one side and *all* the gods of *all* nations on the other. This is because Israel's relationship with her God has now ceased to be tied to a particular area of the earth's surface, and she is no more confronted by the nations and their gods who from time to time menaced that area. The loss of her land had spelt the end of this observable encounter, and the question had now become a general one to be decided on principle: God or the gods. The subject of the trial speeches is this either-or.

The question put to the other gods (v. 9b) is, 'Who among you declares this (the things to come)?' The proof of divinity is, therefore, that a god conducts his people through history on a way which it can tread with confidence, because words which he uttered had shown both the direction to be taken and the end in view. 'And tell us the former things': again the prophet is thinking of a connection between a word and its fulfilment, and the gods are asked whether they can produce evidence of such a connection in the past. If they are in fact in a position so to do—and they are called upon to produce witnesses to attest it—such evidence must be deferred to. In this legal process, the evidence under consideration consists of objective facts, which both sides must accept. If therefore the gods do bring such evidence, then the other side, too—that is, Yahweh and Israel—are bound to listen to it and allow that it is true. What a daring thing to say! Everything staked on one throw! What here decides a religion's title and claim is neither its spiritual or ethical or religious value, nor its enlightenment or high cultural level; instead, it is continuity in history and this alone, the power of a faith to throw a bridge over a chasm torn open by the downfall of a nation. This, however, requires witnesses to testify to it, that is, those who confess the divinity of the god in question.

[10a] In the trial speech, v. 10 represents the endorsement of a testimony in court. To the 'blind' and 'deaf' Yahweh says publicly (v. 9: 'since all the nations are gathered together'), 'you are my witnesses', I acknowledge you as such. The second part of v. 10a says why this is possible: God chose this Israel to be his servant. He can again make the deaf and blind into witnesses, again arouse them from their present deafness and blindness so that they will know and believe and understand (10b). These three verbs refer to one and the same process. It is to be noted that 'to believe' stands between 'to know' and 'to understand'. Therefore, what is meant is not, as our way of thinking might suggest, either a knowledge that leads to faith or, on the other hand, a knowledge which rests on faith. Both views would be a misconstruction of the passage. In order to understand the words, we must leave our modern concept of knowledge aside. What then is here to be known and believed and understood? We are told in terse words which defy translation, but which may be approximately rendered as, 'that it is I.' If we made this into a main clause, it would run, 'I am he'—a cry used in a personal encounter, whose significance depends in each case on the circumstances. In the circumstances in which the Israelites were placed at the time, the words meant exactly what is detailed in the clauses that follow. For

them, God is now the one who is able to create a future out of the ruins of the past. And what they are to know, believe and understand is that he, and he alone, can do this. Therefore, what the prophet has in mind is a fully personal knowledge such as comes only from encounter. Such knowledge embraces belief: it is knowledge that believes, or belief that has knowledge. But whenever Israel knows that God is truly God, she may become his witness; for the one thing which she is to attest is that she has encountered the God who is truly God.

[10b] In the speech in which God now enters his claim to be the one God, vv. 10b–12 and 13 each contains a statement about his being, combined with another about his activity; both together are required to constitute his divinity. Together the two parts of v. 10b predicate God's sole being, but they do this by differentiating him from the other gods and by bluntly challenging them: 'before me no god was formed'. The prophet here uses the language of polytheism, the language of the paganism which surrounded him. That the gods had been created was said often, and quite as a matter of course, in the Sumerian and Accadian myths. In them, as in many other places, theogonies are of the essence of the myths and of the polytheistic theology.[a] Here Deutero-Isaiah feels no need to be polemic or to dispute, but contents himself with the one curt sentence, 'before me no god was formed'. The words demand, however, the addition, 'nor shall there be any after me'. Perhaps we of today can hardly imagine the magnitude of the breakthrough represented by the last two clauses of v. 10b. We may get some inkling of it if we reflect that hitherto Israel had been like the rest of the world in taking for granted that while she had her God, other nations had other gods. Even though the first commandment is the beginning of the road which led finally to Deutero-Isaiah, it does not question the existence of 'other gods'. Before our prophet's time no one had ever spoken so unequivocally or radically on the subject of Israel's God being the only God.

[11a] The first clause, 'I, I, Yahweh' corresponds to the words of v. 10b just discussed, 'that I am he'. The so-called 'formula of revelation', 'I am Yahweh', plays an important part in the Old Testament.[b]

---

[a] Stummer, *op. cit.*, p. 180: 'Here we should remember in particular Enuma Elish I.9ff., which describes "how the gods had been created", how Lahmu and Lahamu "came into being", and how Anshar and Kishar "were created".'

[b] See W. Zimmerli, 'Ich bin Jahwe', *Gesammelte Aufsätze*, pp. 11–40.

It expresses the idea that in the name Yahweh, which was revealed along with Yahweh himself at the beginning of the nation's encounter with him, his relationship with Israel is laid down in its two aspects: the name stands for God's words and God's deeds, which have their unity in it; at the same time, the name also stands for that to which Israel clung, in past and present, as she invoked it in supplication when she was in sore straights or rendered it exultant praise.

This second aspect is expressed in the second part of v. 11. God's unique being is not based on theoretical considerations, but on Israel's actual experience. God has proved himself to be the only saviour; and if in the future anyone can help, it can only be he. Verse 13 repeats this, although in different words.

[13a] The first half of v. 13a corresponds to v. 10b, the second to v. 11. This is the third occurrence in the one passage of the formula of revelation, here in the words 'and today also I am the same' (the translation can only be approximate). The two parts of v. 13 express the fact that God remains, and remains the same, throughout all time. But they do not mean his remaining or his being as such, regarded by itself, but, as comparison with v. 13 shows, what he was, is, and remains for his chosen people, his being there for them, his confrontation of them.

[12, 13b] This, however, only exists in the form of speech and action, and this is the subject of the two other parts of the two utterances in vv. 10b–13. Verse 12a deals with his speaking. In this connection we have to notice that God's eternity—'I am God from old, and today I am the same'—only exists for his chosen people in the form of the continuity between his speech and his action. Words were spoken to Israel, and trust was put in them. With the first revelation of his name, the first 'I am Yahweh', a promise had been united; and from then on there had been a continuous, unbroken series of words of his down to the one now being spoken to the remnant by the prophet Deutero-Isaiah, the word which could make Israel certain of her future. This is beautifully summed up in the simple words, 'I am no stranger in your midst.' This God may be said to be a hidden God (45.15), but never a 'strange God'. Israel knows him, and his hold over her. Her history was a history with God.

It is much more difficult to see the continuity in God's actions (v. 13b); for they took place amid the contingencies of history and its incalculable elements, in which to reckon up his chastising and his saving and reduce them to a common denominator is quite impossible. In consequence, in the case of God's actions, Deutero-Isaiah does not, as with God's speech, point to the continuity experienced; instead, he only emphasizes that God's actions cannot be hindered. Here these are principally related to Israel's actual situation: the political powers at present dominant cannot break the bond between Israel and her God. Destroyed and dispersed as she is, she remains in his hand.

[14-15] Whether these two verses are in their proper context is doubtful. Verse 14a forms the introduction to a new utterance. But a fresh one begins at v. 16a. In this case, vv. 14f. must have been an independent unit. This is extremely unlikely. Only two possibilities then remain. Either vv. 14f. are a fragment of a once independent unit—in that case, the missing part must have fallen out between v. 14 and v. 15, since the latter sounds like the end of an oracle—or else the introduction, v. 14a, did not originally belong to the present passage. In that case, vv. 14b-15 formed part of vv. 8-13. As far as sense goes, they would be better taken with 43.1-7, where they could follow v. 4 or v. 6.

The appositional clause in v. 14a corresponds to the one in 43.3a. The living God is described in the same polar terms: the Holy One of Israel—your redeemer. 'Your redeemer' is explained in what follows. God's intervention in history on Israel's behalf is put concretely: 'for your sake I send to Babylon.' This refers beyond question to Cyrus' capture of Babylon. What followed must have gone on to give a clearer description or proclamation of this, but unfortunately they have not been preserved. Köhler's rendering, 'I break down the prison bars, and the Chaldeans on their ships, full of lamentation', is plausible, but depends on conjecture. Duhm is more cautious, and contents himself with '. . . and break down the bars of the prison, and the Chaldeans . . . their rejoicing into lamentation'. This accords with RSV: 'For your sake I will send to Babylon and break down all the bars, and the shouting of the Chaldeans will be turned to lamentation.' Muilenburg's comment is: 'The reading of the RSV is perhaps the best that can be made of a difficult text.' At all events, this much is certain—here Deutero-Isaiah clearly proclaims the fall of Babylon. Through this event Yahweh shows himself to be the one who had espoused Israel's cause from of old and the one whom she knows. After this open proclamation of the capture of Babylon, predication is piled upon predication in a way that is certainly intentional

—the Creator, the Holy One, Israel's king! This makes it clear that, in Israel's view, such predications differed fundamentally from mere epithets of glorification. As such they would have been no more than something like non-material idolatry. Instead, each of these predications indicates encounter and experience. This was what Yahweh had shown himself to be to his chosen people as they made their way through history.

CHAPTER 43.16–21

A Proclamation of Salvation:
Behold, I am doing a new thing

16 Thus says Yahweh,
    who makes a way in the sea,
    and a path in the mighty waters,
17 who brings forth chariot and horse,
    army and warrior as well.
    There they lie,   they cannot rise,
    extinguished, quenched like a wick.

18 'Remember not the former things,
    nor consider the things of old.
19 Behold, I am doing a new thing;
    now it springs forth, you will perceive it.

    I make a way in the wilderness
    and rivers in the desert.
20 The wild beasts will honour me,
    the jackals and the young ostriches;
    for I give water in the wilderness,
    rivers in the desert,
    to give drink to my people, my chosen ones,
21 the people whom I formed for myself;
    they shall declare my praise.'

Like 41.17–20 and 42.14–17, the passage falls into the literary category of proclamation of salvation; cf. the commentary there. There, the structure of the proclamation of salvation was found to be as follows: (I) Reference to a (community) lament; (II) Proclamation of salvation; (1) God's turning, (2) God's intervention; (III) The end in view. In 43.16–21, this structure is not at first glance easy to discover. Part II—vv. 19f.—and part III—v. 21—are straightforward. But what corresponds here to part I, the reference to a lament?

[16f.] The introductory messenger formula is expanded by means of a series of participial clauses: these form an apposition which in the place of divine predications adduces an act of God, the act which initiated Israel's history, the deliverance at the Red Sea. It is described along two lines: in them the activity of the creator and the lord of history coalesce. For the band of fugitives from Egypt he created a way through the sea (v. 16): he also destroyed the Egyptian troops who pursued (v. 17). (The Exodus is described as in Ex. 6.6.) Deutero-Isaiah here takes up the basic tradition of Israel's faith (called by Noth the original confession), which runs from the Exodus onwards through the whole of the Old Testament. The Exodus is particularly frequently celebrated in the Psalms as God's act of foundation.[a]

[18–19a] Yet, this very thing, God's initial act of deliverance, 'the former thing', 'the thing of old', is, v. 18 appears to say, to be forgotten, so tremendous and overwhelming is the new thing which Yahweh is now on the point of doing (v. 19). This, too, is the preparation of a way: 'I make a way in the wilderness'. And, just as God's new act corresponds to his earlier one, so do its results: the new Exodus corresponds to the original one. But did Deutero-Isaiah really mean this utterance to say that God's new act and the new Exodus which is to be its result are so much to overshadow his past act and the first Exodus as to cause them to be forgotten, obliterated by the new thing shortly to be expected? It would be very strange if he did. More than any other prophet, Deutero-Isaiah holds his nation to their traditions. Over and over again he most emphatically reminds them of God's mighty acts in their past. In the legal process between God and the gods of the nations he gives them the lofty role of being God's witnesses, which means testifying to a reliable continuity between God's words and his action, between proclamations and

---

[a] Cf. K. Galling, *Die Erwählungstraditionen Israels*, Giessen, 1929 (BZAW, 48, 1928); G. von Rad, 'The Problem of the Hexateuch', *The Problem of the Hexateuch and Other Essays*, trs. E. W. T. Dicken, Edinburgh and London, 1966; M. Noth, *Überlieferungsgeschichte des Pentateuch*, Stuttgart, 1948; C. Westermann, 'Vergegenwärtigung der Geschichte in den Psalmen', *Gesammelte Studien*, Munich, 1964, pp. 306–35.

their fulfilment. It would therefore be very strange if here this same man were saying, 'Forget what I did in former days, and consider it no more.'

What is the meaning of 'remember' and 'consider' in v. 18? Here we return to the question raised at the beginning of the present section. The structure of a proclamation of salvation leads us to expect it to start with an allusion to a community lament. The part of the latter to which the allusion is made may vary. Verses 16b and 17 could conceivably correspond to that part of a community lament known as 'the review of God's former acts of salvation'. Now, in extant community laments we do in fact find mention of the deliverance at the Red Sea. A particularly striking example is found in Isa. 63.11-14, in the community lament Isa. 63f., which was very probably written some time after 587. But if in vv. 16f. Deutero-Isaiah relates himself to this part of the lament, then by the term 'remember' in v. 18 he does not have the mere remembering of God's original act in mind, but the expostulation made in laments reproaching God with the contrast between his present attitude towards his chosen people and the great thing he did for them in former days. Thus, Deutero-Isaiah had not the slightest intention of saying that the old traditions are abrogated, and that a new act of God is impending. What he wants to say is rather, 'stop mournfully looking back and clinging to the past, and open your minds to the fact that a new, miraculous act of God lies ahead of you!'

In this case, the prophet's summons in vv. 18f. is in complete accord with the office of witness which he gives to the remnant of his people, whereas forgetting, ceasing to consider God's original deliverance, would be incompatible with it.

The new thing which God proclaims himself to be about to do is the new thing which Israel had ceased to expect, hope for, or believe in. As her laments show, she thought that God's saving acts were now a closed chapter. What is now springing up is a new thing, which means that it is shortly to appear as a reality which Israel herself will experience; 'you will know it, you will perceive it.'

[19b–20] The correspondence between the new thing and the old, the Exodus from the exile and that from Egypt, consists in two things. First, while he takes an entirely new way of doing so, this same God becomes the deliverer and liberator of his chosen people. Secondly, this new deliverance is given effect to and becomes historical reality by means of a new journey through the wilderness, during the course of which the latter is to be miraculously transformed. For God gives water in the wilderness, so abundantly that even the wild creatures living there share in it. This is a further illustration of the way in which God's activity in creation and in redemption are one. Over and over again the prophet Deutero-Isaiah summons his people to faith by appeal to the deliverance which Israel had experienced in her past. She therefore knows it, knows it perhaps only too well, since she is already aware of the form which the divine action assumes. Nevertheless, the prophet takes this deliverance and places it within the wider setting of God's activity in creation, where he is the completely immeasurable one to whom no one dictates (cf. 40.13ff.). The way in which Deutero-Isaiah, in proclaiming the new and now imminent journey through the wilderness, describes the preparation of the way precisely from the point of view of the activity of the creator, squares with the way in which the proclamation itself is phrased, 'Behold, I am doing a new thing' (v. 19a). Israel requires to be shaken out of a faith that has nothing to learn about God's activity, and therefore nothing to learn about what is possible with him, the great danger which threatens any faith that is hidebound in dogmatism, faith that has ceased to be able to expect anything really new from him.

[21] The proclamation of salvation achieves its goal with a forward glance at the result which the new Exodus is to have. Like its predecessor, it is not the final event that is to take place. After it, God is to go on dealing with his chosen people, that is, with the people whom he formed for himself (once more the language of creation). And then the new act of God, the new Exodus, is to be echoed in the praises of the redeemed: 'they shall declare my praise.' Thus, Deutero-Isaiah does not think that the new thing which God is now on the point of doing is to inaugurate a condition of complete salvation. History continues. Praise telling of God's act has no meaning unless history goes on; there are still those who will require to have God's miraculous act told them, and this joyous echo is to be the very means by which its fame will be spread beyond the circle of those who experienced it.

CHAPTER 43.22-28

Trial Speech, Yahweh *v.* Israel:
You have burdened me!

22   You did not call upon me, O Jacob,
       [and did not]ᵃ seek my favour, O Israel.
23   Not to me did you bring your sheep for burnt offerings,
       it was not I whom you honoured with your sacrifices.
       I did not make you serve with offerings,
       or weary you with frankincense.
24   Not for me did you buy sweet cane with money,
       not me did you satisfy with the fat of your sacrifices.

       You made me serve—with your sins;
       wearied me with your iniquities.

25   I, I am he. who blots out your sins;
       for my own sake I remember your iniquities no more.ᵇ

26   Bring a charge against me! Let us together go into court!
       Detail it, that you may be proved right!
27   Your father was the first to sin
       and your spokesmen have transgressed against me.
28   So I deliveredᶜ Jacob to utter destruction
       and Israel to reviling.

43.22-28 and 50.1-3 are the only trial speeches in which Yahweh opposes his chosen people Israel. They are closely akin to disputations.ᵈ

In the trial speeches between Yahweh and the gods, the point at issue is a claim. But the basis of the present passage is a charge brought against God by Israel. It is given in the final verse: 'You delivered Jacob to utter destruction and Israel to shame.' Israel also protested: 'How could you do this, when we faithfully served you by bringing our sacrifices?' This argument (it lies behind vv. 22–24a), God contests by saying: 'In all this you did not really serve me; rather, I

ᵃ Instead of *kī*, read *weˡlō* with LXX and V.
ᵇ Delete the *waw* before *ḥattʾotekā*.
ᶜ Delete *sārē qōdeš weˡettˡnā*.
ᵈ For this group, see 'Sprache und Struktur', pp. 141–4.

was obliged to "serve" you!' This disputation forms the preface to the trial speech proper, which only begins at v. 26. There God challenges Israel to summon him into court. This, however, is never done. In the two final verses God brings charges against Israel and uses them to give the reason why he was obliged to act toward her as he did.

This oracle is particularly important for the understanding of Deutero-Isaiah's proclamation. First, it makes perfectly plain that, while at this particular hour in his nation's history, this prophet of the exile had personally to proclaim salvation, he nevertheless regarded himself as being in the succession of the pre-exilic prophets of doom. For in the present oracle he utters his 'Amen' to the charge which his predecessors had brought against Israel, and that without qualification. The nation's sacrificial worship had lost touch with reality. Deutero-Isaiah here endorses unreservedly the charge brought by Amos, Hosea, Isaiah, Micah and Jeremiah.

Along with this goes the dismissal of the plea made by Israel in her charge against Yahweh, 'yet we truly served you with our sacrifice'. God answers this by saying, 'you did not really serve me. In actual fact you made me into a servant.' This, however, is no more than a clumsy rendering of the Hebrew, which turns on the two forms of the same verb *'ābad* (to serve or to work) in v. 23b and v. 24b: *lo' he'ebadtīka* and *ak he'ebadtānī*: I did not make you work (serve) and you made me work (serve). This key-passage for Deutero-Isaiah's proclamation contains an echo of the catchword of the servant songs (*'ebed*, from *'ābad*). In order to understand this connection, we must realize that the words—and it is God who speaks them—'you have made me serve (made me into a *'ebed*) with your sins' are offensive to, if not indeed impossible for, the Old Testament concept of God. God is lord; in all semitic religions what constitutes the nature of divinity is lordship.[a] If God is made into a *'ebed*, if he is made to serve, he has his divinity taken from him.

Here in 43.24, this reversal of the natural relationship between God and man, in which God is lord and man God's servant, flashes out for just a moment. It fades again immediately, for in v. 25 God again acts precisely and decidedly as a master who can as such simply blot out Israel's guilt. However, what here is the momentary sounding of a note, is to be taken up again in the poems about the *'ebed*, the servant of God: there is to be a servant who, at God's behest, is to

[a] W. W. Graf von Baudissin, *Kyrios*, Giessen, 1929.

take the sins of the others upon himself. This connection between
43.22–28 and the poems about the *'ebed* is, in my view, the clearest
proof that the latter come from Deutero-Isaiah.

[22] Coupled with the address to Jacob-Israel, the series of
disputations in vv. 22–24a begins with a summary and startling denial
or disputation. It makes clear that, in what follows, the subject
is Israel's worship in its entirety. On the part of the men who offer
it, all worship consists in something said and something done, a
combination of speech and action: a call to God or an invocation of
him, and an act, a seeking of his favour, the clearest expression of
which is sacrifice. This speech and act directed to God in worship,
Deutero-Isaiah here says, never in actual fact reached him!

[23–24a] This theme is developed in what now follows: the most
important sacrifices are listed. In v. 23b, the verb already mentioned
sums it up: so it was not a true service that you gave me, Israel; it
was not service of God, worship.

[24b] A positive statement corresponds to the preceding negative,
and at the same time substantiates the disputation in vv. 22–24a:
it was the other way round: you gave me toil and trouble with your
iniquities and sins. The charge which Deutero-Isaiah here makes is a
tremendous one. The reason why it sounds even more thoroughgoing and terrible than the charges made by the pre-exilic prophets
is that, while they protested against particular aspects of corruption
or depravity in Israel's worship, this verdict here, a retrospect, is
passed upon pre-exilic Israel's worship *in toto*.

One qualification, however, needs to be made. Even this verdict
is not meant as an out and out condemnation, or a condemnation in
principle. Deutero-Isaiah would not deny that in the pre-exilic
period there had also been genuine, real and effective worship which
God accepted. Rather, what he says here in God's name to his fellow-
countrymen in the exile is this: 'If, when you come before God, you
depend upon your services of worship as your works, if you now say
by way of objection that, after all, you served him truly, then you
must now be told that there is nothing upon which you can depend
when you come before him, for these services do not alter the fact
that in the monarchical period the road which Israel took was a
mistaken one.'

[27f.] In this mistake of Israel's, what counts with God is that it
was a mistake from beginning to end. This is put in a nutshell in
two most powerful lines in v. 27 which, in the gravity and the sweep-

ing nature of the charges which they bring, might suggest Ezekiel rather than Deutero-Isaiah as their author. They allege that Israel's wrongdoing began as early as the time of her ancestors. The reference is certainly to Jacob, and Deutero-Isaiah takes his stand on a tradition concerning him which is also presupposed in Hos. 12.3-5, a tradition in which, clearly, the Jacob stories are tried and found wanting. The word translated 'spokesmen' (RSV: mediators) in v. 27b occurs only here. Its meaning is uncertain. It could conceivably refer to the prophets of salvation in the monarchical period, but this is no more than conjecture. At all events, the purport of v. 27 is that, in God's sight, the whole of Israel's history had been mistaken. In consequence, he had been forced to let judgment come upon her.

[25] While the subject of this utterance is the vanity of Israel's worship and her mistaken history, it also contains, right at its centre, the proclamation of forgiveness. The contrast to what precedes and follows is glaring. But it is also deliberate. The sole reason for making the proclamation is given in the words, 'for my own sake'. The proclamation is the execution of the God-given task of comforting: 'Say to her that her iniquity is pardoned'. Only as it is seen against the background of thoughts of the past and charges such as are described in 43.22-28 does the significance of this message of forgiveness become clear.

CHAPTER 44.1-5

An Oracle of Salvation: Water on the Thirsty Land

1 But now hear, O Jacob my servant,
   and Israel, whom I have chosen:
2 Thus says Yahweh, your creator,
   who forms you from the womb and helps you:
   Fear not, O Jacob my servant,
   Jeshurun whom I have chosen;
3 For I pour water on the thirsty land,
   and streams on the dry ground.
   I pour my spirit upon your descendants
   and my blessing on your offspring.

4 They spring up [like] the grass [amid waters],[a]
   like willows by flowing streams;
5 This one says, 'I am Yahweh's,'
   and another calls himself by the name of Jacob,
   another writes on his hand, 'Yahweh's',
   and surnames himself by the name of Israel.

The passage falls into the category of oracles of salvation (41.8–13, 14ff.; 43.1–4, 5ff.); its central point is the assurance of salvation, the cry, 'Fear not.' It differs from the oracles of salvation hitherto considered in that this cry is followed not by a substantiation in the perfect tense or by one in the form of a noun clause, but by one in the future tense, vv. 3ff. The absence of substantiation in the perfect and by a noun clause is perhaps to be explained by the fact that the terms in apposition in vv. 1f. are exceptionally large in number, and are to be regarded as replacing them. But a different explanation is also possible. 44.1–5 is loosely attached to the previous oracle, 43.22–28, by means of the words 'but now' (we'attāh). This disputation and trial speech addressed to Israel contains in v. 25 the assurance of forgiveness which properly forms part of the oracle of salvation. Here it is to some extent anticipated; at all events, it points beyond the oracle of judgment with which vv. 22–28 end. It is therefore perfectly possible that this proclamation of God's forgiveness in v. 25 is to be regarded as carrying over into the oracle which follows vv. 22–28— the word of forgiveness makes the new act of God proclaimed in 44.3ff. possible.

This would also provide a better explanation of the other exceptional feature in this assurance of salvation. Verses 3ff., the substantiation in the future tense of the cry, 'Fear not', have as their subject not the event of the return or restoration, but the conditions in the new era of salvation; moreover, strictly speaking, the new salvation is not promised to the recipients of this oracle, but to their descendants. But this promise quite clearly corresponds to vv. 22–28, and in particular to v. 27. These verses gave a summary of Israel's past, speaking of her forefathers; in the same way, 44.3ff. treat of her future, the descendants of the generation then living.

[1] The assurance of salvation begins with the words, 'But now', in contrast to what was said of Israel's past in 43.22–28, in the same way as 43.1ff. contrasts with 42.18–25. Israel is summoned into the new era to hear the new word and, in substantiation of the summons,

[a] Read kᵉbbēn māyim.

is addressed by the parallel terms of God's servant and his chosen one. The two designations supplement each other in that election is more concerned with God's gracious will, and 'servant' refers rather to the end which he seeks to achieve by means of Israel's election.

[2] As is usual, the assurance of salvation is introduced by the messenger formula. Here, however, this no longer has its original purpose of accrediting a message through the messenger: its function is the more general one of conferring the authority of a word of God on an utterance introduced in this way. Once again, the divine name has terms in apposition, taking further those found in v. 1: 'your creator' (the same two verbs, 'make' and 'form', occur in the creation stories in Genesis), 'who helps you' (here the apposition consists in an abbreviated relative clause). We find the same thing in 43.1, 15; 51.13; 54.5. Israel's election which took place in the act of deliverance that set her history on its course is given a still firmer basis by means of a reference to the creation. Muilenburg says, 'Second Isaiah is constantly seeking to ground Israel's unique character in something more ultimate than the Exodus.' Our passage also clearly shows that the creation of Israel must mean not only the historical event through which she became a nation: the addition, 'who forms you from the womb', shows that the prophet is thinking of God's creative activity in the primary sense of the word, and in particular of the fact that every single member of the nation Israel then living was created by him. (Cf. the commentary on 43.1.)

The two words in apposition in v. 1 are repeated along with the cry, 'Fear not'—the only way by which Israel can learn that she is God's servant, chosen by him, and give practical effect to her status, is for her to accept the assurance of salvation now being addressed to the nation. This cry, 'Fear not', says that a new situation has come about. The relationship between God and herself as described in 43.22–28 is at an end, for God has blotted out her guilt (43.25). This is what makes it possible for Israel to have a future, and this is proclaimed in vv. 3ff. The name used to designate her, *yᵉshūrūn* (formed like *zᵉbūlūn*) occurs only here and in Deut. 32.15; 33. 5,26. It may be derived from *yāšār*, the upright, but the meaning is uncertain. It may be intended as a title of honour for Israel.

[3–5] The future is made possible because God is to intervene (v. 3), and the consequences of this are described in vv. 4f. Commentators all agree that this intervention in v. 3 does not refer to the new exodus, the journey home through the desert, but has a more general sense, 'the ever-repeated miracle of growth' (Volz). *Rūaḥ* then expresses 'the divine power which creates life in man and nature', as in Gen. 2.7; Isa. 32.15 and Ps. 104.30; this is the only meaning which can make it parallel to *bᵉrākā*, blessing, which is used in its original sense of vitality or power which bestows fertility. The 'thirsty' and 'dry' are therefore Israel in her present condition.

This proclamation of salvation, different from those hitherto considered, of a new growth for the now dried-up Israel, demands special attention in any consideration of Deutero-Isaiah's preaching, for the increase is not to take effect in the immediate future, but only among the generations to come. Our prophet's preaching does not restrict itself to the proclamation of God's new act of deliverance which was straightaway to usher in the new era of salvation. Rather, the verses before us show that, after the great change in Israel's lot, Yahweh is to continue his workings in history itself, and this means in Israel's history. But his activity is to take a different shape: blessing is added to deliverance, and what was unique becomes the rule. From the very beginning of Israel's faith the God who delivers is also the God who blesses: both aspects have their own time and place, and neither is ever resolved into the other. This also holds true for Deutero-Isaiah; in his proclamation, God's new act on Israel's behalf which transforms her lot is certainly not the end of the chapter. In the future thus opened up by his act, God is to go on blessing and increasing her.

Fuller treatment of this different mode of the divine activity is given later, particularly in chs. 54 and 55 (cf. 54.1ff., and also 49.20f.). The fact that it is intimated here for the first time in the final oracle of the corpus made up of chs. 41–44 is therefore quite deliberate. It shows that the book was put together according to a plan.

[4–5] The increase promised to Israel has two aspects. In v. 4 the common metaphor of trees growing beside streams (cf. Ps. 1) foretells the increase, the natural addition to and prosperity of the descendants of the exiles' own generation. Verse 5 adds something different. It, too, is a form of increase, but not the natural increase in the generations to come, but an increase in and spread of the numbers of the worshippers of Yahweh due to the accession of non-Israelites, i.e., proselytes. Although the abrupt transition from v. 4 to v. 5 does not make it perfectly clear, this is what the majority of commentators take the verse to mean. Some have regarded it as also referring to conversions within Israel itself, but this would almost certainly have been put in a different way. If, however, what v. 5 proclaims is that, after the return, Israel is to increase in numbers because men of other nations and of different religious faiths turn to her and to her God, the significance of this is very great indeed. First, it proves Deutero-Isaiah's expectation that, after the return, Israel was to have a real history within the present world. What he certainly did not look for was that the nations among which she lived would suddenly and in a body turn to Yahweh. Instead, he proclaims that there are to be individuals who turn to Israel's God and thus join in Israel's worship. This is noted by Volz, who draws the inference that 'this gives the prophecy a strong probability of being fulfilled'. In this connection it is not only important that here Deutero-Isaiah proclaims a thing which did in fact take place in the generations following the exile (proselytes are mentioned as early as Trito-Isaiah), but this represents the breakthrough to a new understanding of the chosen people as the community which confesses Yahweh. This, too, is noted by Volz. Now, for this new view of God's people, the terms in which the prophet makes foreigners who join the community of Israel declare their membership of it are of special importance: 'who says . . . who calls himself . . . who writes on his hand.' These verbs all denote avowal of the God of Israel on the basis of a personal decision. As the convert professes his faith, he feels the need to accompany the profession with some form of outward manifestation of it, the adoption of a new name or the writing of God's name on his hand. (In the ancient world the slave cut his master's name on his hand. There is also, as mark of ownership, l*emelek*, 'belonging to the king', often found on the handles of jars from the period of the monarchy.) As Duhm observed, circumcision would have been a very obvious manifestation to mention. 'A later and more legally-minded writer would probably have preferred to speak of circumcision.' Since Deutero-Isaiah does not do so, we can quite safely infer that he did not regard circumcision as a chief mark of membership of the people of God.

One further feature in the description given in v. 5 is important. In both parts of the verse belonging to (or being called by the name of) Yahweh is parallel to belonging to Jacob-Israel. This clearly indicates that turning to Israel's God also involved turning to Israel herself. A man could only confess the God of Israel as his lord if he took his place among the people who served this God. Israel's religion never became something purely spiritual, which could be professed without reference to the history of the chosen people or involvement in it. 'This gives expression to the fact that Israel's religion was historical in character' (Volz).

CHAPTER 44.6–8, 21–22

Trial Speech: the First and the Last

6   Thus says Yahweh, the King of Israel,
    and his Redeemer, Yahweh of hosts:
    I am the first and I am the last,
    and beside me there is no god.
7   And who is like me?
    [Let him come forth and]ᵃ speak,
    let him declare and set it forth before me.
    [Who announced from of old the things to come]?ᵇ
    Let them tell [us]ᶜ what is yet to be.
8   Fear not, nor be afraid.
    Have I not told you from of old and declared it?
    And you are my witnesses:
    Is there a God beside me?
    And there is no Rock that I know of (?).

21   Think of this, O Jacob,
    and Israel, for you are my servant;ᵈ
    I formed you, you are a servant of mine,
    O Israel, you will not be forgotten by me.
22   I sweep away your iniquity like a cloud,
    and your sins like mist.
    Return to me, for I have redeemed you.

The oracle is one of the trial speeches in which Yahweh confronts the nations or their gods (41.1–5; 41.21–28; 43.8–15). Verse 7 is the summons or challenge to the opposite party. The claim made by

---

ᵃ Add with LXX *yaʿᵃmōd wᵉ*.
ᵇ Read *mī hišmīaʿ mēʿōlām ʾōtyōt*.
ᶜ For *lāmō* read *lānū*.
ᵈ Perhaps 'my witness' should be read (with Duhm) instead of 'my servant'.

Yahweh as the one party in the suit is mentioned in advance, being connected with the introduction itself: 'I am the sole God.' The reason substantiating it is contained in v. 7b; this, like the claim itself, is the same as is found in the other trial speeches of this category. In support of this claim, Yahweh appeals to Israel as his witnesses (v. 8b, as in 43.8–15).

In all these parts of it, 44.6–9 agrees with the trial speeches already considered. On the other hand, in the cry here, 'Fear not' (v. 8a), which is in the plural, an element foreign to this literary category enters in, one which properly forms part of an assurance of salvation. The prophet's reason for combining these elements in this, the final, trial speech in chs. 41–44, is his design to show that, in respect of content, the two categories are similar: because Yahweh is the one God, even in the present situation in which he looks as if he were vanquished and stripped of his power he can still give her the assurance of salvation and say to her, 'Fear not'. Her testimony that there is no other 'rock' also makes him once more a rock on which she may plant herself.

The idea of taking vv. 21f. along with vv. 4ff. was Duhm's. It was suggested by the fact that between them comes a passage in prose, vv. 9–20, which most commentators regard as a secondary addition. Such interpolations causing the breaking up of material which was originally a unit are, of course, frequent in the Old Testament. In the present instance, if for the moment we disregard the two imperatives at the beginning and the end of v. 21 ('Remember these things' and 'Return to me'), what is left contains the substantiations of the assurance of salvation in v. 8a, one of them in a noun clause ('you are my servant'), the other in the perfect tense. This makes vv. 6ff. and 21f. into a complete trial speech and a complete assurance of salvation combined to form a single oracle. If this is so, the two summons at the beginning and the end of v. 21 were added only after the separation of the two passages, the purpose being to make what looked like a fragment into a complete oracle (Volz calls it a mocking summons, Begrich an exhortation).

[6a] The introduction is not that of a trial speech (as, for example, 41.1); it is rather a genuine, authoritative oracle introduced by the messenger formula (as 43.1; 44.2). The only explanation of this is the fact that 44.6ff. and 21f. represent the combination of a trial speech and an oracle of salvation; v. 6a is properly the introduction to the oracle of salvation. The impressive opening—the assurance of

salvation was a liturgical form—gives its speaker three predications: Israel's king, her redeemer, and Yahweh of hosts. The third appears again in Deutero-Isaiah in 45.13, where, as here, it has 'says' along with it; apart from this, it only occurs in the stock phrase, 'Yahweh of hosts is his name' (47.4; 48.2; 51.15; 54.5). The presumption is that Deutero-Isaiah took over the term without attaching any particular signification to the designation; to his mind it simply suggested God's majesty. The same is true of the first designation, 'king of Israel'. He uses it in the introduction to the trial speech in 41.21. The designation which comes between the two, 'her redeemer', suggests God's activity in salvation; similarly in 43.1 in the introduction to an oracle of salvation. Deutero-Isaiah has many examples of this polar correspondence in divine predications which show God on the one hand in his majesty and on the other in his will to save. This answers to the two leitmotifs of the psalms of praise.

[6b] The trial speech proper begins with same words as those with which the one in 41.1–5 ended, with the addition of 'beside me there is no god'. The structure of 41.1–5 is, 'Who? . . . I'; in 44.6ff. it is 'I . . . Who?' For our way of thinking, the words 'beside me there is no god',—they reappear at the end of v. 8 in the appeal to the witnesses—present a difficulty. In the trial speeches the gods of the nations are one of the two parties in the suit. In 41.23 they are even addressed with the words, 'that we may know if you are gods'. They must therefore be present, there must be such gods, even in the mind of Deutero-Isaiah—such is our conclusion. To our way of thinking the two sentences just quoted are mutually exclusive. If, however, we are to understand Deutero-Isaiah at this point, we must put our modern category of being out of the picture, for when the prophet was thus expressing himself it had not as yet arisen. The concept of abstract monotheism, in the sense of the existence of one God and one only, would also have been impossible for him. The words, 'and beside me there is no god', constitute a claim, not a statement of fact. The claim is an act or event involving two parties. It has as its counter-claim the one which forced itself on the notice of the Israelites in exile, the claim of the Babylonian gods to be the true gods. This is the reason why the prophet chose the form he did, for what a trial speech turns on is rival claims. In the case of the claim made by God, the issue is whether or not he is the one God as evidenced by his lordship of history in which his word is fulfilled (v. 7b). The inability of the gods of the nations to produce such evidence demonstrates the

nothingness of their claim to lordship. And it is according as this claim stands or falls that the gods' real existence stands or falls. This is what Deutero-Isaiah means when he makes God here say, 'beside me there is no god'.

[7a] The summons or challenge implies that the court is already in session, as described in 41.1 or 41.21. The fact that nothing needed to be said about this implies that the prophet's hearers were familiar with the form of the trial speech.

[7b] The point which is to decide the case is put with the utmost brevity; deity or divinity is proved according as, over a long period of time, the god concerned guides a community's history by means of proclamations whose fulfilment allows the community to know that this god can be relied on to guide.[a]

[8] At this point, the case as it is presented makes a transition to direct address, address to the witnesses who can testify that there is in fact a trustworthy connection between proclamation and fulfilment. This is extremely significant. The personal address is matched by the parallelism God-rock: Israel had experienced this trustworthiness—this is what is said in the figure that God was a rock to them, for in confessions of confidence in the Psalms God is called 'rock'. Thus for Israel, the words 'and beside me there is no god' mean that 'he alone has proved to be our refuge'—he, and no other person or thing. This makes it easy to see why the question to the witnesses in v. 8a is introduced by the formula, 'Fear not'—whenever Israel, past, present or future, hears these words, she experiences in its uniqueness the divinity of God on which he bases his claim *vis-à-vis* the other gods. There is an indissoluble connection between this claim and the authority with which God, when he turns to his chosen people, utters the assurance of salvation. This is what the conjunction of the two forms is intended to make clear. At the same time it safeguards Yahweh's proof (see above) from being misunderstood: what is meant is not the fulfilment of a proclamation made long ago which can be objectively observed and recorded. Of course, that could be so, but it is not the essential point, which is the trustworthiness of the connection between proclamation and fulfilment, i.e., what it signifies for those to whom it had been proclaimed. It would be

---

[a] This claim is also made by the Babylonian gods. In a hymn to Shamash the words occur, 'Shamash whose promise no god makes vain, whose command is not turned back'. Similarly of Marduk in *Enuma Elish* IV, 7, 9, 10 (Stummer, *op. cit.*, p. 182).

nothing without the trust of the people who heard the proclamation and go to meet the fulfilment of what was proclaimed.

[21f.] The verbs in v. 21b correspond to those used in the oracle of salvation in 44.1–4, where similar words (44.1f.) introduce the assurance of salvation. The proper substantiation of the latter comes in v. 22a: God has forgiven his people. It is on this forgiveness that everything depends; it alone can make it possible for Israel to have a future (cf. 43.25).

This assurance, with its verbs in the perfect, occurs within a summons to Israel to 'remember these things'. The words have a backward reference, and must therefore be connected with 44.6–8— there is no god beside Yahweh, and Israel must testify that there is no rock beside him. This, then, is what Israel is to remember. She is indeed Yahweh's servant and can therefore have confidence: 'O Israel, you will not be forgotten by me'—these words probably belong to the framework, which is secondary. The call to 'remember these things', with its backward reference, is then endorsed by means of the assurance of salvation and taken up into the summons with which the passage closes, 'turn to me', or 'be converted to me', is further substantiated by means of the assurance, 'I have redeemed you'.

Taking the utterance as a whole, the most natural explanation of it in context (vv. 21f.), set within the two imperatives, 'remember these things' and 'turn to me', is that it was spoken to men who were at the point of turning away from God and of forgetting his saving activity on their behalf. One would also suppose that the speaker was someone concerned to make them hold on to this or recall it to them. But these are not the circumstances which had confronted Deutero-Isaiah as he uttered his assurance of salvation. In all probability, this framework of admonition and invitation formed by the imperatives was added after the return, when disciples or successors of Deutero-Isaiah were concerned to preserve his message as a living force in the changed circumstances.

[23] The whole of the preceding section, which began at 42.14, is rounded off by the hymn of praise in 44.23:

> Sing, you heavens, for Yahweh has done it,
> shout, you depths of the earth,
> break forth into singing, you mountains,
> the forest, and every tree in it.

For Yahweh has redeemed Jacob, and glorified himself in Israel.

The fact that this hymn forms an end-piece, the conclusion of the whole section which runs from 42.14 to 44.22, was noticed by Duhm, and many other commentators agree with him. The fact that it is an end-piece of itself shows that the book of Deutero-Isaiah must have been deliberately arranged. It is therefore impossible to regard it as a mere stringing together of utterances which were originally without connection.

A sufficient account of the meaning and function of these concluding hymns of praise was given in the commentary on 42.10–13. They are not to be regarded in the way in which Duhm still believed they should: 'they are only a leap for joy, by means of which Deutero-Isaiah occasionally gave vent to the surge of his emotions.' Instead, since these hymns come within the category of psalms of praise, they are response, the note that answers God's sublime act on Israel's behalf. That the farthest parts of the created universe are expected or summoned to strike it up is simply a sign that the act overtops all others and affects earth's farthest shores. The call to rejoice goes forth to the heavens, to (the depths of) the earth, to the mountains and the trees. Notice how it narrows down from the distant to the near. Is the prophet's language mere extravaganza venting itself in lofty rhapsody? Consideration of the literary category of hymn or descriptive psalm of praise, the form in which Deutero-Isaiah clothes these words, leaves no doubt about the answer. Review of the introductory part of such psalms, the call to praise in the imperative taken as a whole, reveals a clear tendency to make the call extend farther and farther— starting from the community of Israel at praise, it reaches out to the other nations and to kings, and then, as in Deutero-Isaiah also, to the whole of creation. This Deutero-Isaiah takes over, the only difference being that with him it is one particular act of God that is to evoke this response from far and wide. There is thus a connection between the phraseology of the proclamation of salvation and the hymns of praise. In the former, the created universe participates in the chosen people's return in that a road is made in the desert, and the latter is watered and transformed into a garden. In the latter, the created universe not only serves, but also praises, forming an immense choir that accompanies the praise of the redeemed. Theologically, this is extremely important. Here it is made perfectly clear that Israel's saviour is in fact the creator of the world. And Deutero-Isaiah says this not only in the light of the activity of this God (40.12f.), but also from the other side, the created universe, which is summoned to make a response to this activity. Hardly any attempt has ever been made to assimilate the daring of this theological statement in Deutero-Isaiah and the vistas it opens up, and to follow it through. Here God's act of deliverance and salvation and the activity of the creator are regarded as identical. The result is that an answer, a reaction on the part of the created universe, is not simply connected as in the psalms which speak of creation (e.g., 148) with the fact of its having been created, but with a saving act of God on behalf of his people. This gives God's saving activity a far wider horizon than the human race (as in Gen. 12.1ff.); the whole cosmos shares in it. How Deutero-Isaiah conceived of this sharing is a question to which there is no answer. What he says here cannot be formulated in concepts; his certainty that the coming act of salvation is to have horizons commensurate with its importance is an 'eschatological' one. How wonderfully Deutero-Isaiah expresses the connection between the central point of the divine action and its farthest horizon, and also, the mighty arch which, *sub specie Dei*, unites the destiny of the chosen people not only with that of the human race, but also, over and beyond it, with that of the entire created universe.

CHAPTER 44.9–20

A Satire on the Manufacture of Idols

9   All who make idols are nothing,
      and the things they delight in can do nothing.
      And as for their witnesses, they are given nothing to see
      and they know nothing – that they may be put to shame.
10   Who fashions a god has cast an image that is profitable for nothing.
11   Behold, all his fellows shall be put to shame,
      and the craftsmen are but men.
      Yea, let them all assemble,
      let them stand forth; they shall be terrified
      and put to shame together.

12   The ironsmith [sharpens]ᵃ the axe
     and does [his work]ᵇ over the coals.
     And he shapes it with hammers
     and forges it with his strong arm.
     He becomes hungry and his strength fails,
     he drinks no water and is faint.

13   The carpenter stretches the line,
     he marks it out with a pencil;
     he makes it with planes and with the compass [   ]ᶜ
     and makes it like the figure of a man,
     like the beauty of a man, to dwell in a house.

14   [He goes forth]ᵈ to cut him down cedars,
     he takes an holm tree or an oak,
     he chooses from among the trees of the forest.
     He plants a spruce, and the rain makes it grow,
15   that it may serve people for fuel,
     and he takes part of it and warms himself.
     Part of it he kindles and makes bread,
     part he makes into a god and worships it,
     he makes it into a graven image and falls down before it.

16   Half of it he burns in the fire,
     he roasts meat over [its coals],ᵉ
     eats thereof and is satisfied.
     Also he warms himself and says,
     'Aha, I am warm, I feel the blaze!'

17   And the rest of it he makes into a god,
     into his idol, and kneels before it.
     He casts himself down and prays to it,
     saying, 'Deliver me, for thou art my god!'

18   They know not, nor do they discern;
                    for their eyes are shut, so that they cannot see,
                    and their minds, so that they cannot understand.

19   And it does not occur to him,
     nor has he the knowledge or discernment to say,
     'Half of it I burned in the fire,

     ᵃ With LXX insert *yāḥēd* after 'axe'.
     ᵇ Read *yippeˤal pāˤolū* instead of *ūpāˤal*.
     ᶜ Delete the second *ytʾrhw*.
     ᵈ With Marti add *yāṣāʾ* at the beginning.
     ᵉ In accordance with v. 19 and the versions read *ˤal geḥālāw* instead of the second
ˤal ḥeṣyō.

and baked bread on its coals,
roasted flesh and ate it,
and made the rest of it into an abomination,
and fall down before a block of wood.'

20   Whoso herds ashes is deluded.
His mind has led him astray
and he will not save his life.
And he does not say, 'Is there not a lie in my hand?'

Bibliography: C. R. North, 'The Essence of Idolatry', *Festschrift für O. Eissfeldt*, Berlin, 1958, pp. 151–60.

This taunt-song differs from all the rest of Deutero-Isaiah in that it says nothing about Yahweh and his dealings with Israel. Neither does the name Yahweh occur, nor does the song contain any allusion to what is, without exception, the theme elsewhere, God's action upon Israel as related to the moment in history at which the prophet uttered his words.

Quite clearly, the point of contact between the song and the proclamation of Deutero-Isaiah is his declaration that Yahweh is the one God; hence the catchword with which 44.9–20 makes the link is 'no god beside me' (44.8b). The matter with which it deals, polemic against idolatry, is also found in Deutero-Isaiah, but his and this are poles apart. Review of the passages of polemic against idolatry in chs. 40–55 (40.19f.; 41.6f.; 42.17; 44.9–20; 45.16f.; 46.1f., 5ff.) shows, first, that the vast majority of commentators regard three of these seven as additions—40.19f. along with 41.6f. and 45.16f. Now, there are two respects in which these three brief passages tally with the long taunt-song in 44.9–20: the subject of all four is the manufacture of idols, and the method of treatment is the same. Thus, as a matter of proper procedure, it is very doubtful whether one should discuss the question whether or not 44.9–20 were written by Deutero-Isaiah without at the same time raising the same question about the three short passages. In any case, even if the four of them are not by the same author, they do all belong to the same strand in the composition of the book. Now, the similarity in subject which links them together coincides with a similarity in form—all of them (and this perhaps includes 46.5ff., which for other reasons is almost universally regarded as an addition) have been inserted in such a way as to cause a break in the context. This was shown above in the case of 40.19f. and 41.6f. 44.9–20 makes a break between 44.6ff. and 21f., which are homogeneous, in just the same way. Such repeated coincidence of arguments from both form and content forces the present writer to believe that all of these passages form part of one strand in the tradition and represent a later addition to the oracles of Deutero-Isaiah.

What is the position of the remaining passages? 42.17 and 45.16f. are not complete units, but endings, both saying the same thing, that the manufacturers of idols, or those who put their trust in them, must be put to shame. They have nothing to tell us about the nature of Deutero-Isaiah's polemic against idolatry, because their content is not express polemic; they only proclaim the downfall of those who either manufacture idols or put their trust in them.

This leaves only 46.1f., and in this case, too, what was said at the beginning of this section holds true—the polemic against idolatry is completely different from that found in 44.9–20 and the three passages which go with it. (For details, see the commentary.) Here only two things need to be said. First, Deutero-Isaiah's oracle contained in 46.1f. bears directly on the situation with reference to which he proclaimed his message. Second, 46.1f. and 46.3f. go together. These verses make a contrast between the actions of the gods who are worshipped by means of images and Yahweh's actions on behalf of Israel, as is made clear by the simple fact of the contrast between 'loaded' in v. 1 and 'borne' in v. 3. Neither in subject-matter nor form do 46.1–4 have any connection with 44.9–20. The terms in which idolatry is discussed are completely different, as will be shown in detail in the commentary on 46.1–4.

The taunt-song contained in 44.9–20 falls into two parts. Verses 9–12 are a general verdict passed on the manufacturers (and wor-shippers) of idols, amounting to the fact that those who make idols are to be put to shame. This first part of 44.9–20 thus agrees with both 42.17 and 45.16f.; it expresses the same sentiments, only at greater length, for the other two cases are only conclusions of utter-ances. 44.9–12 are probably to be regarded as the matrix of the taunt-song. What they say—manufacturers of idols are to be put to shame—was probably a very common sentiment and may have been used in more than one connection. The way by which it is here expanded into a taunt-song is that one of its component parts, that dealing with the manufacture of idols, is elaborated on a broad, colourful canvas. The other part, 'they are to be put to shame', forms the terse, impressive conclusion (v. 20).

[9] In *BH* vv. 9–20 are printed as prose, and a large number of editors have regarded them as such. Recently, however, there has been a tendency (e.g. Muilenburg and others) to take them as poetry. This is correct. Admittedly, they differ from Deutero-Isaiah. They lack his very pronounced, easily recognizable rhythm, and are much freer; their impassioned satire scorns the constraint of rigid rhythms. Nevertheless, one can see a deliberate parallelism, in some places more clearly than in others. In addition, the verses are in the form of strophes (so also Muilenburg); this is indicated in the translation given here.

The song begins with a forceful statement which strikes the key-note of all that is to follow: 'all who make idols are nothing (*tōhū*).' The original meaning of the word here translated as 'idol' was an image hewn out of stone; later it could also designate one carved in wood or a molten image. Idol thus became a general term for an image of a god or gods, and thus also acquired the derogatory over-tone roughly corresponding to that which attaches to our word 'idol'. The 'witnesses' are the worshippers of these idols. They 'see' nothing and 'know' nothing—this is the literal meaning: both verbs have here the sense of 'experience'—the worshippers have no experience of anything done by these home-made gods, and for this very reason they are to be put to shame (*lema'an*, the result viewed as the purpose).

[10] Here *mi* is not the introduction to a rhetorical question. It means 'he who', 'whoever'. As Duhm pointed out, grammatical rules are treated with considerable freedom in 44.9–20.

[11f.] At this point there are textual difficulties which still await their solution. Instead of the translation given here, there is another possibility, that of Duhm, which some adopt: 'Behold, all his exorcisms will be put to shame, and the magicians are but men.' If this was the original text, it alluded to the magical practices ritually used in connection with the manufacture of idols. While this is not ruled out, it is not very likely, considering the tendency shown in the song to write off the manufacture of idols for the very reason that it and religion have absolutely no connection. Verse 11b contains the same words as were used by Deutero-Isaiah to summon the opponents of Yahweh, the gods of the nations, into court (41.21). But here they have lost all connection with the purpose which they served in the legal process. The difference from Deutero-Isaiah is obvious.

[12] The description of the manufacture of idols is structured as follows:

12 the work of the 'ironsmith'
13 the work of the 'carpenter'
14 the procuring of the material
15f. the use made of it: for cooking and for making a god
17 worship offered to the wood
18 a marginal note on the absurdity of such an act
19 he does not know what he does!
20 the conclusion of the whole oracle: the makers of idols are to be put to shame

The series of pictures given in the verses is amazingly true to life. The sharpness and precision of their detail owes its origin to the sharpness of the satire which 'takes off' the manufacturers of idols and, still more, those who worship them. The section is a masterpiece of satirical writing.

The text of v. 12 is uncertain; that the ironsmith should fashion an axe does not suit the context. Torrey changes the word to *maṣṣāb*, 'cuts it out' (so also Muilenburg); it would then be clear that the thing in question is a metal covering for the image. That the smith plies his work so eagerly that he forgets to eat and drink, and so becomes tired and faint, indicates the futility of the exertion. At the same time, however, a contrast can be heard—this is the exertion demanded of a man in order to make a god whose 'might' and 'strength' are then to be glorified!

[13] We are here shown the various processes exactly as they are carried through. It should be noticed that, unlike the manufacture of the statues of the gods in the classical period in Greece, the operation here falls into the category of craftsmanship: the Greek idea of a work of art has not yet arisen; the craftsman is an artist in his craft and not because he transcends craftsmanship. The final statement, 'to dwell in a house', very clearly shows the rationalistic spirit in which the satire is composed. Consider words like 66.1: 'Heaven is my throne . . . where then would be a house which you could build for me?' This is praise of the divine majesty; in the present case the conclusion drawn is, what manner of gods are these that dwell in houses! In this connection, the comparative study of religions shows that the fixed statue, that is, the statue with a base, and the god's

house, the temple, went together from the beginning.

[14] In making each strophe begin with a specific operation, the author shows a fine sense of style. As a result, the poem takes the reader along with it into this series of vigorous processes, and so is able to be all the more effective in pointing to the vanity and meaninglessness of the product. (It is not surprising that the style of the passage reminds one commentator of Schiller's *Bells*.) In v. 14 the master-craftsman himself procures his material and can therefore select whatever tree he wishes. Some commentators have noted that the manufacture of the idol is in fact described in reverse order—in v. 13 the carpenter works the wood, in v. 14 he procures the material, and in v. 14c he plants the tree—but they were unable to give any satisfactory explanation. The character of the poem as explained above provides the explanation. The speaker is not, as in Schiller's *Bells*, someone witnessing the operation, but the man who expands the first clause in v. 9. He views the operation as it were in reverse: in the light of the end-result graven images are all *tōhū*! With this verdict in mind, he looks at the way in which images come into being, and does so by describing the operation in reverse back to its initial stage, 'he plants a spruce'.

[15ff.] Having thus described the manufacture of an idol back to the beginning, the writer now reaches his objective, the satirical contrast between the two uses to which the wood may be put. This (down to v. 17) he does with broad strokes of the brush, and takes relish in his satire. Here, at his objective, the writer of the taunt-song gives the clearest indication of the spirit which inspires him; it is the spirit of rationalism. It is therefore not in the least surprising to find in Roman literature a parallel which exhibits the same ironic contrast —Horace, *Satires* i, 8, 1ff.:

> *Olim truncus eram ficulnus, inutile lignum,*
> *cum faber, incertus scamnum faceretne Priapum,*
> *maluit esse deum.*[a]

A line of thought can be traced, beginning from the second commandment, but breaking away from that commandment's strictly theological language and province and, in protest against the representation of a god in wood, metal or stone worked by hand, resulting in ridicule like this. A similar sentiment, however, can be traced as

---

[a] Quoted by Muilenburg and others.

early as Hosea, in his words, 'They make for themselves a molten image of their silver . . . it is all the work of craftsmen.'[a] This, of course, was said to Israelites. For the history of thought it is significant that this feature, rationalistic sentiments, has beginnings in the Bible itself.

[18] This verse is out of place both in style and content; what v. 19, rounding off the description, puts concretely and directly, appears in v. 18 as a general remark made at some remove. Couched in terms of the piety found in the wisdom literature, it represents the impression which the taunt-song made on a reader.

[19] As he draws his conclusion, the author does not express any surprise he may feel that 'it does not occur' to the manufacturer of idols that he terribly misunderstands the majesty and holiness of the god; he makes his ironic contrast, a god made out of fuel, and leaves it at that. The description has a most impressive ending, the caricature of the idolater's confession of faith, 'I bow down before a block of wood!'

Editors all note that the taunt-song fails to see the real nature of idolatry. Duhm, for example, says, 'There is no need to show that, as is general in later Jewish polemic, the author sees only the externals of idolatry and misses its real point. Even the simplest idolater no more confuses image with *numen* than does the Jew Elijah with his mantle.' There is no denying that, to say the least, the poem makes idolatry out to be coarser than it is. This is due to the nature of the taunt-song—it has no intention of understanding; its desire is to 'take off'. At the same time, there is also no denying that the language used in the trial speeches between Yahweh and the nations is very different. There, the nations' religion is taken so seriously that their gods are summoned into court. They are challenged to produce their proofs, and only thereafter is it demonstrated that their claim to divinity is nothing. The difference between the way in which the gods of the nations are spoken of in the trial speeches and that in the taunt-song is unmistakeable. Again, we must not take it for granted that this rampageous satire in 44.9–20 was uttered or written down within reach of the power of Babylon.

[20] The last verse of the poem, which picks up its beginning (v. 9), takes up a proverb. It is certainly only its first part which remains, 'whoso herds ashes' (Duhm points out that no quotation of this kind occurs elsewhere in Deutero-Isaiah); the second part has

[a] Translation by H. W. Wolff, *Kommentar, ad loc.*

been altered; it perhaps ran, 'his heart is deceived', or something similar. The meaning given it by Duhm is excellent—to herd ashes 'describes an activity that is useless and silly'. Hosea has a similar phrase, 'to feed the wind' (Hos. 12.2 [1]). This proverb for foolish, useless activity is used by the author of the taunt-song on the manufacture of idols to round off the scathing picture he has just given. A note is, however, added on the final result of what is done. Verse 9 ended with the words, 'they will be put to shame;' and here it says, 'he will not save his life'. This final verdict strikes a different note from that of the ironic description itself. Here satire is replaced by deadly earnest. Satire is not given the final say, for idols are not made *in vacuo*, but in the world of men, which has a lord (44.21ff., see above, pp. 138ff.).

CHAPTER 44.24–28; 45.1–7

The Oracle concerning Cyrus

24 Thus says Yahweh, your Redeemer, who formed you from the
  womb:
  I, Yahweh, make all things, stretch out the heavens alone,
  spread out the earth—who is with me?
25 who frustrates the omens of the [interpreters],[a] and makes fools of the
  diviners,
  who turns the wise men back,
  and makes a mock of their knowledge,
26 who confirms the word [of his servants],[b]
  and grants success to the counsel of his messengers,
  who says to Jerusalem, 'Let her be inhabited,
  [and let the foundation of the temple be laid],'[c]
  and to the cities of Judah, 'Let them be built',
  and to their ruins, 'I raise you up';
27 who says to the deep, 'Be dry,
  I dry up your rivers';

---

[a] Read *bārim* for *bādim*.
[b] With the Versions, read the plural instead of the singular, 'my servant'.
[c] The text is deranged in v. 28b; the first part of 26b is repeated in 28b. The simplest solution is to take the second part of 28b along with 26b.

28   who says to Cyrus, 'My shepherd,
      he shall fulfil my purpose' [   ]ᵃ.

45.1 Thus says Yahweh to his anointed, to Cyrus, whose right hand I
         hold:
      to subdue nations before him,
      and I ungird the loins of kings,
      to open doors before him,
      and gates remain unbarred.
  2   I myself go before you and level the [ways] (?mountains),ᵇ
      I break in pieces doors of bronze,   and cut asunder bars of
      iron.

  3   I give you treasures of darkness, secret hoards,
      that you may knowᶜ that I am Yahweh,
      who call you by name, the God of Israel.

  4   For the sake of my servant Jacob
      and Israel, my chosen,
      I call you by name,
      give you a name of honour, who do not know me.
  5   I, Yahweh, and no other,
      beside me there is no god.
      I gird you, and you know me not.

  6   That men may know from the rising of the sun
      and from the west, that there is none besides me.
      I, Yahweh, and there is no other.

  7   It is I who form light and create darkness,
      make weal and create woe,
      I, Yahweh, who do all these things.

Bibliography: M. Haller, 'Die Kyrioslieder bei Deuterojesaja', *Festschrift für H. Gunkel*, I, 1923, pp. 261–77; E. Jenni, 'Die Kyriosweissagungen bei Deuterojesaja', *Die politischen Voraussagen der Propheten*, Zurich, 1956, pp. 100–3.

The oracle concerning Cyrus is unique in its importance for
Deutero-Isaiah's proclamation. Its form, too, that of the royal oracle,

ᵃ See the previous note.
    ᵇ For *hᵃdūrīm*, the meaning of which is uncertain, perhaps mountains, read
haddᵉrakīm.
    ᶜ The 'that you may know' at the beginning is uncertain. Perhaps it should be
omitted.

is unique. There is a considerable tradition of it outside Israel which
also spreads into the Old Testament at several places (Ps. 2 and a
number of smaller units). The so-called Cyrus cylinder, much of
whose phraseology is similar to the present passage in Deutero-Isaiah,
is also based on it.[a]

It may be said with due circumspection that this passage forms the
mid-point in the collection of Deutero-Isaiah's oracles. The utterances which precede it, in chs. 41–44, are for the most part relatively
short, each being a complete unit, while those that follow it, in chs.
46–51, are for the most part considerably longer pieces of writing.
The supreme importance of the oracle can be seen right away: it
ties the prophet's message of comfort to a contemporary event, and
does so in a way that shocks Israel and makes a radical break with
everything of which she had hitherto been persuaded, for it says that
God makes Cyrus, a heathen king, his agent (anointed), through
whom he intends to perform his work of setting Israel free.

The special emphasis put upon the Cyrus oracle is also seen in the
very detailed introduction given in 44.24–28. These verses have even
been taken as an independent unit. This, however, is impossible,
since no more follows the noun clause 'I am Yahweh' than an unbroken series of participles (which cannot be reproduced in the
translation). The oracle itself, although announced in 44.24 ('Thus
says Yahweh'), does not come until 45.2ff. (45.1 resumes the introduction). The words in 44.24 following the introduction, 'I am
Yahweh, your Redeemer', might lead one to expect an oracle
addressed to Israel, but what in fact follows in 45.1ff., after the
repetition of the introduction, is an address to Cyrus. This is quite
deliberate. In the oracle addressed to Cyrus, Yahweh desires to
speak to Israel as well. There are several further indications that
44.24–28 are designed as introduction to 45.1–7. The first words in
the predication following the introduction run, 'I, Yahweh, make all
things.' At the end, the denouement is again a series of predications
(45.6f.), the last of which runs, 'I, Yahweh, who do all these things.'
This cannot be accidental; rather, the placing is quite deliberate—
the end reverts to the beginning.

[24–28] It is easy to see the pattern followed in the introduction
(44.24–28); it is that of descriptive praise. In consequence, the words,

---

[a] For the inscription, see *Documents from Old Testament Times*, ed. D. Winton
Thomas, London, 1958, pp. 92ff. The interpretation given here is substantiated in
detail along with the parallels in my 'Sprache und Struktur', pp. 144–51.

'I am Yahweh', and the participles which follow are praise of God, or, more exactly, praise turned into the first person of self-glorification. As in the descriptive psalms of praise (hymns), God is praised as the creator (v. 24b) and as the lord of history (vv. 25f.). The way in which this section is worked in shows great subtlety and skill, presupposing as it does what was said in the trial speeches about God *vis-à-vis* the gods of the nations. God is lord of history in the continuity of his speech and his action. This continuity is shown in the fact that he 'confirms' (i.e., brings about the fulfilment of) the word spoken by his messengers to his people (v. 26a). In reverse, he makes the words spoken in different ways, as the passage indicates, by the gods of the nations come to nothing (v. 25a and b). He shows himself to be lord of history in what he does—he commands the rebuilding of Jerusalem (v. 26b).

So far everything has been plain, but a difficulty arises in vv. 27f. Haller pointed it out—'the idea of the drying up of the deep which now comes in strikes a foreign note'—and Duhm explained the abyss of waters as a metaphor for the straits in which Israel was then placed. However, the pattern followed in descriptive praise makes the meaning clear. After developing, in vv. 24ff., the two aspects of praise of the creator and praise of the lord of history, the prophet now ends by gathering both up in two powerful lines—

who says to the deep, 'Be dry,'
who says to Cyrus, 'My shepherd,'

which tersely and disconnectedly express the fact that the creator is the lord of history. He who has power to command the deep to dry up is identical with the one who has power to command king Cyrus to fulfil his purpose.

[24a] Israel is now addressed. She is to listen to a word from him who is both her creator ('who forms you') and her redeemer. The prophet uses various terms and combinations of terms to say to his fellow-countrymen that, from the beginning, the end which their God had had in view in all his activity was the redemption of his chosen people, and that this was why he brought them into being. 'Your redeemer'—'your creator': the two predications are linked, and describe a sweep, a history, God's history with his chosen people.

[24b] 'I, Yahweh, make all things' (literally, 'I [am] Yahweh, making all things). The word to Israel from him who formed her and redeems her begins with God's glorifying himself as the creator of all

things, this being exemplified in the primary acts of the creation of heaven and earth. The emphasis is again put on the word 'I'—'I alone'. We have here a very curious form of utterance, which recurs in 45.5 ('I, Yahweh, and no other'); it is the form used when a god glorifies or praises himself. There is no perfectly certain occurrence of it in the Old Testament before Deutero-Isaiah, but he himself uses it remarkably often, particularly in the trial speeches and the Cyrus oracle. We can be certain in saying that he adopted it from his Babylonian environment, for there (as also in Egypt) the self-glorification of the gods was a form in common use. For example:

> My father gave me the heavens,
> and gave me the earth,
> I am the lady of heaven.
> Does anyone, any god, measure himself with me?[a]

A number of hymns of this kind, in which the first person may alternate with personal address, that is, with the normal form of divine praise, show that this is a special form of praise in which the latter is put into the mouth of the god (or goddess) himself. Deutero-Isaiah's adoption of it lets us see something of the boldness of his way of speaking. For this self-praise on the part of the Babylonian gods expresses polytheism in a particularly crude fashion, one god boasting of his greatness and power as compared with the rest. Deutero-Isaiah could see this rivalry among the gods every day, and he reduces it to absurdity by setting over against these rival gods the one God whose glory it is to be God alone—hence the emphasis on 'alone' in v. 24. He proves himself to be the sole God not by being greater and more powerful than all the rest, but by being the one who remains ('I am the first and the last'), and proving himself to be such in the continuity of a history in which his words and his action are connected in such a way as may be relied upon.

[25] This theme is developed in the two verses which now follow. That God alone is creator is proved by his lordship over creation in history. Prediction was not confined to Israel; there were many forms of it in the Gentile world, including Babylon; it does not, however, stay the course, but comes to nothing. What Deutero-Isaiah here says receives striking confirmation from the astonishingly wide knowledge which we now possess of the Babylonian literature of this

---

[a] 'Hymn of Inanna', Falkenstein and von Soden, *Sumerische und Akkadische Hymnen und Gebete*, Zurich and Stuttgart, 1953, p. 67.

period. Among the plethora of oracles addressed to Babylonian and Assyrian kings, not a single one has come down to us proclaiming the complete and final fall of the empire. They are almost entirely oracles of salvation, which were proved to be futile by the events which led to the fall of Assyria and later to the fall of Babylon.

[26a] This is in contrast with the way in which the words of Israel's prophets (God's messengers or servants) were verified. This includes both the pre-exilic prophets of doom and Deutero-Isaiah's own proclamation. The passage is important for the history of prophecy in Israel. Our prophet could certainly never have spoken as he does, had he not had the experience of the fulfilment of the pre-exilic prophets' proclamations of doom behind him. The assurance with which he speaks here of God's workings in history has as one of its deepest bases the knowledge gathered in the terrible years when Jerusalem fell, that God had meant what he said, and that the prophets' oracles of doom had been words of the living God.

[26b] This forms the basis of the proclamation that Jerusalem is to be restored, the first occasion on which such a thing is said directly, with mention of the city's name. God proves himself lord of history by the concurrence of his action and his words. He made his word of doom come true. He will do the same with his word of salvation.

[27f.] The combination of lord of creation and lord of history with which the chapter ends sets two things side by side—a work of the creator which could drastically change the face of the created world (perhaps an allusion to the story of the Flood, for the word for 'deep' or 'abyss' occurs only there) and a work of the controller of history who, as he acts there, can command something new, never heard of before. Thus, the end of 44.24–28 leads directly to the Cyrus oracle which now begins.

[45.1–7] The royal oracle itself is contained in vv. 1–4. Verses 5 and 7 are part of the self-predication of Yahweh, which constitutes the frame in which the whole is set (44.24 and 45.5 and 7). Verse 6 adds a note about the end to be served, 'that men may know'. This royal oracle in vv. 1–4 closely follows the terms used at an enthronement and the ritual enacted there. (The undeviating practice followed in the case of royalty was the regular repetition of the enthronement to confirm the king in his dominion.) Psalms 2 and 110 also reflect the ritual. There have been quite a number of recent studies of these psalms which have shown that words and actions in the rituals connected with the king of Israel were to a large extent taken over from her neighbours.[a] In commenting on 45.1–7, editors all refer to the Cyrus cylinder, an inscription on a clay cylinder dating from about 538, which shows quite astonishingly close parallels with the text before us. On it Cyrus describes how he captured Babylon without the striking of a single blow, and gives the credit to—of all the gods—the Babylonian god Marduk, the 'lord of the gods', who was enraged at the misrule of the last of the kings of Babylon, and then took action out of pity for the oppressed.

> . . . he scoured all the lands for a friend, seeking for the upright prince whom it would have to take his hand. He called Cyrus, king of Anshan. He nominated him to be ruler over all. He made the land of Guti, all the warrior band of Manda, submit to him. The blackheaded people whom he (i.e. Marduk) put in his (Cyrus') power, to them he (Cyrus) tried to behave with justice and righteousness. Marduk, the great lord, compassionate to his people, looked with gladness on (his) good deeds and his upright intentions. He gave orders that he go against his city Babylon. He made him take the road to Babylon and he went at his side like a friend and comrade . . .[b]

Here, too, a god (Marduk) chooses Cyrus as his agent, grants him success in his conquests, calls him to world-dominion, takes pleasure in him, directs his way to Babylon and accompanies him on it. The words, also found in 45.1–7, to the effect that Marduk took Cyrus by the hand and called him by name, indicate an act of enthronement. This clay cylinder was obviously not made until after the capture of Babylon. Deutero-Isaiah cannot then be dependent on it. Both texts presuppose the rites connected with an enthronement and the royal oracle that accompanied them. The amazing thing is that the self-same historical event, Cyrus' capture of Babylon, is in both attributed to the intervention of a non-Persian god who chose Cyrus for this act and equipped him to perform it.

This is what Deutero-Isaiah says about Yahweh's actions with Cyrus:

Cyrus is Yahweh's anointed	(v. 1)
He holds him by the right hand	(v. 1)
He calls him by name	(vv. 3b and 4b)
He gives him a name of honour	(v. 4b)
He girds him	(v. 5b).

[a] Cf. the exegesis of the two psalms in Kraus' *Kommentar* and the literature there given.

[b] Translation by T. Fish in *Documents from Old Testament Times*, ed. D. Winton Thomas, London, 1958, p. 92.

All of these indicate acts connected with the royal ritual, and are attested as such both within Israel and beyond her. The most astonishing, and, for Deutero-Isaiah's audience, the most shocking, is the first, Yahweh's calling Cyrus his anointed. Anointing is also connected with a king's coronation in Ps. 2—'against the Lord and his anointed'. But this is an Israelite king. Naturally, the meaning later associated with the term Messiah, the bringer of salvation, is not to be read into *māšîaḥ* as used here. In the Old Testament the word is never used except of a reigning monarch. The act of anointing signifies that someone is given the ability to do something (here to perform the office of a king).

Grasping the right hand indicates confirmation in the royal office. This, and pronouncing the name, are similarly linked in the Cyrus cylinder (see above). Egypt and other countries furnish ample evidence that, when a king came to the throne, he was given an honorific title. In the Old Testament this act lies behind the honorific names given the king who is to come in the age of salvation (Isa. 9.6). The girding of the king is an act of investiture.

In addition to these acts, there is the oracle addressed to the king. The solemn oracle spoken by God to the king is also found in Ps. 2 (2.7, 'he says to me') and Ps. 110, where it is introduced as a royal oracle ('A saying of Yahweh for the monarch'), in correspondence with Isa. 45.1.

The oracle to Cyrus contains commission and promise. The former was anticipated in 44.28, in the words, 'he shall fulfil all my purpose'. This is the parallel to the words on the Cyrus cylinder, 'he gave orders that he go against his city Babylon' (see above). The promise falls into two parts. God assures Cyrus that he himself will go with him and make his paths straight (the text is not certain). The result of God's presence is that Cyrus will be successful in his march of conquest:

nations are to be subdued   (v. 1b)
doors are to be opened   (v. 1b)
doors are to be broken in pieces and bars of iron cut asunder
                                     (v. 2b)
treasures of darkness are to be bestowed
                                     (v. 3a).

Subjugation of nations is also promised the king in Ps. 2, and the Cyrus cylinder speaks in similar terms. The removal of obstacles has a parallel in words occurring in an oracle spoken by Nini to

Assurbanipal, while one addressed to Esarhaddon says, 'I will go before you.' These show that the promise here made to Cyrus is based on the conventional language of the ancient and widespread royal oracle tradition. There is therefore no need to attempt to link the four things listed above with actual events in the conquests of Cyrus.

[4–5] While the Cyrus oracle is continued here, it is interspersed with clear indications that the commission given Cyrus by Yahweh has limits set to it. To begin with, however, a textual difficulty requires to be looked into. The Hebrew text of v. 3b begins with the words, 'that you may know (that I)'. For various reasons these words are uncertain, and many editors omit them. The verse is too long, and v. 6 begins in practically the same way, a thing without parallel in Deutero-Isaiah. The Hebrew text is kept in the translation given above for the reason that omission of the two (Hebrew) words finds no support in the Mss. or Vss. At the same time, since they are uncertain, we must be careful not to infer anything of importance on their basis. They must never be allowed to influence the interpretation of the verses which follow.

The first bounds set to Cyrus' commission consist in the fact that it is given him for the sake of Israel (v. 4a). The latter is also called God's servant or chosen one, or God's chosen servant. In this connection it is to be noted that, while Deutero-Isaiah calls Cyrus Yahweh's anointed, he never calls him his servant, and this simply because 'servant' implies a mutual relationship in which there is permanence. This does not apply in the case of Cyrus; for what God gives him is a non-recurrent task in one particular set of circumstances. This is all that he is anointed to do. The following verses define the bounds in even stronger terms; in v. 4b, 'I give you a name of honour, though you do not know me,' and in v. 5b, 'I gird you, though you do not know me.' The repetition of the words, 'though you do not know me', underlines their importance. Spoken to Cyrus, they imply a paradox. Yet, the paradox is perfectly deliberate. Cyrus' commissioning, together with the promise made to him, is done for Israel's sake. In no sense is it to further the events in which he himself is involved, those of Persia, as is shown by the fact that Yahweh's actions through the agency of his anointed certainly do not form the beginning of any permanent relationship between the two. This in itself shows that, contrary to the view of a large number of editors, in particular Volz, Deutero-Isaiah had no idea that Cyrus was to be converted and become a servant of Yahweh. Instead, the present passage is the express statement that this will not be true. Had Deutero-Isaiah really meant and believed this, his words in this connection would have been completely wide of the mark, and, in a matter of the utmost importance, he himself would have proved a false prophet.

[6] Deutero-Isaiah now states categorically that the end in view is not the conversion of Cyrus and the nation of Persia to Yahweh. It is something more, and indeed greater—over the whole world men are to know that Yahweh alone is God. Other passages show how Deutero-Isaiah conceived of this. What now occurs in the case of Israel within the context of universal history—the miracle that, with her, a nation's link with its God persisted in spite of the nation's complete ruin—she will attest to others, and people from other nations will turn to this God (cf. 44.5).

What is to inspire the outside world to seek such knowledge of the God of Israel is his commissioning of Cyrus. What is the explanation of this? To see the significance of the Cyrus oracle, we must look at it against the background of the history of the monarchy in Israel. A great prophecy was attached to this (II Sam. 7). That here in Deutero-Isaiah God can declare Cyrus to be his anointed, i.e. his king, in order to carry out a specific task, that of setting Israel free, means the breaking of the link between his actions in the political sphere on behalf of his chosen people and the Davidic monarchy. The corollary is the severance of the link with monarchy altogether, both in Israel and Judah. What God once did through Israel's king he can now do through an alien king, the king of an alien power and a believer in an alien religion. In principle, therefore, God's people is stripped of political power. The moment the Cyrus oracle was spoken, Israel as God's people ceased to be a people with political power. This break did not have to wait for the coming of Christ, but took place now.

[7] The Cyrus oracle represents the farthest that Deutero-Isaiah goes in his proclamation. The same is true of the predications with which it concludes. The way in which the self-predications are put in these final sentences is highly significant; they could only be spoken by God himself: as 'statements made about God' they could never stand up. It is hard to see why this verse does not disturb commentators more than it seems to do. As its introduction it has words which appear more than once in the trial speeches, 'I, Yahweh, and no other' (43.11; 44.6b). Here, however, their logical conclusion is drawn—each and every thing created, each and every event that

happens, light and darkness, weal and woe, are attributable to him, and to him alone. In order to get the meaning of the words correct, we must realize that, in its entirety, the Cyrus oracle represents a statement taken as far as it can go. If we universalize what is said here and draw general conclusions on its basis, we come up against this limit. For, if God's action reaches so far beyond his chosen people, if he calls, equips, accompanies and bestows honour so far beyond it itself, and if a worshipper of foreign gods can be given the approval, help and guidance of the God of Israel, where can it all end? Those who first heard the prophet's words asked the same question. And now the final words here set this action in such vast perspectives that we can only tremble and fall silent as we contemplate them. To push the word 'all' to its full logical conclusion is to land ourselves in difficulties from which there is no way out. The creation story in Gen. 1 shows the utmost care to preserve the limit. Though he is lord over the darkness, God is certainly not its creator. He took it into creation and set bounds to it, but he did not bring it into being. Precisely the same is true of the world of events, as J's version of the creation story makes clear. Evil irrupts into God's creation, but it does so through a creature. And there it is left, without explanation: the limit has once more been reached. In contrast, this oracle of Deutero-Isaiah says, for the one and only time in the Bible and in direct opposition to Gen. 1 and 3, that God created the darkness as he did the light. God brings about woe (the Hebrew word embraces both woe and evil), just as he brings about salvation. This shuts the door firmly on any dualism—if the creator of evil and woe is God, there is no room left for a devil. But what kind of God is this who created evil as well as good, woe as well as weal? In his action upon Cyrus and through him God does a thing which really goes far beyond what he had said to his chosen people about himself and his workings. For this reason the final words of the Cyrus oracle indicate that God's divinity transcends the limit imposed on human speech or thought about him—which means the limit imposed on all theology.

CHAPTER 45.8

Shower, ye heavens

Shower, ye heavens, from above,
ye clouds, rain down salvation,
[let] the earth [open, let salvation bear fruit],[a]
that righteousness may spring up also.
I, Yahweh, have created it.

The importance of the Cyrus oracle in Deutero-Isaiah's pro-clamation makes it appropriate that it should be given a distinctive ending, the short hymn before us. The two hymns contained in 44.23 and 45.8 set it in relief as a distinct and independent part of the oracle. Comparison with the other hymns of praise occurring through-out the book shows that its use along with the Cyrus oracle is deli-berate. This is the one hymn in which the act of God at which men are summoned to exult is called his creation. This obviously re-echoes 44.24, 27 and 45.7. The one who commissions the foreign king Cyrus to perform the saving work on his chosen people's behalf is the creator. And further, what God now does is so unprecedented and new that it falls to be described as creation. This exceptional char-acter is also reflected in the imperatives and jussives. The real role here assigned to the heavens, the earth and the clouds is not to rejoice at this act of God, but rather to let salvation pour forth and down from them. Abundance and more than abundance of gifts resulting from salvation are similarly described in Ps. 85. 12(11) 'faithfulness springs up from the ground, and righteousness looks down from the sky.'[b] What is here described is the pouring forth of blessing, but what is really meant is not blessing, but salvation: the two are deliberately made to coalesce. The result of God's creative deed is salvation for Israel, a salvation to which effect is given in history. Yet—as the language of the hymn suggests—this saving event is to have as its consequence the pouring forth of blessing which is to be described later, in the two final chapters of the book, chs. 54f. The new act of creation brings the renewed blessing.

[a] Read *tippātaḥ* and *wᵉyēper*. [b] Cf. also Hos. 2.21f.

CHAPTER 45.9–13

The Clay and Its Moulder

9 Woe to him who goes to law with his Maker,
   a potsherd among earthen potsherds.
   Does the clay say to him who fashions it, 'What are you making?'
   Does your work say, 'It has no hands?'
   (or, does your work say, 'You have no hands?'
   or, 'I am not the work of your hands.')ᵃ

10 Woe to him who says to a father, 'What are you begetting?',
   or to a woman, 'With what are you in travail?'

11 Thus says Yahweh, the Holy One of Israel, and his Maker:
   [Will you question]ᵇ me about my children,
   or command me concerning the work of my hands?

12 I made the earth and created man upon it.
   It was my hands that stretched out the heavens,
   and I command all their host.

13 I have aroused him in grace,
   and I make straight all his ways.
   He shall build my city
   and set free the captives [of my people].ᶜ
   Not for price and not for reward,'
   says Yahweh of hosts.

This section shows textual disturbances, and the meaning is often extremely hard to see. My own interpretation is no more than tentative. Verses 11ff. have an introduction of their own, and could be an independent text. Taking their opening words, 'Will you question me about my children?', without regard to vv. 9f., one would naturally assume that those to whom the question is put are not the sons themselves, but other people. But who can they be? The only possible

---

ᵃ The text is uncertain in the second half of the verse—C. F. Whitley, 'Textual Notes on Deutero-Isaiah 45.9', *VT*, XI (1961), pp. 458f.
ᵇ Read *ha'attem tiš'ālūnī*.
ᶜ Read with LXX *wᵉgālūt 'ammī*.

answer is the nations, or the gods of the nations, who question Yahweh about his treatment of his sons, that is, of his own chosen people— 'How could you cast off your own sons!' In this case—and vv. 12f. suit this perfectly—the section represents an argument adduced by the foreign nations in their legal contest with Yahweh. It gives Yahweh's argument in refutation of their question, and every clause of it occurs in identical or almost identical terms in the trial speeches. The beginning is lacking.

On the other hand, if we read vv. 11ff. in the light of v. 9f., something quite different is suggested. Here it is Yahweh's creature that revolts against the creator (9a and b), the child against the father. And when we thus connect v. 11 with vv. 9f., we feel instinctively that it, too, is addressed to Israel who (in doubt) questions Yahweh about his actions towards his sons. What is meant here is obvious: the actions are his actions towards Israel through the instrumentality of Cyrus, which greatly offend his chosen people. On this view, vv. 9–13 can be regarded as a single unit constituting a disputation in which the prophet inveighs against hearers who find his description of Cyrus as Yahweh's anointed (45.1–7) intolerable and unacceptable.

A further difficulty now arises. If the utterance of woe in v. 10 beginning with the words, 'Woe to him who says to his father', is taken by itself, it can only be properly understood as expressing the tribulation of an individual person; it is similar to Job's lament in Job 3, and this particular rebellion of the creature against its maker is decisively rejected in the utterance of woe. If v. 10 stood alone, no one would ever imagine that it referred to a resistance offered to a divine act upon Israel. Because of this, Duhm strikes out the entire verse. This does not, however, help much, for if the other word of woe (v. 9a) and the question in v. 9b are taken out of context, they will have to be understood in exactly the same way as v. 10. This means therefore that the only thing which makes the two parts, vv. 9f. and vv. 11ff., into a disputation whose subject is the offence taken by the prophet's hearers at his Cyrus oracle, is their mutual relationship. In addition, while vv. 11ff. are entirely in Deutero-Isaiah's style, vv. 9f. diverge from it widely. This was pointed out by Elliger, and he added an argument based on the subject-matter: this is the only place in Deutero-Isaiah where an utterance of woe is spoken against Israel, i.e., contemporary Israel in exile. Elliger concluded that a genuine utterance of Deutero-Isaiah had been reshaped by a later editor (in his own view, Trito-Isaiah) who made it into a disputation countering the objections to the Cyrus oracle. This is the best interpretation of a difficult passage.

[9f.] The utterances of woe. Oracles of this kind occur particularly in pre-exilic prophecy of doom, e.g. Isa. 5.8ff. They generally appear in series: vv. 9f. are also a series. The words 'Woe to' themselves indicate the pronouncement of doom. Accordingly, the oracles here in 45.9f. ought to be included in the prophetic oracles of doom against Israel. But this would be the one instance of such an oracle in Deutero-Isaiah's proclamation. However, besides this usage, there is a development of these oracles; there the words no longer signify the terse proclaiming of doom, but theoretically and in the abstract condemn an attitude or a fixed mode of action. Such examples occur in the series represented by Isa. 5.8ff., e.g. Isa. 5.21, 'Woe to those who are wise in their own eyes.' Here the utterances of woe are like those found in the wisdom literature. The series here in v. 9f. is very similar. The terms are again general and akin to those of the wisdom teaching. But if the verses do form a series of such secondary 'woe words', it is perfectly possible that the three sayings represented by vv. 9a, 9b and 10 have a slightly different meaning, just as they are also different in form; vv. 9a and 10 are 'woe words', but v. 9b is a reprimand in the form of a question, such as is also commonly found in the wisdom teaching. In this case, the probability is that in order to achieve his design of turning the edge of the offence of the Cyrus oracle, the man who combined vv. 9–13 into a single unit used sayings already current and well known. This explains why the quotations in vv. 9–10a can indicate this situation without, however, fitting it exactly: the three sayings were originally coined with reference to entirely different situations.

Verse 9 assumes previous knowledge of the metaphor of the potter's work for the creation of man, a metaphor frequently found in poetry and in the wisdom literature, as, for example, in Job 10.9. It expresses the artist's unlimited power in disposing of his material. Although it admits of secondary application to the situation set out here, its primary reference is to the personal fate which overtakes a man who is determined to rebel against his maker. Verse 10 expresses the same sentiments, but it is more like a simile: 'as little as a man can ask his father or mother'. In all three utterances such rebellion against the creator is decisively rejected. As far as content is concerned, there is no difference between the 'woe words' and the reprimand in question form.

In vv. 11ff., however, this rebellion is referred to a specific set of circumstances of which not the slightest trace is to be found in vv. 9f. In v. 11 the rebellion of the creature against his creator is applied to Israel's rebellion against God's treatment of his children (11b), which, after the allusion to God's power as shown in creation (v. 12), is in v. 13 expressly stated to be the summoning of Cyrus to set Israel free and to rebuild Jerusalem. This is what the man who combined vv. 9f. with vv. 11ff. had in mind, and this is how the majority of editors take it. Volz, for example, says: 'The prophet inveighs against his fellow-exiles' assertion that it is out of the question for a pagan to be the *māšiaḥ*. Verses 9f. reject the murmuring as such, vv. 11f. set against it Yahweh's sovereignty in general, and v. 13 his sovereign power in a specific instance.'[a] At first sight this appears to be clear and obvious. If, however, the context is more carefully considered, the real difficulty appears. This can never originally have been meant as a disputation of the objection that 'it is out of the question for a pagan to be the *māšiaḥ*', for the argument with which Yahweh counters it in v. 13 is identical with the objection itself. To put it another way, there is no disputation whatsoever here, merely the countering of the objection that God makes a pagan the messiah by Yahweh's being made to say, 'Yes, I make a pagan the messiah, for', and we may go on to add in terms of v. 12, 'I have the power so to do.' A disputation which only consists in the vociferous repetition of the subject under debate is hardly to be presumed. This shows that when vv. 11ff. stood by themselves, they must have meant something different.

[11] The two predications, 'the Holy One of Israel' and 'his Maker', occur in 43.15 in a trial speech. They are followed by a number of further parallels to the latter. Without directly quoting it, v. 11b alludes to an argument of the opposite party's—'Do you (the gods of the nations) mean to say in reply to me that I destroyed my chosen people, that I brought about the fall of Jerusalem and drove them into exile?' While this argument is not actually found in the other trial speeches, it might very well have been adduced; it would be astonishing if in the entire literary category there were no trace of it, for this is the very point at which the other gods could prove their superiority to the God of Israel. One must assume that this argument had been given at greater length; Elliger is correct in supposing that something has probably been omitted before v. 11b. At all events,

---

[a] Volz, *op. cit., ad loc.*

this argument on the part of Yahweh's opponents can easily be reconstructed from the two questions in v. 11b.

[12f.] Assuming this to be the argument, then the two verses which follow make good sense as an answer to it. It runs as follows: 'I have not abandoned my chosen people. I am on the point of restoring their homeland to them.' This answer is substantiated in v. 12 by the self-predication of the creator. Here praise of God as creator is particularly detailed: he created the heavens and the stars in them, the earth and man upon it (cf. 44.24ff.). As creator, he is lord of his creation; he commands the host of the stars (cf. 40.26). This is the basis of his lordship of history (so also Duhm and Volz, *ad loc.*). It is brought into relationship with one particular point, the rousing up of Cyrus to set Israel free. The first part of v. 13a is the same as 41.25 and similar to 41.2 (both occur in trial speeches), the second is very close to 45.2a. Verse 13b corresponds to 44.26b, the only difference being that in 44.26 the rebuilding of Jerusalem is directly attributed to God himself. This is the one place where it is stated thus directly and openly that the one who is to build Yahweh's city, i.e. Jerusalem, and set free the captives of his chosen people, is Cyrus.

The meaning of the concluding words, 'not for price and not for reward', is not certain. Elliger regards them as an addition made by Trito-Isaiah. The simplest interpretation is that Cyrus is to derive no profit from performing this work of setting Israel free; the sole reason for this liberation is the will of God.

CHAPTER 45.14, 15, 16–17

God is with you

Thus says Yahweh:

14 'The wealth of Egypt and the produce of Ethiopia,
    and the Sabeans, men of stature,
    come over to you and are yours,
    they follow you, they go in chains,
    they bow down to you, they pay homage to you, saying:
    "God is with you and there is no other, no God." '[a]

[a] N. H. Snaith, 'The Meaning of the Hebrew אך (45.14)', *VT*, XIV (1964), pp. 221ff.

CHAPTER 45.14, 15, 16–17

15 Truly, thou art a God who hidest thyself,
    O God of Israel, a Saviour.

16 All of them will be put to shame and brought to nothing,
    the makers of idols go in confusion together.

17 But Israel finds help in Yahweh, help for ever.
    You shall not be brought to nothing or put to shame
    to all eternity.

Most editors regard 45.14–17 as a single unit. After repeated
examination of the verses I find this impossible. The three component
parts are too different in style, vocabulary and intention. The
astonishing exclamation in v. 15, 'thou art a God who hidest thyself', is quite out of keeping with v. 14; if anywhere, God's workings
with his chosen people are *revealed* in the confession of those who come
to him from afar. Nor do I see a connection between the words in
vv. 16f., 'the makers of idols will be put to shame, but Israel will not
be put to shame', and what precedes them. Examination of the
form also leads to the same conclusion: in this respect, too, there are
no indications that vv. 14–17 make up one single unit.

In that case, we must reckon with the possibility that the verses
are a combination of fragments which could only have been preserved as fragments. Each part has therefore to be examined separately in the light of its own characteristic features.

[14] This oracle seems strange in Deutero-Isaiah, because it
visualizes a state of well-being for Israel still lying in the future, a
thing which occurs nowhere else in the prophet's work. The many
attempts on the part of editors to change the text or delete parts of it
are evidence of this uniqueness. On the other hand, the description
given here perfectly accords with that of the state of well-being in
Isa. 60, where the nations and their treasures come to Zion to be
Israel's servants in her new state of well-being, and to pay homage to
her God (Isa. 60.3–14). One feature in particular is exactly the same
as in Isa. 60, and it is a feature that does not suit Deutero-Isaiah: the
ambassadors of the nations come *with their treasures* and appear all
together, as in a procession, to pay homage (cf. Isa. 60.13–14). Even
the words, 'in chains', which editors find difficult and which are
often deleted out of hand, have their counterpart in Isa. 60.14, 'the
sons of those who oppressed you shall come bending low to you.' I
cannot explain how the verse, which, as we have seen, properly

belongs to the description given in Isa. 60, came to be placed here. The likelihood that it was originally connected with Isa. 60 is supported by the fact that here in Deutero-Isaiah 45.14 it is a fragment without connection with either what precedes it or what follows it. It can therefore only be commented on in the context of Isa. 60.

[15] The reading *'itteka* (with you) has been suggested in place of *'atta* (you). This is evidently an attempt to link the verse with v. 14. There is no justification for such a change, and of itself the fact that such a course is felt necessary shows v. 15 to be an independent unit unconnected with what goes before. Nor does v. 15 in any way go along with vv. 16f. Nevertheless, independent as it is, it does go with the Cyrus oracle in 44.24–45.7. As we have already seen, 45.9–13 are to be regarded as a disputation composed with reference to this oracle about Cyrus, whose subject is the baffling proclamation of Cyrus as Yahweh's anointed; as we noted, however, the verses represent the working over of an oracle of Deutero-Isaiah which originally had a different intent. 45.15 is also a reaction to the Cyrus oracle, but of an entirely different kind. Here this unprecedented act of God is given a favourable reception: the writer bows down in astonishment at it. The exclamation literally says, 'Truly, thou art a God who hidest thyself.' It expresses an insight of the highest importance. The action of Israel's God on behalf of his people by means of a pagan monarch, as now announced by Deutero-Isaiah, represents a breakthrough, leading to a change in the mode of his action. The way for it had for long been in preparation in the pre-exilic prophets' message of doom. There, for example, Assyria could be called the rod of God's anger: even as early as this, we find him acting with reference to his chosen people through the political power of a pagan monarch. The breakthrough meant the end of that era in the divine action during which God's activity in history had been discernible, when he was openly on his chosen people's side in their wars and smote their enemies. Deutero-Isaiah's Cyrus oracle terminated this for ever. Henceforward God's action in history is a hidden one. But one further thing needs to be said. There is one place at which the God who hides himself is revealed—the place where he becomes his chosen people's saviour. This is here indicated in the predication with which the verse ends, 'God of Israel, a helper (or, a saviour)'.

We cannot be sure whether this isolated saying in v. 15 is from Deutero-Isaiah himself or from some reader of the Cyrus oracle who wanted to confront the disbelief challenged in vv. 9–13 with an utterance of faith. However it may be, it is a word after the prophet's own heart; it shows real understanding of Deutero-Isaiah's proclamation. If it is a later addition, it forms one of the many 'Amen' glosses running through the whole Bible. (By 'Amen' gloss is meant words added by a reader, or someone who heard the text read, saying an Amen to what he had heard.) If that is the case here, 45.15 would exemplify the truth that a gloss can often be of the utmost importance for the context in which it occurs, for the words here are a theological summary of Cyrus oracle which Deutero-Isaiah made the central point of his proclamation.

[16–17] Editors who suppose vv. 14–17 to be a unity, pay too little heed to the fact that the subject of vv. 16f. is 'making idols', i.e., the manufacture of images. There can be no question that these verses—and they alone in the present section—form part of the well-defined set of texts in the book of Deutero-Isaiah whose subject is the manufacture of idols. These were treated as a group in the exegesis of 44.9–20, but it was not decided there whether 45.16f. was to be included among them. A review of all the passages which make up the set shows that 45.16f. is parallel to 44.9 and 20, the general statement to the effect that the makers of idols are to be put to shame, which serves there as the framework for the description of the manufacture of images. 45.16f. says exactly the same thing, the only difference being that here the fate which is to overtake those who put their trust in idols is contrasted with that of those who rely upon Yahweh. Since the passages which describe the manufacture of idols are often later insertions into other contexts, there is no difficulty in regarding 45.16f., too, as an originally independent unit.

CHAPTER 45.18–19

He did not create it a chaos

18 For thus says Yahweh, who created the heavens, he, God,
    who formed the earth and made it, he established it:
    he did not create it a chaos,
    he formed it to be inhabited:
    'I am Yahweh, and there is no other.

19 I did not speak in secret,
in a land of darkness.
I did not say to the offspring of Jacob,
"Seek me in chaos."
I am Yahweh, who speaks salvation,
who declares what is true.'

From 45.18 onwards, i.e. after the Cyrus oracle, the book of
Deutero-Isaiah is mainly composed of units of considerable length,
which cannot be clearly assigned to any precise form. For the most
part, they are composite pieces which either unite motifs taken from
several forms or have small, relatively complete units placed alongside one another. This is also true of the passage beginning with
45.18. 45.18f. is relatively complete in itself, yet it cannot be called
an independent unit. It is, however, so obviously meant to be connected with 45.20–25 and 46.1–13 that it may be taken as an introduction to them. Its similarity to 44.24–28, the introduction to the
Cyrus oracle, also points in the same direction.

In their general character the verses remind one of the disputations.
This is due to the emphatic 'not' which appears three times in
vv. 18f. But what is the position here disputed? This is not easy to
see, and it can only be discovered from the detailed exegesis.

[18] The introduction with the predication of God as creator is
reminiscent of 44.24ff., except that there these words are self-predications. The fact that God is creator of heaven and earth has great
stress put on it here, and, as the forceful noun clause at the end of the
first line brings out, it is this very thing that makes him the only, the
sole God (the words *hū' hā 'elōhīm* can hardly be translated: literally,
'he: the God'). The end of v. 18 comes back to the proclamation that
God is the only God; here it is put in the form of a self-predication,
which means that it is the beginning of the address to which the first
clause in v. 18 forms the introduction.

Between the introduction and the self-predication comes an
expansion which adds to the general predication of God as creator the
particular point—and this is the only mention of it in the book—'not
as a chaos (*tōhū*), but to be inhabited'. Taken by themselves, the
words sound like a commonplace, something self-evident. To mean
anything, they must be thought of as a reply. However, the position
which they combat cannot be ascertained from v. 18 and v. 19 alone,
but only becomes apparent in vv. 20–25. Here we need only anticipate to the extent of saying that the writer is obviously thinking

primarily of the other nations of the world. They form part of God's creation, and God created the world for them to dwell in. The words are directed against a position which calls in question this positive attitude on God's part towards the other nations. In countering it, Deutero-Isaiah here displays the same universalistic attitude as also determines what is said of God in the primaeval history, and in particular, in the tables of the nations.

[19] Here something slightly different is added, but, as the recurrence of the same term *tōhū* in the denial in v. 18 and v. 19 makes clear, it must be connected with what precedes it. The two lines vv. 18a and b are obviously to be taken as parallel, for they say the same thing. But to what do the words, 'Seek me in chaos (or nothingness)' allude? *Tōhū*, meaning nothingness, that which is empty, can also have the sense of 'futile'—the meaning would then be, 'Seek me in vain'. In this case, 'in secret' and 'in darkness' in v. 19a would not refer, as most editors interpret them, to mystery cults, cult practices in secret, etc.; instead, they would refer to the hiddenness and darkness of what God said. In that case, v. 19 is not a contrast between the luminous, clear word of God as found in Israel and the dark, mysterious oracles of other cults. Instead, the words are directed against the attitude which Deutero-Isaiah encounters in the other disputations as well, namely, that God had left his chosen people in the lurch, and that his words, meaning the earlier prophecies, had led to darkness and nothingness. This the prophet disputes, and he counters the attitude with an 'I am' saying in which God designates himself as the one who really announces salvation. Thus interpreted, v. 19 deals with almost the same subject as the conclusion of the great disputation which comes at the beginning of the book, 40.27–31.

How then are the two entirely different disputations in vv. 18 and 19 related to one another, and what do the two positions challenged have in common? This cannot be gathered simply from the two verses themselves. Instead, the question shows that something must still be to come, to which vv. 18f. are really an introduction. So far, this much is clear: v. 18 is related to the first of the passages introduced by vv. 18f. (45.20–25) and v. 19 to the second (46.1–13), the former being a word spoken to the nations, the latter one spoken to Israel.

CHAPTER 45.20–25

All the Ends of the Earth

20 Assemble yourselves and come,
draw near together, you survivors of the nations.
They have no knowledge to carry about their wooden idols,
they pray to a god that cannot save.

21 Declare and present your case,
yes, take counsel together!
Who told this long ago?
Who declared it of old?
Was it not I, Yahweh?
And there is no other god besides me.
There is no righteous and helping God beside me.

22 Turn to me and be helped,
all the ends of the earth!
For I am God, and there is no other.
23 By myself I swear.
From my mouth truth goes forth,
a word that does not return:
To me every knee bows, every tongue swears:
24 [Truly],ᵃ in Yahweh there is salvation and strength.
To him [come]ᵇ in shame
all who were incensed against him.
25 In Yahweh all the offspring of Israel have salvation and glory.

The utterance is one of the trial speeches in which Yahweh confronts the nations or the gods of the nations, and it is to be interpreted in the context of the rest of the texts in the group.ᶜ

[20–21a] These verses represent the challenge to appear in court. This is as found in the other texts of this category, but it differs from them in that the people here addressed are, as is emphasized, the 'survivors of the nations'. The Hebrew word for 'survivors' always

---

ᵃ Instead of *lī'āmar* read *lē'mōr* before *'ak*.
ᵇ Instead of *yābō'* read the plural. But the text is uncertain.
ᶜ 41.1–5; 41.21–29; 43.8–15; 44.6–8. Cf. Westermann, *Forschung am Alten Testament*, Munich, 1964, pp. 134–41.

presupposes a battle, and a lost battle at that, from which those concerned have made their escape. Thus, the people here addressed and
summoned into court are such as have escaped from a lost battle,
from the downfall of a state. In the light of 45.1–7, there can be no
doubt that the prophet was thinking primarily of the Babylonians,
and in particular, of those who had escaped when the city itself fell.
They stand, however, for the 'survivors of the nations' in general.
Now that disaster has overtaken them, they are to state their claim
and substantiate it. The predicament in which this puts them owing
to the complete change of circumstances is indicated in the last words
of v. 21a, 'Yes, take counsel together.' They can certainly no longer
adduce the victorious might of their gods!

[20b] At this point, between vv. 20a and 21, which go together, a
gloss has been inserted, once again a condemnation of idolatry
similar to 44.18 and, therefore, a marginal gloss of the same kind.
But this censure (v. 20b) does not fit in 45.20–25. It is obviously a
marginal gloss on 46.1–2, whose subject is likewise idolatry, and a
copyist has inserted it at the wrong place in the text.

[21b] Addressing himself to the entirely new circumstances,
Israel's God now once more adduces in support of his claim to be
God the argument, 'Who told this long ago?' But whereas previously
this was one assertion set against the other, now, because of the
changed situation, it has the staggering facts of history to lend it
weight. Why, this very event by which the 'nations' were made
survivors was foretold by the God of Israel! This is a fact which can
no longer be evaded. Note that those to whom he proclaimed it
were his own chosen people, and in so doing he proved himself 'a
righteous and helping God' to them. Thus, the trustworthiness of
this God in speech and action extends beyond the small band of his
own people; this proclamation affects universal history; it was made
to the Israelites as 'survivors' outside their own land and in the sphere
of influence of another power. And there, in a foreign country, God
shows them that he is a righteous and helping God, since, faraway
there amidst other powers, his action in history continues as though
they had never met with disaster.

[22] Now, however, comes the amazing thing: the victor does not
glory in his feat. Now that those who yesterday were still powerful and
victorious have themselves become survivors, since the same fate,
defeat and exile, has overtaken them as overtook Israel, there is no
jubilation on the victor's part over the defeated gods, no triumphant

'I told you so'. Instead, something entirely different takes its place, the invitation to those from among the nations who survived the avalanche to participate in salvation! This invitation signs and seals the fact that God's intervention by means of Cyrus involved a radical change in the divine *modus operandi* in history. And at the same time it elucidates the first 'not' in the introduction (v. 18): God is the creator of the whole world, and therefore it cannot be his purpose to destroy the nations, *vis-à-vis* whom he has shown himself to be the real God. His victory in the lawsuit against their gods involves something entirely new; there is no longer overthrowing and destroying, but convincing!

[23–25] What God's oath means is this: the goal to which God's dealings with mankind are directed is free confession, the assent which springs from conviction, on the part of those who have realized that the only true God is the God of Israel. The only thing which leads to this goal is invitation, free and open access to this salvation for all nations on earth. In the final words of v. 23, 'to me every knee bows, every tongue swears', the note struck is not at all the sum-total of all men everywhere; 'every' means every individual. This is the novel aspect. Bowing the knee to Yahweh and confessing him to be the one God demands the free assent of the individual to his claims. In the confession, 'Truly, in Yahweh are salvation and strength', the distant and the near now meet: those who once were his enemies and fought against him (v. 24b) arrive on the scene and together with Israel participate in his salvation (v. 25).

This text is taken up into the New Testament (in Rom. 14.11 and Phil. 2.10f.). No violence is done to the subject-matter and both citations strictly adhere to the sense of the original. The crucial change in the concept of the people of God is already present here in Deutero-Isaiah. As the verses before us make clear, he believed that in his day a final break had been made between the people of God and any form of its existence as a political entity. All men are invited to partake in the divine salvation, and membership of the people of God is based on the free confession of those who have discovered that he alone is God. These two factors, of crucial importance for the Christian concept of the Church, are already present in Deutero-Isaiah.

CHAPTER 46.1–4

Bearing and Being Borne

1   Bel bows down   Nebo stoops
    Their idols have become   burdens for cattle!
    Burdens for cattle   burdens for the weary![a]

2   They stoop, they bow down together,
    they cannot save the burden,
    and they themselves—they go into captivity!

3   Hearken to me, O house of Jacob
    and all the remnant of the house of Israel,
    who have been borne from your birth,
    carried from the womb:
4   even to your old age I am He,
    and to grey hairs I will carry you.
    I have [borne][b] and I will bear,
    and I will carry and will save.

46.1–13 is the second part of the longish poem which was introduced by 45.18f. The clearest indication that these two sections go
together is the address in 46.3, 'the remnant of the house of Israel'.
This is the sole occasion in the book that Israel is thus addressed; it
corresponds to the address to the nations in 45.20, 'you survivors of
the nations'. Both of these, therefore, the nations and Israel, are
addressed as those who have survived the downfall of a state. Just as
first part of the introduction, 45.18, referred to the nations and their
fate, and this was the subject of 45.20–25, so too its second part, 45.19,

---

[a] The text is in disorder. Some transposition of the transmitted text allows it to
be kept. In doing this the strong 2.2. rhythm is a help.

   hāyū ʿaṣabbēhᵉm maśśāʾ lahayyā
   nisuōʾtēkem labbᵉhēmmā ʿammusōt laʿayyēpā

C. F. Whitley, 'Textual Notes on Deutero-Isaiah (46.1)', *VT*, XI (1961), p. 459.
   [b] Read *nāsāʾtī*; J. J. Rabinowitz, 'A Note on Isa. 46.4 (*sābal*)', *JBL*, 73 (1954),
pp. 237ff.

refers to Israel and her fate, and this is the theme of 46.1–13. Whereas
the introduction uttered the divine 'No' to Israel's despondency ('I
did not speak in secret'), 46.1–13 now present the positive message of
salvation. 46.1–13 form a unity (so also Muilenburg), as is made
clear by the way in which its various sections begin:

> v. 3   Hearken to me
> 9   Remember the former things of old
> 12   Hearken to me

This stylistic device of making sections or strophes of a longish poem
begin with imperatives which correspond to those found in the
address, occurs several times in Deutero-Isaiah, and is particularly
characteristic of his style. The way in which the two parts of vv. 1–4,
1f. and 3f., are related to one another is especially artistic; it shows
considerable thought on the prophet's part, and makes of the verses
a relatively self-contained unit within the body of 46.1–13.

[1f.] The rhythm of the first two verses is 2:2 throughout, the
rhythm of the shortest possible stichos, and it always indicates special
agitation and excitement; it is the rhythm used for brief, rapid ejacu-
lations. This, as well as the diction, shows that the prophet had here
taken over and adapted a well-defined fixed form. It is that used for
bringing tidings of victory, or an imitation of it: the enemy's rout is
proclaimed. Here the place of a human enemy is taken by the two
chief gods of Babylon. While Deutero-Isaiah's oracles of salvation
and his trial speeches are somewhat cryptic in what they say about
future events, here, as in 44.28 and 45.13, specific facts and names are
given. Bel was originally the god of heaven and, as such, father of the
gods, having his shrine at Nippur. At a later date he was merged
with Marduk, the god of the city of Babylon, who was then given the
double name Bel-Marduk. Nebo, the god of Borsippa, was worshipped
as Marduk's son. His importance is shown by the many names com-
pounded with Nabu, such as Nebuchadnezzar, Nabopolassar, etc.
He was the chief god of the neo-Babylonian or Chaldean dynasty.
The empire represented by these gods is on the point of falling, and
at the eleventh hour an attempt is made to remove the gods' images
from their temples, where they are in danger. The statues are taken
down from their pedestals and loaded on beasts of burden. Deutero-
Isaiah here describes what was probably a not uncommon happening
in the world of history, *vide* an account found in an inscription of
Sennacherib relating to Merodach-Baladan on the occasion of a
military defeat: 'the gods, the protection (?) of his land, he gathered

in their shrines, shipped them on vessels and took himself off to the city Nagiti-Rakki.'[a]

The vignette of the carrying away of the images which these brief, truncated lines conjure up may also have been suggested by a contrast to it, namely, recollection of the great New Year procession from Babylon to Borsippa, in which, too, the statues of the gods were borne along the processional way and then loaded on to ships. Now, however, all their pomp and splendour has deserted them, as they topple down from their pedestals, are loaded on to beasts, and carried off. It should be noticed that v. 2 clearly differentiates between the gods and their statues: 'they cannot save the burden', that is, the gods do not manage to save their statues. They themselves, the gods, are entangled in the downfall of their people, and forced to go into captivity along with them. This itself makes clear that the conception of the relationship between the Babylonian gods and their images found here is quite different from that suggested in the satire in 44.9–20, where the two were identified without qualification.

However, we have not yet reached the climax of the verses. With an amazing conciseness this short poem combines two statements. The first is clear, and is expressed in the contrast made in every one of the brief lines—the two supreme ones in the Babylonian empire have collapsed; those who towered so mightily have had a fall! But when the prophet says this, and strikes up this song of victory, the statues are still standing in their places, and day in and day out, eloquent hymns are extolling these gods as the high and mighty ones! The song is therefore in fact proclamation, with never a note of doubt in its anticipation of the fall of Babylon—this is inevitable. If we try to put ourselves into the position of the prophet's hearers, these verses will let us see that the exilic prophet's oracles were regarded and pre-served as authoritative.

Something else, however, is said in the verses, but this time it only becomes clear when we take the total content of the prophet's preaching into account. What does it mean for a god to be bound up with his image? This is only revealed now, at the moment when disaster is engulfing a country. Then, in the hour of disaster, it is suddenly made plain that, even if the god is not identical with his image, he is connected with it beyond hope of separation. Where the only possibility is flight, the statue is not mere symbol; the fugitives

[a] E. Schrader, *The Cuneiform Inscriptions and the Old Testament*, London, 1885–8, Vol. II, p. 36.

must take it along with them. This tells its own story. It means the sudden, fantastic reversal of roles. The worshippers are obliged to save their gods, for the gods cannot save themselves. Instead of the gods bearing their people at the time when ruin threatens to engulf the latter, they themselves require to be borne, they become a burden.

This passage constitutes the Bible's most profound utterance on the representation of a god by an image. Here the second commandment has borne its richest harvest. For Deutero-Isaiah, the difference between Yahweh and the gods who can be represented by images is not an intellectual or conceptual one; he holds that the one factor which decides between them lies in the realm of history. When disasters happen there, the image, the representation, is seen to be committed to human hands to carry. What circumscribes a god who is to be represented by an image is the fact that he cannot save the latter. Verses 3f. are then to show that this is actually the exact point of difference between such a god and the God of Israel—precisely in the hour of his people's downfall, *he* bears *them*.

There is a further respect in which this brief oracle is important. One can see from it that Deutero-Isaiah did in fact deliver it *before* the fall of the Babylonian empire; for things did not turn out exactly as he here proclaimed they would. The images of the gods of Babylon did not require to be loaded on animals, because Cyrus not only allowed them to remain in place, but even showed reverence for them. Deutero-Isaiah could not therefore have spoken as he does here *after* the fall of Babylon. This is a particularly fine example of the fact that prophetic utterances were sometimes not fulfilled exactly, without this in any way detracting from their intrinsic significance. Even if Babylon did not fall in precisely the way that Deutero-Isaiah proclaimed here, nevertheless, the fact that she was captured without the striking of a blow meant the downfall of her gods. The merest glance at the Babylonian hymns shows that the gods stood or fell according as the Babylonian empire itself did. Even if worship of them did continue for some little time, the fall of the empire had spelt the fall of the gods.

[3–4] The voice which proclaimed the downfall of the Babylonian gods turns to the exiles there. They are addressed as 'the remnant of the house of Israel', being thus reminded of the catastrophic events from which they had escaped (cf. 45.20). Every word now spoken to them echoes the leitmotif of vv. 1f., and says that God is the God who can bear, and who does not require to be borne. 'I have borne and I

will bear.' The remnant of the house of Israel, who were asking—
the downfall of all that they had held dear still ringing in their ears—
whether the former prophecies had vanished into the void and the
darkness (45.19), are reminded, 'I carried you from the womb'. This
carrying, which the survivors had kept in remembrance, still held
good even though Jerusalem had fallen. In the case of the gods of
Babylon, the downfall of the empire demonstrated how weak was the
mighty, imposing relationship in which they stood with their worshippers (vv. 1f.), whereas in the case of the God of Israel, the self-
same thing demonstrated that his power to bear persisted.

The metaphor used at this particular point, the span of one man's
life, 'from your mother's womb even to grey hairs', is a remarkable
way of expressing the prophet's view of the history of the chosen
people, his own nation's history, as something that had suffered no
interruption. The metaphor was very far from obvious! Great faith
was needed to look beyond the fall of Jerusalem, the final destruction
of Israel as a political power, and the downfall and end of the house
of David, and see the history of the people of Israel as an uninterrupted
life-span in which God's bearing of her was a matter of past and
future alike.

The words show us the other side of what, in the legal process with
the other gods, Yahweh adduced as his sole but clinching argument in
support of his being God, the dependable connection between his
speech and his action. The trial speeches had shown what this meant
as regards the other gods ('who among you declared this?'); the
present verses show what it means for his chosen people: only God's
faithfulness in bearing gives their history its continuity.

At this point this present oracle of salvation has close affinities with
43.22–28. There, in opposition to a perverse form of worship within
Israel, God was obliged to say, 'you have not served me, but I you.'
The present passage makes a similar pronouncement about idolatry
outside of Israel, to the effect that even the mightiest gods cannot bear
their people over the collapse of their nationhood, since they themselves require to be borne in the shape of their images. Ability to bear
his people rests with the God who, precisely in the hour of collapse,
proves that he bears faithfully. The two central terms of both passages,
serving and bearing, point beyond themselves to the servant songs. In
these, because of forgiveness (43.25) and bearing (53.4), servant-
ship becomes historical reality through the servant who does service
for others by his vicarious suffering.

The final words in the passage, 'I will carry and will save', emphasize afresh the idea of God's bearing Israel into the future. This does not, however, mean as Israel's future an age of salvation that is always to remain the same. It is a continuing history in which the nation will give her God occasion to bear her, and in which renewed dangers call for renewed deliverance.

CHAPTER 46.5–8

To whom will you liken me?

5 To whom will you liken me and make me equal,
  and compare me, that we may be alike?[a]
6 Those who lavish gold from the purse,
  and weigh out silver in the scales,
  hire a goldsmith, that he should make it into a god;
  they bow, and even cast themselves down before it.
7 they lift it upon their shoulders, they carry it around;
  they set it down, and it stands there,
  it does not move from its place.
  If one cries to it, it does not answer,
  or save him from his trouble.
8 Remember this, and be [ashamed][b] in face of one another,
  recall it to mind, you transgressors.

[5–8] These verses are one of the series of oracles which declaim against the manufacture of images. So similar are they all in diction and attitude that they must have the same author. In each instance their place of insertion into the text has been deliberately chosen—at points where Deutero-Isaiah either says something about the gods of the nations, or speaks of the incomparability of God. Verse 5 is almost the same as 40.18, which has similar polemic against idolatry appended (vv. 19f.). The attraction of such additions to 46.1–2 is only to be expected: two actually—one preceding (45.20b) and one following (46.5 –8)—have been taken into the text here. It is hardly necessary to point out how very greatly their polemic differs from Deutero-Isaiah's own

---

[a] DSS Isa.[1] has 'that I may be like him'.

[b] In spite of various proposals, $hit'ōšāšū$ remains unexplained. The translation reads b for $'$, corresponding to the Vulgate.

in 46.1–4. One only needs to put the texts side by side to see this. In 44.9–20 the whole emphasis is put on the manufacture of images as such, whereas the present utterance merely devotes a word to this: what it stresses is the absurdity of the idea that, the material being available, a man can order a god at the goldsmith's! Thereafter the main part speaks of the worship offered to this made-to-order god. A description is given of the three most important acts in it: the obeisance or proskynesis, the procession, and the prayer. Incidentally this shows why this particular utterance was chosen for insertion here—while 46.1f. have a different frame of reference, they, too, speak of the carrying of gods. Prominence is given here to the inability to move or the passivity of the god who is represented by an image: he is carried about on men's shoulders, but when he is put back in his place, he once more stands motionless. In connection with the description of the prayer before the image (v. 7b), it is important that the typical form of prayer is regarded as supplication in time of trouble—praise of the god is probably thought of as forming part of the obeisance—and the god's reaction—here said to be none—as answering and helping. This corresponds to the two parts of prayer in a psalm of lamentation. The polemic concludes with a reprimand (v. 8) and an admonition.

CHAPTER 46.9–13

Remember the former things of old

9   Remember the former things of old;
    for I am God and there is no other,
    I am God, and there is none like me.
10 I declare what is to come from the beginning,
    and from ancient times things not yet done.
    I tell my purpose, and it comes about,
    all that I will I accomplish.

11 I call the bird of prey from the east,
    the man of [my][a] purpose from a far country.
    I have spoken,   I bring it to pass,
    I have purposed   and I do it.
                a Read ʿaṣātī.

12   Hearken to me, you [dejected]ᵃ in heart,
     you who are far from deliverance.
13   I bring near my deliverance, it is not far off,
     and my help does not tarry.
     I will put salvation in Zion,
     for Israel my glory.

'Remember' in v. 9 takes up 'hearken' in v. 3. What was only a hint in the appositions in vv. 3f. is now developed in vv. 9ff. Verse 12 repeats the first words of v. 3, 'Hearken to me', and the proclamation of salvation which it introduces (v. 13) brings the chapter to its goal. The appositions in this closing appeal, 'you dejected in heart, who are far from salvation', refer back to the lament alluded to in the introduction (45.19). It may now be taken as proved that 45.18–46.13 (omitting 46.5–8) forms a single unit, divided up by the inter-related imperatives at 46.3, 9, 12.

[9–10] The words with which Israel is addressed, 'Remember the former things of old', remind her of her history. This had already been anticipated in the clauses in apposition in v. 3b. What follows, a development of the metaphor in v. 3b describing Israel's experience in her history, adduces, in identical terms, God's argument in the trial speeches against the gods' claim to divinity. What had there been addressed to the nations here becomes a word spoken to Israel: God's claim to be the only God is based on the fact that there is a connection between his word and his action upon which Israel can depend. And, as in the trial speeches, this reliability is evinced at this very moment—God is commissioning Cyrus to execute his purpose proclaimed to his chosen people, the 'remnant of Israel', in the oracle of salvation.

The opening words of the oracle of salvation to Israel, 'remember the former things of old', form the only link between it and the argument of the trial speech; all the rest of vv. 9–11 could be part of one of the trial speeches exactly as it stands. But these opening words, too, correspond to one of the parts of the trial speeches, namely, the summons to Israel to be God's witnesses (43.10; 44.8b). 'Remember' here corresponds to 'You are my witnesses' there. The call to Israel in v. 12, 'Hearken to me', summoning her to accept the message of salvation, is based on the 'remember' of vv. 9–11. The prophet thus rests faith's present 'Yes' to the future on the nation's experiences with God in the past (cf. the metaphor in v. 3b). This is of the utmost

     ᵃ Read with LXX *'ōbdi* instead of *'abbīrē*.

significance for Deutero-Isaiah's concept of faith. When he summons his audience to put their faith in his message of salvation, he does not mean a 'strong faith' which they now needed to bring into play as something achieved by themselves. Rather, the call to have faith means bringing the nation's experience with God in history to bear upon the present. The fact that they accord recognition to this and say 'yes' to it makes them free to accept the message of salvation. In Deutero-Isaiah's view, there is no such thing as faith divorced from history; it is never an individual or existential attainment. Rather, when faith says 'Yes' to the future, this is the affirmation that God can be depended on, as is proved in the chosen people's history. Now, since 'remembrance of the former things of old' is not possible without a handing on of the facts, tradition is here brought to bear immediately and directly upon faith. But with Deutero-Isaiah, tradition does not mean tradition ossified in an institution, but something living, as exemplified in that part of a psalm entitled 'the review of God's previous saving actions'. For instance, in v. 5 (4) of Ps. 22 the suppliant says, 'In thee our fathers trusted; they trusted, and thou didst help them;' this represents the accomplishment of the very thing to which Deutero-Isaiah here summons his fellow-captives when he says, 'Remember the former things of old.'

[11] Such remembrance of the former things does not, however, mean a clinging to them. If Israel is serious as she remembers God's former acts, then she expects fresh action from him (cf. 43.19). Thus, acceptance of God's activity by the hands of Cyrus can be based on a remembrance of the past in which God wrought miracles.

Attention to Deutero-Isaiah's view of the connection between past, present and future could lead to a rethinking of the concept of tradition current in the Church today. This kind of view of tradition does not exclude, it rather includes, the resting of faith upon the word alone.

[12–13] The summons to hear takes up the summons in v. 3: the people called there the 'remnant of Israel' are the same as those now addressed as 'you dejected in heart, you who are far from deliverance'. Their complaint, indeed their arraignment of God, had been hinted at in the introduction (45.19): God's prophecies had been spoken into the darkness and the void. Now they are told, 'I bring near my deliverance, it is no longer far off'. And—this is the meaning of the whole poem contained in 45.18–46.13—this proclamation of speedy deliverance is now firmly based on the divine action in history viewed in its entirety. The central point is the victorious cry that the gods of Babylon have fallen. This proves the limitations of the gods of the other nations: in the hour of crisis they are shown to be bound to their images; they do not bear, but are themselves borne. For 'the survivors of the nations' this event opens up access to lasting salvation (45.20–25), while to the 'remnant of Israel' it opens the door to the future, for her God is the God who truly bears (46.3f.), and who gives effect to the salvation promised her (46.9–13).

CHAPTER 47.1–15

Come down into the dust

Preliminary note. This translation of ch. 47 is Köhler's. I take this means of drawing attention to his very valuable translation of Deutero-Isaiah (*Deuterojesaja stilkritisch untersucht*, BZAW, 1923), which is not as well known as it deserves to be. I adopt the translation without change. For its basis, see the above-mentioned work.

1   Come down! sit in the dust, you virgin daughter of Babylon!
    Sit on the ground without a throne, O daughter of the Chaldeans!
    For you are no more called the tender, the delicate one.
2   Take the millstones, grind fine meal! Away with your veil!
    Strip off your train, bare your thigh, pass only through rivers!
3   I take vengeance inexorable, says our Redeemer,
4   Yahweh of hosts is his name, the Holy One of Israel.

5 Sit in silence and go into the darkness,	O daughter of the Chaldeans.
For you are no more called	the mistress of the kingdoms.
6 I was greatly wroth with my people,	I abandoned my heritage,
gave them into your hand,	you showed them no mercy.
Heavily you laid on the aged	your hard yoke.
7 You said, 'I am for ever	mistress for ever!'
You did not lay this to heart	did not think of the end.
8 And now: hear this, you lover of pleasures	who dwell securely,
Who say in your heart,	'I, and there is none besides me!
I do not sit as a widow, and I	know nothing of childlessness!'

9 These two things shall come to you in a moment and in one day!
Childlessness and widowhood in full measure come upon you,
however mighty your sorceries be, however many your enchantments.

10 But you trusted in your wickedness, you said, 'No one sees me':

Behold your wisdom and your knowledge led you astray.
You said in your heart, 'I, and there is none beside me'.
11 Now evil comes upon you, you know of no sorcery.
Terror falls upon you, your boldness is gone from you.
All of a sudden there comes upon you ruin of which you know nothing.
12 Yet, stand fast in your incantations, your many enchantments.
Perhaps you may be able to bring yourself help, perhaps you inspire terror—

13 Those who mark out the heavens[a] will help you, those who gaze at the stars,
who month by month tell you whence it comes.
14 Behold, they are like stubble, so that fire consumes them.
They do not deliver themselves from the power of the flame.
15 Such have your sorcerers become for you, who have been your care from your youth.

They reel one against the other, none helps you.

First, the structure of the poem:

1–4 First strophe: Come down into the dust!
   1–2 Orders for Babylon's abasement
   3–4 Substantiation: Yahweh's retribution
5–7 Second strophe: the charge: ruthlessness
   5 Go into the dark!—loss of dominion
   6 God gave Israel into the hand of Babylon. She showed no pity
   7 Babylon boasted that she would be mistress for ever
8–9 Third strophe: the proclamation: childlessness and widowhood
   8 A summons to hear, expanded: Babylon's presumptuousness

[a] E. Ullendorf, 'Ugaritica Marginalia II', *JSS* (1962), pp. 339–51; J. Blau, *VT*, vii (1957), pp. 183f., both translate 'worshippers of heaven'.

9   Proclamation: childlessness and widowhood come upon
     you
9b   in spite of all your sorceries and enchantments
10–12 Fourth strophe: Disaster comes in spite of all Babylon's wisdom
   10   Babylon relied on her wisdom and her knowledge
   11   In spite of it, ruin suddenly comes upon her
   12   Defence by means of incantations and enchantments is
        of no help
13–15 Fifth strophe: Babylon's wise men and scholars perish along
     with her
   13   Her astrologers ought to help Babylon
   14   They perish along with her in the conflagration of the
        empire
   15   The sorcerers are of no help, they perish themselves

Chapter 47 is unique among Deutero-Isaiah's utterances. While
there can be no doubt that the prophet himself is its author, its
literary form occurs nowhere else in the book. In itself the fact that
the chapter contains about forty words not found elsewhere in
Deutero-Isaiah (C. R. North) shows its special character. Duhm
designates it as a triumph song, and Muilenburg as a mocking song.
While both descriptions suit some of the features found in the poem,
they do not suit its literary category. Chapter 47 is the one poem in
Deutero-Isaiah that falls into the category of oracles against foreign
nations. Such oracles, spoken against foreign nations hostile to Israel,
constitute a main form of prophecy of salvation, and are found from
the earliest days of the monarchy (with roots even further back in
time) right down until, in the post-exilic period, they pass over into
apocalyptic. Here in ch. 47, then, Deutero-Isaiah speaks as a prophet
of salvation, using the language of prophecy of salvation in the traditional sense of that term. The chapter forms one of the many oracles
against Babylon handed on to us in other prophetic books, the
majority being anonymous prophecy which have been added to other
collections of oracles. Among them are Isa. 13 and 14, and the
oracles against Babylon collected in Jer. 50–51. These have many
points of contact with ch. 47, but they also show considerable divergencies from it. It is only when ch. 47 is set against the background
of these numerous oracles against Babylon that its own peculiar
features stand out. Even when he uses this traditional form, prophecy
of salvation, the word which Deutero-Isaiah speaks is his own particular word, part and parcel of his prophecy viewed in its entirety.

What renders this all the more noteworthy is the fact that, as shown by the numerous oracles against Babylon that have been preserved, Deutero-Isaiah was far from being alone in proclaiming the fall of Babylon as such; many contemporary prophets of whom we know nothing were doing the same. Once it is realized that ch. 47 is one among numerous oracles against Babylon, it also becomes clear that this is genuine proclamation, and therefore, exactly like 46.1–2, delivered before the fall of Babylon. For this reason designations such as 'triumph song' or 'mocking song' are unsuitable. The imperatives with which it begins, 'come down', 'sit in the dust', 'go into the darkness', etc., presuppose that what is proclaimed has already been fulfilled, and they describe its consequences. Thus, from the first verse to the last the prophet speaks of an event which has still to come to pass: he proclaims the fall of the Babylonian empire.

The structure of the poem also agrees with this. The lengthy description of the collapse of the empire, in which Babylon is personified, reveals the elements of the prophetic word which constitute the skeleton of the poem: the prophetic word of doom has its two usual parts, a substantiation (the charge and its elaboration), and a proclamation of doom (God's intervention and its consequences). The introduction to the proclamation of doom ('thus says Yahweh') comes at the end of the first strophe, in v. 4 (taking along with it the last word of v. 3, which should be emended into '*āmar*). The thing proclaimed itself is contained in the words preceding '*āmar*, 'I take vengeance inexorable'; Yahweh proclaims that he is to intervene. Then, as is so characteristic of Deutero-Isaiah, this part is expanded by a series of imperatives, the closest parallel to which is the diametrically opposite kind of imperative addressed to Israel in 51.9–52.2. The consequences of God's intervention form part of its proclamation, though these are not stated until the third strophe (vv. 8f.): childlessness and widowhood. As is frequent with prophetic oracles of doom, this section (beginning at v. 8) is introduced by the words, 'but now' and a command to hear. This is a slight, but quite certain, proof that it has the diction of the prophetic oracle of doom as its basis. In the second strophe (vv. 5ff.), v. 5 continues the imperatives of vv. 1f. This is followed, in v. 6, by the first of the two substantiations, the ruthless treatment meted out to the exiles. The other substantiation is Babylon's presumptuous self-assurance, given in vv. 7–8 (this introduces the proclamation of doom) and v. 10. In the fourth and fifth strophes (vv. 10ff. and 13ff.) this motif, Babylon's presumptuous self-assurance, is united with another often found in a proclamation of doom, namely, that the doom is inevitable, and that there is no evading of it. This Deutero-Isaiah here took up; the vast religious and intellectual means of security at Babylon's disposal through her cult, her magic, and her mantic are to be of no help to her: they are all to be caught up into her downfall.

[1–4] Strophe (1). The poetic force displayed in the proclamation of Babylon's fall is quite extraordinary. In this chapter, Deutero-Isaiah speaks in a form of discourse traditional to prophecy, whose skeleton, as we have just seen, can be clearly recognized. Yet we are at once aware how, out of this, his poetic genius shapes a little drama whose verve makes it into more than just proclamation by a prophet: it is, in fact, a prophetic poem. In the first strophe this effect is achieved by means of the series of imperatives, which are spoken to a person, the virgin Babylon (Israel is often similarly personified in the pre-exilic prophets of doom, e.g. Amos 5.1f.), and by the terse, abrupt and rough orders for Babylon's humiliation, which so vividly conjure up the harsh reality that awaits the lady of high degree once she is humbled and reduced to slavery. Her coming down from her throne into the dust is paralleled in the Ugaritic *Baal and Anath*:

Thereupon Ltpn, God of Mercy,
Goes down from the throne,   Sits on the footstool,
and from the footstool sits on the earth.[a]

Thus, the opening words of the poem depict the humiliation of Babylon in terms of movement, a human figure moving directly before our eyes, and it is this introduction which imparts the convincing sense of movement to the whole. It is also promoted by means of a contrast; she (as often, Babylon is designated as 'she') is no no longer 'the tender, the delicate one'—the terms conjure up the idea of luxury, the refinements of the court, the elegant life of care-free enjoyment—she is now a slave, brusquely ordered about and forced to do the most menial tasks. Her humiliation extends even to her dress: veil and train, the apparel denoting high rank, are torn off her; she works with her clothes tucked up, like a servant girl.

These orders for Babylon's humiliation are followed by an equally abrupt 'I' (God). For the factors which bring about Babylon's fall into the depths are the word and will of the 'Holy One of Israel'. To get some idea of the audacity of what is said here, we need to realize just how quite fantastic it is for vv. 3f. to follow immediately upon the orders for Babylon's humiliation—the vanquished God of a petty,

[a] Cyrus H. Gordon, *Ugaritic Literature*, Rome, 1949, p. 42.

vanquished nation takes vengeance on the mighty colossus Babylon! The prophet's audacity is the product of what God stands for in his eyes, and this is stated in v. 4, the only one in ch. 47 which is found in identical terms elsewhere in Deutero-Isaiah: the two poles in the divine being as represented by the words, 'our redeemer . . . the Holy One of Israel'. His addition here of 'Yahweh of hosts' is deliberate; he was thinking of the importance attaching to the heavenly bodies in Babylon (v. 13); but they are no more than the creatures of God, who obey his command (40.26).

[5–7] Strophe (2). The movement from the exalted throne down to the dust at the beginning of the first strophe is now followed by the other, Babylon's translation from the glory and blare of world-dominion to silence and darkness—what a description of an historical event! And now into the silence and the darkness come the words that substantiate her fate. It should be noted that the charge brought against her is not that of destroying the kingdom of Judah, carrying off its king, and razing the temple to the ground. This is the substantiation of God's wrath against Babylon given in other similar oracles. Here a totally different theology is propounded. It was God himself who delivered his own people into the hands of Babylon! (Similarly in 43.28, and also Jer. 27.6.) The charge is therefore simply an offence against common humanity—her treatment of those whom she took captive. The hard fate which overtook the aged is also mentioned in Lam. 1.19; 2.21; 5.12, but these certainly must represent isolated cases. In general, the treatment meted out to the exiles in Babylon was not particularly cruel. For v. 7, too, shows that the treatment is to be taken as indicative of a general attitude; this is the thing upon which the whole emphasis is put in the charge, 'You said, "I am for ever mistress, for ever." ' It is Babylon's attitude of arrogant self-assurance that is the real object of the divine chastisement. And yet: it is here cast in the teeth of the Babylonian empire and its rulers that they did not lay 'this' (v. 7a) to heart and did not think of the end, that is, that the Babylonian mastery might come to an end. But is this not naïve and absolutely unrealistic? This is the gist of Duhm's comment on the verse. But there is more to it than that. During the entire period of the monarchy Israel had constantly to listen to one man or another proclaiming the divine word that she might cease to exist as a nation. Even the promise to the house of David was not absolute. And the parenesis in Deuteronomy is very emphatic in making clear that for Israel her statehood was a gift which might be taken away again. In the light of all this, the charge here brought against Babylon—the same as that alleged against the Assyrian empire in Hab. 2—is to be taken quite seriously: for Israel, any attempt to perpetuate power, or render it absolute, was blasphemy.

[8–9] Strophe (3). The proclamation which begins in v. 9 is prefaced by the words, 'And now: hear this.' In their expansion, the address to Babylon, the charge made in v. 7 is again taken up. This, too—the development of the charge by means of citation—is a feature of the prophetic proclamation of doom. The one made here and repeated in v. 10b as 'I, and there is none besides me', the declaration of the way in which Babylon regarded herself, excellently expresses our political term absolutism. (The same claim is made in Zeph. 2.15.) In opposition to any doctrine of two kingdoms which is neutral towards the way in which the terrestrial power regards itself, the passage here condemns power which regards itself as absolute.

Now comes the proclamation of doom. The result of God's intervention (v. 3) is childlessness and widowhood, cf. Israel's lament in 54.1–6: 'the two greatest evils that can befall a woman', they signify 'unprotectedness and loneliness' (Duhm). They befall the one who had been quite certain that this could never happen to her. Verse 9 adds the motif which becomes the dominant note in the two following strophes; God's judgment spells the complete breakdown of all Babylon's intellectual ascendancy and of her science.

[10–12] Strophe (4). Not one of the many other oracles against Babylon has as its subject what is Deutero-Isaiah's here, the intellectual resources at Babylon's disposal. The prophet had keenly observed it all, and, as we may see, taken it with the utmost seriousness. There is absolutely no suggestion of mockery. Rather—and for the time this was a magnificent achievement—he saw the connection between Babylon's absolute power and her intellectual eminence:

Your wisdom and your knowledge led you astray,
so that you said in your heart, 'I, and no other!' (Duhm's translation)

This is probably the first occasion in world-history when the way of making power absolute was not conceived in material terms such as armies, armaments, and financial resources, but in terms of the intellectual substructures of power. The literature of the neo-Babylonian empire furnishes us with enough knowledge of the diversity and profusion of Mesopotamia's intellectual and religious life during the period to let us to understand this. Deutero-Isaiah mentions sorceries, enchantments, expiatory rites, and astrology. Nowadays we are prejudiced against all this, and our prejudice also involves criticism of Deutero-Isaiah. Leaving this aside, however, the extant documents from Mesopotamia give us some idea of the immense intellectual efforts expended both to influence the present by means of a plethora of magical formulae, and to safeguard the future, or control it for one's own advantage, by means of a whole body of knowledge devoted to prediction, and, in particular, to astrology. As we know, the widespread preoccupation with astrology also led to a very considerable knowledge of astronomy.

The two main uses to which these practices and sciences were put are named in v. 12b—help and defence. We must realize that the roles played in the enlightened world of today by science and technology had a kind of prelude in the later developments of the great religions. The simple cultic forms such as sacrifice, prayer, the giving of oracles, and proclamation, assumed exaggerated forms in which the entire emphasis was concentrated on such branches of knowledge and such practices as furthered or safeguarded existence. This is the way in which we should view the cultic magic and the traffic in prediction in the late forms of Babylonian religion and elsewhere.

[13–15] Strophe (5). Finally Deutero-Isaiah mentions astrology, which was of course exceptionally important in Babylon. The words, 'you who divide the heavens' refer to the houses into which the heavens are divided by the constellations—in this matter our present-day astrologers remain the heirs of the Babylonian astronomers—and, as still happens, some periods were foretold as favourable, others as unfavourable: 'who month by month tell you'. In practice this worked out as follows:

When Mars approaches the moon and stands, the moon will cause evil to inhabit the land. When a planet stands at the left horn of the moon, the king will act mightily. When Virgo stands at its left horn, in that year the vegetables of Akkad will prosper. . . . On the fourteenth an eclipse will take place; it is evil for Elam and Akhanu, lucky for the king, my lord; let the king, my lord, rest happy . . .ᵃ

The two final verses (14.15) again have very much the ring of the pre-exilic prophets' oracles of doom. As there, fire is a metaphor for God's chastisement and destruction; as there, those whom these overtake are 'as stubble'. The conclusion let us see very clearly how

ᵃ Given in G. E. Wright, *The Old Testament against its Environment*, SBT, 4, London, 1950, p. 81.

seriously the prophet took Babylon's intellectual and cultic methods of safeguarding her existence. There is no word of sarcasm or jeering. Instead, he indicates the tragic element in her complete breakdown: what fails in the hour of disaster is the wisdom and scientific knowledge elaborated in the course of a long and glorious history ('from your youth'). 'They do not deliver themselves'—Deutero-Isaiah uses similar terms of idols in 46.1ff.—and, without being able to help the empire in its collapse, 'they stagger into one another'.

CHAPTER 48.1–11

The Former Things and the New

1 Hear this, O house of Jacob, who are called by the name of Israel,
who came forth from the body (? from the loins) of Judah,
who swear by the name of Yahweh,
and confess the God of Israel
but not in truth or righteousness;
2 for they call themselves after the holy city
and stay themselves on the God of Israel,
Yahweh of hosts is his name:

3 The former things I declared of old.
They went forth from my mouth, I made them known.
Suddenly I did them and they came to pass.
4 Because I knew that you are obstinate,
and your neck an iron sinew,
and your forehead brass.
5 From of old I declared them to you,
before they came to pass I announced them to you,
lest you should say, 'My idol has done them,
my graven image and my molten image commanded them'.
6 You have heard all [this];[a]
must you not yourself [attest][b] it?
From this time forth I make you hear new things,
hidden things which you have not known.
7 They are created now, not long ago,
and before [his day][c] you have not heard of them,
lest you should say, 'Behold, I knew them.'

[a] Read *hazzeh* instead of *hazzōʾt*.
[b] Read *tāʿīdū*. [c] Read *lipnē yōmō lō*.

8   You have never heard, you have never known,
     hitherto your ear was never opened;
          for I knew that you were altogether faithless,
          and that from birth you were called a rebel.
9   For my name's sake
          I defer my anger.
          And for the sake of my praise
          I spare you and destroy you not.
10   Behold, I refine you [as]ᵃ silver,
          I [try]ᵇ you in the furnace of affliction.
11 For my own sake, for my own sake, I do it [ ],ᶜ
     and I give my glory to no other.
          For how it would be profaned!

There are more difficulties than usual here, and so far editors have not succeeded in finding any convincing solution. The chief of them is not actually the fact that 'here Deutero-Isaiah, the prophet of consolation, speaks in unusually harsh tones, much harsher than, for example, in 43.23ff., and 42.18ff.' (Volz, repeated almost word for word by C. R. North in his recent commentary). These words harshly accusing Israel occur in an utterance in which they seem to have no place—this is the real difficulty. As I made clear in my essay on Deutero-Isaiah,ᵈ the three passages, 46.3–13, 48.1–11 and 48.12–16, all show the same general pattern. Common to all are (1) a summons to hear along with an address to Israel, (2) God makes a proclamation and gives effect to it, (3) the calling of Cyrus. In 48.1–11 this general pattern is worked out as follows: The summons to hear along with the address to Israel (v. 1) is expanded (vv. 1–2) in seven clauses, appositions to Israel. The utterance announced in v. 1a begins in v. 3 and continues until v. 11. There is a clear division into two parts. Verses 3–6a: the former things I declared to you and they came to pass, as Israel herself is bound to admit; vv. 6b–11: now I announce new things of which you have never before heard, and I am on the point of bringing them to pass. This I do for my honour's sake. But the utterance announced in vv. 1f. does not end here. It is continued in vv. 12–16 and, at the end of the chapter (48.20–21), issues in the summons to depart from Babylon.

What does this utterance mean, and what end does it serve? The

ᵃ Instead of *wᵉlō bᵉ* read *kᵉ*.
ᵇ Read *bᵉḥantīkā*.
ᶜ Perhaps *kī 'ēk yēḥal* is a gloss?
ᵈ 'Sprache und Struktur', p. 155.

argument used in the trial speeches against the other gods, the reliable connection between what God proclaims and what he performs, is here spoken to Israel, the purpose being to give her confidence in the new proclamation and in its fulfilment. Verses 20f. leave no doubt about the end which the utterance is designed to serve. Its purpose is to help Israel to step out on the way home.

These sentiments cannot possibly be reconciled with the harsh charge brought against Israel in vv. 1 (the last clause), 4, 5b, 7b, and 8–10b. The latter can never have been uttered in order to strengthen Israel's confidence that the fresh action of God now proclaimed served for her salvation and was leading to her release. Their *raison d'être* is quite different—it is the purpose of preaching judgment or repentance. Had the whole of 48.1–11 been intended as preaching of repentance or judgment, this would put a very different complexion on the question of its authorship. What makes it certain that the speaker here is someone other than Deutero-Isaiah is the fact that, when the words of accusation are omitted, 48.1–11 form a well-constructed utterance meant to serve a different purpose. To assume different authorship renders both the prophet's utterance and that of the other speaker more lucid and straightforward.[a]

[1–2] 48.1f. is a particularly emphatic address with numerous appositions, and is of the kind used by Deutero-Isaiah to introduce passages of some length or of particular importance, e.g. 44.24–28 and 46.3f. Here 48.1f. introduces the entire chapter, which issues in the call to go forth from Babylon, vv. 20f. As in 43.3f., the appositions in the chapter all refer to Israel, and this is in keeping with its purpose, which is to make clear to *Israel* that God's fresh action is designed for her salvation. The people addressed are the 'house of Jacob'. Strictly speaking, this means Jacob's own family. This is then explained in the first two appositions—those who bear the name of the patriarch Jacob and are descended from Judah. This indicates the first basis upon which the history of Israel rests—that solidarity, initiated by the blessing, which reaches back beyond the clans (north and south) to unite the generation now alive with the patriarchs who had received the promise of a future for the chosen people. The further appositions all refer to the other basis of Israel's history—her worship. The following acts of worship are mentioned: 'swearing by

---

[a] I have given more detailed reasons for my view in 'Jesaja 48 und die "Bezeugung gegen Israel" ', *Studia Biblica et Semitica Theodoro Christiano Vriezen Dedicata*, eds., W. C. van Unnik and A. S. van der Woude, Wageningen, 1966, pp. 356–66.

Yahweh', the confirmation of something by appeal to God as judge; 'remembering', or appealing to, God, in particular remembering his acts in praise, the focal point being the holy city, to which they are designated as belonging; 'they stay themselves on the God of Israel', which is a way of describing the 'confession of trust', the central part of supplication. Very significantly, the only aspect of worship here mentioned by the prophet is its spoken element. This agrees with Deutero-Isaiah's regular practice in his proclamation of making use of this spoken element in worship, in particular of the psalms of lamentation and of praise as well as of the oracle of salvation. On the other hand, consider his judgment on Israel's sacrificial worship in 43.22–28. Here, therefore, the prophet regards Israel's converse with God throughout her history as a continuing factor which, from the human angle, sustained that history.

At its end v. 1 has the addition, 'not in truth or righteousness'. These are the first words of the added matter which runs from here onward through the entire passage. As comparison with the appositions in 46.3–4 or 44.24–28 makes clear, a sudden interruption by a negative statement is completely out of harmony with the purpose which these introductory appositions are meant to serve. As regards content, too, it is quite certain that Deutero-Isaiah had no intention of judging one of the two bases of Israel's history negatively (from the human angle, cf. for the divine, 46.3f.).

[3] Because of her history Israel knows well the mutual relationship between God's word and his act. There might be a very long lapse of time between the proclamation and its fulfilment. Then God would act all of a sudden, and the thing proclaimed would come to pass. That is to say, the matter of fulfilment rested entirely with God; as well as the proclamation there was a separate and independent event which could not possibly be deduced from the proclamation.

[5] Verse 5 emphasizes the other side of this. A proclamation, too, made a long time before had an independent significance. On the basis of the word communicated to her, Israel could prepare herself for something that would come.

[6a] Verse 6a forms the conclusion of this section. It gives a particularly clear indication of the purpose of the utterance. Deutero-Isaiah strives to make his hearers understand. 'You have heard all this. Must you not yourselves admit it?' For when they see and acknowledge how God's word and his act were united in their history, and how the latter was the product of that unity, then they

will also be able to see the fresh and entirely different proclamation in the context of this. Thus, what Deutero-Isaiah takes up and re-directs to Israel herself in v. 6a is the very office of witness-bearing which she had in the trial speeches.

[4, 5b] This section (vv. 3–6a), too, has the harsh charges against Israel appended. The reason given in v. 4 for God's declaring of the former things and bringing them to pass (v. 3) is Israel's obstinacy. But if we narrow it down and ask how this can be so, we run into difficulties. This kind of reason is not in place in Deutero-Isaiah. This is the language of charges against Israel such as we find in Ex. 32.9; Deut. 9.6, 27; Jer. 3.3; Ezek. 3.7. The terms here used are very closely reminiscent of Ezekiel (v. 8b). In v. 5b the clause added is a final clause, 'lest . . .'. This again makes a bad link with what precedes (v. 5a). (Duhm pointed this out both in the case of the present addition and the others.) The real purpose of the addition is simply accusation as such, in the present case, the charge of idolatry.

[8b–10] Here again a charge is appended. As Duhm noticed, every single part of the utterance has an accusation appended, almost as it were by way of commentary. Again it denotes purpose, at all events in v. 8b. Once more, v. 8b cannot properly give the reason for v. 8a. The charges are loosely added, and v. 8b represents the most comprehensive and radical of them all, being very reminiscent of Ezek. 16 and 23; cf. 43.27. The statement there made, 'your first father sinned' (43.27), is similar; Israel's sin is carried back to her earliest days. In ch. 43, however, the words serve to give the reason for the punishment which God had been forced to bring upon Israel (43.28). But this was not the final word, for God had now blotted out this sin (43.25), and this had transformed the whole situation. The case is completely different in 48.8b–10. Here Israel's sinfulness is a permanent state (8b). She deserved to be cut off (9b). But for his name's sake God defers his anger (9a), and the judgment which he brings upon her is only a refining (10).

[11] The words, 'I do it', relate to 'they are created' in v. 7, that is to say, the fresh act only now proclaimed, on which vv. 12–16 are to comment. God's honour, which he does not give to another, is involved in the act he now does, which is an intervention in world-history on his chosen people's behalf that is without precedent. The brief insertion in v. 11, 'for how should it (the name) be profaned', is one of the charges. As Duhm supposed, it may indicate that vv. 9f. were originally an addition to v. 11 and ought properly to follow it.

A final note on the connection between the charges and what Deutero-Isaiah himself says here: As we know from Trito-Isaiah, the message of salvation and nothing but salvation which Deutero-Isaiah had been commissioned to declare and which Trito-Isaiah also proclaimed had additions made to it after the return in the shape of admonitions, reprimands and oracles of doom. The writer who expanded 48.1–11 is connected with this process. In his day it seemed no longer possible to proclaim salvation and nothing but salvation. At the same time he wished to preserve and transmit Deutero-Isaiah's message. He therefore added charges against Israel. Just as chs. 56–66 with their many charges and censures were appended to the message of Deutero-Israel which ended at ch. 55, so 48.1–11, one single utterance of the latter's, had an accusation added to and inserted into it. In this connection, the words 'genuine' and 'spurious' are beside the mark. Their use is false to the facts and obscures them. But it is important for Deutero-Isaiah's message that, while he can and does make a charge against *pre-exilic* Israel (43.22–28), the time at which he himself had to preach was entirely under the aegis of God's word of forgiveness (40.2; 43.25). This is the reason why his message is salvation and nothing but salvation.

CHAPTER 48.12–17

I called you

12 Hearken to me, O Jacob, [my servant],[a]
and Israel, whom I called.
I am He, I am the first, and I am also the last.
13 My hand laid the foundation of the earth,
my right hand spread out the heavens,
when I call to them   they stand forth together.

14 Assemble, all of you, and hear!
Who among them has declared these things?
Yahweh loves him, he performs his purpose
on Babylon and on the [seed][b] of the Chaldeans.

[a] Add with some MSS. *'abdī*.
[b] Read *ūbᵉzeraʿ*.

15   I, even I, have spoken, and also called him.
     I have brought him, and [make]ᵃ his way prosper.
16c   But now, the Lord Yahweh has sent me and his spirit . . .

16a Draw near to me, hear this;
17a Thus says Yahweh, your Redeemer, the Holy One of Israel:ᵇ
16b From the beginning I have not spoken in secret,
     from the time it came into being I have been there.
17b I, Yahweh, am your God, who teaches you to profit,
     who makes for you the way in which you should go.

In this part of the chapter, too, there are serious textual difficulties, although they only appear towards the end. The summons which comes at the beginning, 'Hearken to me, O Jacob', carries on that of v. 1. The proclamation, 'from this time forth I make you hear new things', is explained at greater length in vv. 12–17. Here the affinity with the trial speeches is even more marked than it was in vv. 1–11— witness in particular the various summonses in vv. 14 and 16a to assemble for a trial. At the same time, there is an obvious difference. The arguments which God had adduced in the legal process with the nations in support of his divinity—that he was the first and the last, that he was the creator, as well as the connection between proclamation and fulfilment, and the calling of Cyrus—he now addresses to Israel, who were then his witnesses. Why does he do this? In order that she may recognize and understand that he is at work, at work both in his prophet's proclamation and in contemporary history. Verses 12f. are introductory. Self-predication on God's part expands the summons (cf. 44.24ff.). He speaks to Israel as the one who is everlasting (v. 12b), and as the creator (v. 13). As creator, he is the lord of history (vv. 14f.). He is the only one of the gods (v. 14a) who proclaimed what Cyrus was to accomplish (v. 14b). He makes Cyrus perform his work (vv. 14f.) and grants him success in it. But this whole thing is done for the sake of Israel. Thus, in the second part, which is introduced in the same way as the first (v. 16a), what the latter says of God, that he is the creator and the lord of history, is now supplemented by his being called the redeemer (v. 17a; as in 44.24ff., we can once again see that the basic structure is that found in descriptive praise). From the beginning he had not spoken in secret (v. 16b). And now the event attests that he had been present (v. 16b). And through-

---

ᵃ With the Vss. read *wā'aṣlīaḥ*.
ᵇ Read 17a between 16a and 16b.

out he has acted in order to benefit Israel and prepare the way for her
(v. 17b). On this way the conclusion of the whole section (vv. 20f.)
summons Israel to set out.

[12f.] The summons to Israel, God's servant, the one whom he
called, to hear, links on to v. 1, and is at once followed by self-
predications on God's part. The terminology is the same as in the trial
speeches, but, addressed as it here is to Israel, its purpose is to exalt
God in his chosen people's eyes, abased as Israel then was. He is the
everlasting God, and creator of heaven and earth. His people have
been overthrown, but he who now appeals to them is the one who
at the beginning called heaven and earth into being. Here, at a date
earlier than P, we meet with the concept of creation by the word.
Thus it is earlier than Gen. 1, or else, in this respect, too, Gen. 1 is
based on an older tradition.

[14] The words 'who among them' can only refer to the gods of
the nations. Omit the emphatic address to Israel, and all four verses
(12–15) could be part of a trial speech. In explicitly repeating to his
own nation what had had to be said against the foreign nations and
their gods, Deutero-Isaiah's purpose was so to impress them with
God's sovereign power that they would regain confidence. They are
oppressed. They have been made insignificant. They are without
prospects. Yet, this is the very moment at which God proves himself
to be the everlasting one, and the creator and lord of the universe.
The thing, however, to which they can hold fast, and which can tell
them something of the immense compass of his actions in history, is
his word. The drama now being enacted before their eyes on the
stage of history had been proclaimed to them beforehand. The words
'Yahweh loves him, he does his will' are textually uncertain. Many
editors change into the first person: 'my loved one (he whom I love)
performs my will.' This would suit the context very much better. But
even if the break into the third person is kept, the meaning is still
clear. God's 'loving' Cyrus is a variant of the other terms which
express his relationship to him, 'my shepherd', 'my anointed', 'the
man who fulfils my purpose'. All these designations are simply meant
to express the fact that God is with Cyrus, the fact which the Israelites
found so incomprehensible and offensive. All of them allude only to
the non-recurrent and limited function which Cyrus has in God's plan
with his chosen people, and through them with the world.

[15] The emphatic 'I' standing at the beginning of v. 15 and continuing throughout it (cf. vv. 12f.) means this: 'It is I, the God who

is known to you, of whom you have had experience, who am at work here, even if this fresh work does shatter an old concept of the old God.'

[16f.] The second part goes on to relate this fresh act to Israel's history, her way. It begins in the same way as v. 14a, which shows that the two parts are clearly connected in form as well as content. God speaks now as Israel's redeemer, who has used his sovereign power on his people's behalf. The theme of the first part (vv. 14f.) had been his speech and his action, and how these went together, and v. 16b goes on to relate this specifically to Israel. From the beginning God had not spoken to her 'in secret', which means that the preceding proclamation may be attested. 'Ever since the prophecies became reality, "he has been there"; that is to say . . . he has shown himself to be the one with the power to give prophecies their fulfilment.'[a] But the point for Israel is, 'I, Yahweh, am your God.' And he is this in that he 'teaches her to profit'. The terms are too general for any certain interpretation, but the meaning probably is that in this fresh act Israel is experiencing an entirely new way in which God can help her. It is only the final words of the utterance, 'I am your God . . . who makes for you the way in which you should go,' that reveal its objective. The *hiph'il* of *dārak* properly means 'to make solid by treading', and so 'to make a way'. This is the same preparing of the way as is spoken of in the prologue (40.3f.). It is the way by which the people are to travel home, and upon which the hymn which ends this chapter summons them to set foot.

Chapter 48 makes one feature of Deutero-Isaiah's theology particularly clear. The reason why God's action with his chosen people, which finally emerges as the point of the chapter (vv. 16f.), is set within the wide horizon of his work as creator is that Israel must be brought to see that one part of her traditional concept of God is now shattered. God's being with Israel, as shown in the fact that he prepares the way home for her, must cease to be construed as 'opposition' in principle to the other nations. Instead, God can prepare the way for his people by granting a foreign nation and a heathen king success. The reason why Deutero-Isaiah reiterates this part of his message is the difficulty of breaking down a tradition of Israel's faith which was antagonistic to it.

As was stated above, at the end of the chapter there are disturbances in the text. The text as here translated and commented on

<hr />

[a] Elliger, *op. cit.*, p. 215.

was arrived at by omitting part of a verse (16c) and transposing v. 17a to come between vv. 16a and 16b. No emendation is necessary. The text adopted assumes that v. 16a, a small fragment, and vv. 18–19, which form a unit, are later additions.

[16c] Editors are unanimous that the words, 'The Lord Yahweh has sent me his spirit . . .' (the verb is lacking), cannot possibly be explained in their present context. At the same time, they are not an addition to vv. 12–17. They represent a fragment similar to 61.1 which has found a place here. The speaker is someone who is certain that he has been sent by God and endowed with his spirit. Precisely the same sentiments are expressed in the Servant Song in 49.1–6, which suggests that the words may have been added in the margin at 49.1b (perhaps by Trito-Isaiah, as Elliger supposes), and were then inserted into the text at a wrong place. At the same time, to begin with, they may conceivably have formed part of 49.1–6.

CHAPTER 48.18–19

Then your peace would be like a river

18   O that you would hearken to my commandments!
     Then your peace would be like a river,
     and your salvation like the waves of the sea.
19   Your offspring would be like the sand,
     and your descendants like its grains;
     their name would never be cut off
     or destroyed from before me.

This is a wish incorporating an admonition to keep God's commandments and drawn up in the familiar conditional style. The utterance has a remarkably close parallel in Ps. 81. In addition, as Elliger has shown, there are reminiscences of Trito-Isaiah. Ps. 81.14 (13) contains the same wish as here: 'O that my people would listen to me, that Israel would walk in my ways', which is followed, again as here, by a contingent promise of blessing: 'Your happiness would last for ever. I wished to feed you . . . and satisfy you.' Now, if we look at the context in which these words occur in the psalm, we find, to our surprise, that the oracle of salvation suggested in vv. 6b–8 (5b–7)—it is in answer to a community lament, the psalm preceding—is followed (v. 9 [8]) by a new section, 'Hear, O my people, I will admonish you.' The admonition thus introduced is built up as follows: vv. 10f. (9f.) confront Israel with the first commandment, in terms almost identical with those of the Decalogue. This is followed, in v. 12 (11), by the charge, 'But my people did not listen to me.' Then comes the divine judgment (v. 12 [11]), and, finally (vv. 14–17 [13–16]), the wish with its admonition. This admonitory passage following upon the oracle of salvation contains the same component parts as do the additions throughout ch. 48. Psalm 81 undoubtedly reflects an act of worship. To an oracle of salvation given to the community at worship is added an admonition—no doubt by a cult prophet. This furnishes an excellent explanation of the additions in ch. 48. As in Ps. 81, Deutero-Isaiah's words, which spoke solely of salvation (cf. the oracle of salvation in the Psalm) have been supplemented by an admonition delivered as an act of worship. We should therefore regard the additions in ch. 48 as evidence of the fact that, very shortly after they were first uttered, Deutero-Isaiah's words were read in the post-exilic community's services of worship.

CHAPTER 48.20–21

Go forth from Babylon

20 Go forth from Babylon!   Flee from the Chaldeans!
    Declare this with a shout of joy,
    proclaim it,
    send it forth to the end of the earth, say:
    Yahweh has redeemed   his servant Jacob.
21 He leads them through deserts   but they thirst not.
    Water from rocks   he makes flow for them,
    He cleaves the rock   and the waters gush out.

There is no peace, says Yahweh, for the wicked.

The section composed of chs. 46–48 is rounded off by this hymn of jubilation. It is at one and the same time a summons to go forth from Babylon and a call to extol the act of God whereby he redeemed his chosen people. Both anticipate the actual event itself. As things are there is no possibility of Israel's going forth, and as things are there is no sign of Yahweh's act of redemption. Nevertheless, the strains of jubilation at both are to be raised right away, in order that the prophet's word of salvation (a promise of salvation in the perfect tense) may be re-echoed in the answer of the community, its responsory. Elsewhere the summons (in the imperative) to exalt and declare introduces descriptive praise of God. Here, however, the praise is declarative. God has already redeemed his people! This is a form of psalm found only in the prophecy of Deutero-Isaiah and is the product of his prophecy. It is an 'eschatological' hymn of praise, since Israel's answering exultation assumes that God's final act has already taken place.

In the Psalter, the range of those summoned to render praise tends to grow wider and wider. It is the same here; 'send it forth to the end of the earth'. God's action towards Israel is done in full view of the Gentile world. In addition, in this case the exultant praise of the redeemed is an actual way by which the nations may come to know of the act. Volz draws attention to Ps. 126.26; there, too, the praise of the redeemed is re-echoed by the wider world.

The final verse goes beyond the release and tells of how the exiles are to be cared for on the journey through the desert. This is parallel to what took place at the exodus from Egypt. The prophet does not mean the simple repetition of the events at the beginning of Israel's history. Chapter 48 itself leaves no doubt about the complete difference in this new deliverance of the nation from the exile. The meaning is, instead, that, just as at the Exodus, the miraculous deliverance is to be accompanied by miraculous guidance and care; the God who cared for and protected them then will also care for and protect them now.

The final words of v. 21 (v. 22 in English) are an addition. What makes one sure of this is the fact that they recur in 57.21 (again at the end of a chapter). They were added by a reader in whose eyes the division into the godly and the wicked was an axiom of theology, and who was anxious to prevent the wicked from claiming such words of salvation for themselves.

CHAPTER 49.1–6

The Second Servant Song

1   Listen to me, you coastlands,
    and hearken, you peoples from afar!
    Yahweh called me from the womb,
    from the body of my mother he made mention of my name,
2   he made my mouth like a sharp sword,
    in the shadow of his hand he hid me.
    He made me a polished arrow,
    in his quiver he hid me away.
3   He said to me, 'You are my servant,
    Israel, in whom I will be glorified.'

4   But I thought, I have laboured in vain,
    spent my strength for nothing and vanity;
    nevertheless my right is with Yahweh,
    and my recompense with my God.

5   But now, [thus]ᵃ says Yahweh,
    who formed me from the womb to be his servant,
    to bring Jacob back to him,
    and that Israel might be gathered [to him:]ᵇ
    (and I was precious in the eyes of Yahweh, and my God was my
       strength.)

6   [   ]ᶜ 'It is too light a thing that you should be my servant,
    to raise up the tribes of Jacob and to restore the preserved of Israel,
    therefore I make you a light to the nations,
    that my salvation may reach to the ends of the earth.'

For bibliography, see that on 42.1–4, p. 92.

The words are addressed to the foreign nations. They are built round three sentences:

ᵃ Add *kōh.*
ᵇ Read *lō* for *lo'.*
ᶜ Delete *wayyō'mer.*

Listen to me, you coastlands;
Thus says Yahweh (to me);
I make you a light to the nations.

Therefore, exposition of the song has always to remember that everything it says has reference to the nations. Its pattern as shown above (summons to hear, the messenger formula, and Yahweh's word to the speaker) is of the nature of a prophet's report about himself. However, another pattern is added. The speaker reports how there came to be the word which God now speaks to him, what went before it. Three stages of development are described:

   I   1b–3   The election, call and equipment of the Servant
  II   4   His despondency
 III   5–6   His new task.

These three stages are clearly marked off by the *waw*-adversative in v. 4 ('but I') and v. 5 ('But now'). This lets us see clearly how this servant song is constructed. The Servant declares to the nations, 'God said to me, "I make you a light to the nations." ' He explains the meaning of this in what he tells about himself. 'God called me to be his Servant that he might perform a work on behalf of his chosen people through me (vv. 1ff. and 5b, 6a). I, however, became despondent, and regarded the work as in vain (v. 4). But then—in spite of this—God extended the scope of my commission to include the Gentiles (vv. 5f.), in order that his salvation might reach to the ends of the earth.'

[1] The speaker is the one whom God pronounced to be his Servant in 42.1–4. Addressing the Gentiles, he summons them to listen to him. He has a word from God to speak to them which, while it concerns him personally, also concerns his audience—God has made him a 'light to the Gentiles'. Two main points in 42.1–4 are taken up again in 49.1–6, his installation as God's Servant and the commission that embraces the Gentiles. The two passages therefore clearly go together. The Servant's discourse begins in v. 1. He gives an account of his call (v. 1b), his equipment (v. 2), and his installation (v. 3). The account of his call in v. 1b reminds one of Jer. 1.5, a verse in the account of Jeremiah's call. This makes clear that the Servant's call approximates very closely to those of the prophets. The same terms can apply to Servant and prophet alike. As called, the Servant is called forth. His entire life is affected by the call. He is called in every part of his existence (cf. 42.1a).

[2] In 42.1–4 also, the Servant's designation (v. 1a) is followed by

his equipment (v. 1b). The earlier chapter only describes this in quite general terms, but here details are given. First of all, as v. 2 makes perfectly clear, the servant's work is a work with the word (so in 50.4 as well). This is a further point of contact between himself and the prophets. Thus, the two metaphors in vv. 2a and 2b, c must mean that God has endowed the Servant's word with the power to penetrate (a 'sharp sword') and to range far and wide ('a polished arrow'). This is exactly the same thing as is said of a prophet's word in Jer. 23.29 (cf. also Jer. 1.9f.), and, in the New Testament, of God's (Heb. 4.12; Rev. 1.16; Eph. 6.17). Now, a sword and an arrow are definitely weapons of offence. This then implies a work by means of the word that is in some sense aggressive (exactly as in Jeremiah). But these metaphors ill suit the work of Deutero-Isaiah himself.

What does the second part of v. 2 mean? Most editors (Duhm, Volz, North) take it as signifying that the servant's life fell into two parts—for a while God kept him hidden, in order afterwards to install him for his work. But, taken in this way, the parallel clauses almost defy understanding, for the second half-verse of 2a and b must one way or another give a parallel to the first half. The latter tells of the Servant's equipment. The former must have some connection with this. This view is also supported by a number of parallels in the Psalms. 'Hid' has exactly the same meaning as in Pss. 17.8; 27.5; 64.3 (2), and, in particular, in 31.21 (20): 'in the covert of thy wings (*text. emend.*) thou hidest them.' Being hid with God, 'in the shadow of his hand', forms part of the servant's equipment. The same thing was also promised to Jeremiah at his call (Jer. 1.19b).

[3] Not until v. 3 does the Servant tell the Gentiles the purpose for which he was called by God. 'God pronounced me to be his *'ebed*, his servant'. While v. 3 takes up v. 1 and is its continuation, the nuance is different. Verses 1f. bear clear traces of the call of a prophet. But never on such an occasion is a prophet given anything in the nature of a title. Verse 3 reminds us of Ps. 2.7. This suggests the call of a prophet combined in some measure with the designation of a king, as in 42.1–4. Again, in the case of a prophet, it is never said that God will be glorified in him. On the assumption that the relative pronoun in the second half of the verse refers to the Servant in the first half, the whole thing turns into a paradox that no one could ever have imagined—a servant is to glorify his master! In this case, the paradox would point to the mystery attaching to this Servant—what manner of servant is it in whom God, the lord of all lords, is able to

be glorified? This sense would also fit in very well with the whole corpus of the servant songs—in all of them the whole thing turns on the mystery attaching to this Servant. In MT, however, the word 'Israel' comes in the middle of the two half-verses. From the point of view of grammar and metre alone, it raises difficulties. But these are not the most important thing. At all events, there is no need of the word, and the verse makes good sense without it. The important thing about the question whether 'Israel' stood in the original text or whether it is a later addition is that it could in fact resolve the long-standing debate—it has been going on for centuries and even thousands of years—as to the identity of the Servant of the songs. 'The Servant is Israel'—here it is, plump and plain. Yes, but it is not so easy as this. And none of the critics who support the so-called 'collective interpretation' (the servant is Israel) has the hardihood to found on this uncertain 'Israel' in 49.3 alone. There are several weighty reasons for supposing it to be a later addition. (1) One argument, a very weak one, comes from the history of the text. 'Israel' is absent in one of the MSS. of the LXX. But it does stand in the new Isaiah MS. from the Dead Sea. Thus, the history of the text rather favours its retention. (2) Form itself is quite important here. It has been noticed that, apart from 49.3, Deutero-Isaiah never uses 'Israel' except in parallelism to 'Jacob'. (3) A feature in all the other servant songs is that the 'ebed is never given a name. (4) The greatest difficulty, however, in that the Servant whom v. 3 calls Israel is in v. 5 given a mission to Israel. This is strengthened by the fact that anyone reading the song without prejudice has no doubt that the 'I' in vv. 1ff. and v. 4 refer to a single person. How could Israel possibly say, 'from the body of my mother'? Or what is meant by Israel's mouth? 49.1–6 is one of the cases where retention of the text as handed down is actually much harder than allowing 'Israel' in v. 3 to be an addition. The reason for its addition is easy to see. 'Israel' in v. 3 is the earliest witness to the collective interpretation of the Servant, one gloss among the many that seek to interpret the text. It has justification in the fact that elsewhere and in a different context (44.23), Deutero-Isaiah can say that God is glorified in Israel.

On the other hand, the content of the two passages is rather different. The present passage does not imply straightforward self-glorification on God's part, plain for all to see in his deliverance of Israel. Here the glorification is a hidden and paradoxical one; partly because the lord's purpose is to glorify himself at the hands of his

Servant, and partly because only the opposite of glory can be discerned in the Servant, as is indicated in v. 4 here, and will be shown more clearly later, in 50.4–9 and ch. 53.

[4] The Servant now contrasts his high calling (1b–3) with the results of his efforts in its performance. In his view, it has been in vain, for nothing. This should remind us of the fact that, in the accounts of prophets' calls, God's summons is frequently followed by a disclaimer on the prophet's part (Isa. 6.5; Jer. 1.6). Here, however, what the Servant does is to give a review of his work up to date, which he can only regard as having been without result or value. The form which the words take here, 'But I thought (lit., said): in vain . . . for nothing', is the same as is found in an individual psalm of praise, Ps. 31.23 (22), 'but I said in my alarm, "I am driven far from thy sight" ' (similarly in Ps. 66.18 and Jonah 2.5). Here the man to whom deliverance has come looks back over his troubles and the effect they had upon him. He regarded himself as already lost. Deutero-Isaiah's words thus allude to the lament which he uttered when he was troubled. But, unlike the passages cited from the Psalms, the subject of Isa. 49.4 is not troubles affecting the Servant himself, but troubles concerned with his office and task. To this extent, his words reflect not the lament of an individual suppliant, as do the passages from the Psalms, but 'the lament of a mediator', as in the case of Moses, Elijah and Jeremiah. The troubles were those of one commissioned to a task and despairing of it. Nevertheless, the parallels with the Psalms put exegesis on the right track. For the speaker, v. 4 is in the past. The present is represented by vv. 5f. Verses 1ff. in their turn ante-date v. 4. The call of the Servant to an office involving the word (vv. 1b–3) is subsequently (vv. 5b and 6b) defined as an office on behalf of Israel. In the Servant's own view, this has been unsuccessful (v. 4). But he is now given a new task, the greater one of becoming a light to the Gentiles. And this implies God's approval of the earlier task on behalf of Israel which, as the Servant thought, had had no success.

Verse 4b says that something did, however, remain over when the task proved unsuccessful, his 'right' and his 'reward', by which are meant that, although men thought that his task had miscarried, God vindicated and accepted it. This indicates the divine confirmation of a work which had seemingly ended in failure. This failure has not broken the relationship between God and the Servant.

[5] Verse 5, a new word of God to the Servant, sets the new task

afoot. The word itself is not given until v. 6, v. 5 being a longish introduction to it in the shape of appositions to Yahweh. This formulation, the messenger formula as the introduction to a word, then appositions, then the word itself, is so typical of Deutero-Isaiah as to make it one of the strongest arguments in favour of his being the author of the songs. The appositions link on to vv. 1ff., and take them up. Their first words, 'who formed me from the womb', correspond to v. 1b, while the second clause, 'to bring Jacob back to him' corresponds to v. 3b. Verse 5 thus recapitulates the Servant's task up to date, and is the first mention of what is involved in it. This is then repeated in v. 6, and a conspectus of the four verbs used to describe the task up to date will repay study. Each of them has the same object, Jacob-Israel. But, as between v. 5b and v. 6, the task they describe is not precisely the same. The one in v. 6, 'to restore the preserved of Israel', could apply exactly to the work of Deutero-Isaiah himself. On the other hand, v. 5b could not. Bringing Israel back to Yahweh would be much more applicable to the words of the pre-exilic prophets. This would also suit v. 4 and give it its meaning. Its subject is the earlier prophets' lack of success in bringing Israel back to Yahweh, and it is a direct reflection of their lament. They could do no other than look on their work as having been in vain, cf. Jeremiah's laments. The proclamation of the prophets, with its restricted goal of bringing Israel back to God and its apparent unsuccess, to which the Servant looks back as he is given a new and wider task, can only be the ministry of the prophets of Israel. This interpretation is confirmed by the fact that the people to whom the prophet here speaks are the Gentiles. The new task which he proclaims and explains is on their behalf.

This is the point at which the alternatives usually proposed, an individual or a collective interpretation, prove inadequate. If there had to be a choice between them, then 49.1–6 would rule out the latter. Of course it is a single person whom God calls from his mother's womb (1b), to whose word God gives effect (2), and whom he keeps safe (2). It is a single person who had had to regard his work as a failure (4a), while at the same time knowing that God had approved it (4b). But the point at issue in connection with these various individuals is not they themselves, but their office, their ministry, their being servants. The change in the ministry described in v. 6 allows the particular servant in a series of them to be spoken of as *the* Servant, the Servant who at this moment is given a new task. If, especially in v. 6, this is contrasted with Deutero-Isaiah's ministry, this may be meant to suggest that the new era in the Servant's life, in which he becomes a light to the Gentiles, has some kind of connection with Deutero-Isaiah. It must, however, be emphasized that the whole thing is put very cryptically. On certain points there is no doubt. First, there is the proclamation of a change in the Servant's office. Its scope is extended to include the Gentile world. Secondly, this is preceded by a ministry to Israel aimed at bringing her back to God. In the Servant's own view, this part of his task was a complete failure. Nevertheless, and strange to say, God showed his approbation of his Servant by giving him a new and greater task, the purpose of which is that the servant whose work had been unsuccessful but though whom God intends to glorify himself, may bring God's salvation to the ends of the earth.

CHAPTER 49.7–12

In the day of salvation I help you

7a Thus says Yahweh, the Redeemer of Israel, his Holy One,
   To one deeply [despised],ᵃ abhorred by the nations, the servant of
      rulers [   ]ᵇ
8 ᶜIn a time of favour I answer you,
   on the day of salvation I help you
            and I form you and make you a covenant to the peoples,
   to establish the land,ᵈ
   to apportion the desolate heritages,
9 to say to the prisoners, 'Come forth',
   to those who are in darkness, 'Appear'.
   They shall feed along [all]ᵉ the ways,
   on all bare heights shall be their pasture.
10 They hunger not, nor thirst.
   Scorching and sun do not smite them.

ᵃ Instead of *libzō* read *libzūy*, so see IQ Isa.[1]
ᵇ Read 7b after v. 12. See the commentary.
ᶜ Omit 'thus says Yahweh'.
ᵈ After 'land' an adjective has probably dropped out.
ᵉ Read *'al kol dᵉrākīm*.

For he who has pity on them leads them,
he leads them to springs of water.

11 I make all mountains [   ]ᵃ a way
and my highways shall be raised up.

12 Lo, these come from afar,
and lo, these from the north and south,
and these from the land of Sᵉwēnîm.ᵇ

7b Kings see it and arise,
princes, and they prostrate themselves;
because of Yahweh, who is faithful,
the Holy One of Israel, who has chosen you.

Exegesis has to take as starting point the fact that this utterance is appended to the second servant song in the same way as 42.5–9 are to the first (42.1–4). In both cases, the addition is followed by a hymn of praise (42.10ff. and 49.13). As we have already seen, after they were appended, 42.5–9 were made to refer to the Servant. The same is true of 49.7-12, although with a certain difference. Further, there is a certain amount of verbal agreement. The words, 'and I form you and make you as a covenant to the people' (42.6) are identical with 49.8, while 42.7 is very similar to 49.9a.

Again, editors are almost unanimous that 49.7–12 contain additions, and that we have to take account of transpositions, and also omissions. Primarily, it is the words of v. 8 just quoted which are almost universally regarded as an addition. It is they which made the person whom God here addresses into the Servant. We should notice how obvious such a reinterpretation was. The attributes of the one addressed in v. 7 can be straightway transferred to the Servant, for in actual fact 53.3 also calls him 'abhorred by the nations'. In addition, in 49.6 the Servant's task is 'to raise up the tribes of Jacob'. The same verb, with the same meaning, follows immediately in the insertion (v. 8). Thus v. 8 makes the meaning and purpose of this addition abundantly clear.

The second difficulty is the new beginning made in v. 8, 'thus says Yahweh'. Its solution is both easy and certain. We have only to ask what kind of utterance has been thus later reshaped to make it into an utterance concerning the Servant. Its structure is obviously that of a proclamation of salvation (as in 41.17–20):

7a   Introduction, with indication of a community lament.

ᵃ Read *hārîm*.
ᵇ Read *sᵉwēnîm* for *sînîm*.

8a   Proclamation that God is to turn in favour.

8c–12 Proclamation of his intervention.

7b   The object—awestruck recognition by kings and princes.

This arrangement of the verses presupposes that v. 7b was the passage's original ending. Comparison with the other proclamations of salvation at once shows that v. 7b is a concluding line such as is normal in this literary category. This is the solution of the difficulty caused by the new beginning, 'thus says Yahweh', at the start of v. 8. The shifting of the ending, to come after v. 7b, obscured the fact that the divine utterance introduced in v. 7a begins with v. 8. The introduction has therefore to be repeated.

These two changes allow us to rediscover Deutero-Isaiah's original utterance. In all respects it corresponds with the rest of the proclamations of salvation, and this makes it certain that from first to last Israel is the one addressed. She is told of God's new turning towards her in favour and of the return which is contingent on this. As with most of the other proclamations of salvation, what is emphasized is the miraculous preparations for the journey home.

[7a] God speaks to his chosen people Israel, and what he says reveals the tension indicated by the two titles, 'Holy One' and 'Redeemer' (cf. on 43.3). It is not just the 'gracious God' who is at work here, but the holy God who acts with a grace that is both incomprehensible and in no sense conditioned by his gracious nature. He speaks to an oppressed ('servant of rulers') and despised nation. As often in the attributes he applies to Yahweh, Deutero-Isaiah takes up the lamentation made in the exile by his fellow-countrymen. Once again the background here is expressly words in the book of Lamentations which call God's attention to the fact that Israel has been made to do service (1.1, 3; 5.8), that she is despised (1.8b, 11), that she has become filthy (1.8; 3.45), and that she has been brought into disgrace (5.1). We have already seen that, in the case of the other proclamations of salvation, only one motif of the community lament is struck up at the beginning. Here this is the disgrace of suffering. As we see from the Psalms, in ancient Israel suffering and shame went together beyond possibility of separation in a way which we today fail to understand. Yet, this is what we must realize if we are to appreciate the radical nature of the change involved in giving a positive evaluation to the Servant's suffering, this Servant to whose suffering, too, as ch. 53 says emphatically, is attached disgrace. When the later editor who made 49.1–7 apply to the Servant gave the

latter this attribute of disgrace, he touched on a very close relationship indeed.

[8] The first words addressed to the oppressed and despised nation
are closely akin to a promise of salvation in the perfect tense—the
tense also used here. They proclaim God's turning in favour towards
the one despised. They begin with the granting of the prayer, the
answer to the nation's lament. To this the second half of the verse
adds God's help (corresponding to the prayer in its two parts). This
is then developed at length in vv. 8c–12. Corresponding to the two
verbs are the two indications of time. 'The time of favour', i.e., the
hour at which God once more turns in grace towards his people
(40.1ff.), is co-ordinate with his answering them, while the 'day of
salvation', i.e. the hour when he intervenes to deliver them, is co-
ordinate with his helping them. The emphasis thus put upon the
definite point of time, throwing it into bold relief, is entirely similar
to the prologue. The time of service is past, that of salvation is dawning. When Paul took over these words of v. 8 and used them in II
Cor. 6.2, he gave them the exact sense that they have here. On the
addition in v. 8b, cf. the commentary on 42.6.

Verse 8c is the start of the detailed development of God's intervention to deliver which continues until the end of v. 12. The term
'development' both here and in corresponding passages is to be given
its literal meaning. That is to say, the topic here is not all manner of
things connected with the intervention to deliver. This latter itself is
developed in its constituent parts. The verses result in a whole
developed according to its components. The arrangement of this
section is particularly subtle. The two clauses with infinitives, to
establish the land (v. 8c) and to free the prisoners (v. 9), are directly
dependent on the verbs in v. 8a. Their sequel can only be v. 11, since
it resumes discourse in the first person—God will prepare the way
(similarly in 40.3f.). This—'being led in the way'—is what vv. 8c and
9a had designated as the object of God's work. In vv. 9b–10b the
proclamation changes into a description of the journey home. Using
the old figure of shepherd and flock, it says of the journey home of the
released the very same thing as Ps. 23 says of the righteous man who is
protected by the good shepherd—he will not lack food and drink;
they are to be protected and led in safety. Once again and quite
obviously, the background is the Exodus at the beginning of the
nation's history. It, too, gives accounts of God's miraculous bestowal
of food and drink, and of his guidance on the way. However, the new

Exodus is to be much more miraculous in character than was this.

Since its meaning places v. 11 between vv. 9a and b, v. 10b is the end of the description. Verse 12 could possibly be an addition bringing in some other features of the journey home. But Volz and North are correct in their view that it properly goes with the motif of 'gathering the dispersed', and would therefore come more naturally after v. 18 in the next section. As long ago as 1775 Michaelis proposed to read *Sᵉwēnîm* for the last word of the verse. Numerous editors have accepted the conjecture, and it has now been confirmed by the Isaiah MS. from Qumran. Thus the reference is to the Jewish colony in Syene (Assuan) in the south of Egypt (cf. Ezek. 29.10; 30.6), which we know from the Elephantine papyri.

[7b] The concluding words of the utterance indicate the object of God's present action. The latter has an effect on the nations. Astonished and awestruck, kings and princes are to witness how a nation that had been overthrown and dispersed for years comes home again and begins anew. But what compels their awestruck attention is not this nation's vitality and toughness. It is the faithfulness of its God who, when disaster overtook it, stood by it from first to last.

CHAPTER 49.13

Sing for joy, O heavens!

Sing for joy, O heavens, and exult, O earth!
Break forth, O mountains, into singing!
For Yahweh has comforted his people,
he has compassion on his afflicted.

Here we have another of the hymns of praise that accompany Deutero-Isaiah's proclamation. God has 'comforted' his people—and here 'comfort' obviously has the meaning, as shown on 40.1, of intervention to put an end to the extremity. But this has to have a response made to it, and this not only by all the nations of the world (v. 7b). The whole of creation is involved. This summons to creation to sing for joy reveals the same motif as occurs in several of the descriptive psalms of praise. God's sovereign power is so great, and his kindness so miraculous, that the whole of creation has to join in Israel's praise. Strains must come from further and further. We today speak of the beauty of nature. But here nature is still the creation of God. Beauty is contingent. It results from the comparison of the act of creation with its results, as Gen. 1 says, though in a different way.

CHAPTER 49.14–26

I have graven you on my hands

14 And Zion said, 'Yahweh has forsaken me, the Lord has forgotten me.'
15 Does a woman forget her little child,
     that she should have no compassion on the son of her womb?
     Even if these forget, I forget you not.
16 Behold, I have graven you on my hands;
     your walls are continually before me.
17 Your builders make haste to come;
     your destroyers and those who laid you waste go forth from you.[a]
18 Lift up your eyes round about and see:
     they all gather, they come to you. (Insert v. 12 here.)
     As I live, says Yahweh, you shall put them all on as a garment,
     you shall bind them on as a bride does.
19 For your ruins and your desolate places
     and your devastated land—
     now you will too narrow for your inhabitants
     and those who devastated you are far away.
20 The children born in the time of your bereavement
     will yet say in your ears:
     'The place is too narrow for me;
     make room for me to dwell in.'

21 Then you say in your heart:
     'Who has borne me these?
     I was childless and barren [   ],[b]
     and who has brought up these?
     Behold, I was left alone; whence then have these come?'

[a] A. Bertholet. 'Textkritische Bemerkungen zu Deuterojesaja', *Marti Festschrift*, 1914. D. Flusser, 'The Text of Is. 49.17 in the DSS', *Annual of the Hebrew University Bible Project*, 2, 1962, pp. 140ff.
[b] 'Exiled and put away' was added as an explanatory gloss.

22   Thus says the Lord Yahweh:
'Behold, I lift up my hand to the nations,
And raise my signal to the peoples,
and they bring your sons in their arms,
and carry your daughters on their shoulders.
23   And kings shall be your foster fathers,
and princesses your nursing mothers.
With their faces to the ground they bow down to you,
and lick the dust at your feet.
And you will know that those who wait for me, Yahweh,
will not be put to shame.'
24   Can the prey be taken from a strong man?
or the captive be rescued from the [tyrant] ?[a]
25   For thus says Yahweh:
'Even captives shall be wrested from the strong man,
and the prey of the tyrant be rescued.
And I myself contend with those who contend with you,
and I myself help your sons.
26   I make your oppressors eat their own flesh,
they drink their blood like wine.
And all flesh shall know
that I, Yahweh, am your Saviour,
Your Redeemer, the Mighty One of Israel.'

Once again in 49.14–26 we have a somewhat lengthy unit composed of three parts, vv. 14–20, 21ff. and 24ff. As we can see, each of
them begins by disputing an assertion made by Israel—v. 14: you
maintain that God has forsaken you; v. 20: you had thought, I am
childless, left alone; and v. 24: you thought, how can a strong man
be robbed of his prey? But all three parts pass over into a proclamation of salvation. To counter Israel's despondency she has it proclaimed to her that God takes care of her and will restore her. The
connection between disputation and proclamation is contrived thus:
the assertion made by Israel, which is disputed, is presented in the
form of a lament, and the disputation is the word of salvation in
answer to the lament. What makes a unity of the three parts is the
fact that the introduction to each of them takes the form of one of the
three sections of a lament—the charges brought against God (v. 14),
the lament in the first person (v. 21), and the lament because of
enemies (v. 24). This is very clear evidence of conscious construction.
Apart from the form used in the introductions, that of the disputation,
the three sections are drawn up as proclamations of salvation. Each

---

[a] *ṣaddīq* is a mistake for *'āriṣ*, cf. v. 25.

begins by suggesting the community lament (vv. 14, 21f. and 24). This is followed by God's answer disputing the terms of the lament and at the same time proclaiming salvation. The theme of God's turning towards his people is the theme particularly developed in the first section, vv. 15f. and it goes for the whole. The subject in vv. 17–20, 22f. and 25f. is God's intervention; in each case it takes its tone from the lament in question. The object is distributed over sections I and II. Thus, the balance of 'you shall know' (v. 23) and 'all the world shall know' is evidence of conscious composition of 49.14–26. 40.12–31 are similar in structure. They stand at the head of the first division of Deutero-Isaiah as do 49.14–26 at the head of the second.

[14–20] The starting point of Deutero-Isaiah's entire proclamation is the despondency and despair of the remnant of Israel. They imagine that God has forsaken and forgotten them. This is the mental attitude which addresses us with such first-hand poignancy in Lamentations. We need only recall the last verse of ch. 5, with which the book ends: 'or hast thou utterly rejected us? Art thou so exceedingly angry with us?' Exactly the same idea is found following 40.27. Thus, as well as affinity in form as between chs. 40 and 49, there is also affinity in subject matter. What Deutero-Isaiah then quotes in v. 14 is a lament that was actually made. They are words that were used in worship, and well-known to everyone who heard them. This lament he disputes. He opposes this religion that harked back to the past.

[15] Once we are aware of this, and realize the way in which Israel persisted in making such wistful lamentation—it was the sole surviving link with her past—then we can form some idea of the force of the attack and the pent-up passion which lie behind the present verse. And here comparison with ch. 40 has something to tell us. In 40.26 Deutero-Isaiah had directed his hearers' despairing gaze to the stars and, by their means, to the creator. Similarly in 49.15 he points it to a mother and her child. There can be no better way of representing what faith in the creator meant for Deutero-Isaiah. For him the creator and the redeemer were absolutely the same person. As vivid and ever-present tokens of the work of the creator the exiles still had these two things—the stars in heaven and a child in his mother's lap. The stars and a nursing mother, the sovereign power of God and his goodness, and all the range of his creative work that they betoken— 'Look to these,' the prophet cries, 'stop clinging to the past and lamenting. Step out into a wider world'. Here, however, in v. 15 he at the same time indicates that everything pertaining to the created,

even the love of a mother, has limits beyond which it cannot go. He bases trust in the new thing on that faithfulness which can never fail.

[16] The latter, God's absolute faithfulness, is now pictured in a different way.

The section dealing with God's turning towards Israel continues until the end of v. 16, where there is a suggestion of the promise of salvation. Thus, the proclamation proper comes only now. Here we should note that in all three sections it is stressed that this is a word of God. This is clear in v. 22a and v. 25a (which is in no case to be struck out, as Köhler, for example, does) though it is less so in the first section, where it takes the form of *nᵉ'um yhwh* added towards the end (18b). The construction would be made much more clear if v. 17 were read immediately before v. 19, with which it goes in point of subject matter. In the first section (vv. 14–20) the proclamation of salvation announces (1) the gathering together of the exiles and their return home (v. 18) and (2) their increase into a great nation (vv. 17, 19 and 20).

[18] The summons to 'lift up your eyes round about and see' is in the highest degree characteristic of Deutero-Isaiah. Imagine it spoken to men and women in a village in Babylon. What a demand the prophet makes of his hearers! There is absolutely nothing to be seen. He is therefore summoning them to join with himself in his vision of the return home even though, situated as they are, there can be no idea of it! (If, as North suggests, v. 12 should be inserted at this point, the vision would gain in realism and vividness.) Yet, with Deutero-Isaiah such visions of the future are at best secondary; first and foremost is always God's design to alter his chosen people's lot (vv. 15f.). This is taken up again in v. 18b. God takes an oath that those who return from many lands (v. 12) are to be ornaments of the new Israel. Here the term 'ornament' is not really an aesthetic one. Adornment is 'what renders someone beautiful in the sight of others', splendour or dignity. It is not here conceived in terms of its objective value or beauty. It means making beautiful and dignified in the eyes of others. The reason why Israel regains her honour and standing in the world's eye is the vast number of those who return.

[17, 19f.] The second section of the word of salvation begins with the restoration, vv. 17 and 19b. Little is said of it, however. The purpose of the picture given in v. 17—and it is almost over-strained— is to highlight the miraculous and sudden change from destruction to reconstruction. Its background is doubtless words taken from a lament such as we find in Ps. 74.3, 'direct thy steps to the perpetual ruins'. With v. 19b, however, there is a quick transition to another aspect of the new salvation: the mighty increase of the people in the devastated land, which will soon be too narrow. Verse 20, a quotation which is almost as overstrained as v. 17, puts this very vividly indeed.

[21–23b] The second section. Here the lament is changed into a question, so astonishing that one can hardly believe it. The subject of the lament is childlessness, the same thing as we find in Lamentations (1.5, 20b; 5.3). To begin with it was undoubtedly a cry made by individuals—*vide* early narratives—and was then transferred to the nation personified.

The question which lies behind the exiles' lament over childlessness is answered by the proclamation that God is to intervene. He has Zion's children brought back to her. Strictly speaking, the intervention (v. 22a) and its consequence (vv. 22b, 23a) are not in entire agreement. When God lifts up his hand against nations and raises his signal against them, this is a sign to join battle with them. At this point, then, Deutero-Isaiah makes use of an old oracle, an old method of God's answering supplication in time of war, adapting it to meet the situation confronting himself. (It can be discerned in vv. 22a, 23b, 25b and 26a.) This is the explanation of the slight inconsistencies (cf. vv. 22b and 23a with 26), as well as of the words used of the enemies in vv. 23b and 26a, which are unusually ferocious and cruel for Deutero-Isaiah. In vv. 22f. what he really wants to do is answer Zion's lament and her question—she is given her children back. Volz is correct in his comment that in vv. 22b and 23a Deutero-Isaiah does not imply that the nations are to serve Zion in perpetuity. He gives metaphors for the careful protection, and the deference and attention, to be accorded to those who return home.

[23c] Yet, there is more to it than this. The people on whose behalf this action is taken are to be moved to make a response, to know something. God's saving act here proclaimed is designed to tell the despondent and despairing who God really is. He may be relied on unconditionally. Those who hope in him will not be put to shame.[a] Thus the act of deliverance is the prelude to a new history in which the redeemed will always be aware of this.

[24–26] Section three. As before, the question which introduces the section clearly indicates the reproach which the disputation is to

[a] On the concept of 'hoping in Yahweh' cf. Westermann, 'Das Hoffen im Alten Testament', *Forschung am Alten Testament*, Munich, 1964, pp. 219ff.

combat. In vv. 14–20 this was a charge brought against God. In
vv. 21ff. it was a lament in the first person. Here the lament is
because of enemies. They are the source of the trial. 'We have
become the prey of a mighty one.' It was inevitable for the exiled
Israelites to think of it in this way. So there was nothing that could be
done about it. All hope was gone. This has been the fate of countless
other men and nations in the ancient world. Now, it is our turn. We
must put up with it, like all the rest so stricken. To this God makes
answer. (The introduction to it, v. 25a, should not be transferred to
come before v. 24, as suggested by the *apparatus criticus* in *BH*.) The
answer is that this very thing that seems impossible comes about all
the same. The mighty one is in fact to have his prey torn from him. I
myself contend with those who contend against you. The last words
undoubtedly formed part of the older answer made by God mentioned
above. They correspond to the prayer in Pss. 74.22 and 35.1, psalms
of lamentation. It was shown above that v. 26a also formed part of
the old oracle. While the breaking of the power of Babylon obviously
forms part and parcel of Deutero-Isiah's proclamation of Israel's
release, the punishment, destruction and castigation of the Babylonians does not interest him. Even ch. 47, that great poem, says not
one word about the destruction of the city's inhabitants. One of his
main reasons is undoubtedly the fact that he can say that the Babylonians who survive the overthrow of the empire are to be invited to
participate in the divine salvation (45.20–25). This being so, we can
assume that, while Deutero-Isaiah might make use of a traditional
ferocious oracle of destruction such as 49.26a, the things just mentioned do not represent what interested him personally.

[26b] Israel is not alone in having conferred on her by the coming
event a knowledge which she is to take with her into her future
history (v. 23c). Such knowledge, the response to the event, is to go
forth far out into the world. 'All flesh' is to know who is at work here.
As in v. 23c, the thing to be known is summed up in the words, 'I am
Yahweh'. The subject of the knowledge is God's divinity, v. 23c
stating what this means for Israel and v. 26b what it means for the
world. This is summed up in two attributes which, as so often in
Deutero-Isaiah, co-relate the two aspects of divinity, both of which
must be present before it can be said who God is—the one who
wields sovereign power (amazingly, the very ancient designation
found in the patriarchal stories [Gen. 49.24] appears again here;
previously only once, Isa. 1.24) is at the same time the saviour of

Israel. Yahweh's act in redeeming Israel speaks a language that attracts attention among the Gentiles, too.

CHAPTER 50.1–3

Where is your mother's bill of divorcement?

1   Thus says Yahweh:
    'Where is then this bill of divorce
    with which I am supposed to have put your mother away?
    Or which of my creditors is it
    to whom I am supposed to have sold you?
    Behold, for your iniquities you were sold,
    and for your transgressions your mother was put away.

2   Why, when I came, was there no man,
    when I called, was there none that answered?
    Is my hand too short for it to release,
    or have I no power to deliver?
    Behold, by my rebuke I dry up the sea,
    I make rivers a desert,
    their fish [dry up]ᵃ without water,
    [their animals]ᵇ die of thirst.
            I clothe the heavens with blackness
            and put sackcloth on them as a covering.'

If we are really to understand this utterance, the particular thing of importance is to know the class of Deutero-Isaiah's utterances of which it forms part. Begrich ranks it with the disputations. But, while it certainly has affinities with these, its diction, particularly in v. 2a, shows that it is better classed with a smaller group of utterances, the trial speeches in which there is a confrontation between Yahweh and Israel, Yahweh being the defendant (43.22–28; 42.18–25[?]; 50.1–3).ᶜ Its similarity to the other two passages in the group is shown (1) by v. 1a as compared with 43.28, and (2) by the fact

ᵃ Read *tībōš* (LXX) for *tibʾaš*.
ᵇ Insert *bᵉhemtām* before *baṣṣāmā*.
ᶜ On this see Westermann, 'Sprache und Struktur', pp. 141–4.

that Yahweh's rejoinder in v. 1b is the same as there. Also, v. 2 corresponds to 43.22–24.

[1] As is often the case with Deutero-Isaiah's trial speeches, the
opening leads straight into the middle of the legal process, which is
very conventionalized and only just suggested. The charge made
by the plaintiff stands at the head. Israel accuses God of having re-
pudiated her, in spite of the fact of having bound himself to her
in the covenant. This charge is contained in the two metaphors in
v. 1a,b. In content it is the same as that implied in 40.27. The first
metaphor is found in a community lament in Jer. 14.19: 'Hast thou
utterly rejected Judah? Does thy soul loathe Zion?', the second in
Ps. 44.13 (12): 'Thou hast sold thy people for a trifle.' Verse 1c gives
the rejoinder to the charge. This does not dispute the fact of repudiation. Since this is a legal process, the point at issue is whether the
accused's action was justified. And this is what the rejoinder avers:
I was obliged so to act—because of Israel's transgression. This is
exactly the same as 43.28, 'therefore I had to put Israel under the
ban.' This shows that, contrary to the opinion of many recent editors,
the repudiation of the mother and the selling of the children signifies
Israel's destruction as a nation. This is what is bewailed in the community lament presupposed in v. 1a, and it is this rejection of Israel
that is substantiated in v. 1c. Thus, it is the sins of Israel as a nation,
and not those of the present generation of Israelites, that were the
cause of the divine judgment.

[2] After God's rejoinder in these terms (v. 1b), the plaintiff
remains silent. This is shown by v. 2a, words similar to which are
found in other trial speeches, and with the same meaning, e.g., 41.28,
'But when I look, there is no one'. This decides the case. Verse 2b is
an expansion of the rejoinder. As in 40.12ff., its presupposition is the
other aspect of Israel's charge, that God no longer had the power to
help her. Here, too, Deutero-Isaiah refers to a community lament,
e.g., Jer. 14.9, 'like a mighty man who cannot save'. As in 40.12ff.,
what is to overcome this doubt about God's might is his all-embracing
power as creator. In this connection, it should be noticed that the
reference is not to the work of creation in general, but to a specific
motif found in praise offered to the creator—God is the one who in
every quarter, even the most remote, has power to effect mighty
transformations: at a spot where, from time immemorial, there was
the sea or a stream, he can violently intervene all of a sudden, and
make it into a desert. Ps. 107 is a striking example of this. The setting

there is praise of God with the theme, 'he turns rivers into a desert and springs of water into thirsty ground' (v. 33), and the psalm includes a series of declarative hymns of praise in which men who have been delivered from death tell of their deliverance. Their import is the same as here in 50.1ff.—Israel can rest assured that this God who effects such violent transformations in his creation can deliver and release her by the might of his arm.

[3] As Budde observed, we should expect v. 2 to be followed by an utterance of the kind proclaiming Israel's release, such as we have in 43.22–28 and 42.18–25. In addition, these two passages are both followed by explicit promises of salvation. Instead, v. 3a continues the description of God's transforming action in a way that suggests apocalyptic. Yet, this description, too, breaks off for no apparent reason. The presumption is that the final part of 50.1ff. fell out, and that the insertion of the next servant song (50.4–9) had something to do with this. The insertion of these songs has disturbed the original text in more than one place.

CHAPTER 50.4–9

The Third Servant Song

4 The Lord Yahweh has given me the tongue of those who are taught,
   that I may know how to [answer]ᵃ the weary
with the word . . .
Morning by morning he wakensᵇ my ear,
   to hear as those who are taught.
5 The Lord Yahweh has opened my ear . . .ᶜ

But I was not rebellious,
   I turned not backward.
6 I gave my back to the smiters,
   my cheeks to those who pulled out the beard,ᵈ

ᵃ Read *laᶜanōt* with LXX.
ᵇ The first *yāᶜîr* is doubtful.
ᶜ A half-verse has probably been dropped after the first part of v. 5.
ᵈ On 50.6: J. Hempel, *ZAW*, 76 (1964), p. 327 follows DSS and translates *limtillîm* as 'to those who lay me low'.

I hid not my face
from shame and spitting.

7 But the Lord Yahweh helps me,
therefore I shall not be put to shame.
Therefore I set my face like a flint,
and know that I shall not be made ashamed.

8 He who vindicates me is near; who will contend with me?
Let us come forward together.
Who is my adversary? Let him come near to me.

9 Behold, the Lord Yahweh helps me;
who will declare me guilty?

Behold, all of them wear out like a garment
that the moths eat.

Bibliography: see above on 42.1–4, p. 92.

Of all Deutero-Isaiah's servant songs this is probably the easiest to understand, because it is possible to ascertain the provenance of all its component parts. Begrich[a] recognized its form to be that of the individual lament. This, which has since been largely accepted, put exegesis of 50.4–9 on a solid basis. In two respects, however, it can be somewhat improved. Where there is neither lament or prayer, the term 'psalm of lamentation' is not appropriate. Certainly, as Begrich saw, there is a suggestion of a lament in vv. 5b and 6. At the same time it is here changed into something different (see below). But if there is neither lamentation nor prayer, the form which serves as base for 50.4–9 is not the individual lament, but the individual psalm of confidence. Verses 7ff. are a broad development of the two motifs of such a psalm, the confession of confidence and the certainty of being answered. The relationship of vv. 4ff. to these has still to be determined.

A glance at vv. 4–5a and 5b–6 suggests the second improvement. Verses 5b–6 resemble an individual lament (cf. Begrich). They are like the protestation of innocence and contain allusions to the lament. But vv. 4–5a have absolutely nothing to do with an individual lament. What is the explanation? As well as laments on the part of an individual righteous man the Old Testament contains laments on the

[a] *op. cit.*, p. 48.

part of a mediator,[a] whose subject is suffering in consequence of the office of being a mediator (Moses, Elijah and Jeremiah). While there is only a small number of such laments, there must have been several kinds of them, with a history. The best-known examples are Jeremiah's laments, and there we find the same combination of speech about a task and lamentation as in 50.4–9.

The background of vv. 5b–6 is grievous assaults that had been made on the Servant. The equivalent in Jeremiah is his complaints about his enemies, 11.19, 21; 18.18; 20.10. The most of what is here said corresponds to the motif found in the psalms of lamentation, e.g. Jer. 11.19, 'they devised schemes against me', 18.22, 'for they have dug a pit to take me'. But Jeremiah's office also comes into it. In 20.8 he says, 'the word of Yahweh has become for me a reproach and derision all day long.' And even where Jeremiah speaks only of himself, there are words which are only intelligible in the context of his office: 'I never sat joyful in the company of merrymakers' (15.17). These words bring us very close to the servant songs. Both tell of a commissioning with the word of God which involves its recipients in loneliness and suffering. Jer. 20.9, too, where the prophet confesses that he would fain have cast off the heavy burden involved in his office, but could not, is not altogether unlike 50.5b, 'I was not rebellious, and turned not backward.'

The most obvious points are the affinities between 50.4–9 and the confidence motifs in Jeremiah's laments (11.20; 15.15, 16; 17.14; 20.11, 12; 18.23); the affinities with the 'certainty of being answered', which approximates to the motif just mentioned (11.20; 20.11, 12) and to the fact that a protestation of innocence is often combined with a confidence motif (11.19; 12.3; 15.10, 16; 18.20; 20.12). But these are the very three motifs which we found built into 50.4–9.

In his examination of Jeremiah's laments, Baumgartner saw that quite an amount of what is there said can only be explained in the context of the situation in which Jeremiah was placed and of his task —15.16, 19; 17.15f.; 18.18, 20; 20.8f. Direct correspondences between our present passage and Jeremiah are as follows.

Isa. 50.4   The Lord Yahweh has   Jer. 15.16   Thy word was found,
given me the tongue of those who   and I ate it.
are taught . . . he wakes my ear   18.20   Remember how I
to hear as those who are taught.   stood before thee.

[a] On this see my essay, 'Struktur und Geschichte der Klage im Alten Testament', *Forschung am Alten Testament*, Munich, 1964, p. 269.

Isa. 50.5b

Isa. 50.6a   I gave my back to the smiters, my cheeks to those who pulled out the beard.

Isa. 50.6b   . . . Shame and spitting.

7a   But the Lord Yahweh helps me.
8–9a   He who vindicates me is near.
9b   Behold, all of them wear out like a garment.

20.9   (see above)
The complaints about his enemies 11.18,19; 15.15; 18.20, 22; 20.10. Protestation of innocence, 11.18; but I was like a gentle lamb. Jer. 20.8   . . . a reproach and a derision . . . 20.7, 8; 15.10.
11.20; 20.12; to thee have I committed my cause.
11.20   I shall see thy vengeance upon them: 20.12.
20.11   Therefore my persecutors will stumble.

This supplies the answer to the question raised above as to the connection between 50.4–5a and vv. 5b–9. The one who in vv. 5b–9 confesses his unshakeable confidence in God is a man commissioned with an office of the word; he says so in vv. 4–5a. This is the same combination as we find in Jeremiah's laments, and it shows that, to be properly understood, at least 50.4–9, if not all the songs, must be taken in the context of these. 50.4–9 represent the confession of confidence spoken by a mediator of the word. While this does not prove that the Servant is the prophet Deutero-Isaiah, it does show that he regarded his task, his sufferings and his relationship to God as those of a prophet.

[4] The whole of v. 4 (together with the first clause of v. 5) is the utterance of a man whose being is governed by hearing and speaking. In both respects he is 'like a disciple', which means that in both his hearing and his speaking he is concentrated on God, and that these have God as their source. He could hear nothing if God did not open his ear—and this morning by morning—and he could say nothing if what he was to say were not told him. 'Morning by morning' holds true for his speaking also; he also resembles a disciple in the fact that he is told the times at which he has to speak. 'That I may know how to answer the weary' means that his words are spoken with reference to particular situations (so Köhler, 'that I may have an answer to give to the weary'). 'Weary' or 'prostrate' is undoubtedly to be given the meaning it has in 40.28ff., where it is three times repeated. There, too, 'the weary' has a word spoken to him, and there the one who is 'weary' is Israel. The same will apply here. There may, however, be a further implication. The Servant has to be awakened, aroused, in order to hear the word. The word which he has to pass on is addressed

to the weary, the prostrate. As such, Israel is not in a position to hear the word. Therefore, like the Servant, she, too, must be aroused before she can hear the word that applies to her case.

As we know from our decision on the nature of the passage taken altogether, vv. 4–5a represent the call of the one who in vv. 5b–9 attests his faith in the office committed to him. Let us disregard this for a moment and consider vv. 4–5a in independence. They are, every single word of them, an exact description of prophecy in Israel—not, of course, of prophecy's subject matter, but of prophecy as event between God and his chosen people. The prophetic office can be described in just the way in which it is summed up here, as hearing and speaking 'like a disciple', *limmud* being understood 'in the sense of a person at school' (Volz). The special characteristic of the prophetic office is the very fact that the prophet wakens his ear 'morning by morning', and must continually allow it to be opened by God, in order to have 'an answer to give to the weary'. The entire inability to exercise any control over the reception and transmission of a word that has no establishment in which it is at home, is here the expression of the chief characteristic of the prophetic office of the word. The verses also mention a second distinctive and entirely appropriate feature. Elsewhere in the Old Testament *limmud* only designates the disciple of a human master or teacher (e.g. Isa. 8.16). Its use here to describe the reception of God's word directly from himself points to the unique way in which precisely the prophets of the eighth century speak of the word which they receive and have to transmit. We can therefore only conclude that when the speaker in the opening verses of the present song—the Servant—appeals to the office to which he has been commissioned, this is absolutely the same prophetic office as we find in the case of the writing prophets before Deutero-Isaiah. In this connection, it should be noticed that the designation *'ebed* does not appear in 50.4–9. Instead, here the *'ebed* is the *limmud*. God's servant is here described as God's 'disciple'. The implication is this. The term *limmud* does not say all that might be said about the Servant. 'God's servant is God's disciple.' This expresses the most important feature in the picture of the Servant. But it is not the complete picture. The Servant is more than a *limmud*.

[5b–6] The second part begins with *waw* adversative. What does this 'but' oppose? All the clauses in vv. 5b–6 presuppose that the speaker had experienced hostility, attacks on his person, even blows and abuse. This is what 'but' refers to: in spite of it all, I was not disobedient nor did I shrink back. If the lament says nothing about the attacks, the blows and the insults, one reason for this is the form which it takes: 50.4–9 resemble a psalm of confidence, and there, while the lament is still there in the background, it is no longer uttered, because what it complains of has been allayed. Another reason is the content, the particular character of this part of the song— the protestation of innocence found in a lament, which is the background of vv. 5b–6, has been changed into an asservation. The Servant avers that, in spite of all attacks and abuse, he has been true to his task. In this respect what the Servant says in 50.4–9 shows a distinct and decided divergence from the laments of Jeremiah, for here suffering for the sake of the task (of the word) is assented to and accepted. Here the cry of the mediator so passionately and wildly voiced by Jeremiah is silenced. Some radical change has come about, and a new factor entered into God's dealings with his chosen people— the lament of the mediator who is attacked and defamed because of his task here develops, for the first time, into assent to and acceptance of this suffering. The first verse, 5b, refers directly to the hearing and transmission of the word (vv. 4–5a); in spite of the attacks and abuse, the Servant has not rebelled against receiving the word from God, nor has he shrunk from coming forward with it to those for whom it was designed. He has not been deterred into ceasing to hear and to speak. Verse 6a and 6b show an element frequently found in laments, suffering and its shame. This, however, is the one passage in the Old Testament where these are spoken of in such terms as here. These two lines in Isa. 50.6 are truly revolutionary in their importance, not only in the history of Israel, but in the ancient world in general, because in terms of that world's thought what the Servant here says of himself, that he allowed himself to be smitten, means that he regards the attacks, blows and insults as justified, and so concedes that God is on the side of his opponents. Any other way of taking the Servant's behaviour as expressed in v. 6 was quite impossible for the times. To see this one only needs to recall Jeremiah's laments.

[7] For the thought of the time, the new 'but' (RSV 'for') at the beginning of the confession of confidence in v. 7 constituted a sharp contrast to v. 6. The words say something that is strictly impossible— the Servant is certain that God is on his side, although his own conduct as expressed in v. 6 apparently indicated the reverse. This is the start of the new factor—his conviction that God himself wills his Servant's suffering and its acceptance. The glaring contradiction

between v. 6 and v. 7 extends even to the words used. The last verb
in v. 7a is from the same root as the second last noun in v. 6c: 'I hid
not my face from shame'—'I shall not be put to shame'. This contradiction must not be resolved by making it simply a matter of
succession in time—'I take this shame upon me now, but God will
take it away from me later.' Even if such a succession in time is
implied, what is emphasized is that God is to bring the past and
present acts of hostility and abuse into constructive connection with
the Servant's justification. The latter accepts them because he
knows that this is God's will for him. The main thing is that, as
sufferer, he knows that 'I shall not be made ashamed'. Therefore
'he makes his face like flint'. Something very similar is said in the
call of Jeremiah (1.18) and of Ezekiel (3.8f.). But there is a characteristic difference. With these two, this forms part of God's equipment
of the prophet at his call: 'like diamond harder than rock I make your
forehead'. Here, on the other hand, the prophet says it of himself. The
reason for the difference is that in the case of the Servant the hard-
ness (or power of resistance) derives from his acceptance of the blows
and shameful treatment with which he meets. It is this complete
acceptance, and it alone, that enables him to make his face hard as
flint. This single feature again clearly shows both the Servant's
connection with the earlier prophets and the new factor.

[8–9a] The certainty that God is on his side (corresponding to the
'certainty of being answered' in the Psalms) is now expressed in a
different, and very forceful, way, by means of terms taken from a
legal process. The same form was used by Paul in a similar situation
to express the same conviction (Rom. 8.31ff.). The legal terms are so
suggestive of the trial speeches as to make them another pointer to
Deutero-Isaiah's being the author of 50.4-9. To be accurate, v. 8 is a
challenge to take part in a legal contest. The Servant summons those
who oppose him—the same people as smite him and shame him and
spit upon him—to come into court, for he is convinced that God
justifies him and that no one can condemn him. This is only comprehensible if the situation is seen from the opponents' point of view. In
their eyes, the contest is already decided, the Servant's case is lost,
and he has admitted defeat by the acceptance of the blows and acts
of shame. In the opponents' view there is nothing left to settle. Seen
in this light, a special significance attaches to the words which express
the Servant's certainty at the beginning of v. 7 and reappear at the
end in v. 9a, 'the Lord Yahweh helps me.' How is this to come about?

In such a situation, is there the slightest possibility of any justification
or rehabilitation for the Servant? In 50.4–9 the question is left open.
The last line (v. 9b) expressing the Servant's conviction that his
opponents who can now mock and smite him with impunity will
perish, is after all no real answer to the question. The words are also
taken over from the tradition represented in the Psalter. (The two
parts of v. 9 have affinities with the double wish.) The question is left
open and points forward to the final servant song.

CHAPTER 51.1–2, 4–8 (along with 50.10–11)

My deliverance is for ever

51.1a Hearken to me, you who pursue deliverance,
    you who seek Yahweh.
50.10 Who among you fears Yahweh,
    listens to the voice of his servant?
    He who walks in darkness and has no light,
    let him trust in the name of Yahweh and rely upon his God.
11 But all of you, who kindle your fire
    and set brands [alight],[a]
    walk into the glow of your fire,
    and into the brands which you set alight.
    This you have from my hand,
    you shall lie down in the place of torment.

51.4 Give heed to me, [you peoples].[b]
    Give ear to me, you [nations].[c]
    For teaching goes forth from me,
    and my justice as a light to the people.
5   [Now][d] is my salvation near,
    my salvation goes forth [like light]. [   ][e]
    The coastlands hope for me
    and for my arm they wait.

[a] Read *me'îrē* (with the Vss.).
[b] Read plural.
[c] Read plural.
[d] Read *rega' qārōb* with LXX.
[e] Add *kā'ōr* with LXX and omit the last three words of the line.

6   Lift up your eyes to the heavens
     and look at the earth beneath;
     for the heavens vanish like smoke,
     the earth falls in pieces like a garment,
     and they who dwell on it die like gnats.
     But my deliverance is for ever,
     and my salvation will not be shaken.

7a   Hearken to me, you who know salvation,
     you people in whose heart is my teaching:
1a   look to the rock from which you were hewn,
     and to the quarry from which you were digged,
2   look to Abraham your father,
     and to Sarah who bore you;
     for when he was but one I called him,
     and I blessed him and made him many.
7b   Fear not the reproach of men,
     and be not dismayed at their revilings.
8   For the moth eats them up like a garment,
     and the cockroach consumes them like wool.
     But my salvation remains for ever,
     and my help from generation to generation.

Editors are all aware of the difficulties in the verses that come between the servant song in 50.4-9 and 51.9ff., which is a unit with the clear marks of Deutero-Isaiah upon it. In the case of the first two *ebed* passages, 42.1-4 and 49.1-6, we found that the verses which followed them presented difficulties. We discovered the following schema. The servant song is followed by an addition that is clearly related to it, and the addition is followed by a hymn of praise. A similar addition is also to be found here, either 50.10f. or, along with it, parts of 51.1-8 as well. But there is no hymn of praise to round it off. However, 51.3 has a substantiation in the perfect tense, which forms the second part of these hymns, and it is possible that the first part, the call to praise, has been dropped.[a] At all events, 51.3 cannot have gone along with 51.1f. originally (notice the *kī* in vv. 2b and 3a). It is a unit in itself, and therefore best taken as a fragment of a hymn of praise which followed the *ebed* song and the addition to it.

This does not clear up the difficulties, however. The disturbance in the text goes deeper. The beginning of 50.10, 'who among you', implies that people have been previously addressed. 51.1b and 2 do not fit in with the address in 51.1a. If, first, we examine the form for

---

[a] For the reason for this, see 'Sprache und Struktur', pp. 162f.

some indications of a unit, we find the same imperatives in 51.1, 4 and 7. The one who saw this most clearly was Budde: 'vv. 1–8 form a passage composed of three parts introduced in each case with "hear (hearken to) me" '. If, next, we consider the people to whom this summons to hear is addressed, we find that in each case they are quite different—obviously, this is deliberate. In v. 7 they are 'you who know salvation', in v. 4 'you peoples and nations', and in 51.1a 'you who pursue deliverance'. This shows that in vv. 1b and 2 those addressed are Israel, as in v. 7. But it is not certain that vv. 1b and 2 are linked directly with v. 1a, and v. 3 is an independent unit. However, if we take the summons contained in 51.1 and put it before 50.10 where, as we have already seen, there is no address, we find, to our surprise, a solution which removes all the difficulties. The people addressed in 51.1, who pursue deliverance and seek Yahweh, are the people whom v. 10 calls those who fear God. But this is a term later used for proselytes. This is the key to the poem with its three strophes each addressed to different people. In 51.1a and 50.10f. these are the proselytes, in 51.4ff. the heathen, and in 51.7f. and 1b and 2 the chosen people. Is this venture—thus rearranging the text—essential? And can it be accounted for? See the commentary.

[**51.1a and 50.10f.**] Those who already know salvation and who 'have the *tōrā* in their heart' (v. 7) are differentiated from those who pursue salvation and seek Yahweh. The latter are called upon to listen to the one who is speaking here, who asks them, 'who among you fears Yahweh?' This reminds one of the term later used for proselytes, 'God-fearers' (so also in the New Testament). The question goes on, 'obeys the voice of his Servant'? This catchword clearly links the passage before us with the servant songs, and makes it correspond to the additions to 42.1–4 and 49.1–6. The use of the word 'Servant' in v. 10 undoubtedly represents an interpretation of the 'Servant' in 50.4–9 or in the songs in general, but the way in which it is to be taken is not absolutely plain. It is best to take the most cautious explanation—the person meant is the one of whom v. 4 says that he has been commissioned to promulgate God's word; the proof of 'fear of God' is obedience to the word of the Servant. *'ašer* in v. 10b refers to 'you' in v. 10a. The people addressed are those who 'walk in darkness', for the reason that as yet they do not know the light of salvation. Verse 10b also makes it particularly clear that the people to whom it refers cannot be the same as those addressed in v. 7. The promise (v. 10b) is made to the one who pursues salvation and seeks

Yahweh. For the present he can trust in the name of Yahweh and rely on him as his God. A similar promise to proselytes is to be found in 56.3–8.

[11] In contrast to the promise made to those who fear Yahweh and obey his Servant's voice, the transgressors have judgment proclaimed to them. The way in which this is put is difficult and obscure, but one can gather its gist. It is addressed to those who 'kindle fire and set brands alight'. As the Psalms show us, these are metaphors to describe the action of the transgressors against the righteous. Ps. 57.5 (4) is similar, 'among those who spit flames, whose teeth are spears and arrows'. In those Psalms whose subject is the action of the godless, the punishment measures up to the action (57.6 [5] 'they dug a pit and have fallen into it'). Similarly here, 'walk into the glow of your fire and into the brands which you set alight'. That is to say, they are to perish by means of the weapons they had used against the righteous. Verse 11c expressly adds that this retribution comes from Yahweh and leads to the transgressors' death. North explains this as ' "to lie down" must have the meaning "die" . . . *ma'ăṣēbā* means "a place of (fiery) torment", very nearly "Gehenna". The conception is late'. In this first part of the section those who come from the dark and seek salvation are promised that they will obtain it in the name of Yahweh, but the transgressors are threatened with destruction by their own weapons, those that they had used against the righteous. This makes it certain that these words are post-exilic.

[4–6] The second strophe addresses the peoples. They, too, are summoned to hear and give heed. The reason given for this in v. 4b is a paraphrase of what the Servant says in 42.3f. about his task for the nations; v. 5b is almost word for word the same as 42.4. This strophe addressed to the peoples is a striking example of the way in which the servant songs lived on and were handed down. The post-exilic community—or a section within it—took up the possibility of salvation for non-Israelites which 42.1–4 had opened up, and in the Servant's name proclaimed to the heathen that Yahweh's salvation was available for them, and that the light which they had been awaiting was now there.

The first strophe contained a threat of doom corresponding to the offer of salvation. The same holds true here. The nations' gaze is directed to the coming world-judgment in which heaven, earth and those who dwell in it are to be destroyed. When the end of the world comes, there is only one continuing security, God's salvation which continues for ever. Verse 6a and b uses the language of apocalyptic, cf. in the Isaiah apocalypse, chs. 24–27, ch. 24 in particular. It, too, has the contrast between the end of the world and God's salvation which continues for ever.

[7a. 1b. 2] Israel herself is not addressed until this third strophe— 'you who know salvation, in whose heart is my teaching'. The second clause presupposes Jer. 31.31–34, where this very thing is prophesied. In the case of Israel, a prophesy is made which bears on her present oppression. It hints at two things: verses 1b and 2 apparently imply that Israel has become few in number, while vv. 7b and 8 imply that she has enemies who oppress her. Once again the situation thus described indicates the post-exilic period. It is described in similar terms by Trito-Isaiah. It is very curious to find the mention of Abraham and Sarah in vv. 1b and 2. Its purpose is to give present significance to God's dealings with the two of them. What Deutero-Isaiah recalls to his fellow-countrymen's minds are not God's dealings in delivering them, in particular the Exodus, but his activity of blessing them. The metaphors of the rock and the quarry cannot, as de Boer suggests, refer to God. They are allusions to very ancient mythological ideas about the birth of mankind from a rock or a quarry (Volz). The reason why the poet uses the metaphors is not simply 'because he wants to mention something very ancient' (Volz). He also wishes to give Israel's descent from Abraham and Sarah the status of an act of creation, on a par with Deutero-Isaiah's description of the nation's election at the Exodus as creation.

[7b–8] The two words 'reproach' and 'revilings' are found, in a very similar context, in Zeph. 2.8. There it is the nations which dwell round about Israel, Moab and Edom, who abuse and malign her in her smallness and weakness. Here, however (v. 7b), the agent is not specified; but since vv. 7ff. address Israel as a nation and remind her of her descent from Abraham, v. 7b can only refer to people who are her enemies, exactly as in Zeph. 2.8. And this indicates the condition of things after the exile as history depicts it. In face of it Israel is told, 'Fear not . . . your enemies will perish, but God's salvation is for ever'. These final words are a further example of the way in which Deutero-Isaiah's proclamation continued in being. The words 'fear not' take up the oracle of salvation, although it is very much altered. Verse 8a is almost the same as the last verse of the song (50.9b).

In order to bring out the elaborate and imaginative build-up of the three strophes, the proposed rearrangement of the text is essential. The final parts of the second and the third strophes correspond exactly: the promise of God's salvation which is for ever comes at the end of both like a refrain.

CHAPTER 51.3

A Fragment of a Hymn of Praise

. . . .
for Yahweh has comforted Zion,
all her waste places are comforted.
He makes her wilderness like Eden,
her desert like the garden of Yahweh,
that joy and gladness may be found in her,
shouts of praise and the voice of song.

In all probability, imperatives calling for exultation and praise have fallen out before the substantiation in the perfect tense. The hymn of praise followed the expansion of the servant song in the same way as 42.10–13 and 49.13. The repetition of 'Yahweh has comforted' makes it perfectly plain that in Deutero-Isaiah 'comfort' means a turning towards a person that definitely alters a distressful situation, and not just words of sympathy. 'Zion' is parallel to 'waste places', the meaning being the Zion at present lying in ruins.

The second and third lines give the consequences of Yahweh's turning towards Zion to help her. In this case the motif 'change' does not refer to the journey home, but to Jerusalem, now lying in ruins, and to the territory surrounding it. Hence—and this is exactly the fit and proper place for it—the comparison with Eden, the garden of Yahweh. This may be an allusion to Gen. 2. But it may also be due to some other tradition connected with Eden, the garden of Yahweh, of which we are ignorant. The reason why other people will realize that Zion has been restored is that they will once again hear joy, songs and praise ringing out from the city, cf. Jer. 7.34.

CHAPTER 51.9–52.3

Stand up, Stand up!

9 Awake, awake, put on strength, O arm of Yahweh!
Awake, as in the days of old, the generations of long ago.
Was it not thou that didst cut Rahab in pieces, that didst pierce the
    dragon?
10 Was it not thou that didst dry up the sea,
the waters of the great deep;
that didst make the depths of the sea a way
for the delivered to pass through?
11   And the redeemed of Yahweh return,
                they come to Zion with singing.
                Everlasting joy is upon their heads,
                they obtain joy and gladness,
                sorrow and sighing are fled away.
12 I, I am he that comforts you,
who are you that are afraid
of men who die,
of the sons of men who pass away like grass,
13 and forget Yahweh, your Maker,
who stretches out the heavens, who lays the foundations of the earth,
and you tremble continually all the day
because of the fury of the oppressor?
Even if he sets himself out to destroy,
where is the fury of the oppressor?
14 He who is in fetters shall speedily be released;
he shall not die in the grave
and his bread does not fail.
15 But I am Yahweh, your God,
who stirs up the sea, and its waves roar,
Yahweh of hosts is his name.
16 I stretch out the heavens, lay the foundations of the earth,
and say to Zion, 'You are my people.'
                And I put my words in your mouth
                and hide you in the shadow of my hand.

17 Rouse yourself, rouse yourself, stand up, O Jerusalem,
you who have drunk at the hand of Yahweh
the cup of his wrath,
drunk to the dregs the bowl of staggering.

18 None guides her among all the sons she has borne,
    and none takes her by the hand among all the children she has
    brought up.
19 These two things have befallen you—who makes lament for you?—
    devastation and destruction, famine and sword—who [comforts]
    you?[a]
20 Your sons lie fainting at the corners of every street
                                    like an antelope in the net,
    Full of the wrath of Yahweh,   the rebuke of your God.
21 Therefore hear this, you who are afflicted, who are drunk, but not
    with wine:
22 Thus says Yahweh, your Lord,   Your God who pleads the cause
                                    of his people:
    Behold, I take away from you   the cup of stunning,
    the bowl of my wrath you shall drink no more.
23 I put it into the hand of your tormentors, who say to you,
    'Bow down, that we may pass over,'
    so that you make your back like the ground,
    like a street for people to pass over.

52.1–3
1 Awake, awake, put on your strength (?), O Zion!
   Put on your beautiful garments, O Jerusalem, the Holy City!
   For henceforth there shall no more come into you
   the uncircumcized and the unclean.
2 Shake off the dust, arise, sit up, O Jerusalem,
   loose the bonds from your neck, O captive[b] daughter of Zion.
3 For [   ][c] you were sold for nothing
   and you shall be redeemed without money.
   . . . .

Bibliography: H. L. Ginsberg. 'The Arm of YHWH in Is. 51–63', *JBL*, 77
(1958), pp. 152–56.

A number of editors (Volz, Budde, Elliger, Muilenburg etc.) take
the view that 51.9–52.2(6) represent a single consciously designed
unit. The start of each of the three parts of it (51.9, 17; 52.1) is very
clearly marked. The repetition of the imperatives there is strangely
reminiscent of the prologue. There the twofold 'comfort' at the
beginning introduced a series of operation orders. The last of them,

[a] Read third person with DSS Isa[1].
[b] On this verse see M. Dahood, 'Some Ambiguous Texts in Isaias', *CBQ*, 20
(1958), pp. 41–49.
[c] Omit 'Thus says Yahweh'.

as we pointed out, was not as yet stated; it comes later in 52.11f. Leaving aside the hymn of praise in 52.7–10, 51.9–52.5 is the final poem before this command to depart. It brings Deutero-Isaiah's message to a final point of culmination just before it ends. The urgent summons to Jerusalem, 'rouse yourself' (51.17), 'awake', necessitates a further imperative—for what is she to rouse herself, for what is she to awaken and put on her beautiful garments? The only possible answer is that this entire poem represents the preparation of the way for the final summons in 52.11f., 'depart, depart'. It is thus easy to see why this poem once more magnificently gathers up the main motifs of the message of Deutero-Isaiah. How is this done? The lamentation made by Israel, enslaved and in exile, is finally and con-clusively given its quietus. This involves the two series of motifs which go to make up the poem's three parts—the community lament and the promise of salvation with the proclamation of the same. It begins (51.9f.) as a community lament, which is set down without alteration, and the motifs of such a lament are continued throughout the entire poem. The lament is answered by the oracle, or answer, of salvation beginning with the reiterated 'I' in v. 12. The component parts are easy to see. Verses 12f. are a paraphrase of 'fear not', v. 15a gives the substantiation by means of a relative clause, v. 15b the substantiation in the perfect tense, and 52.1f. the expansion relating to the future, that is to say, the proclamation of salvation. However, the poem also introduces another form that has an important place in Deutero-Isaiah's proclamation, the disputation in vv. 12ff. It must be emphasized that, regarded as a single unit, the poem does not represent any one of these forms. The different forms have been fused together to make up an entirely new entity, which might perhaps be called a lament assuaged. But the deliberate way in which they have been worked up is seen in the fact that each of the poem's three sec-tions has its lines given to it by a main element in an oracle of salvation, vv. 9–16 by the promise of salvation, 'fear not', vv. 17–23 by the substantiation in the perfect, and 51.1f. by the proclamation relating to the future.

[9ff.] Elsewhere in Deutero-Isaiah the stricken and humiliated nation's laments are only suggested, or at best have a few words of them quoted (as in 40.27). Here, however, in this concluding poem, it is given plainly, for vv. 9f. are, word for word without change, the beginning of a community lament, consisting of the introductory cry for help (v. 9a) and the review of God's saving actions in the past

(vv. 9b–10). With the first of these cf. Ps. 44.24 (23) (the same verb); Pss. 44.27 (26); 74.22, and frequently. With the second cf. Pss. 44.1–9 (1–8); 80.9–15 (8–14); 83.10ff. (9ff.); 85.2ff. (1ff.); 126.1ff.; Isa. 63.11–14. In these cases the community reviews either the nation's previous history (44.2–5 [1–4]; 80.9–12 [8–11]; Isa. 63.11–14) or creation (74.12–17). Of these, 74.13f. with its language taken from myth closely resembles the passage before us.[a] Our verses make a very characteristic link between creation and redemption. God's action as creator—pictured as a victory over the powers of chaos—is combined with the deliverance of Israel at the Red Sea in such a way that the transition from the one (v. 9b) to the other (v. 10) is barely noticeable.[b] Appeal is made to the 'Arm of Yahweh' (40.10, 11; 51.5; 52.10; 53.1). Significantly enough, we today feel that this expression smacks much more strongly of anthropomorphism than do the 'face of God' or the 'word of God', although undoubtedly it does not. Instead, it throws into relief that activity in history on God's part which for Deutero-Isaiah and the entire Old Testament alike so largely decides his divinity. The imperative 'put on strength' of itself suggests the pictures of events taken from myth which follow—arming with weapons that lend strength plays an important part in the epics telling of the struggle with chaos. The cry for help in present trouble makes the transition to the review, by means of the words 'as in the days of old' (cf. Ps. 83.10[9]). In a community lament, the function of the latter is to conjure up the contrast between God's previous actions in history and his present non-intervention, his being silent or asleep (hence the initial imperatives that seek to arouse him). The 'days of old' are the time when God worked so mightily, and may therefore represent both the primaeval creation and the first beginnings of the nation's history. The language of vv. 9b and 10 describing God's act of creation in terms belonging to myth is amazingly directly taken over from myth and unsafeguarded. There is an accumulation of mythological names—Rahab, Tannin (Isa. 27.1), Yām (sea), Tᵉhōm rabbā (the great deep). And there can be no mistaking the fact that v. 10b describes the victory over the

[a] Cf. Westermann, 'Vergegenwärtigung der Geschichte in den Psalmen', *Forschung am Alten Testament*, Munich, 1964, pp. 306ff.

[b] This was correctly noticed by Volz: 'There is no doubt that v. 9b refers to the creation of the world, and v. 10b to the passage of the Red Sea; 10a.... forms a transition, since to begin with it continues to speak of creation, but leads on to the second miraculous act by speaking of the drying up of the sea' (*Commentary, ad loc.*)

chaos-dragon in exactly the same way as the Babylonia epic *Enuma elish*[a]. This idea of the struggle with chaos leading to the creation is found more than once in the Old Testament. It occurs in a similar context, again as a review, in a community lament, Ps. 74.13f., and in praise in Ps. 89. 11 (10); Job. 26.12; 9.13. More frequently, there is simply an allusion to it. How was it possible to say of Yahweh, the God of Israel, 'was it thou that didst cut Rahab in pieces, that didst pierce the dragon?' Why is the answer not 'No'? The one who did this and the God of Israel have not the slightest thing in common. Editors are all quick with the explanation that this is merely figurative language. This is to some extent correct, but it does not go far enough. For in other places, such as Gen. 1; Ps. 93.1–5 and Job 38.8–11, the same myth has become so colourless that no one could object to it. It might, of course, be said that here Deutero-Isaiah has borrowed from a community lament where the terms were already fixed. But how can he do so without change? And how can Israel's psalms use such language? There is no getting away from it; here ideas taken straight from myth are applied to the Yahweh who is elsewhere the mortal foe of myth. This ought to be taken with greater seriousness than it generally is. The explanation may perhaps lie along the line that the Old Testament has no uniform theology about first and last things. This is seen particularly in the fact that very different ideas about creation were able to maintain themselves side by side; mythological and pre-mythological ones were not ousted by creation by the word. We have also to bear in mind that v. 9b presumes knowledge of the Babylonian creation myth. As is shown by the numerous tablets found at many widely different spots, this knowledge must have been widespread. And, as we now know, the Babylonian creation myth has a long pre-history of ramifications of creation stories and myths about the struggle against the monster that inhabited chaos. This is indicated here in the four different names given to it. At one time they all belonged to separate traditions. For example, *Yām* (sea) is Ugaritic.

[10a] In v. 10a, which still speaks of the primaeval creation, the verb 'to dry up' makes the transition to that act which laid the foundation of Israel's history. The fact that God's act in creation can be thus put together with his salvation at the Red Sea shows the strictly theological line of development—it is from his actions in history that Israel knows the God to whom she here appeals. When he

[a] *ANET*, pp. 66f.

is extolled as creator, the praises given him show the unbounded range of the workings and the power, in time and space, of the God who is Israel's deliverer. In this connection, the way in which v. 10b speaks of the miraculous deliverance at the Red Sea suggests the way of the redeemed which for Israel is now not only in the far past, but also in the immediate future. This, once again, contains an echo of the prologue.

[11] Verse 11 is almost word for word identical with 35.10. Duhm felt this to be the proof that v. 11 was an addition taken from 35.10. Subsequent editors have been divided without being able to come to any conclusion. Verses 9–10 constitute a community lament's review of God's previous saving acts, and therefore there must be some kind of transition before they can continue as a proclamation of salvation. To put it in another way, the 'redeemed' of v. 10 are the Israelites who departed from Egypt, while the 'ransomed of Yahweh' of v. 11 are those who depart from Babylon. It is not possible for the two events to be linked merely by the one word, 'and'. On the other hand, the addition of v. 11 at this point because the 'redeemed' of v. 10b were taken to be Israel in the exile in Babylon, is at once intelligible. Deutero-Isaiah's authorship of v. 11 is not only possible but probable. Only, this is not its original position (cf. on 52.1f.).

[12–16] The community lament quoted in 51.9f. is followed in vv. 12ff. by the divine answer, the mode of utterance being as before, impassioned and urgent.[a] It is not simply an oracle of salvation, as Begrich says, but presupposes this, and paraphrases it, reshaping it freely in its own way. The answer begins with the noun clause which is such a central feature of Deutero-Isaiah's style, but which unfortunately defies translation, 'I, I am he.' It is a response to the cry for help made in the imperative in v. 9—'I, I am he that comforts you' (40.1)—and it then proceeds by way of disputation and reproof, 'who are you that are afraid?' The mode of speech used to dispute Israel's lamentation is the same as is found in 40.12ff., 'Do you not know, have you not heard?' Reproof for being afraid is underlined in v. 12b, 'who are those of whom you are afraid? They are mortal men.' This now brings us to the real substantiation of the reproof: Israel, in fearing mortal men you forget God, your creator. This is once more reminiscent of 42.12ff., and also of Isa. 31.1ff. Verse 13b gives the verb parallel to 'you are afraid'—'and you tremble because

[a] This was recognized by Begrich (*op. cit.*, pp. 167–70). But this is not, as Begrich says there, 'a prophet's lament'. Without any doubt it is a community lament.

of the fury of the oppressor'—and counters it by proclaiming the change in Israel's fortunes, 'where is the fury of the oppressor?' Then v. 14 proclaims the release without circumlocution. The conclusion, vv. 15f., returns to the 'I am' with which the divine answer had begun (v. 12). In the answer just given in outline, Deutero-Isaiah shows amazing artistry in the way in which he works up the motifs of the oracle of salvation like the theme of a fugue. Verse 12a gives the promise of salvation, 'be not afraid', with substantiation in two noun clauses, vv. 12a and 15a. The self-predications come in the expansion of the introduction to the oracle of salvation, in vv. 13a, 15b and 16. The part referring to the future is contained in v. 14. All that is lacking is the substantiation in the perfect tense, which does not appear until the next section, vv. 17–23. All the things that have just been mentioned are found in oracles of salvation, and so need no further comment here. But while the object of the first verb, 'you are afraid' (v. 12), is only couched in general terms, mortal men, that of the second, 'you tremble' (v. 13b), is the 'fury of the oppressor who sets himself out to destroy'. This takes up the lament that was broken off in v. 10, although this is not done directly, but by means of the rejoinder to it. The whole of v. 14, too, proclaiming the release, echoes words and phrases of the lament. It indicates the lament in the first person plural, and v. 13 the lament because of enemies.

[15f.] As is so often the case in utterances of Deutero-Isaiah, the concluding part of the divine answer goes back to the beginning: the sum-total of what his chosen people are to be told and what they are to accept is contained in the words, 'I am Yahweh, your God.' And these are summarized in the two basic propositions of creation and election—the one who elected you is the creator—again as in promises of salvation. Verses 15f. are a unity in respect of both subject-matter and form, and how v. 16a, 'and I put my words in your mouth, and hide you in the shadow of my hand', made its way into them defies explanation. The first part is similar to 59.21, and the second quite like 49.2. It is difficult to take the words otherwise than as a word of God addressed them to the Servant. They could quite easily come after 42.1. As a displaced fragment v.16a could also indicate that there was once another servant song which has not come down to us.

[17–23] The cry which introduces the laments (51.9) has as its counterpart a cry designed to arouse Israel out of her depression and lamentation. It comes in v. 17, and is taken up again in 52.1 and 2. While the imperatives are alike in respect of form, the notes which they strike are entirely different, although we today cannot appreciate this as the original hearers must have done, with the cry of the lament still ringing in their ears from its use in worship. Verse 17b begins with the relative pronoun, 'You who have drunk'. The relative clause of which this is the start continues until v. 20 (hence the participle in v. 20b), even if from v. 18 it goes on as principal clauses. The words 'because you', in vv. 17–20 thus link on to 'therefore' in v. 21, which in turn introduces the divine utterance spoken to meet the situation (vv. 22f.). This makes it easy to see that the verses are parallel in their structure to vv. 9–17. The lament in vv. 9f. has as its counterpart the long relative clause composed of vv. 17b–20, God's answer in vv. 12–16, his utterance in vv. 22f.

Verses 17b-20 continue the community lament, here practically without alteration: it is simply put in the form of God's addressing Israel. The original is perfectly easy to reconstruct: ..

> Thou didst give us, Lord Yahweh, the cup of thy wrath to drink,
> made us drink to the dregs the bowl of staggering.

Zion makes lamentation:

> None guides me among all the sons I have borne,
> And no one takes me by the hand among all the children I have
>   brought up.
> These two things have befallen me—who makes lament for me?
> Devastation and destruction, famine and sword—who comforts me?
> My sons lie fainting at the corners of every street like an antelope in
>   the net,
> full of the wrath of Yahweh, the rebuke of our God.

It is a lament in the first person plural set within the charge levelled against God. In vv. 17b and 20 the subject is the whole nation, in vv. 18–20a Zion. The close affinities with the Book of Lamentations are quite obvious. The latter is also a lament made by the daughter of Zion (1.6). 2.21b–22 and 4.11 speak of Yahweh's anger and wrath, and 3.15, 19 say 'Thou hast given me wormwood to drink' (cf. Ps. 60.5 [3]). 1.18b and 20b lament the loss of Zion's children', there is none to comfort her, 1.2b, 16b, 17b and 21b. For v. 20a, cf. 1.15 and with 20b, 2.19 and 4.1. For 'full of wrath' cf. Ps. 123. We can therefore be quite certain in saying that here Deutero-Isaiah takes up the words of a community lament such as was made both in the exiles' worship and in that of the people who were not deported. These sentiments, expressed word for word, were perfectly familiar to everyone who heard them. But a change has now come over them.

Here they are the words of God addressed to Israel. And in the long relative clause (vv. 17b–20) he turns them into comfort for her. 'Yes, this is what you are in actual fact! All that you say in your laments is true. I have heard it all and seen it. I know all about it. This is the state you are in at present. But now . . . !'

[21] Here begins the oracle proper. Verse 21 is introductory, and the word 'therefore' and the expansions in the address gather up the lament which has gone before in vv. 17b–20. In v. 22a 'your' points to God's turning in favour towards his people, and the relative clause, 'who pleads the cause of his people', to his intervention (Ps. 35.1). The thing thus impressively introduced, and with emphasis, is the substantiation in the perfect tense of this promise of salvation (v. 22b and c); God has already given effect to the change. But this can only be forthcoming from God himself; it therefore begins in the charge brought against God (see on v. 17b, c above): God desists from his wrath against Israel, and turns to her enemies. The reason for so doing is repeated at the end of the passage—the oppressive and shameful treatment which Israel had experienced at their hands (v. 23b, c). Once again words of a lament are echoed here, a lament because of enemies. We thus find that this section, vv. 17–20, con-tains the three component parts of a lament—the charge brought against God (vv. 17b and 20b), the speakers' lament over their present plight (vv. 18–20a), and the lament because of enemies (v. 23). This poem forms the conclusion of Deutero-Isaiah's message and sums it up. Its background is quite clearly a community lament. This shows that his work bore directly on the lamentation made by the remnant of his people in worship.

[52.1–2] As most editors say, the final part of the poem has not been preserved in its entirety. Like 51.9 and 17, 52.1 begins with the twofold imperative of the same verb. In 51.17 the call to Zion sum-moned her to rouse herself from mourning. 52.1 adds that she is to adorn herself, which means to make herself ready for a festival. Since it is as a festival, an exultant procession, that Deutero-Isaiah pictures the nation's return, the imperatives in 52.1 and 2 are continued in those of v. 11, 'depart, depart'. A difficulty is presented by the words, 'put on your strength, O Zion.' They could have the meaning of 'rouse yourself and become strong'. But what follows makes this unlikely. It is altogether probable that a copyist had 51.9 still running in his mind when he repeated the word 'strength' here—the opening words of the two passages are the same. This furnishes good grounds for reading *'edyēk*, your adornment, instead of *'uzzēk*. Jerusalem is holy as the city chosen by God, and by him freed and destined for new life. While v. 1c represents genuine cultic language, Deutero-Isaiah's meaning cannot be, or cannot only be, that 'uncircumcised and unclean' are to be barred from the holy region. These stand for the enemies of Israel who destroyed the city and temple.

Verse 2 continues the imperatives of v. 1a. Literally, the first says, 'Shake yourself from the dust' (Duhm), a very graphic picture. Although it is Zion-Jerusalem that is actually addressed as 'captive' in v. 2a and b (*šebiyā* is to be read in v. 2a as in v. 2b), the people whom the prophet has chiefly in mind are the exiles—he often gives them the name Zion. In 1a, b and c, however, he is obviously thinking rather of the city. The loosing of the bonds does not then relate to the city but to the exiles.

Unfortunately, the third part of the poem breaks off at this point. To make it correspond with v. 1 we should have expected a *ki*-clause after v. 2, and its subject must have been the release and the return. Verses 3–6 are, in the view of most editors, an addition which is not due to Deutero-Isaiah himself, although it makes use of several phrases and expressions of his. One of these is v. 3, the direct continuation of vv. 1f., and if we omit 'Thus says Yahweh', there is no difficulty in regarding it as such. This also furnishes an explanation of vv. 4ff. If v. 3 forms part of the original text, vv. 4ff. are a marginal gloss on the catchword 'for nothing'.

But while this certainly gains the poem another line, v. 3 itself cannot have been its original conclusion. The way in which the whole thing is built up demands a further part referring to the future, a proclamation of salvation. In actual fact its beginning is v. 1c, and it is continued in the last verb of v. 3. But there it breaks off. I suggest the addition of 51.11 at this point; its present position is certainly not original. Then the conclusion of the poem would read, beginning with v. 2, as follows:

Shake off the dust, arise, sit up, O Jerusalem,
loose the bonds from your neck, O captive daughter of Zion;
for you were sold for nothing,
and you shall be redeemed without money.
And the ransomed of Yahweh return,
they come to Zion with singing.
Everlasting joy is upon their heads,
they obtain joy and gladness,
sorrow and sighing are fled away.

CHAPTER 52.4–6

Egypt, Assyria and Babylon

4 For thus says the Lord Yahweh:
   My people went down at the first into Egypt
   to dwell there as strangers. And Assyria oppressed them for nothing.
5 But now, what have I here? says Yahweh,
   for my people are robbed for nothing,
   their rulers wail, says Yahweh.
   And continually all the day my name is blasphemed.
6 Therefore my people shall know my name,
   therefore in that day they shall know
   that it is I who speak, behold, I.

This is a marginal gloss in prose linking on to the word 'for nothing'
in v. 3. The whole story began with the sojourn in Egypt. Then came
oppression at the hands of Assyria—this too, without justification.
And then Babylon, whither the chosen people have been deported 'for
nothing'. Why then should God still remain there (in Babylon with
the exiles)? Where his name is continually blasphemed by the con-
querors and oppressors! Thus far the meaning and purpose of the
marginal gloss is clear. By means of the catchword 'for nothing'
(whose meaning here is very indeterminate), it ranges the Babylonian exile alongside the previous occasions of subjection to a foreign
power. On the other hand, the text of vv. 5b and 6 is so corrupt that
the original meaning cannot now be made out. Taking the usual
meaning of the verb, the words 'their rulers wail' can only refer to
the rulers of Israel. But this barely makes sense here. So it probably
means that her overlords put on airs, or something of that nature.
Verse 6 may take over one or two phrases of Deutero-Isaiah's own,
but the whole thing is scrappy and yields no clear meaning. In
particular, the reiterated 'says Yahweh'—similar to what we find in
Hag. 1—suggests a later addition. The formula 'in that day' occurs
nowhere in Deutero-Isaiah himself. Only the general meaning is
clear: through the release from Babylon Israel is to know that it is
Yahweh who is here at work—for the honour of his name.

CHAPTER 52.7–10

Your God is King

7 How beautiful upon the mountains are the feet of him who brings
     good tidings,
    who publishes peace, who proclaims good, who publishes salvation,
    who says to Zion,   'Your God is King.'
8 [All]ᵃ your watchmen lift up their voice,
    together they sing for joy:
    for eye to eye they see
    the return of Yahweh to Zion.

9 Break forth together into singing, you waste places of Jerusalem,
    for Yahweh has comforted his people,
    redeemed Jerusalem.
10 Yahweh has bared his holy arm
    before the eyes of all the nations,
    and all the ends of the earth see
    the salvation of our God.

Bibliography: F. Fichtner, 'Jes. 52.7–10 in der christlichen Verkündigung', *Festschrift für W. Rudolph*, Tübingen, 1961, pp. 51–66.

The words radiate exultation, an exultation which can only be very imperfectly conveyed in translation and commentary, for the force of the original is lost. They are to be thought of as sung. They form the responsory to the last great poem in the book, 51.9–52.3. The latter put an end to Israel's lamentation, and this hymn's exultation is the answer.

Verses 9f. make up one of the hymns which form the conclusion of a section (like 42.10–13; 44.23; 45.8; 48.20f.; 49.13; 51.3). It has the same structure and vocabulary as these. Here, however, it is united with the tidings that the event which all these hymns take as the substantiation (in the perfect tense) of the cry to rejoice, Israel's release—as in v. 9b here—has now come to pass. But what is described is not the event itself but the coming of the *tidings* of it. It can

ᵃ Read *kol* for *qōl*.

be truly said that Deutero-Isaiah is here a poet. He proclaims the hour of fulfilment by giving a picture of the moment when the messenger announcing the triumph arrives. This enables him to avoid any delineation of the actual return itself, and what he says remains completely concentrated on God's part in the act. The event which he has to proclaim is not resolved into a picture, but stays event pure and simple. As has been recognized by a large number of editors, 51.7–10 form a deliberate counterpart to the final section of the prologue, 40.9ff. We only need to read the one after the other to see the extent to which they say the same thing, even if the metaphors which they use are different.

In 40.9ff. God is the shepherd. Here he is the king. Both are extremely ancient predications of deity, and both were taken over by Israel. Verses 7–12 take over not only the title itself, but also an extremely ancient *schema* for extolling a king—the one here extolled is the divine king who has overcome the foe (v. 10a), who comes in triumphal procession to his city (v. 8), mounts the throne and is extolled with the 'jubilation accorded to a king' (v. 7). The importance even in Israel's worship of such extolling of God's kingship is made clear in Pss. 93–99. We cannot here take up the question of a possible Enthronment Festival (Mowinckel) and—what is connected with this—the 'royal ideology' (Engnell and others). For Isa. 52.7–10 the points of importance are as follows: (1) while the old *schema* for extolling a king clearly forms the background of vv. 7–12, it is completely assimilated to Deutero-Isaiah's message of salvation; (2) what these verses describe is not an act in the cult, but the act of God in history by which he delivered Israel and reversed her fortunes. God's assumption of kingship (v. 7b) goes along with his having compassion (v. 9)—elsewhere in Deutero-Isaiah and in the Psalms God's sovereign power always goes along with his goodness. Thus, although using different terms and metaphors, 52.7–10 say exactly the same thing as had earlier been said at the end of the prologue (40.9–11).

[7] 'How beautiful . . . are': the *pa'el* of *na'āh*, the only other occurrence being Song of Solomon 1.10. The *qal* means 'to adorn'. North comments laconically, 'but feet are hardly beautiful'. But this fails to see that 'the beautiful' means something different in Hebrew thought than it does for us. The beautiful is something that comes about; and 52.7 is a particularly clear example of this idea of it. The messenger's feet are not objectively beautiful. Their beauty consists

in their intimation of the beauty of the coming of the tidings; and this is beautiful because it awakens jubilation (cf. in English, 'how charming of you to come'). 'Upon the mountains' is practically the only factual touch in the description, but it is quite enough to make the scene of the messenger's arrival come to life for the people in Babylon, cf. Ps. 125.2, 'as the mountains are round about Jerusalem'. The messenger of good tidings (40.9; 41.27; in the vast majority of cases the verb *bissēr* indicates glad tidings) has to proclaim something that has already taken place, and this marks him off from the messenger who has to announce something still lying in the future. This is salvation for Israel, as all three clauses of v. 7b say in different ways, v. 7c giving the tidings proper, that God is, or has become, king. For the people who listened to them, Israel in exile, they say that it is now manifest to all men that Israel's God is king, just as is said later in v. 10.[a]

[8] The voice of the messenger of good tidings is joined by the voices of the 'watchmen' on the walls—or, rather, on the waste places (51.3) of Jerusalem. Seeing is added to hearing, the watchmen see 'eye to eye'. Thus, what for so long a time Israel had been unable to believe or comprehend now turns out to be a real thing that men can plainly see. Here, at the end of the book, we once more meet with 'Yahweh's return to Zion', a subject hitherto mentioned only in the prologue. The phrase is an amazingly concise expression of the fact that the exiles' coming back home and their restoration are one and the same as God's coming, his return. The background is the old form used to describe an epiphany and celebrating God's advance to aid his people, his advent.

[9–10] To begin with (v. 7) it was a single voice, that of the messenger of good tidings. Then the exultant voices of the watchmen come in as well (v. 8). Now, in the hymn which chimes in at this point, it is the whole choir composed of the 'waste places of Jerusalem', a paradox whose exaggeration is typically Deutero-Isaianic. The waste places stand for the suffering, bewildered and weary remnant of the nation in the exile and the Diaspora. Now the time has come to shout for joy. Everything is now put right, for 'Yahweh has comforted his people'. One is specially aware here that the perfect

---

[a] This cry extolling God as king is also found in Babylonian texts. The gods hail Marduk with the cry, 'Marduk is king' (*Enuma Elish*, iv. 28). Similarly in several hymns to Ishtar, 'Ishtar is glorious, Ishtar is queen' (Stummer, *op. cit.*, p. 185).

tense in the hymns which gives the reason for the summons to exult is the same in form and content as the one which gives the reason for the summons, 'Fear not', in the promises of salvation.

[10] The metaphor of God's arm is found throughout Deutero-Isaiah's proclamation. We last met with it in the first words of the poem composed of 51.9–52.3. There it came in a plea for help. Here its function is to indicate that God's intervention is both a fact and the decisive fact. Everyone can now see what God is doing to his chosen people, and the time of trial—due to the fact that his sovereign power had been kept concealed—is now past.

CHAPTER 52.11–12

Depart!

11   Depart, depart, go out thence!
     Touch no unclean thing!
     Go out from the midst of her, purify yourselves,
     you who bear the vessels of Yahweh!
12   For you shall not go out in haste,
     and you shall not go in flight;
     for Yahweh goes before you,
     and the God of Israel is your rear guard.

Bibliography: B. W. Anderson, 'Exodus Typology in Second Isaiah', *Israel's Prophetic Heritage (Festschift for Muilenburg)*, London and New York, 1962, pp. 177–95.

This command to depart is that to which the entire message of Deutero-Isaiah has been leading up. It started with God's call, 'Comfort my people'. And the final operation order is the one here, 'go out hence'. It would be quite wrong to regard its development in vv. 11f. as a literal description of the departure from Babylon. The fact that its diction is shot through with suggestions of old traditions makes this clear. Two things go to make up the description. First, in v. 11b there is a procession representing the journey of the Holy One. Here the figure is more important than the details. In spite of many of his editors, it is not the case that here, in his final words, Deutero-Isaiah displays an interest in cultic practices and vessels which he has never shown before. Instead, his intention is to make clear that this miraculous departure is distinctive in its holiness. Separation from all that is unclean is therefore to be taken as meaning the final and complete severance from the unclean land of the foreign gods; the bearing of the holy vessels, which is certainly to be understood literally (II Chron. 36.7, 10, 18f.), then has perhaps the more general meaning of bringing back the worship *in toto* that had been kept up in Babylon.

The second thing describes the Exodus with a change in it. The reminiscences of the first Exodus are plain to see (Ex. 12.11; Deut. 16.3; Ex. 13.21, Deut. 1.30–33, etc.). But the new Exodus which from beginning to end has God as its leader and protector, and in which no one interferes, is to be a journey in peace and security.

CHAPTER 52.13–53.12

The Fourth Servant Song

13 Behold, my servant shall prosper,
     He shall be exalted, lifted up, and very high.
14a As many were aghast at you (? him), [　]ᵃ
15 so many nations shall be [astonished]ᵇ at him,
     kings shall shut their mouths;
     for that which was never told them they see,
     and that which they never heard they perceive.

53.1 Who could have believed what we have heard,
     and to whom has the arm of Yahweh been revealed?
2 He grew up before himᶜ like a young plant,
     and like a root out of dry ground.
     He had no form or comeliness
     that should have made us give heed to him;
     there was no beauty that should have made us desire him;

ᵃ Read v. 14b after 53.2.
ᵇ Instead of *yazzeh* read *yirgᵉzū* (LXX).
ᶜ *lᵉpānayw* is not certain.

52.14b his appearance was so marred, beyond human semblance,
     and his form beyond that of the sons of men.
53.3 He was despised and rejected by men,
     a man of sorrows, and humiliated by sickness.[a]
     He was like one before whom men hide their faces,
     despised—we esteemed him not.

4   Yet *ours* were the sickness that *he* carried,
     and *ours* the pains *he* bore.
     Yet we supposed him stricken,
     smitten of God and humiliated.
5   Yet he was pierced on account of our sins,
     crushed on account of our iniquities.
     Chastisement that led to our welfare lay upon him,
     and by means of his stripes there was healing for us.[b]

6   All we like sheep have gone astray;
     we have turned everyone to his own way,
     but Yahweh laid on him the iniquity of us all.

7   Tortured, he endured it submissively,
     and opened not his mouth;
     like a sheep that is led to the slaughter,
     like a lamb before its shearers,
     he was dumb and opened not his mouth.
8   He was carried off from prison and judgment,
     and who gave a thought to his stock?
     For he was cut off from the land of the living,
     [put to death][c] because of [our] sins.
9   And they made his grave with transgressors,
     and his [place of burial][d] with [miscreants],[e]
     although he had committed no crime
     and there was no deceit in his mouth.

10   Yet Yahweh took pleasure in him [who was crushed],
     and [healed][f] the one who made his life an offering for sin.
     He will see his seed, he shall prolong his days
     and the purpose of Yahweh shall prosper in his hand.

[a] *widūaʿ* from *ydʿ* = humiliate (so Driver, Thomas).

[b] The translation of vv. 4f. here given is based on C. R. North, *Isaiah 40–55*, 2nd edn., London, 1964.

[c] Read *mippešāʿēnū* as suggested in *BH, app. crit.*, following the versions, and then *nuggaʿ lammāwet*.

[d] Read *bēt mōtō* instead of *bemōtayw*.

[e] Instead of *ʿāšīr*, 'with the rich', read *ʿošē raʿ* = with evildoers.

[f] With Elliger read *dakkāʾō* instead of *dakkeʾō*, and then with Begrich, *hehelīm et-šām*.

11　Out of the travail of his soul he sees [light]
　　he is satisfied . . .[a]
　　As a righteous one my servant shall justify many,
　　for he bore their sins.
12　Therefore I will give him a portion with the great,
　　and he shall divide the spoil with the strong;
　　because he poured out his soul to death
　　and let himself be numbered among the transgressors.
　　Yet he bore the sins of many
　　and made intercession for the transgressors.

Bibliography: Cf. 42.1–4. H. W. Wolff, *Jesaja 53 im Urchristentum*, 3rd edn., Berlin, 1953; G. Fascher, *Jesaja 53*, Berlin, 1958; H. W. Hertzberg, 'Die "Abtrunnigen" and "die Vielen", ein Beitrag zu Jesaja 53', *Festschrift für W. Rudolph*, Tübingen, 1961, pp. 97–108; H. H. Rowley, *The Servant of the Lord and Other Essays in the Old Testament*, London, 1952; S. Mowinckel, *He that Cometh*, Oxford, 1959, pp. 187–260; J. Scharbert, 'Stellvertretendes Sühneleiden in den Ebed-Jahwe-Liedern und in altorientalischen Ritualtexten', *BZ* (1958), pp. 190–213.

Structure

　　The fourth servant song is in two parts. What certain people say, 53.1–11a, is set within the framework of something that God says, 52.13ff. and 53.11b–12. Both parts speak of the Servant in the third person. The utterance contained in the framework bears the stamp of an announcement, and its subject is the Servant. The central portion is a report, the Servant again being its subject. What links the two is the fact that both tell of the Servant's humiliation and exaltation.

52.13　　Announcement of the exaltation
　14–15　The development of this
　　　14　Earlier: many were aghast at him (humiliation)
　　　15　Now: king and nations are astonished at his exaltation

53.1–11a　Report on the Servant's suffering and exaltation

　　1　　Introduction: we never dreamt of what we have been told

　2–9　　Report on the Servant's sufferings
　　　2　he grew up parched and was insignificant
　　　3　he was despised
　　　4–6　*his* suffering had been caused by *our* guilt
　　　　4　he (bore)—we (supposed him)
　　　　5　he (was smitten)—we (because of our sins)

　　　[a] Add *'ōr* with LXX. What follows is obscure.

> 6 we (each his own way)—he (Yahweh laid our iniquity on him)
> 7 he suffered submissively (was made to appear in court)
> 8 he was killed (put to death for our sins)
> 9 buried with transgressors (although there was nothing guilty about him)

10–11a Report on the Servant's deliverance
> 10a God turned to him (took pleasure in him)
> 10b God's intervention on the Servant's behalf (he healed)
> 10c and 11a The consequence for the Servant of the intervention (future tense)

53.11b–12 the divine oracle (continuation of 52.13ff.)
> 11b my Servant will procure righteousness, bear sins
> 12a I will give him a return for his work
> 12b because he gave up his life and accepted shame
> 12c thus he bore sins and became intercessor.

1. The utterance in the framework

In 52.13ff. God proclaims the success of his Servant's work (v. 13a); this is to bring about his exaltation (v. 13b). Verses 14f. develop this. He is to suffer greatly and be humiliated, with the result that many are aghast at him (v. 14). Thereafter, however, 'kings and nations' are to be astonished at his exaltation (15a), and to understand something that they had never dreamt of (v. 15b).

This proclamation is continued in 53.11b–12. We are now told what the success and the exaltation consist in. The Servant (so God proclaims) is to effect righteousness for many and bear their sins (v. 11b). For this it is God's will to give him the return for his work ('portion' and 'spoil'), because he gave up his life and so became intercessor for many (v. 12).

This utterance links directly on to the designation of the Servant in 42.1–4 and shows its purpose.

2. The report about the Servant's suffering and exaltation

The first point of contact between this report and the divine utterance in which it is set is the fact that it presents the contrast between the Servant's humiliation and his exaltation (vv. 14f.), thus developing the proclamation of v. 13. Verses 2–5 correspond to v. 14, and vv. 10–11a to v. 15. Secondly, in 51.3 what ends vv. 13ff., 'that which they have not heard' (v. 15c) becomes the introduction to the report. Thus introduced the report proper begins in v. 2. As Begrich

says, its two main parts (vv. 2–9 and vv. 10–11a) point to an individual psalm of thanksgiving (declarative psalm of praise), where the
central portion is made up of the same parts as here, a report on the
suffering and a report on the deliverance. Nevertheless, while many
of the words, too, suggest this category of psalm, the latter does no
more than form the background, for it has been altered in two ways.
First, the narrator is not the man himself who experienced deliverance—this man's story is given in the third person; and secondly,
those who tell of the Servant's anguish and deliverance have themselves been given salvation by what happened to and through the
Servant. Thus, the part formed by the report (53.1–11a) contains a
second strand which is closely woven into it—the report is also a
confession on the part of those who experienced salvation. This second
strand comes out particularly clearly in vv. 4ff.; those who report on
the Servant's humiliation and exaltation confess that his suffering
had been caused by their guilt. And there are a number of echoes of
this confession later on.

The drift of the report on the Servant's sufferings is as such
perfectly clear. He grew up with nothing to commend him, and disdained (vv. 2f.). He was smitten with pains and disease (vv. 4f.). He
suffered submissively (v. 7 may mean that he was taken before a
court). He was put to death, and buried with the accompaniments of
shame (vv. 8f.). This drift makes a further deviation from the reports
made in psalms of lamentation and thanksgiving. In laments and
declarative praise, the suffering brought to God's notice always has
limits set to it. Here, however, the drift involves an entire life-span:
he grew up . . . he was buried. On the other hand, here there is
point for point correspondence with the Church's confession as it is
given in the Apostles' Creed—born, suffered, died and was buried.
This similarity in structure (the Creed, too, is the confession of men
who had been given salvation) is far more important than quotations
from Isa. 52f. here and there in the New Testament.

Verses 10–11a of the report of the deliverance have a structure
that is mentioned frequently—of God's turning towards a person
(Yahweh took pleasure in him), and his intervention on his behalf
(he healed him who), as well as the consequences of the latter—the
Servant sees salvation. The verses also furnished the third point of
contact with the divine utterance preceding the report (52.13ff.)
—the reappearance of the verb with which v. 13 begins: 'the purpose
of Yahweh will prosper in his hand.'

The divine utterance with which the poem ends (vv. 11b and 12) is an oracle attesting the truth of the statement made in their confession by the people whose attitude had changed: 'he bore the sins of many and made intercession for the transgressors.'

[52.13–15] Quite obviously, the opening words hark back to the designation of the servant in 42.1–4. This began, 'behold my Servant, whom I uphold'; and 52.13 also begins, 'behold my Servant'. There can be no doubt that this is deliberate. The two songs go together in that 42.1–4 show the origin of the Servant's work—his designation to his office by God—and chs. 52f. its culmination—God proclaims the success of his Servant's way and work. Of this, too, the success, a hint had been given in 42.4 (where it is put negatively). Here it is expressed clearly. Verse 13 hardly goes much beyond 42.4, but vv. 14f. do add that the way to the Servant's exaltation (v. 13b) is one of profound humiliation. Here the last servant song takes up the central part of 50.4–9.

Following LXX and the Vulgate, Luther translated the first verb as 'will do prudently', 'will act wisely'. This is a perfectly possible rendering. It is one of the Hebrew verbs which denote both an action and its results. This wider meaning enshrines the lesson taught by experience, that prudence in action leads to success. However, the way in which the song develops shows that in this case the verb only refers to the result—my Servant will succeed, achieve what he proposes (as in Josh. 1.8). This consists in his exaltation. The verbs are very strong ones. In the vision at the call of Isaiah (6.1) God's throne is 'high and lifted up'; and expressions referring to Jesus' exaltation (such as Acts 2.33) probably go back to the passage before us. The exaltation of the humiliated from the dust is an important occasion for praise of God in Israel.[a]

Verses 14f. give an indirect description of the Servant's humiliation and exaltation—they tell of the effect of these on people who had had part in them or learned of them (except v. 14b). The effect is set forth in a contrast. The astonishment with which men later greeted the Servant's exaltation was exactly as great as had been their previous horror at the way in which he suffered and was treated with scorn. 'As' in v. 14a corresponds to 'so' in v. 15. On the other hand, 'so' in v. 14b gives the reason for the horror in v. 14a, so that v. 14b has to be read as a parenthesis. Since the repetition of 'so'—at the

[a] See especially Ps. 113.

beginning of v. 14b and v. 15—is difficult, many editors since the time of Duhm (now, for example, Mowinckel) have placed v. 14b between 53.2 and 3. The verb 'to be horrified at' is used, e.g., in I Kings 9.8 of horror at a divine judgment pronounced on the temple at Jerusalem. Instead of 'at you' we should read 'at him'.

The reason for the horror is the disfigured appearance of the Servant, of which two forceful descriptions are given—'beyond human semblance', 'beyond that of the sons of men'. This can only be understood against the background of a characteristic feature in the view of man here presupposed—grievous suffering and, in particular, suffering that disfigures, can cut a man off from his fellows. The shuddering or horror which we today feel at the sight of a badly disfigured face still has here the full effect of cutting off or ostracizing one so 'horribly' marked. The psalms of lamentation and, in particular, Job, allow us to hear the pathetic cries of men cut off from their fellows because they had been disfigured by suffering. In fact, they are no longer regarded as genuine, normal human beings. They no longer belong. This is the terribly serious overtone of 'beyond that of the sons of men' in v. 14b. And the horror at the Servant is to be taken as being as true to life as the description of it.

[15] Now comes a sharp contrast, called in v. 15b 'something unheard of'—the effect of the Servant's exaltation on those who had had part in it or learned of it. The exact meaning of the verb *yazzeh* in v. 15a is not known. Literally it means 'to leap', and several editors have taken this as the basis of a suitable meaning here (see Muilenburg, *ad loc.*). But in the context it would be better to assume a verb with the meaning of 'startle', which is very often found parallel to 'to shut the mouth'. 'Many' in v. 15 corresponds to the same word in v. 14. The people who are so astonished at the Servant's exaltation and rendered dumb by it are called 'nations' and 'kings'. This finds its explanation in the Psalms, where nations and kings are called upon to praise God for his mighty acts. The meaning is that his work which consists in the exaltation of the Servant is so stupendous that people hear of it with astonishment in far-distant places (nations) and exalted circles (kings). Deutero-Isaiah is thinking of the widespread publicity to be given to the work, but not of heathen spheres outside of Israel.

[15b] The event in question is literally 'unheard of'—this has never taken place or been told of hitherto! Verse 15b does more than just accentuate the high degree of astonishment. Instead, the Servant's

exaltation is a thing without precedent. It is epoch-making in its importance. That a man who was smitten, who was marred beyond human semblance, and who was despised in the eyes of God and men should be given such approval and significance, and be thus exalted, is in very truth something new and unheard of, going against tradition and all men's settled ideas. Verse 15b also makes clear that the thing reported in this servant song is thought of as something absolutely unique. It cannot therefore be explained as arising out of anything that recurs, such as the cult of a dying and rising God (Gressmann, Dürr, Engnell, etc.).

[53.1] 'Who could have believed what we have heard (what we were told of)?' 53.1 is the beginning of the report made by a group of people and set within the framework of the divine utterance (52.13ff. and 53.11b–12). Who the 'we' are is not stated. But the report beginning at 53.1 links so perfectly on to 52.13–15 that the transition from divine utterance to report is scarcely noticeable. The introduction (v. 1) makes a direct link with 52.15b and takes up its final words, repeating that what is now to be related has never before been heard of, and doing this now from the standpoint of those who learned of the change (vv. 14f.). For them the event is a $š^e mū^c ā$, a thing of which they have heard (I Sam. 2.24; 4.19), and, as such, tidings which they themselves have to pass on to others. To them themselves the thing was just as unbelievable as it had been to the people who actually witnessed it (v. 15b). 53.1, where the tidings are passed on, continues v. 15b, stressing the element of the unheard of and the unbelievable in the event. The second half of the verse, 'to whom was the arm of Yahweh revealed?', or, 'who could have seen the arm of Yahweh in this?' (Mowinckel) gives a hint as to the reason why the thing was unheard of—the power of God was revealed in this weakness (II Cor. 12.9b). In order to appreciate what comes afterwards it is important to remember that this introduction to the report sets the key-note for the entire passage—that of an astonishment that is still unable to comprehend what has here come about.

[53.2–9] This first part of the report tells of the Servant's humiliation. Here the reader must keep in mind the analysis of the song as given above. Verses 2–9 are not to be regarded as a list of the various things which went to make up the Servant's humiliation. We have to stand back and see the picture as a whole. The verse by verse exegesis must always take as its starting point the total effect of the Servant's humiliation as stated in 52.14. Viewed in the light of 53.11a, 52.13ff.

is a summary by way of introduction, such as we find in declarative praise in the Psalter.

[2] When the psalms of lament and of praise speak of suffering, this is invariably restricted, only an incident in the life of a healthy man. Here, however, there is a difference. The thing described is an entire life-span with the stamp of suffering upon it. Hence at the beginning, 'he grew up', and at the end, 'he was buried'. The meaning of the words 'before him' is uncertain. Many editors change the text and read 'before us'. But this does not make it any the clearer. One would expect the 'growing up' to be made most precise, parallel to 'out of a dry ground' in the second half of the verse. However it may be, both half-verses imply his growing up parched and without strength or sap. 'Dry land' is mentioned in 41.18. The description in vv. 2–9 of the Servant's suffering uses the language of the psalms of lamentation (Begrich). The first simile here, the shoot or root out of dry ground, is in keeping with these, and while there is no direct parallel in the Psalms themselves, there is in Akkadian.[a] Verse 2b describes other people's reaction to this feebleness—the Servant seemed insignificant. Luther's rendering, 'he had no form or beauty', well expresses the meaning. The words go closely with what is said in v. 2a. They continue the description of how this man came to be the man he was, or they describe the prelude to what afterwards befell him. A similar thing is seen in the case of Joseph (Gen. 39.6b), and of David (I Sam. 16.18; here, too, the word *tō'ar* occurs)—one prerequisite of what is subsequently told about them is their beauty. In order to understand this we have to remember two things. First, in the Old Testament beauty of the person is a concomitant of the blessing; Joseph's beauty thus indicates that he is a man with a blessing. Of the Servant, however, it is said that there was nothing beautiful about him; he was a man without a blessing. Secondly, in the Old Testament beauty is first and foremost something that comes about—here clearly a person's beauty is experienced as something conjoined with what happens to him. Thus, for the Servant lack of beauty means that no regard will be paid to him.

[3] Clearly, v. 3 goes beyond this—this life without blessing or regard given it is assailed with blows. The structure of the verse is as follows. Its main statement comes in the second of the four half-verses—'a man of blows, and humiliated by sickness (pain)'. This is

[a] Cited in North, *The Suffering Servant*, 2nd ed., London, 1956, pp. 220f., and also by Muilenburg.

set within three half-verses which state the effects of the Servant's being stricken, the emphasis falling upon the word 'despised', the repetition of which is deliberate. Now, in this verse there is no mistaking the language of the psalms of lamentation, a considerable number of which mention illness—the word here used for pain *mak'ōbā*, is found, for example, in Ps. 38.18 (17), 'and my pain is ever with me', Ps. 69.27 (26); Job 33.19; while there is a close parallel to the present passage in Lam. 3.1, 'I am the man who has known pains.' As here, in the Psalms the pain is always accompanied by being despised and rejected, e.g. Pss. 22.7 (6); 119.22. Hiding of the face along with despising and disgust at the sight of wretchedness, as here, is also found in Ps. 22.25 (24). This close affinity with the language of the psalms has one important consequence. We cannot look for the various statements made in v. 3 to furnish us with an exact and literal description of the Servant's suffering. What we have is the same stereotyped way of speaking about suffering in general terms as is used in the psalms by those who bring their suffering to God in a lament. This was not recognized by the attempts that have been made to pin-point some particular form of suffering (Duhm suggested that the Servant was a leper, and this one or two recent editors have revived). The term which supplements 'despised' in v. 3a, *ḥªdal 'išīm*, means literally 'shunning men'; however, alongside the passive *nibze* it can probably take on a passive meaning. At all events, this verse is emphatic that the Servant's suffering isolated him in the community—this is also the case in the psalms of lamentation— and that he was despised and held in loathing. As a result—this is what is meant in the context—he had lost all positive significance for the community.

[4–6] Now comes the confession on the part of the men who had changed their opinion. It is a masterly piece of writing, amazingly forceful and direct. We have only to notice the way in which the converts' discovery of the new thing of which they had never dreamt is expressed in the rhythm called forth by the changing pronouns (he . . . we) (Muilenburg).

It is best to begin with v. 4b. It looks back to the past, and gives the explanation of the contempt and abhorrence which the Servant encountered—we supposed that he had been smitten by God. This is not hardened sinners and superciliousness. Instead, for the ancient world, this attitude was the orthodox, correct, indeed the devout, one. Job's friends, too, thought in exactly the same way about the blows which had fallen upon him. Like the speakers here, they could do no other, because in the ancient world's way of thinking suffering as such indicated God's smiting and his wrath.

The new thing of which they had never dreamt and which shattered an almost primeval iron law was that the cause of the blows was now viewed in a different light. This comes in v. 4a: *our sicknesses*—he bore them. The Servant's bearing and being burdened both makes the whole thing vivid, and at the same time shows how incomprehensible it all was; one who was laden, bowed down because of the burden of his own agonizing suffering, becomes by that very fact a bearer. In this connection it should be noticed that two things are involved in what the Servant bears, what he has loaded upon him—the sins of the others and the punishment which results upon them. Thus, the healing gained for the others (v. 5) by his stripes includes as well the forgiveness of their sins and the removal of their punishment, that is to say, the suffering. Luther's rendering once more expresses this well—'the punishment lies on him, in order that we might have peace (*šālōm*)'. Exegesis of this confession on the part of the unnamed 'we' in vv. 4ff. must bring out that every word of its represents an experience revolutionary in its novelty. Certainly, substitution in various forms had obtained both in Israel and in the world about her and before her, as has often said in exegesis of the present verses. But the thing that was new and revolutionary for the present speakers was the fact that in this case suffering which gave power to be a substitute and to atone was found residing in a quite ordinary, feeble and inconsiderable person whose suffering, disfiguring as it was, had brought him into contempt and abhorrence. This raises the question which in fact goes much deeper than the one generally discussed, namely, who is the Servant? The real question is this: what led the speakers in 53.1–11 to make the discovery they did? There is as little answer to it as to the question of the Servant's identity. To point to his subsequent exaltation is not the answer. For as such this has nothing to tell us about the work done in humiliation and exaltation. Instead, if we wish to see the significance of these, humiliation and exaltation, our only source of information is the divine utterance within which the report is set (11b–12).

All we can say about the discovery made by the speakers in 53.1–11 amounts to no more than what they say in v. 6, namely, that they themselves had been changed. These same people who, together with all the devout, had hitherto regarded the Servant as one smitten by God now confess—and in so doing dissociate themselves from what all the devout believe—that they themselves had gone astray, and had each and all of them been intent only on his own way, whereas the despised sufferer took their iniquity upon himself, and so procured healing and peace for them.

Confession always has a reference to something that has been done. Here, too, something must have been done to produce the change and the confession which was its outcome. It must be connected with the Servant's exaltation. This, together with its interpretation, i.e. 'for us', must have been the source of the present speakers' conviction. This is all that we can say. The actual way in which it came about remains secret. And where the report is silent we must defer to it.

[7–9] The report, interrupted by the confession in vv. 4ff., now continues in v. 7. Verse 3 corresponded to 'was born' in the Apostles' Creed; vv. 7ff. correspond to 'suffered, died and buried'. The use of these four verbs to describe a human life results in a structure corresponding to that of the Creed, and this itself makes it perfectly certain that the servant song thinks of the Servant as an individual. No further arguments are here required.

Comparison of vv. 7f. with vv. 4ff. reveals that the two passages speak of the Servant's suffering in very different terms. Reading vv. 4ff. we think of an illness, even if the word *ḥºli* in v. 3 is to be given the more general meaning of suffering. On the other hand, there is nothing suggestive of illness in vv. 7f. Instead, everything points to suffering at the hands of others. About *nāgaś* in v. 7 North says, 'the word implies the use of physical violence', and he refers to Ex. 3.7 (cf. also Isa. 58.3). The second part, 'and he opened not his mouth', too, is only meaningful in the context of violent action on the part of other people. Attention has often been drawn to the similarity between v. 7 and Jer. 11.19; the latter, too, is concerned with hostile action on the part of men. The sentiment is found in an individual lament, the context being the same as here—Ps. 38.14 (13), 'But I am . . . like a dumb man who does not open his mouth'; where it is preceded by 'those who seek my life lay snares' (13 [12]). The second verb in v. 7, *'ānā*, is often found in psalms of lamentation, e.g. 116.10; 119.67, 71, 107. The metaphors in v. 7b suggest being taken into court or something of the kind. At all events, the repeated 'he was dumb and opened not his mouth' is to be taken as meaning the same as the words which resemble them in v. 7a.

The meaning of the first two parts of v. 8 is not certain. The rendering usually adopted, 'he was carried off from prison and judgment', makes a good connection with v. 7b, and this commends it (so e.g. North, too). Köhler modifies this slightly—'by reason of oppression and judgment he was taken off'. Engnell takes the two nouns as an example of hendiadys and translates 'a judgment of violence', which amounts to the same thing. Mowinckel, on the other hand, is completely different—'from protection and right he was taken away' (for this meaning for *ʿōṣer* he takes I Sam. 9.17 as his basis). In whatever way they are taken, the words speak of violent action by others against the Servant within the context of a court of law. The second part of the verse, too, has very different interpretations given it. In this suffering, too, the Servant is alone, with no one concerned about him—this is certain. But the meaning of *dōr* is not certain. Its usual meaning is not impossible and could stand—the Servant's death also means the cutting off of his line, and no one was concerned about this. Driver takes *dōr* as meaning 'lot' (or 'state'), which fits in considerably better. Similarly Nyberg. This is adopted by Mowinckel and North. Köhler, Elliger and others render 'and as for the men of his time'. But this does not run very easily. Sellin changes to 'his release', others to 'his way'. We can only say that the exact meaning of *dōr* is uncertain, but that the general sense is perfectly clear—no one was concerned about him.

Verses 8b and 9 tell of the Servant's death and burial. Mowinckel is correct in saying that 'the text does not make it clear whether he died of the disgraceful disease, or by violence . . . or by normal condemnation and execution'. The difference in the description of the Servant's suffering as between vv. 3–6 and vv. 7f. is due to a reason which is extremely important for the exegesis of Isa. 53. Here we find the same two different aspects or strands in the description of suffering as in the psalms of lamentation. On this see the *Einleitung in die Psalmen* by Gunkel and Begrich. We need do no more than refer to Ps. 22, where the suffering bemoaned shows the very same two aspects—it is illness (or at least suffering described in bodily terms), and it is also persecution and hostility. This shows that Isa. 53, too, portrays the Suffering Servant as the typical sufferer in terms of the two basic modes of suffering as given by tradition. There is therefore no reason for taking either the one (illness, e.g. leprosy) or the other (violence or conviction) as a literal, true to life description.

Nor does the brief and very reserved report of the Servant's death —'he was cut off from the land of the living'—go beyond what is said in psalms of lament; cf. here Lam. 3.54. In the second half-verse of v. 8 the text is in disorder and, as it stands, cannot be translated, as all editors agree. The emendation proposed in *BH* on the basis of the versions, 'stricken to death because of our sins', is still the best available (so now also Mowinckel). The Servant's death is to be regarded as the end appropriate to his suffering, for a speedy end had been in prospect from the beginning. The suffering and the death constitute one single thing. This is the reason why the ends of v. 9 and v. 10 make the same observation on his death as had been made earlier about his suffering—it was the death of the guiltless, that is to say, it was a violent death not due to guilt incurred by himself, and it was a death which the Servant suffered because of the sins of those who now report it.

[9a] Shame was part and parcel of the Servant's suffering. Shame also attaches to his death. He was buried with malefactors and miscreants. This is the verse that makes two things clear. First, the report has an individual, one single man, in view. And at the same time it shows perfectly plainly that the one about whom the report is made had actually died and been buried—that is to say, from the narrator's point of view, the Servant's death is a thing of the past. And since his burial involved a further act of contempt and putting to shame, this puts it beyond doubt that, right up to the last moment, up to the grave itself, the Servant's life gave absolutely no indication at all of the supremely positive significance which was later attached to it.

[10–11a] Now comes the 'report about the deliverance'. What makes the basic difference between it and the declarative psalm of praise (psalm of thanksgiving) is the fact that here the one who reports that God miraculously delivered him from his troubles is not the man himself. Since the trouble had encompassed the Servant's life from start to finish and can therefore only be told of by others, the 'deliverance' here is something lying outside the span from birth to death and burial, and in consequence it, too, can only be declared by others.

Verse 10 begins with *wāw* adversative which in the psalms of lamentation so frequently marks the turning-point in a lament. Verse 10a is corrupt, but Begrich's restoration based on a very slightly altered proposal of Elliger's carries conviction—'but Yahweh took pleasure in his humiliated one' (adopted by Köhler in his *Lexikon*). Two things are said here: first, that in spite of all appearance Yahweh had all along been ranged on the Suffering Servant's side; and secondly, that after the latter's death he gave his turning towards him practical effect—he intervened on his behalf. He revived him (*hehelim*, cf. Isa. 38.16) or healed him. But what is meant by this? Many editors (e.g. Mowinckel) are quite sure that what is here reported is the Servant's resurrection from the dead. As against this it should be noticed that this is not clearly said to be the case. There is no doubt that God's act of restoring the Servant, the latter's exaltation, is an act done upon him after his death and on the far side of the grave. But no attempt is made to be precise or to explain. Instead, the concepts and expressions used to describe God's act of restoring the Servant and exalting him are simply taken from tradition, and none of them is really appropriate to what took place here. The text thus draws a line here, and exegesis ought not to overstep it. While the Servant's exaltation assuredly took place, and while it forms an essential part of the report about his death and exaltation, what it actually was cannot now be ascertained.

Verses 10b and 11a indicate the consequences of God's act of restoring his Servant, but the terms used are merely general and taken from tradition. He is to have a long life and see his offspring; after the 'travail of his soul' he is to see light, that is to say, happiness, salvation, and to be satisfied . . .; what follows is so corrupt as to defy reconstruction. According to MT the end in view is 'by his knowledge'. North translates 'and have fullness of knowledge', Mowinckel 'and be satisfied with what he desires', (*bir ͑ūtō*). Clearly, vv. 10b and 11a state that, in consequence of God's intervention, the Servant obtains 'life' in the sense that this word has in the Old Testament, life happy and satisfied.

[11b–12] The conclusion of the divine utterance (the continuation of 52.13ff.). The introductory part of the song (52.13ff.) had proclaimed, to the astonishment of many, that after his humiliation the Servant would be exalted. 53.11b–12 join directly on to this. The text of the first half-verse is not certain. The usual translation is 'as a righteous one my Servant will procure righteousness for many'. But the Hebrew rules out such an arrangement of the words. Mowinckel's explanation is better adapted to both the context and the words themselves (the subject in v. 11a is *͑abdi*): 'My Servant will show himself to be righteous [*yasdiq*, internal causative] (and so stand) as righteous before the many', that is to say, my Servant will stand as righteous before the many because he bore their sins. The words then express God's justification of the Servant previously condemned in shame, and his declaring of him as righteous. God rehabilitates the Servant and restores his honour.

[12] The rehabilitation is followed by the reparation made to him —again this is expressed in general terms taken from tradition. The one who had been deprived of all the good things of life is now to receive them in abundance.

The reason for the restoration of honour and good things is given in vv. 12b and c as follows: in v. 12b God utters a final endorsement of the Servant's work, and in v. 12c of the 'wherefore' of it. These concluding words are of the utmost importance. 'In this divine utterance vicarious suffering is mentioned in no less than five places' (Volz). Verse 12b takes the Servant's suffering and his death together and views them as a single act or process. At the same time, however, it once again sets out the two aspects of the act—the Servant's death is a death in shame. The first part could also be translated, 'because he poured out his blood (*nepeš*) to death'. This suggests a sacrifice of expiation, corresponding to the sacrificial term *'āšām* (guilt offering) in v. 10. These two clear pointers to an expiatory sacrifice as the explanation of the meaning of the Servant's suffering and death deserve to have particular attention given them. They are never, of course, to be taken in the sense of a revival of something correspond-ing to human sacrifice, although this would not have been beyond the bounds of possibility for the contemporaries of this song's author —it was not so long ago that Jeremiah had protested against the resurgence of child-sacrifice. Instead, these pointers to the sacrificial character of the Servant's sufferings and death are to be understood along the lines of the prophets' criticisms of the cult. Since the suffer-ing and death of the Servant is absolutely once for all in its character, the same holds true of the expiatory sacrifice which he offered— because it is a once for all act, it takes the place of the recurrent expiatory sacrifice, and so abolishes this. Here, of course, this is not carried to its logical conclusion. But the ἐφ'ἅπαξ of the Epistle to the Hebrews and its logical conclusions are already implicit here. Along with this, however, goes something else. If a man despised and dis-figured by suffering, and his death in shame and his grave with the wicked, can be explained as an expiatory sacrifice, this involves a radical desacralization of sacrifice.

'And let himself be numbered with the transgressors.' Here translation by a reflexive is preferable to translation by a passive,

because the terms of v. 12b*a* suggest that, in this final divine utterance, the emphasis is meant to fall on the Servant's own active part in
what was accomplished by his suffering. He offered no resistance to
being numbered with the transgressors, he actually accepted it. We
may estimate the significance of this by reference to the psalms of
lamentation, where so large a part is played by the differentiation of
the righteous from the transgressors.

[12c] The word 'yet' which begins this final line presupposes
something left unsaid. Yes, he let himself be numbered with the
transgressors; but in reality he was no transgressor, but . . . Here,
as the termination of the whole thing, two brief but weighty statements sum up the meaning of the Servant's work. The first is, 'he bore
the sins of many'. The really miraculous thing about the Servant's
path in life, his suffering and his death, is this. The suffering which
overtakes an ordinary man without priestly status, a man buffeted
and despised, makes it possible for him to take the sins of others
upon himself, and so to avert from them the consequences of these,
punishment. In the final words—this is the second statement—this
same thing is subsumed under the concept of representation or intercession. The *hip'il* of the verb *pāga'*, 'to light upon someone', means
'to cause to light upon', as in 53.6 (see above); and with *b*^e (in a
request) 'to make entreaty', as in Jer. 36.25. Used absolutely it means
'to intervene', as in Isa. 59.16. This elucidates the meaning here, 'he
interceded for the transgressors'. This does not mean, as some
editors imagine, that he made prayers of intercession for them, but
that with his life, his suffering and his death, he took their place and
underwent their punishment in their stead.

CHAPTER 54.1–10

Sing, O barren one!

1   Sing, O barren one, who did not hear,
       break forth into singing and cry aloud, you who have not been in
          travail!
     For the children of the desolate one are more
     than the children of her that is married, says Yahweh.

2 Enlarge the place of your tent
  [stretch out your curtains],[a] hold not back,
  lengthen your cords, make your pegs fast.
3 For you spread abroad to the right and to the left,
  your descendants possess nations, settle in desolate cities.

4 Fear not, for you will not be put to shame;
  be not confounded, for you need not blush;
  for you will forget the shame of your youth,
  and the reproach of your widowhood you will remember no more.
5 For your maker is your bridegroom, Yahweh of hosts is his name,
  and the Holy One of Israel is your redeemer,
  the God of the whole earth he is called.
6 For he has called you [   ][b] like a wife forsaken and grieved in
      spirit,
  and like a wife of youth who had been cast off,
  says Yahweh, your God.
7 For a brief moment I forsook you,
  but with great compassion I gather you.
8 In overflowing wrath I hid
  for a moment my face from you,
  but with everlasting love I have compassion on you,
  says Yahweh, your Redeemer.
9 For this is like the days of Noah to me:
  as I swore that the waters of Noah
  should no more go over the earth,
  so I swear to be no more angry with you,
  no more to rebuke you.
10 For even although mountains depart and hills remove,
  my grace shall not depart from you,
  and my covenant of peace does not remove,
  declares Yahweh, who has compassion on you.

This poem is an exceptionally impressive example of Deutero-Isaiah's poetic art. Yet, it is proclamation throughout, and what gives the utterance its brilliant tone is the perfect unity achieved between poetry and proclamation. But to appreciate it fully, we must be familiar with the whole of Deutero-Isaiah. A whole range of motifs is here fused into something quite new: a hymn of praise ('sing, O barren one'), a promise of salvation ('fear not') and a proclamation of salvation ('my grace shall not depart from you'), are made into a unified whole. We may note one or two features in it. The double imperative 'sing . . . cry aloud' (the stylistic device which Deutero-

a With LXX read *wīrī'ōtayik hattī.*
b Read *yhwh* after *'āmar.*

Isaiah employs so frequently) is answered by the double imperative in v. 4, 'fear not . . . be not confounded'. The same is true of the substantiation of the summons—the change from suffering (increase and enlargement, vv. 1b, 2, 3) is balanced by the change from the shame of it (taking back of the one who had been left alone, vv. 4ff.). But in the last analysis the reason for this change is God himself: his wrath is changed into fresh compassion which is now permanent and everlasting. The poem might well have ended at this point. It is given an expansion, however, in vv. 9f., which connects the whole thing with an earlier change, the change from the flood to the time after the flood. This expansion (vv. 9f.) is in harmony with the exceptional nature of ch. 54 as compared with all that precedes it— the thing proclaimed is not God's act of deliverance, but the new state of salvation to which this gives rise. As far as diction goes, a telling connection is made between this expansion (vv. 9f.) and what precedes it—the words which end v. 8 and v. 10, 'says Yahweh your Redeemer' and 'declares Yahweh, who has compassion on you' correspond as if in parallelism. But in addition, the three parts of the poem, vv. 1ff., 4ff. and 7–10, can be seen to be a single unit, deliberately constructed, in that they are based on the three component parts of a lament: the charge brought against God (vv. 7–10, 'why hast thou forsaken us? Why dost thou hide thy face from us? Why does thine anger boil up against us?'), the lament in the first person singular in vv. 1ff. (the lament of the childless woman, like the lament made by Jerusalem in Lamentations), and the lament over the shame of the suffering, as in many community laments, vv. 4ff. Once again, then, in this final proclamation, Israel's lamentation is turned into a shout of joy.

[1–2] The various summonses at the start, 'Sing . . . break forth into singing and cry aloud', correspond to the hymns of praise comprised by 44.23, 49.13 and 52.9. The summons to sing, which is antiphonal and responsive in the hymns, is here placed parallel to the call to salvation (v. 4). This is designed to bring out the cry which changes Israel's suffering, the cry that God has now again turned towards her in favour, must awaken joy and evoke loud exultation. In 44.23 and 49.13 it was the whole of creation that was summoned thus to sing because of God's saving act towards Israel. Here it is Israel herself. This shows that, exactly like the Psalter's summons to praise and rejoicing, the cry here represents an expansion pushed to its greatest possible limits. The one here summoned to rejoice is the 'barren one who did not bear . . . who had not been in travail'. Here the age-old lament of the childless woman (e.g. Rebekah's lament) is transferred to a corporate body, the city bereft of its inhabitants or its male population, as in Lamentations, 'how lonely sits the city' (1.1). It is not enough then to say that Deutero-Isaiah here employs the same metaphor, the city personified as a woman. Instead, he takes up words and metaphors from laments in actual use at the time and familiar to his hearers from the services of lamentation held by the exilic community. Deutero-Isaiah takes up the metaphor only to change it completely. To those who heard it, the summons, 'Sing, O barren one', must have sounded extremely paradoxical. The word *ᶜᵃqārā* suggested expiry beyond recall. How could a barren woman be summoned to sing? This was both meaningless and pitiless. But these are the exact feelings of shock which Deutero-Isaiah wishes his metaphor to evoke, for he has something undreamt of and quite incredible to proclaim. The substantiation of the summons in v. 1 is the promise which God now makes, that the barren one is to be given many children. But in its hearers' ears this substantiation no longer suggests the impossible, for in their services they sang the praises of that very God who 'makes the barren and childless one the joyous mother of children' (Ps. 113). This is a good example of the way in which Deutero-Isaiah's proclamation echoes not only laments, but motifs from the hymns of praise as well.

[2-3] The series of imperatives in v. 2, 'enlarge . . . stretch out . . . lengthen', is a perfect example of the exuberance which distinguishes Deutero-Isaiah's style of preaching and is such a marked feature of his prophecy. In respect of form, these summonses are parallel to those to sing in v. 1. In respect of content, however, they are the substantiation of the summons to sing—'yes, I mean it. You can sing. For you will soon require to enlarge your habitations, so greatly are you to grow again.' But the prophet finds it so urgent to convince Israel of the reality of this glorious future in which she is to thrive that he even now summons her thus to enlarge her habitations as an action prompted by the joy of the renewal! The substantiation proper is delayed until v. 3, which now gives the reason for the summons to enlarge the tents. What here re-appears in all its pristine freshness—the range of Deutero-Isaiah's topics and of his theology leaves us marvelling—is the old promise of increase so well known from the stories told of the patriarchs. This also lets us understand the use of the tent metaphor in an age when Israel had for long had

houses as her dwelling-places—Deutero-Isaiah deliberately recalls the days of old when the promise of increase mattered so much. This now makes it perfectly clear that in ch. 54 the prophet's promise goes beyond what he had had to proclaim hitherto. The promise of deliverance is supplemented by the promise of blessing in the particular form of promise of increase. This, too, is amazingly parallel to the promise which was made at the beginning of Israel's history in Ex. 3.7f., where along with deliverance, release from Egypt, Israel is promised blessing—in this case, of course, not in the form of a promise of increase, but of the land.

[4–6] Along with the removal of Israel's suffering goes the removal of the shame of it. In order to appreciate the plethora of verbs (v. 4a) and nouns (v. 4b) expressing the shame, ignominy and humiliation, we must remember that, with Israel and the nations round about her, suffering and shame went together as the outside and the inside of the same phenomenon. Thus, in the case of the childless woman's suffering, it is not anything she does, such as behaving immorally, that involves her in shame, but childlessness as such. It is exactly the same with a vanquished nation—its defeat costs it its honour in the eyes of the rest of the nations. This is the desperate shame in face of which the prophet cries, 'Fear not' and makes the promise of salvation which takes away not only the suffering, but the shame as well.

The turn to salvation in vv. 5f. takes up the metaphor of vv. 1ff. It again stresses the new state of salvation—God takes the woman forsaken and grieved in spirit back again, and she once more has a husband. The state of forsakenness, loneliness and shame is past, and she who was solitary is given back the happiness and honour of the married state and status.

[7–8] It is to be noticed that the metaphor which plays the leading part in vv. 1–6 fails to re-appear in vv. 7–10. In verses 7f., which point out the real reason for the great change, Deutero-Isaiah speaks directly, without metaphor. Nevertheless, the subject is the same. Verses 1–6 expressed it by contrasting two states; vv. 7ff. do so again by using a motif taken from the Psalms, and vv. 9f. by means of the comparison with the covenant with Noah.

In the psalms of praise the exultation of a person who has been delivered may be expressed as follows: as he looks back at the distress, this now seems to have lasted but a little, while the life restored to him by the deliverance seems to stretch far on in a future free from trouble (Ps. 30.6 [5]):

For his anger is but for a moment; but his favour is for a lifetime.
Weeping may come in the evening, but in the morning there is joy.

This is the very same motif as Deutero-Isaiah takes up here, the only difference being that he makes God the speaker: 'for a brief moment I forsook you.' This motif also allows the proclamation of the averting of God's wrath to emphasize the lasting and abiding element in the new salvation—'but with everlasting love I have compassion upon you'; this, too, corresponds to a motif in the psalms of praise, 'for his favour endures for ever'. Frequent reading of 54.1–10 shows that the rhythm itself marks off vv. 7f. as the poem's climax. Here we have the heart of the matter, the basic factor in Deutero-Isaiah's proclamation—with God himself and in God himself the change has already taken place, and therefore everything must alter. A change has come over God. He ceases from wrath, and again shows Israel mercy. This makes everything all right again. This is clearly a re-echoing of the words of the prologue. These verses, the climax of the last great poem in Deutero-Isaiah, show how largely his proclamation is couched in the diction of the psalms—what the men who there lament want is this same turning of God's wrath into compassion, while those who praise him tell how they have experienced it. Such sentiments draw their inspiration from the language of prayer, and for this very reason their artless lack of reserve allows us to feel something of the way in which old Israel's heart throbbed as she stood before her God. They also tell us something about the way in which she understood her own existence. A small band of people whose destiny is bound up with the immense complexities of world-history has no reserve in regarding that destiny as absolutely, and absolutely simply, dependent on the action of God.

[9–10] The construction of vv. 9f., which close the poem, is as follows: Verse 9 makes a comparison with what was said in vv. 7f. The change which is now coming about is compared with a former one. Verse 10 substantiates the comparison by giving the assurance that the new salvation will be a lasting one. But at the same time it brings the whole poem to its end. Verse 10 might equally have come after v. 8.

[9] The comparison with the covenant with Noah is a separate utterance, although most certainly added by Deutero-Isaiah himself. Another reason why it stands out in relief from its context is the fact that it is practically prose, while v. 10 reverts to the distinctly rhythmical language of the verses preceding v. 9. Verse 10 is in fact

something like a historical comparison whose content is extremely different from what comes both before and after, and this at once leaves its mark on the diction. For the thought or the theology of the Old Testament this comparison represents a bold advance. As Deutero-Isaiah looks back into the past in search of a turning-point comparable with the one which now confronts Israel, he finds none in the history of Israel herself. He has to go further back to that turning-point in primaeval times which marked the end of catastrophic events involving the whole human race! This is also Muilenburg's understanding of the passage: 'the imminent events are of essentially the same order as the promise to Noah after the universal flood.' There is no place in Deutero-Isaiah which indicates more clearly—though this is not said in so many words—that the turning-point which he had to proclaim had a significance which far transcended Israel herself, and affected the whole world. This comparison is to be read in the context of the many passages in which Deutero-Isaiah emphasizes that Israel's redeemer is the creator.

Without any doubt the promise of salvation contained in vv. 9f. is the promise of something that is to continue, a new condition of things. This could scarcely have been more clearly expressed than by means of the comparison of the covenant with Noah, for it is just this very element of continuance and permanence that God promised to the world after the flood, Gen. 8.22. The counterpart of this continuing element is the term *berīt šālōm*, 'covenant of peace', in v. 10. *šālōm* is a term denoting a condition and belongs to the vocabulary connected with blessing; properly speaking, it denotes the well-being of a community. The two verbs, 'not depart', 'not remove', correspond to this—these, too, are reinforcements of the element of continuance in the new salvation. This is also the context in which we have to take the term 'covenant', both here and again in 55.3. It occurs in Deutero-Isaiah only in these two places—chs. 54 and 55. Thus, he uses it when, and only when, he speaks of God's salvation as a condition of things, something permanent. This shows us a matter of great importance for Old Testament theology. Strictly speaking, God's saving act on behalf of his chosen people is not the making of the covenant, but the deliverance. For God's saving action in the Old Testament, the covenant is not foundation, but confirmation. These two passages in Deutero-Isaiah made it perfectly clear that what the covenant does is confirm the new relationship established between God and the chosen people. This is exactly the same as in Ex. 34 and Josh. 24—

through the covenant the new relationship which *anterior* divine
saving acts had created between God and the chosen people is given
its confirmation, that is to say, made into something permanent.
This idea of the covenant, the making of an event into a permanent
condition, is expressed in 55.3 by describing it as an 'everlasting
covenant', and in 54.9 by the repetition of the verb 'to swear'. In
Gen. 8 the latter is not used by either J or P, indicating that they
handled the tradition with freedom. If God here swears to cease from
his wrath against Israel and not to vent it any more, and also promises that now his grace is not to depart from Israel, and that peace,
well-being, are to continue for ever—this promise goes far beyond the
actual facts of history. We have to admit quite freely that it was never
fulfilled in the post-exilic period. But it also goes far beyond the fulfilment in Christ. Deutero-Isaiah's promise of an interrupted
condition of salvation points far beyond history, or far beyond the
path trodden by God's people on their journey through history.

CHAPTER 54.11–17

The New Salvation

11   . . .ᵃ O afflicted one, storm-tossed, and not comforted!
        behold, I set your stones in antimony
        and your foundations in sapphires,
12   your pinnacles I make of rubies,
        and your gates of crystals,
        and all your wall of precious stones,
13   and all your [builders]ᵇ shall be taught by Yahweh.
14a In salvation you shall be established,ᶜ
13b and great is the prosperity of your sons.
14b You shall be far from oppression,
        for you need have nothing to fear;
        and from terror,
        for it shall not come near you.

ᵃ In all probability a half-verse has been dropped before 11a.
ᵇ Read *bōnayik* instead of *bānayik*.
ᶜ V. 14a is better taken before v. 13b.

15 Behold, if any one attacks, it is not from me,
   whoever attacks you falls because of you.ᵃ
16 Behold, I create the smith
   who blows the fire of coals,
   and produces the weapon for its purpose;
   and I create the ravager to destroy.
17 No weapon fashioned against you shall prosper.
   You shall confute
   every tongue that rises against you in judgment.
   This is the heritage of the servants of Yahweh,
   and their salvation from me, says Yahweh.

The passage is made up of two parts which are independent of one another. Verses 11–13a describe the new, splendid Jerusalem, and vv. 13b–17 assure Zion or Israel of peace and security for the future. In this second part of ch. 54 the subject of the promise is again not deliverance and restoration, but the new condition of salvation. This is what gives the passage, or the two of them, their peculiar stamp. It cannot be decided for certain whether they and 54.1–10 form a single unit (as is the view of Elliger, who believes that chs. 54 and 55 come from Trito-Isaiah), or whether they are independent units. But at all events they go together with vv. 1–10 in that their subject is not the saving event, but the era of salvation.

[11–13a] This part is akin to 51.21ff. and is similarly constructed. There, too, Zion is addressed as 'O afflicted one'. There, however, the address is preceded by the words, 'therefore hear this, O afflicted one', and it is probable that a similar introduction has dropped out here. The address is reminiscent of the lament made by Jerusalem after she had been destroyed. Not only is she promised restoration (as e.g. in 49.8b), but she is also to be raised up in supernatural splendour. Very strikingly, this description has nothing to say of her size or security or strength. Its sole theme is the glittering splendour of her buildings. It makes no difference whether, as the text suggests, the pinnacles are thought of as actually constructed of rubies and the gates of crystals (the various precious stones mentioned cannot be determined for certain) or whether they are merely adorned with such stones. The sole thing of importance is that the accent falls on the city's splendour, and on it alone. Before this time, the only reason for Israel's mentioning splendid buildings had been the desire to put these forward as evidence of the wealth and power of the

ᵃ For *mē'ōti* read *mē'ittī* and for *'ittāk* read *'ōtāk*.

sovereign. For the most part, such splendour in buildings in Israel was condemned by the prophets. It is a different story with the temple. But a temple is the last thing Deutero-Isaiah is speaking of here! What then is the splendour of the new Jerusalem intended to signify? The only real possibility is that the new Jerusalem is God's city in a completely new way, and its glittering splendour points directly to the divine majesty. This also gives point to the final words, that the builders of this new Jerusalem are to be taught by Yahweh: these buildings arise out of God's plan and will.

In this connection Deutero-Isaiah may have been thinking of a feature found in royal inscriptions in Babylon. Stummer remarks,

> we may think of how the neo-Babylonian kings, above all Nebuchad-nezzar, often say that they had erected such and such a building in precious stones. Mention is often made in particular of the *ūnknû* stone, that is, the lapis lazuli or azure stone. In actual fact, of course, what came in question were perfectly ordinary bricks overlaid with blue glass paste.[a]

Still, Deutero-Isaiah's description goes far beyond this; Stummer says that 'the stones mentioned in the passage in Isaiah are not just *lapides pretiosi*, but *gemmae*'. Does Deutero-Isaiah mean to say that 'chock-full of splendour as was Babylon, the magnificence of the new Jerusalem is to surpass it' (Stummer)? This might perhaps square with the fact that in the trial speeches Yahweh proves himself to be the sole God as over against the gods of the nations. In any case, in the whole of Deutero-Isaiah's proclamation this description of the new Jerusalem is the odd man out; its context is the description of salvation, of which there is hardly any other trace in our prophet.

[13b–17] In this section Deutero-Isaiah employs a form of whose provenance we can be quite certain. It is a promise of blessing, which elsewhere is made only to an individual. And it is a fixed form, which certainly had some particular act of worship as its basis. There are instances of it in Pss. 91 and 121 and in Job 5.17–26, and suggestions of it in other places as well. Verse 14b corresponds to Ps. 91. 5a, 10 and to Job 5.9b; 54.13b is similar to Job 5.25. There is a difference between the promise of blessing and the promise, or oracle, of salvation. The latter is God's answer to a lament, and it promises the removal of the suffering there lamented. The former, on the

[a] 'Einige Keilschriftliche Parallelen zu Jes. 40–66', *JBL*, XLV (1926), pp. 171–89.

other hand, promises God's constant presence, help, protection and blessing. This is the one occasion on which it is used by Deutero-Isaiah, and the one occasion when its reference is to Israel—only here in ch. 54, throughout which the subject is the condition of things in the era of salvation. The structure is simple. Verses 14a and 13b are general assurances of well-being for those addressed and their children. Verse 14b promises safety from all oppression and terror. Verses 15 and 17 explain this—anyone who attacks is to fail (v. 15); the reason for this is that God has his weapons and his plans to destroy under control. Verse 17a resumes v. 14b: no weapon or word that rises in judgment is to succeed in harming those addressed (similarly Job 5.23). Verse 17b rounds it all off: 'this is the heritage of the servants of Yahweh.' In the original promise of blessing, its recipient was the righteous man, the man who trusts in God (Ps. 91.14). And here, too, we can still read between the lines that this is strictly speaking a promise made to an individual (e.g. 'the tongue that rises against you', cf. Job 5.21, 'you shall be hid from the scourge of the tongue'). This is also the origin of the plural, 'the servants of Yahweh', the only occurrence of the term in Deutero-Isaiah. Because of all this, it is impossible to interpret the various things said in this promise of blessing to Israel as referring to her present situation or to her situation in the immediate future. Deutero-Isaiah has taken the promise of blessing used in worship and, with hardly any, or even no change, adapted it to the nation in order to say that God's new turning towards her (54.7f.) means not only the removal of her extremity, but a new era of divine blessing. The prophet does not in fact give a detailed description of the era. Instead, he achieves his purpose by means of the *personal* promise of blessing well known to his hearers.

As we look back over ch. 54, we find there a particularly clear example of a characteristic of Deutero-Isaiah's prophecy. As well as promising deliverance, in this chapter Deutero-Isaiah also wants to say that with and through the deliverance comes a new era of salvation for Israel. The renewed turning of God's grace towards her (v. 8) means the introduction of a new condition of things which is to be a permanent one. The prophet's whole interest, however, is concentrated on the theological aspect of this new state of salvation. The climax of it all is quite plainly the proclamation in vv. 7f.—for Israel the new salvation means that God turns towards her in mercy.

As far as concerns Israel, Deutero-Isaiah places the whole emphasis on the fact that Zion is freed from her solitude (vv. 1ff.) and the shame which this occasions (vv. 4ff.). In the matter of factual description of the new era Deutero-Isaiah is reserved; he takes up practically unchanged existing traditions which refer to the new splendour (vv. 11–13a) and the new peace (vv. 13b–17) rather than gives a concrete picture of these. This very fact, however, suggests (as against Elliger) that the speaker in the whole of ch. 54 is Deutero-Isaiah himself. It is only with Trito-Isaiah that we find very concrete and elaborate description of the new era.

CHAPTER 55.1–5

Come, all you that thirst

1 Ho, every one who thirsts, come to the waters,
   and even he who has no money, come!
   Buy and eat, come and buy
   wine and milk, without money and without price!
2 Why do you spend money for bread that has no worth,
   the wages of your labour for food that does not satisfy?
   Hearken diligently to me, that you may have what is good to eat,
   that your soul may regale itself with fatness.
3 Incline your ear, come to me,
   hear, that your soul may revive.

   I will make with you an everlasting covenant,
   the steadfast, sure promises of grace to David.
   Behold, I made him a witness for peoples,
   a leader and commander of nations.
5 Behold, you call a nation that you know not,
   a nation that knows you not, they run to you
   because of Yahweh, your God,
   and of the Holy One of Israel, for he glorifies you.

Bibliography. O Eissfeldt, 'The Promises of Grace to David in Isaiah 55. 1–5', *Israel's Prophetic Heritage*, ed. B. W. Anderson and W. Harrelson, London, 1962, pp. 196–207.

Chapters 54 and 55 are closely akin; thus the imperatives in vv.

1-3a follow on those of 54.1 and 4 and the one which was probably dropped before v. 11. There is an unusual accumulation of imperatives here (vv. 1-2a, come and buy, vv. 2b-3a, come and hear), and what they serve to introduce is a proclamation of salvation (v. 3b). This is expanded by means of a twofold 'behold'. The first, in v. 4, looks back to the old covenant with David, the second, in v. 5a, makes a contrast between this and the new covenant in which the 'graces bestowed on David' are now promised to Israel. The proclamation of salvation proper (v. 3b) is couched in the first person (the divine intervention), and the development in v. 5 as an address to Israel (the consequence of the intervention). The object to be attained (v. 5b) is stated to be: this takes place because of God, the Holy One of Israel.

[1-3] The opening words of this are both unique and very strange in the proclamation of Deutero-Isaiah. In respect of form, they are in entire accord with the various other introductions with imperatives, and elsewhere in Deutero-Isaiah a doubled or repeated imperative is a characteristic of introductions (40.1ff.; 51.9ff.). What is different and strange here is the thing which the imperatives summon men to do—to buy and eat. No doubt the imperatives in vv. 1 and 2a are to be taken metaphorically—they are (to some extent) departed from in the summons to hear, vv. 2b and 3a. All the same, strangely and almost paradoxically, this summons to hear, too, has satisfying and reviving as its object. The exceptional nature of the imperatives in vv. 1-3a is due to the character of chs. 54f. As was shown above, their language throughout is the language used in blessing. The thing to which men are here called is not primarily the saving event, but the new condition of salvation. This co-ordination of deliverance and blessing in a promise goes back to the very earliest times that Israel had promises made her. We find it as early as the promise in Ex. 3.7f., where the deliverance has as its concomitant the promise of entry into the 'good land', that 'flows with milk and honey'. Begrich gives an excellent explanation of the form of the first verses which sheds a great deal of light upon them:

> In respect of form, 55.1-5 is an invitation on the part of Wisdom to be guests at her table. She begins with the characteristic public invitation to the hungry and thirsty to come (Prov. 9.5; Ecclus. 24.19) and partake of food and drink at her table, where both can be had without money . . . Notice that, as in Prov. 9.11, this invitation culminates in a promise of life.

While I have no wish to challenge this explanation, I should like to ask whether these cries in v. 2a might not have as good, or even better, a prototype, in the cries of the water-sellers and others who shouted their wares in the market—these certainly had a fixed form and were familiar to everyone. There would be a gain in this. The majority of editors delete parts of vv. 1–2a, or transpose them, in order to make the text run more smoothly and evenly. With my suggestion there would be no need of alteration. The repetition of the imperatives 'come' and 'buy' would be perfectly deliberate, in imitation of the cries of the vendors. Set this alongside Wisdom's invitation to her banquet, and the original form in the passages which Begrich adduces looks extremely polished and stylized. Additionally, there is in actual fact a difference between a cry of the vendor in the market and an invitation to a banquet.

What is the meaning of this loud 'market-place' invitation? The clue to this ought to be the surprising variation between protasis and apodosis in vv. 2b and 3a, 'hearken to me . . . that you may be satisfied', 'incline your ear . . . that your heart may revive'. It must again be stated emphatically that never before has Deutero-Isaiah given any comparable substantiation of his urgent, impassioned appeals to hearken to his message. In actual fact, here he says something different from what he has said hitherto. What this is we cannot, in my opinion, see if we make our present-day distinction between spiritual and physical. Volz explains vv. 1f. by saying, 'in the name of his God, the prophet says, "do not set your heart on earthly things . . . instead, strive for what is spiritual, invisible and eternal" '. But this does seem to me to be what the text is really trying to say (Muilenburg and North also reject such a distinction). As against this, the translation of v. 3a suggested by North, 'that you may have life in its fullness', seems to point in the right direction. What Deutero-Isaiah had previously proclaimed in the discharge of his task was in the main the deliverance from Babylon and the return home. He now adds to this words to the effect that life in its fullness is awaiting you! As well as delivering you, God gives you blessing. The fullness of this blessing that God works for you is awaiting you if you now close with the invitation given in his word of salvation. This interpretation is also suggested by the crescendo from the things essential to life, water and bread (v. 1a; the imperative 'buy' is a denominative of grain and properly means 'buy grain') to what is superfluous, wine and milk. For the other figure, 'bread that has no worth' (literally, 'not bread'), 'food that does not satisfy', the precise meaning can hardly be fixed. Since in v. 2b the acquisition (of good as well as of bad food) is interpreted as hearkening, v. 2a ought to refer to voices opposed to that of the prophet. The address in v. 1a is clearer—those concerned are hungry and in need. This corresponds to the usual address in Deutero-Isaiah's proclamation of salvation, where Israel in exile is addressed in similar terms (the allusion to a community lament at the beginning of the proclamation). In the light of this v. 2a may be taken more generally—the prophet is speaking of all efforts to get out of the privations of the period of exile.

[3b–5] We now arrive at the proclamation, the object of the invitation of vv. 1–3a, and what people are summoned to hear in vv. 2b and 3a. With his chosen people God intends to make a lasting (or permanent) covenant, the content of which is defined in the words that follow, the steadfast, sure tokens of grace vouchsafed to David (II Sam. 7.8–16; 23.5; Ps. 89.28–38 [27–37]). The thing signified is put very briefly—it is hardly more than suggested—but there is no dubiety. The tokens of grace which the prophecy of Nathan conferred on David and his house are now promised to Israel. This is a radical change on the prophecy of Nathan or the covenant with David, as is brought out particularly by Volz. 'The thing to be noticed here is . . . that the promise to David is transferred to the nation Israel.' The theological significance of this is emphasized by von Rad. 'He does not, however, interpret . . . in the traditional way, for he understands them (the promises) to have been made not to David but to the whole nation. It is, therefore, for all Israel that the promises made to David are to be realized.'[a] As well as II Sam. 7.8–16 and I Kings 8.23–26 and II Sam. 23.5, Ps. 89 is particularly important for the understanding of the present passage. (In his commentary North draws attention to the many points of contact between Ps. 89 and Isa. 55.3f., as does also Eissfeldt in his essay mentioned above.) There the actual subject of a community lament (probably composed during the exile) is the breach of the divine promises made—and that by oath—to David. Psalm 89 itself shows how greatly this breach disturbed Israel. It called everything in question (cf. also Lam. 4). It gave rise to two entirely different new hopes or proclamations. The first was that a new and completely different king would come into being from the house of David (the

[a] *Old Testament Theology*, II, Edinburgh and London, 1965, p. 240.

'shoot', the Messiah). The second was this transformation of the old prophecy in Deutero-Isaiah. We have to take it that laments such as that contained in Ps. 89 were known to our prophet, and also that the great disturbance caused by the breach of the old promise to David formed part of the misery, to counter which he had to speak his message of comfort. Because of this, an utterance on the subject was indispensable. And what he does say is extremely bold. Unlike the messianic predictions, he does not take as the way of comforting his people telling them of some supernatural king who is to come at some time in the future and effect their salvation. Instead, he is daring enough to proclaim that, with the imminent divine act of the release, the tokens of grace vouchsafed to David are transferred to Israel. Bearing Ps. 89 in mind, we see that this is the reason for what is so much emphasized in the proclamation in v. 3b, a *lasting* covenant (*bᵉrīt ʿōlām*), the *reliable* (or, sure and steadfast) tokens of grace vouchsafed to David. These words are a direct refutation of the lament at the breach of the covenant with David. This once again makes it perfectly plain that what chs. 54f. are concerned with is the element of continuance and permanence, the enduring. This is also the reason for the mention of the covenants with Noah and David, both of which involve promises of blessing.

[4–5] In order to understand vv. 4f., which develop v. 3b, the first important thing to realize is that while Deutero-Isaiah's re-adaptation of the old promise made to David is a bold one, when he comes to develop this, he is reserved in the extreme. After the invitation given in vv. 1–3a, one would look for the development of the new thing which Deutero-Isaiah proclaims, and to which so loud an invitation is given, to contain some description of the fullness of the life and blessing held out. In actual fact, the promise once made to the house of David applied to the nation as well, for in it the king is the mediator of blessing. It is through him that the nation receives blessing, peace and fullness of life. Of this, however, the development in vv. 4f. has, surprisingly enough, nothing to say. Instead, one point, and it alone, is brought out in connection with the transfer of God's tokens of grace from the king (David) to the nation. But precisely this one small part of the fullness of life and blessing which the king mediated to the nation is the very thing on to which Deutero-Isaiah might have been expected to fasten. As was shown in the first paragraph of the present section, the word 'behold' (*hēn*) at the beginning of v. 4 and of v. 5 is meant to make a contrast.

This being so, v. 4 must refer to the past, to the tokens of grace which God vouchsafed to David; the new promise, now transferred to the nation Israel, only comes in v. 5. God made David 'a leader and commander of nations'. Ps. 18.44 (43), 'thou didst make one the head of nations; people whom I had not known served me', directly reflects the astonishment which this evoked. But while in v. 4b Deutero-Isaiah does no more than adduce a fact of history, in his first designation of David, in v. 4a, 'I made him a witness for peoples', he adds an interpretation of his own. The only possible meaning is that David's victories and conquests gave evidence of the God of Israel and of his espousing of his chosen people's cause. The similarity between this and the now imminent realization of the promise to Israel is only very remote—although in an entirely different way, Israel is to become a witness to God among the nations: 'you call people that you know not . . . they run to you.' The allusions to the actual words of Ps. 18.44 (43) underline the similarity with God's actions in the case of David. The verbs are reminiscent of the introduction (vv. 1–3a), while the things described are the same—an invitation and its acceptance now extend beyond Israel to distant and foreign peoples —in entire agreement with 45.20–25 and 44.5.

The oldest concept of the blessing includes growth (increase of population) and victory over one's enemies (e.g., Gen. 24.60). The one side of this is developed in ch. 54 and taken up again in the introduction to ch. 55 (1–3a), the other, victory over one's enemies, is radically transformed. What is promised to the nation once it is delivered from Babylon are not new victories or the subjugation of foreign nations, but increase in numbers because of the distant and foreign people who come to Israel and want to belong to her because of the God of Israel.

[5b] Verse 5b brings this section to its end. The new, lasting covenant with Israel is made 'because of Yahweh, your God'. The covenant is altogether an act of God's grace towards Israel; there is no suggestion of Israel's being laid under any obligation. In it 'the Holy One of Israel' is at work (44.5; 45.19; 49.7), and by this means he glorifies himself through his people (in 49.3 the same verb is used with reference to the Servant). The idea that in all that is done God intends to glorify Israel (and this for his own sake) is particularly emphasized. Precisely this glorification is the object of the loud summons in vv. 1–3a. But as vv. 4 and 5a make clear, the glory envisaged is not the same as that which had once accrued to Israel

because of David's dominion and his victories. The promise is taken out of the political sphere and the sphere of kingship and is transferred to the nation. It is to prove itself true is this—in an entirely new way there is an increase from abroad in Israel's numbers, and to the rest of the nations she becomes a witness to the miraculous workings of her God.

CHAPTER 55.6–11

The word that goes forth from my mouth

6 Seek Yahweh, since he may be found,
  call upon him, since he is near!
7   Let the wicked forsake his way,
        and the unrighteous man his thoughts,
        and return to Yahweh,
        that he may have mercy upon him,
        and to our God;
        for he is abundant in mercy.

8 For my thoughts are not your thoughts,
  and neither are your ways my ways, says Yahweh.
9 But as the heavens are higher than the earth,
  so are my ways higher than your ways
  and my thoughts than your thoughts.

10 For as the rain and the snow come down from heaven
  and return not thither,
  but water the earth,
  making it bring forth and sprout,
  giving seed to the sower and bread to the eater,
11 so is my word that goes forth from my mouth;
  it does not return to me empty,
  but it accomplishes that which I purpose,
  and prospers in the thing for which I send it.

While the book ends with a prophecy (vv. 12f.), this section is in fact the tail-piece. It might even be called an epilogue, for, as many editors have pointed out, its close connections with the prologue, especially with 40.6ff., are obvious. It structure is very simple: there are the imperatives in v. 6, the last of the many that have been addressed to Israel, and the substantiation in two parts that rounds off and gathers up all the rest. To counter the questions asked by Israel now reduced to doubt, vv. 8f. substantiate the promise by reference to the loftiness of the thoughts and ways of God, while vv. 10f. do the same by saying that there can be no doubt that the saving word which God speaks to Israel will prosper. As in 40.12–31, the reason why this final substantiation of the call to partake in God's salvation is divided into two parts is that descriptive praise is similarly divided—God is praised in respect of his sovereign power and of his condescension. That 55.6–11 are in the nature of a conclusion and summary also comes out in the fact that the terms used are those of a summary. In vv. 8f. God's thoughts and ways are grouped together and contrasted with those of men, and in vv. 10f., the words of God spoken to Israel, his promises and proclamations of salvation, are subsumed under the term, *the* word of God, a synthesis found only in the prologue, in 40.8.

[6] The summons in the final section of the book of Deutero-Isaiah to 'seek Yahweh' means essentially the same as do its fellows in the earliest writing prophets, Amos (5.6) or Jeremiah (29.12f.). Basically, it is a cultic summons, a summons to approach God and to seek him with sacrifice and prayer in the temple. But even as early as the time of Amos it had lost its connection with the temple, and taken on the broader meaning of turning towards God. The same is also true here, where the summons continues the invitation extended in 55.1–3a (in Jer. 29.12f., too, the summons is accompanied by the promise, 'so will you live'). Since Isa. 55.6ff. form a conclusion and summary, the verses cannot possibly have been intended, as is the view of Volz, Begrich and North, to be a general invitation to seek God and invoke him. Instead, they are to be taken in exactly the same way as the invitation in 55.1–3a—now, at this present moment, you, Israel, are given the offer of salvation, God's turning towards you, the return home, and the new life! He can be found *now, now* is he near! The offer of salvation to Israel is here couched in the form of a summons that could be quite general and without reference to any particular time. But the general terms are perfectly deliberate. It was of set purpose that Deutero-Isaiah clothed this offer in a form associated with the solemnities of Israel's worship. He wanted to make her see what was now at stake. Verse 6 itself gives a hint about the substantiation of the summons, to be developed in vv. 8–11; he may be found, he is near. For. . .

[7] But how is the sense of the passage as just given to get over v. 7? If we follow Begrich and take vv. 6f. as a unit, then the verses are undoubtedly a general exhortation without reference to any particular time. But, so taken, they would be absolutely out of keeping with the rest of Deutero-Isaiah's proclamation, and their summons to trans-gressors to repent would have no bearing on the situation to which the prophet addresses himself. Duhm's objections to v. 7 in its present context are still valid. In particular, the 'thoughts' and 'ways' of mankind in v. 7 mean something entirely different from what they mean in v. 8. In v. 7 they are the transgressors' thoughts and ways, but in v. 8 they are those of Israel, whose doubting and lack of faith are contrasted with the thoughts and ways of God. 'For' in v. 8 may substantiate v. 6, but not v. 7.

We must therefore regard v. 7 as an addition made by a reader, either suggested by the words 'thoughts and ways' in v. 6, or as an expansion of v. 6, which he took as a general exhortation.

[8–9] Here 'thoughts' does not have the meaning of 'reflections', but, as often in the Old Testament, of plan or design. The ways are appropriate to the execution of these plans or designs. The subject is, what God purposes and how he carries it out. The general terms, 'thoughts and ways', allow of the very apt parallel between God and men, which excellently brings out the contrast. This utterance, Isa. 55.8f., is remarkably typical of the way in which the Bible speaks about God and man. The sole way the Bible has of speaking about God is in terms and concepts related to man. Its language is through-out anthropomorphic—God thinks his thoughts as men thinks theirs, and he goes his way as they go theirs. 'As the heavens are higher than the earth'—this is the one and only way of expressing the contrast between God and man. The Bible never speaks of God without this reference to man.

At first sight the contrast between God's thoughts and ways and those of man has the appearance of being quite general, but the reason for this lies in the nature of the passage—it forms the conclusion of the book. And even if the words are in fact as general as they seem to be, they nevertheless refer on the one hand to one specific thing which God is planning and to its execution, and on the other to a specific way of thinking and acting on the part of men—God's design at this very time to procure Israel's salvation, and, as against this, Israel's lassitude and acquiesence because of the situation in which she found herself. That this is what he means is shown by the way in which vv. 10f. re-echo 40.6ff. And when he goes on to say in the vivid way he does that God's thoughts and ways are not men's, but are as high above them as the heavens, or poles asunder, these sentiments take us extremely close to those of 40.12–31, where, in order to counter Israel's resignation and weariness (40.27), Deutero-Isaiah extols God and magnifies him as creator and lord of history. He does the same thing here. By pointing to the boundless horizons of God's designs and ways, immeasurably greater than men can think them to be, he gives his hearers confidence. Though they are no longer able to believe it, all things are possible with God.

[10–11] Verses 10f. state the other factor; his word can be depended upon. While this, too, is again put in perfectly general terms, still, what the general statement made about God's words alludes to is the word of salvation now being spoken to Israel, on which people can depend—what God wills with it, it accomplishes. What is here said is given its force by the comparison in which it is formulated. This was taken from the sphere of the blessing. Strictly speaking, the two processes set side by side and compared are in themselves not at all of the same nature. The word expressly spoken to the needs of a particular situation and meeting with faith or lack of faith in it, understanding or lack of understanding, is an entirely different matter from rain or snow in the world of nature. Nevertheless (just as with the parables of Jesus) it is precisely this difference in kind that makes the comparison possible, for what it tries to say is this—these two very different matters have, still, one thing in common: with both something is effected and achieves its purpose. This factor which links the two must then be something that Deutero-Isaiah regards as characteristic of the word and of its understanding—through the word something takes place between an I and a Thou, a speaker and a hearer. For our prophet the word is not primarily something with a content, but the instrument by means of which something is effected. God's word is a word that does things. When God speaks, something comes about. This view of the word dominates the whole of prophecy—before Deutero-Isaiah it finds expression in Jeremiah. But in addition it is the basic view in the Old and the New Testament alike. One can very well see why this view of God's word is given its classical expression by Deutero-Isaiah at the end of the classical period of prophecy, and also why he puts it in the very last words of his message. The special feature in the word of God as the prophets proclaimed it was that it had nothing to safeguard it. It had no connection with the tradition to be found in an establishment, and rested solely on its having been transmitted to the messenger who, on this occasion and that, came on the scene with it. As such it might be doubted, disdained, even silenced. But the very fact that it was without safeguard threw its character as an entirely personal word, and a word that came to a particular man, into bolder relief than can be seen anywhere else than in prophecy, or at any other time.

But this is only the one aspect of what is here said about God's word. The other is the certainty that what it proclaims will be fulfilled. The particular word envisaged is the word of salvation in the form, promise of salvation or proclamation of the same, which runs through the whole of Deutero-Isaiah's proclamation and forms its heart.

First, we must beware of a wrong idea. Editors often say that the present passage makes of the word of God almost (or entirely) a hypostasis, an agency that brings something about by means of actions on its own part. This forgets the fact that the word of salvation spoken to Israel, the primary concern here, does not work automatically. It is spoken to men who have the power to accept it or refuse it. It is always an entirely personal word in which something happens between two persons. God's word does not magically call a new state of salvation into being. The only way by which it effects what God designs it to do is the hearkening to, and acceptance of, the message of salvation. Verses 10f. are indeed the substantiation of the invitation given in v. 6 to accept by so doing.

It is only as we realize this that the assurance in vv. 10f. comes into its proper focus. It is a tremendously bold one. It takes up a motif found in the trial speeches with the other gods—that of the dependable connection between what is proclaimed (by God) and its fulfilment ('did I not proclaim it to you beforehand?'). Israel had been summoned to attest this. And now the final words of Deutero-Isaiah's message are that this state of affairs still continues in being. Now—in his own message—a fresh word of God is uttered. It, too, achieves its purpose and fulfilment. There is no other possibility—what he has proclaimed as God's word must be fulfilled, as will be attested by subsequent generations.

The assurance is, we said, very bold. The reason for saying so is that the prophet had no sure knowledge about this or that in the future. While he proclaims, he is not a foreteller. There is a fundamental distinction between the two. A great deal of what was said by Deutero-Isaiah, which means a great deal of what he proclaimed as the word of God, was not fulfilled in the way in which he said it would be. Israel's return home was no triumphal procession through a desert transformed into a garden. In the matter of many of his utterances one can point a finger and say that this is not in fact what actually took place.

But this makes no difference to what he said in 50.10ff. about the word of God and its efficacy. (We must, of course, take vv. 10f. in the light of what vv. 8f. say about God's plans and his activity.) Ever and always are God's thoughts and ways higher than those of men— as much higher as heaven is in relation to the earth. This holds true also of the fulfilment of his promises. When ascertainment of it is possible, the fulfilment may well be different, very different even, from what the prophet led people to expect. The only thing that is absolutely certain is that prophecy inevitably results in fulfilment. The word never returns void. But the God who fulfils his promises is always one whose thoughts and ways are immeasurably greater than those of men.

What Deutero-Isaiah here says in the utterance which brings his message to its end forms in actual fact a bridge between the exile and the new Jerusalem. But at the same time it made no exact statement of the fulfilment's precise nature.

CHAPTER 55.12–13

You shall go out in joy

12 For you shall go out in joy
   and be led forth in peace;
   Mountains and hills before you shall break forth into singing,
   and all the trees of the fields shall clap their hands.
13 Instead of the thorn shall come up the cypress,
   instead of the brier shall come up the myrtle.
   It is to the praise of Yahweh,
   an everlasting sign that shall not be cut off.

On what is properly the final passage of the prophecy, the epilogue in 55.6–11, ensues the simple, direct proclamation of the departure from Babylon and the return home. After the repeated variations of the prophecy of salvation which reaches its climax in 56.6–11, we once more find the simple basic motif struck up. Deutero-Isaiah's purpose in so doing is to say that 'this is what all that I had to say was driving at—the hour of departure, the joy of the way back home'.

The joy to which the prophet summoned his fellow-countrymen in the hymns of praise which accompanied his preaching, the singing to which he summoned those still in captivity, still cut off from any future that might spell salvation for them, and in which only a faith that anticipated the future could join ('eschatological' hymn of praise)—this singing is to be the one, and the necessary, reaction on the part of the people now setting forth for home. It is the joy of a man who has for long been in a foreign country and now steps out on the way back home. Here, however, the opening of the road that leads to the homeland is an event which so 'shakes the world' that it not only has consequences that leave their mark on world-history (Cyrus): it has a bearing on creation itself. For the one who frees Israel is the lord of history. This is the reason why she may go forth in joy. But further-more, this one is also the creator. And because of this the whole of creation, the universe, shares in the joy of those set free. Hence the possibility of using the magnificent, if exaggerated, picture, 'the trees shall clap their hands'. This is exactly what we find in the psalms, where the singing of the redeemeds goes on to summon the whole of creation to render praise. The terms are exaggerated. None the less, they are based on the belief that holds true for the whole of the Bible—in the mind of God, creation and history are a unity and can never be separated.

[13b] The book's final words point away from the redemption to the redeemer. In the last analysis, whatever comes about comes about for God's honour, just as all creation exists in order to render him praise.

PART TWO

TRITO-ISAIAH

Chapters 56–66

INTRODUCTION

THE PERIOD

IN THE YEAR 538 Cyrus, King of Persia, issued the edict concerning the rebuilding of the temple in Jerusalem. He allowed the Jews to return home from Babylon, and gave back the temple vessels carried off when the city was captured. The text of this edict is preserved in Ezra 6.3ff. It is dated in 'the first year of the reign of Cyrus', which means the first year of his sovereignty over the empire of Babylon. In the following year, 537, a small number of Israelites returned from Babylon to Jerusalem. Soon afterwards came the laying of the foundations of the new temple (Ezra 5.14ff.). But it also stopped short at this; nothing more was done towards the building. The reason was given in Hag. 1.1–11. Things were so uncertain, circumstances so straightened, and economic troubles so severe, that the vast operation which needed a common effort was discontinued. When in 522 the king of Persia, Cambyses, died without leaving an heir to the throne and the kingship fell to Darius, disturbances throughout the whole of the empire were the occasion of a new movement in Jerusalem. The prophet Haggai appeared with his message that all progress and prosperity depended on the rebuilding of the temple. Work on it was resumed towards the end of the year 520 (Hag. 1.12ff.). These are also the circumstances and the time in which the prophet Zechariah delivered his proclamation. Darius, who was soon in full control, gave his approval to the further work on the temple. The newly erected sanctuary was consecrated in 515.

Nevertheless, there was no thoroughgoing change for the better, as Haggai and Zechariah had proclaimed there would be. We are given a vivid description of the difficulties and confused state of things by the prophet Malachi, whose activity lies in this period (perhaps about 470), a period about which we have scarcely any other information.

Change only came with the reform of Nehemiah and Ezra, which began in 445. There can be no doubt that the activity of the prophet

Trito-Isaiah falls within the period between 537 and 455. The reason for the involved discussion about a nearer determination of its actual point within these limits was due to the fact that efforts to determine the strands from which the collection of writings grew up had met with no success. Taking what is clearly the nucleus (chs. 60–62) as the basis of enquiry, it is at once perfectly evident that the point in history at which Trito-Isaiah made his proclamation is the beginning of the period, that is to say, the years between 537 and 515. Haggai's description of them tallies exactly with what can be gathered about them from the proclamations contained in chs. 60–62. Since 60.13 says that the temple had not as yet been rebuilt, we may infer a date previous to Haggai and Zechariah, that is, before 521. Thus, Trito-Isaiah's activity fell between 537 and 521, perhaps about the year 530. Of its duration we have no idea. It was certainly not more than a few years, and perhaps less than one.

It is impossible to determine the dates of the later strands in chs. 56–66. The one which shows a division into the transgressors and the devout cannot be very much later than Trito-Isaiah, because of the clear picture it gives of the beginnings of the cleavage.

STRUCTURE AND COMPOSITION OF CHAPTERS 56–66

I

There is a large measure of agreement on the following points. Chapters 60–62 form the nucleus of the message contained in the book of Trito-Isaiah. They reproduce the message of a prophet of the period after the exile. They also form a literary unit. Two characteristics in particular make it possible to be certain about all this. First, chs. 60–62 contain a message of salvation and nothing but salvation. Secondly, this message shows from first to last a provenance from, or a harking back to, that of Deutero-Isaiah. There are also a number of additional characteristics, but for the moment we shall confine ourselves to these two. Are there parts other than chs. 60–62 to which they also apply? The answer is that there are three, and that these, too, can be reckoned |as forming part of the nucleus of Trito-Isaiah's message. They are 57.14–20; 65.16b–25; and 66.6–16. These, too, are a message of salvation and nothing but salvation, and they also presuppose Deutero-Isaiah's proclamation. This does not preclude the possibility that still more passages may form part of the nucleus. But scholarship is on firmer ground if, for its starting point, it takes only those passages which beyond any doubt form part of the nucleus. The common factors in this proclamation of salvation may now be defined more precisely.

1. It is very easy to see the circumstances with reference to which it was delivered. The words of salvation are not now spoken in the exile and to the exiles, but after the return, in Judah and Jerusalem. Nevertheless, it is clear that the return of the first exiles after 537 did not prove the mighty, all-transforming turning-point to salvation that the message of Deutero-Isaiah might have led people to expect. Instead, even now men were still looking to the future for this. The circumstances of those who did return are wretched, straightened and vexatious. So few did in fact come back that an important point in Trito-Isaiah's proclamation of salvation is the return of those still in the diaspora. The change to salvation, the shining forth of God's glory over his chosen people (60.1f.), is to transform a state of things determined by economic hardship (60.17; 62.8f.), insecurity in political life (60.10, 18), ruins and devastation (61.4), and the burden of continuing shame (61.7; 62.4).

2. What this proclamation of salvation says about the foreign nations is particularly its own. The prophet makes a peculiarly close link between these and Israel's now changed lot—in the role of servants they are given part in the great transformation which, when it comes, God's salvation is to effect. Nations and kings come to the light that rises over God's people (60.3). They bring back the dispersed of Israel (60.4b, 9b; 66.12). They bring their treasures and riches to Jerusalem (60.9b). They have to acknowledge the mighty acts of God (60.6; 61.9; 62.2). Their association with Israel, serving her in this manner, in her new condition of salvation, and the way in which they directly or indirectly serve to glorify Yahweh, give them a positive, if limited, part in the change to salvation—the negative statements made about them, as, for example, that those who once oppressed them now come bending low to them (60.14), are less prominent. At all events, it is absolutely clear that the great turning-point which means salvation for Israel does not automatically mean the destruction of her foes. Quite possibly this attitude to the foreign nations goes back to Deutero-Isaiah, although Trito-Isaiah does considerably damp down the former's universalism.

3. The recipient of the promise of salvation is Israel, Israel taken

all together and addressed as a single unit. One of the main things which helps to give the promise the tone it has in the fact that this form allows the chosen people to be addressed in the second personal singular—'Arise, shine: for your light comes' (60.1)—just as one addresses a person. This is one of the most important points of agreement between Trito-Isaiah's promise of salvation and that of Deutero-Isaiah. Both are directed to Israel, Israel as a single unit. This at once marks off two characteristics of the former. First, as with Deutero-Isaiah, the promise has no conditions attached to it. It is not bound up with any mode of action on the part of the nation as its antecedent. Secondly, in no part of the nucleus of Trito-Isaiah is anything said of a division within the nation which would mean that only one section of it would benefit by the salvation which the prophet proclaims.

4. Without laying any special stress upon it, Trito-Isaiah's message of salvation assumes that in the era of salvation there will be worship and sacrifice. For example, in 60.6f., the treasures which the foreign nations bring contribute, among other things, to the restored worship. They bring incense with them, sheep and rams come on the altars, and God's house is to be glorified (60.7, 13; 62.9). Apart from this there is no mention of worship (61.6 has nothing to do with this subject). It cannot be said that Trito-Isaiah puts any special emphasis on the part which worship is to play in the salvation to come.

5. From the first to last, the salvation which Trito-Isaiah proclaims is conceived in terms of this world. That is to say, the great change which inaugurates it brings about a state of affairs which is still tied to the realm of history. Its scene is the earthly Jerusalem. Where she has been devastated she must be rebuilt (61.4), including her walls and gates (60.10f., 18). Israel is once more to possess her land (60.21). And, while the nation is to increase in numbers (60.22), it does not cease to be one nations among the rest (61.9ff.), and its livelihood depends on its own efforts (62.8f.; 65.21–23). No doubt it is a life of richest blessing in peace (65.19; 66.12). Israel exalts and rejoices (65.18). She has security (65.23), glory and honour, and also wealth and abundance. But none of this goes beyond the conditions applying to life in space and time.

There are, however, a few passages which do go beyond this, and where the salvation promised has traits incompatible with the realm of history. They are as follows: 60.19–20: Yahweh is to be an everlasting light for Zion, and there is to be no further need of sun and moon; and the two utterances within are set 65.16b–25, i.e. v. 17, about the new heaven and the new earth, and v. 25, depicting the animals as living together in peace. Both may be due to later expansion. Yet, even if they are to be thought of as part of Trito-Isaiah's own proclamation, they are not characteristic of it.

6. We have now outlined the main elements in the nucleus of Isa. 56–66. But there are only two parts of it which tell us anything of the prophet who proclaimed this message. They are 61.1ff. and 62.1, 6. The former represents the declaration of the messenger who tells his hearers of his authorization and equipment to proclaim the message of the salvation to come, while 62.1, 6 add that he is not to be silent until the actual arrival of the salvation. These passages let us be quite certain that the unknown figure whom we call Trito-Isaiah was a definite person, a prophet of the early post-exilic period, whose primary task was to reawaken Deutero-Isaiah's message of salvation for a small band of people living in a time of disillusionment after the end of the exile and the return. While this is all that we know of him, these passages show us a man deeply involved in his task, conscious of being God's messenger, and one who, like the pre-exilic prophets, prepared the way for the message of salvation in defiance of the apparent logic of facts and at a time when men were depressed and resigned to things as they were. To the best of our knowledge, he was the last person in Israel to say of himself—and say it with assurance— that God sent him as a messenger to his fellow-countrymen.

7. The preceding paragraphs show the relationship in which he stood to Deutero-Isaiah. He was the latter's disciple, as Elliger emphasized and proved. His desire was to revive his master's proclamation for his own day. However, the change in the situation involved an alteration in the message. He is unable to connect the advent of the salvation with a definite event in the clear way that his predecessor did. When he speaks of the exiles' being brought back, this is not the unique, eagerly awaited miracle of the return home, but the continuance and development of something that had already begun. In his hands his master's exact proclamations concerning historical events are replaced by promises of a more general and abstract kind, and he paints in stronger colours. The promise of salvation in the perfect tense, the central feature of Deutero-Isaiah's proclamation, is wholly lacking, the proclamation of salvation often passes over into a description of the latter, and there is more about the state of things in the era of salvation than about the event which inaugurates it.

Accordingly, the note which the proclamation strikes is not so much the miraculous new act of deliverance (the new Exodus) as the overwhelming splendour of the new condition that is soon to begin; glorifying and glorification are constantly on his lips. As with Deutero-Isaiah, a large part is given to the response consisting of joy, singing and praise.

II

Quite obviously, Deutero-Isaiah's proclamation was related to the laments made by Israel—the oracle of salvation is an answer to them, and the proclamation of salvation contains a reference to them. There is certainly something corresponding to this in Trito-Isaiah also. But with him the link between proclamation of salvation and lament is only a vague and superficial one. The nucleus, chs. 60–62, is set within the framework of two laments, chs. 59 and 63f. The purpose is to connect the proclamation with the nation's laments: it gives God's answer to the supplication. But even although the relationship with the lament is not such a complex and carefully contrived one as it is in Deutero-Isaiah, still, the climax of the psalm of lament in 63, 19b (64.1), 'O thou that rendest the heavens', can be perfectly well related to the beginning of the message of salvation in 60.1f. That which was the subject of supplication in the one case is promised in the other.

1. This shows, first, that, as with his master, there is some connection between Trito-Isaiah's proclamation and the worship of his day. But a reservation must be made. The connection is confined to one aspect of worship, lamentation. As the commentary will show, even the promise of salvation contained in chs. 60–62 has many connections with community laments. In particular, the structure of the three chapters is based on the three parts of a lament (see below). We know that the special services of lamentation instituted after the fall of Jerusalem still continued even after the return of the first exiles, which means that they were still taking place in Trito-Isaiah's time. We can thus very well understand why the prophet brought his promise of salvation into relationship with them. As to whether he made his utterances during the course of such services, we are in the dark. But it is perfectly possible.

2. It follows that chs. 59 and 63f. are genuine community laments. If so, they cannot be compositions of Trito-Isaiah himself. Like all psalms of lamentation, their birth-place was Israel's worship. This

squares with what a considerable number of editors have recognized
—that chs. 63f. are psalms which came into being as the direct result
of the fall of Jerusalem, and fairly soon after that event (so Volz,
Kessler, etc.), even if, in all probability, they were expanded and
altered before Trito-Isaiah included them in his book. The prophet's
incorporation of these psalms into his message indicates two things.
First, he took his stand alongside the people who, since the fall of
Jerusalem, had been making this lament as they came before God.
But secondly, he answered the anxiety represented in the verse which
concludes the psalm (64.11 [12]) with an impassioned 'No'. God is
no longer to be silent in face of his chosen people's extremity—'the
glory of Yahweh rises upon you!'

3. It is different with the lament in ch. 59, because here the lament
has the utterance of a prophet associated with it. It comes at the very
beginning (59.1f.), to answer a community lament, and, in particular,
the charges brought against God. The prophet substantiates what he
says by bringing a charge against the sinful nation (3–8). The
answer is a confession of sin on its part (12–15a). Thereupon God
begins to speak and intervenes to effect deliverance (15b–20). The
chapter thus resembles what Gunkel called prophetic liturgies. It
cannot be so closely connected with Trito-Isaiah's promise of
salvation as can be chs. 63f. God's intervention to save is very different
from Trito-Isaiah's promise of salvation, and this is even truer still of
the charge made by the prophet in vv. 3–8. Of the latter there is no
trace in the nucleus of Trito-Isaiah's proclamation. What marks it
off is that its style is not the same as that of the charge usually made
by the prophets, since it goes on to a 'description of the transgressors',
and the place where this is at home is the lament of the individual.
Thus, in ch. 59 we have discovered an element not to be found in the
nucleus of the proclamation of Trito-Isaiah.

III

Chapter 59 thus forms a means of connecting two strands in chs.
55–66. As a lament, it is part of the framework of chs. 60–62, and the
prophetic charge which goes on to give a picture of the transgressors,
connects it with a different strand. What is it?

The first part of it is composed of the small amount of material
gathered together in 56.9–57.13. This contains three prophetic oracles
of judgment, 56.9–12; 57.3–6; and 57.7–13a. Ewald, Volz and others

saw that these are pre-exilic, and the commentary here will verify this. This little group of oracles is the most certain proof that Isa. 56–66 is not a unity, the work of one single prophet, but that the nucleus had other pieces of various kinds added to it. In respect of form and subject-matter, the three pronouncements of judgment contained in 56.9–57.13 are absolutely similar to those found in pre-exilic prophecy. In 56.9–12, it is the nation's corrupt leaders, the watchmen and shepherds, who are accused, and in 57.3–6 the adulterous people itself (apostasy). The nation is also the subject in 57.7–13. With all three, the verdict passed is destruction. In each case it is the whole nation, or the leaders who represent it, who are addressed. The proclamation has no conditions attached.

The utterances within which all this is set, 57.1f. and 13b, bear a very different stamp. Verses 1f. are a lament over the increase in number of the transgressors, which is bringing about the ruin of the devout and the upright (cf. Ps. 12). The same words are used in the description of the transgressors in Micah 7.2. There, too (Micah 7.1ff.), this lament is connected with a prophetic accusation. Closely associated with 57.1f. is 13b, a promise made to the righteous. These additions which form the framework of the oracles of doom serve to show the way by which these pre-exilic oracles of doom came to be taken up into the post-exilic document. The post-exilic community drew a distinction. One section regarded themselves as the devout and the others as transgressors. In this changed situation, prophetic oracles of doom of the pre-exilic period were revised and directed against these transgressors.

We may therefore assume that the charges which ch. 59 makes against the transgressors form part of the same strand, and are due to the same situation as led in 56.9–57.13 to the transformation of earlier oracles of doom into charges brought against transgressors. We also find utterances against transgressors in the shape of an addition to the promise of salvation in 57.14–19, which link directly on to the material gathered together in 56.9–57.13. Verse 20 describes the transgressors as 'like the tossing sea', and v. 21 adds that there is no peace for them. The fact that the same words occur elsewhere as an addition (Isa. 48.29), and many other reasons, too, lead the majority of editors to regard vv. 20f. as an addition. If, as was shown above, 59.14–19 form part of the nucleus of Trito-Isaiah's proclamation, this proves that the accusations and condemnations of transgressors in 57.20f. and in the other passages form parts of a separate strand.

They are due to the situation in which a cleavage was beginning, when it ceased to be possible to proclaim salvation to all alike, as Trito-Isaiah was still in a position to do. Now the promised peace could not apply to the transgressors.

That part of the book which follows chs. 60–62, namely 65.1–16a, forms part of this same strand and is due to the same situation. There is, however, a difference. In the material so far considered traditional forms or simple additions were employed in speaking about the transgressors. But 65.1–16a is an utterance expressly devised for this new situation. It is obviously intended as a prophetic word. It represents the new type of utterance, a proclamation going in two directions. The devout have salvation proclaimed to them and the transgressors ruin. This very circumstantial utterance clearly reveals a further difference from Trito-Isaiah's promise of salvation. The malpractices for which the description of the transgressors reprimands them are excessively cultic: 65.3b–5, 7, 11. The matters added in 66.17 also come in here. In 65.11 the transgressors are addressed thus, 'but you who forsake me, who forget my holy mountain'. This implies a purely cultic standpoint on the part of the speaker, which obviously differs from that of Deutero-Isaiah's proclamation of salvation. Correspondingly, 65.1–16a have no echoes of the former prophet's proclamation.

In 65.8 there is an express substantiation of the parting of the way as between proclamation of salvation and proclamation of ruin. This suggests that the cleavage was felt to be a new departure, and that the passage before us dates from its beginning. This is even more apparent in the final utterance in this strand, 66.5. This is a word of salvation for those 'who tremble at his word' because of oppression by 'brethren' who scoff at them because they hold fast to the promises. This gives us direct insight into the way in which the community, of which both sides are members, is developing a cleavage, resulting in the presence of a new situation in which the same divine word can no longer apply to everyone alike.

IV

An admonition is found in 58.1–12 on the subject of what is, and what is not, proper fasting. While the passage is made up of elements of different kinds, it is nevertheless obviously a unity. Unlike chs. 60–62, the promise of salvation which lies at the heart of it is a conditional one. But, as opposed to those passages which imply the division into devout and transgressors, this utterance agrees with chs. 60–62 in being addressed to everyone in the nation. In that it declares the kind of fasting proper and pleasing to God to be love of one's neighbour, and not ritual observance of fast days, it takes up the social proclamation of earlier prophecy. Of all the utterances that lie outside the nucleus (57.14–20; 60–62; 65.1–16a and 66.6–16), ch. 58 is the closest to it. We may therefore safely assume that it formed part of the proclamation of the prophet Trito-Isaiah. This is supported by the presence of several reminiscences of utterances in chs. 60–62. Further, the opening (58.1), which corresponds to that of 61.1ff., may represent an exceptional commissioning to deliver the exceptional utterance contained in ch. 61.

Similar to ch. 58 are 66.1f. They, too, are critical of the cult. Chapter 58 called fasting in question. Here the same is done for the temple as God's house. However, the present utterance has closer affinities with the language of the Psalms and is similar to Ps. 50. Since in what he says in ch. 60 Trito-Isaiah takes it for granted that the temple forms a part of the new Jerusalem of the era of salvation, it is improbable that 66.1f. were also delivered by him. The verses cannot be fitted into any of the strands distinguishable in Trito-Isaiah. They stand quite apart. The connection between 66.1–2 and 3–4 is a loose one. The former has the temple as its subject, the latter sacrifice. Much in vv. 3f. recalls the cultic malpractices enumerated in ch. 65; 66.4b and c are practically the same as 65.12b and c. Thus, 66.3f. are to be reckoned to the strand to which 65.1–16a belong.

v

The words of judgment against the foreign nations form a well-defined and obviously homogeneous group apart. They quite clearly represent a strand later than chs. 60–62. There the nations are given a portion—even if it is only as servants—in the salvation which is coming to the chosen people. The present oracles of judgment against the foreign nations represent a deliberate correction of this made from a standpoint which regarded God's judgment on the nations as an article of faith. It is therefore no accident that the harshest and most circumstantial oracle of judgment against the foreign nations, 63.1–6, was appended to the nucleus itself, chs. 60–62. The intention is perfectly plain; the attitude towards the nations expressed in chs. 60–62 is amended by the addition of 'but thereafter God begins his great battle with them to destroy them!' 63.1–6 resemble apocalyptic. Couched in the language of myth, the metaphor of the treader of the vine-press depicts the final destruction of the foreign nations, the hostile power of myth. This makes it certain that 63.1–6 form part of one of the latest strands in chs. 56–66.

The same attitude was responsible for the addition of 60.12, at the very point where the theme is the nations' and kings' participation in Israel's salvation in the capacity of servants. Here again, it is quite obvious that the destruction of the nations is proclaimed in order to amend. This was also the purpose of setting the promise of salvation in 66.7–14, which forms part of the nucleus of Trito-Isaiah, within the framework of an epiphany of judgment, vv. 6 and 15f. Verse 6 describes the advent of Yahweh, 'who renders recompense to his enemies', and this is continued in vv. 15f.—he comes to judge all the earth. The final words, 'and those slain by Yahweh are many', clearly suggest 63.1–6. Finally, mention has still to be made of the last words of the addition represented by 66.20–24: v. 24 envisages the destruction of all God's enemies. It is extended to include the idea of an eternal destruction, an idea which belongs to the latest parts of the Old Testament canon.

VI

Practically all editors, even those who—as, for example, Kessler—regard Isa. 56–66 as a unity, look on the opening and the closing verses (56.1–8 and 66.18–24) as later additions.

The two utterances comprised in 56.1f. and 3–8 are not real prophetic utterances. They merely wear the garb of them. 56.1f. is an exhortation to act rightly, especially to keep the sabbath, while 56.3–8 are a regulation concerning membership of the community that worships Yahweh. Of the two utterances 56.3–8 is the more important. In terms of Deut. 23.2–9 (*BH*) eunuchs and foreigners were excluded. But here a newly issued divine oracle expressly admits them. A decision in the realm of sacral law is here given its sanction by means of a word from God. This means a radical change in the idea of the chosen people. Membership ceases to be based on birth, and now depends on resolution, the resolve to take as one's god the God of Israel. The purpose of adding this resolve to the book of Trito-Isaiah was to fit it into the prophetic tradition and confer on it the authority of the prophetic word.

The importance attaching to the sabbath, exemplified in this regulation of sacral law, is further emphasized in 56.1f. and, later on, in the addition 58.13f. In both places the admonition to keep the sabbath has a promise attached to it. Now, since these two additions form the setting, at its beginning and end, of the part of the book of Trito-Isaiah which precedes chs. 60ff., we can here clearly see another strand of tradition. The part comprised by 56.9–58.12 had been preserved and transmitted by a group of people who thought it particularly important that the post-exilic community should be ready to receive foreigners and to be missionary (56.3–8), and who also laid stress on the keeping of the sabbath.

Three verses, 66.18f., 21, probably originated in the same circle. Their position suggests this—this utterance, too, forms the conclusion of a section; and so does the subject-matter—here again the community which worships Yahweh is proclaimed to be missionary and ready to receive foreigners. In this case, its outreach is very much wider, universal in fact. We may therefore assume that this was the group which gave the book of Trito-Isaiah the form in which we have it today (with the exception of 66.20, 22ff. and 59.21)—they put chs. 59–66 together with chs. 56–58. It was a group which had revived the universalism of Deutero-Isaiah, and was thus well adapted to transmit the legacy of Trito-Isaiah.

The last addition, 66.20, 22ff. (along with 59.21), makes a link with Trito-Isaiah (v. 20: the foreign nations bring back Israel's sons and daughters), but goes on to seek to amend the universalism with which the book ends by countering it with a dualism derived from apocalyptic, in terms of which the end to which God's ways are directed is the everlasting worship of God in Jerusalem and the everlasting annihilation of his foes. This addition is in line with the oracles of judgment on the foreign nations, but is later.

VII

Last of all, something still falls to be said about the apocalyptic additions in 60.19f.; 65.17, 25; and 66.20, 22ff. While they show the influence of the rise of apocalyptic, they also show that in all essentials the book of Trito-Isaiah had reached its final form before the era of apocalyptic. The fact that the apocalyptic additions and oracles of judgment upon the nations are only found in chs. 60–66 supports the view that chs. 56–58 and 60 (or 59)–66 were once separate units.

To sum it all up: the following stages can be traced in the origin of the utterances collected in Trito-Isaiah.

The nucleus was formed by chs. 60–62, the proclamation of salvation made by the prophet Trito-Isaiah. This was set within the framework of the two community laments, chs. 59 and 63/64. This corresponds to the relationship that existed between the prophet's proclamation and the exiles' services of lamentation. Together with this block were transmitted a few unconnected utterances of Trito-Isaiah's (57.14–20; 65.16b–25; 66.6–16; and perhaps 58.1–12). These were later joined to the collection, and along with them other utterances, the author of which was not Trito-Isaiah. The latter had been transmitted separately, as is shown by the fact that they were all given additions or insertions.

A second strand is made up of a number of independent utterances and additions, in all of which the main feature of the situation in face of which they were uttered is the rise of a cleavage between the devout and the transgressors (56.9–57.13; 57.21; 59.2–8; 65.1–16a; 66.3f.; 66.5, 17).

A third strand, found only in chs. 60–66, seeks to amend Trito-Isaiah's friendly and open disposition towards foreign nations by proclaiming judgment upon them (60.12; 63.1–6; 66.6, 15f.; 66.20, 22ff.). Similar to it is a series of apocalyptic additions to the oracles of salvation; again, these are found only in chs. 60–66 (60.19f., 65.17, 25; 66.20, 22ff.).

A fourth strand consists of additions at the beginning and the end of the book (56.1f., 3–8; 66.18f., 21.) These are of particular importance as witness to the openness of the community to Gentiles and its missionary character, and to the keeping of the sabbath. 66.1f. may also form part of this strand, but this is not certain.

The importance of Trito-Isaiah lies not so much in his actual proclamation as in the fact that, in the days following the end of the exile, a time of profound disillusionment when there was the utmost lack of common aims and ideals, he revived the promise of salvation.

In the matter of his proclamation he is a disciple of Deutero-Isaiah, and his message is in large measure drawn from the latter's well. This is a sign that we are in the era of post-exilic prophecy which throughout rests upon the tradition of pre-exilic and exilic prophecy, and is more interested in preserving this than in saying anything fresh. This may incline us to feel that Trito-Isaiah is lacking in creative force of his own, and lead us to set no great store by him. But we must reflect on the other hand that, as Deutero-Isaiah's disciple, he made an important—probably the most important—contribution towards the preservation of the latter's message. In the first decades after the return from exile, this was largely regarded as having failed to be fulfilled. But Trito-Isaiah caused it to be preserved as a still valid word of God.

Both Deutero-Isaiah and Trito-Isaiah set us the same problem. Neither the end of the exile nor the years and decades after it spelt the dawn of the era of salvation for the chosen people. Trito-Isaiah's proclamation of salvation was not directly fulfilled, especially in the matter of the details in his description of the era of salvation to come. The failure to be fulfilled, which throughout in the Bible determines the relationship between prophecy and fulfilment, makes itself exceptionally felt in this case. Nor can we get out of it by saying that, while Trito-Isaiah's promises were not fulfilled at the time, they were so in the coming of Christ. Even that can only be said in so far as, here too, the failure to be fulfilled is clearly recognized. For even with Christ the details did not come to pass in the way that Trito-Isaiah proclaimed them.

None the less, the use made of 61.1ff. in Luke 4.16ff. shows the importance which Trito-Isaiah actually had for God's people. The proclamation made by the messenger, in which the prophet of the return declared his authority to proclaim salvation to come, was taken up again by Jesus of Nazareth as his own authorization. This shows the limits of Trito-Isaiah's work—he did not usher the fulfilment in. At the same time it also shows his importance in the positive direction, as the voice of a messenger proclaiming salvation on the way which led to Christ. In Luke 4.16ff., Jesus of Nazareth finds that his task can be summed up in the same words as, five hundred years before, Trito-Isaiah had used to describe his. This reveals besides a clear material connection between the tasks of the two men:

> He has sent me to bring good tidings to the poor,
> to bind up the brokenhearted,
> to proclaim liberty to the captives,
> and for those who are bound the opening . . .

CHAPTER 56.1–2

Keep justice!

1 Thus says Yahweh;
  keep justice   and do righteousness,
  for my salvation is near to its coming
  and my righteousness to its revelation.

2 Salvation to the man who does this,
  and to the son of man who holds its fast,
  who keeps the Sabbath, not profaning it,
  and keeps his hand from doing any evil.

[1–2] This utterance has a prophetic proclamation of salvation as its middle-point: 'my salvation is near to its coming' (or, as Kessler renders it, 'the coming of my help is near'). These words (v. 1b) make an excellent link between the part of the book which begins at ch. 56 and the proclamation of Deutero-Isaiah. They even suggest a specific utterance of his, 46.13; the author of 56.1f. may have had the verse in his mind, and used it deliberately to form his link. At the same time this also shows the difference between the two men's situation and what they sought to achieve. Both proclaim that God's salvation is near. But while with Deutero-Isaiah this substantiates a summons to the despondent to hear (46.12), in 56.1 it is an admonition to act righteously. Omit v. 1b from vv. 1f., and what remains is an obvious admonition. Indeed, the connection between it and the proclamation of salvation is such a loose one that the pronouns and suffixes in v. 2a take no account of v. 1b and relate to 'justice' and 'righteousness' in v. 1a. Further, the point of the connection is not perfectly clear. The probable meaning is, 'act thus, that you may have part in the salvation to come'. But the catchword which makes the connection, 'do ṣᵉdāqā, for my ṣᵉdāqā comes', is a strange one, for the same word has a different meaning in the two parts of the sentence. All of this shows that the proclamation of the salvation to come as made by

Deutero-Isaiah is to be re-issued in times that are different from his, times in which the emphasis is on the parenesis which accompanies the proclamation—an exhortation to 'act righteously' combined with a blessing upon the man who holds to justice and righteousness, in the same way as in Ps. 1.

[2b] As the meaning of devout conduct is explained, there is an awkward parallelism which combines a concrete and particular demand, the keeping of the Sabbath, with a warning against evil-doing in general. Once again the link is a merely formal catchword ('who keeps the Sabbath—who keeps his hand'). The dissimilarity in kind as between the two halves of the verse discloses the emphasis put upon the particular admonition, the keeping of the Sabbath. In itself, the awkwardness in the drafting of the verse makes one feel that the real point which the admonition wants to make is that the only real indication of whether a man truly holds to 'justice and righteousness', whether he is truly devout, is strict observance of the Sabbath. It is precisely the same in the passage which follows (vv. 3–8), and also in the addition 58.13f. (and 66.23). This reveals a new situation. During the exile the Sabbath had become a badge denoting membership of the community that worshipped Yahweh. Now, after the return, it is given a further significance: it is made a clinching criterion of orthodoxy. This significance attaching to the Sabbath, maintained down to the time of Jesus, shows how the nation changed into a religious community; whether one holds to Yahweh or not is a matter for the individual to decide for himself, and the most conspicuous sign of decision is observance of the Sabbath.

The primary purpose of the passage (56.1f.) is not comfort, as in the proclamation of salvation contained in chs. 40–55, but admonition. The announcement of the salvation is a means employed to serve the ends of this admonition. Its being introduced as a divine utterance does not primarily relate to the announcement of the salvation: it gives the admonition authority. The real point of this admonition to do justice and righteousness lies in the exhortation to keep the Sabbath which, for the speaker here, was the most obvious indication of decision for Yahweh and for the community which worshipped him. One sees a deliberate link with Deutero-Isaiah, but at the same time a considerable difference from him as well.

CHAPTER 56.3-8

I give you monument and name

3 And let not the foreigner who has joined himself to Yahweh say,
'Yahweh has altogether separated me from his people.'
And let not the eunuch say, 'Ah, I am a dried up tree.'[a]
4 For thus says Yahweh
to the eunuchs who keep my sabbaths
and have chosen the things that please me
and hold fast my covenant:
5 I give them in my house
and within my walls monument and name,
better than sons and daughters.
I give [them][b] an everlasting name,
which shall not be cut off.[c]

6 And the foreigners who join themselves to Yahweh,
to minister to him and to love the name of Yahweh,
to be his servants,
everyone who keeps the Sabbath and does not profane it,
and holds fast my covenant—
7 these I bring to my holy mountain,
and prepare joy for them in my house of prayer.
Their burnt offerings and their sacrifices
are accepted on my altar;
for my house shall be called 'house of prayer for all peoples'.

8 Oracle of the Lord Yahweh,
who gathers the dispersed of Israel,
I will gather yet others of [his banished ones][d]
besides those already gathered.

The construction of 56.3-8 is clear and plain. Verse 3 reproduces the laments of two sets of people, foreigners and eunuchs, and rejects their complaint. In vv. 4-7 this rejection is substantiated by means of

[a] B. D. Eerdmans, *OT Studies*, I, Leiden, 1942, pp. 1ff.
[b] Read the plural, with Vss. and DSS Isa.[1].
[c] On v. 4, see K. Galling, 'Erwägungen zum Stelenheiligtum von Hazor', *ZDPV* 75 (1959), pp. 1-13.
[d] With the Targum, read *gōlāyw*.

an oracle, vv. 4f. being addressed to the eunuchs, and vv. 6f. to the foreigners. Both of these have a promise made to them, admittance to a place in the community that worships Yahweh. The oracle contained in vv. 4–7 is rounded off in v. 8 by means of a predication, 'who gathers Israel'. The utterance is couched in the messenger-formula used by the prophets; as such it is set between vv. 4 and 8 and given the form of a speech made by Yahweh. In actual fact, what comes in point is a decision in the realm of sacral law. Are two sets of people expressly excluded from the worship of Yahweh by Deut. 23.2–9 (*BH*)—hence their laments in v. 3—now to be admitted to it? The passage is a perfect example of the way in which, in the post-exilic period, priestly and prophetic forms of discourse became mingled. Sanction is conferred on a decision taken purely on the basis of sacral law by dressing it up as a divine oracle. This decision was of great importance for the form assumed by the community of the worshippers of Yahweh in post-exilic days—was it to be open and missionary, or wholly restricted to Jews?

[3] Verses 3–8 are independent of vv. 1f., and not their continuation. The word 'and' shows that as between vv. 1f. and vv. 3–8 there is similarity of content. This we shall take up below. *bēn-hannēkār* is the foreigner; Duhm, 'the foreigner by birth'; Volz., 'foreign in the nation'; Köhler, 'the alien'. The term reappears with the same meaning in 60.10; 61.5; 62.8. 'Who has joined himself to Yahweh': this is obviously a designation for a proselyte current at the time. It occurs with the same meaning in Isa. 14.1: 'aliens will join them', a verse which may have roughly the same date as Trito-Isaiah. So also Zech. 2.11; cf. Esther 9.27 and Dan. 11.34. The subject is the possibility, only recently opened up, of a foreigner's taking part in Israel's worship. This has two preconditions. The first is external, the severance of the connection between the worshipping community and statehood. The second is internal, Yahweh's offer of salvation to the nations as proclaimed by Deutero-Isaiah, especially in 45.20–25.

The foreigners' lament in v. 3 presupposes a wish on their part to continue as members of the community which worships Yahweh, and the intention on the part of others to debar them. The latter exclusive tendency can be very plainly seen in Ezra and Nehemiah, who demand a total separation from foreigners (the same word is used in Ezra 9.1f. and Neh. 9.2). Here, this comes to light in the words, 'Yahweh has separated (or, will separate) me from his people.' This points to a section or a court who, in Yahweh's name, put this severance into practice. These were the very people who, as we see from Ezra and Nehemiah, eventually gained the upper hand. They must, however, have been in existence long before this. But in the passage before us, 'Yahweh' may stand for 'Yahweh's word'. In this case, the lament would refer to Deut. 23.2–9.

The connection here made between the two classes derives from Deut. 23.2–9, which determines those who may not be members of the community that worships Yahweh. There is no point of contact between the eunuch's lament and that of the foreigner except that, according to the regulation in Deut. 23.2–9, the former, too, is debarred from being a member. This lament points in the same direction as Abraham's in Gen. 15.2: life without posterity is life without blessing. Because blessing cannot be bestowed upon a man who is unable to have issue, he may not take part in worship, either, Deut. 23.2. This shows the revolutionary nature of the change here made on the Deuteronomic regulation, and why it had to be substantiated by means of an oracle.

[4–5] The old regulation given in Deut. 23.2 is cancelled. Henceforth the eunuch is expressly and solemnly granted a place in the community which worships Yahweh. This brought about a fundamental change on the form that the community had had in pre-exilic times, and it required to be made known by changing regulations about its membership. New conditions are named. Two of these are formulated in the case of two sets of people in identical terms, 'who keep my Sabbaths, who hold fast my covenant'. As in v. 2b, the keeping of the Sabbath is a primary condition; in this respect the two utterances, 56.1f. and 56.3–8, coincide. This specific condition is accompanied by one that is quite general; here with 'holding fast my covenant' (cf. the same verb in v. 2a) the idea is probably 'the precepts of my covenant'; in a late stage of its use *berit* may have the meaning of 'law'. Hallowing the Sabbath and keeping the law— these are the two basic conditions of membership of the community. In the case of the eunuchs there are also the words, 'who have chosen the things that please me'; this corresponds to 'who love the name of Yahweh, minister to him, and are his servants' in the case of the foreigner. These verbs make it perfectly plain that membership of the community which worships Yahweh is now based upon resolve, a free affirmation of this God and of his worship. No longer is it thought of in national but in individual terms. The chosen people has turned into the confessing community. But now confession ceases to be the confession of praise, that is to say, the recital of God's mighty acts. It is now indirect, by way of observing the law and keeping the Sabbath.

[5] The promise made to the eunuchs, 'I give him in my house a monument (literally, hand) and a name', is explained by reference to II Sam. 18.18. The monument (*maṣṣēbā*) which Absalom had set up to keep himself in remembrance, since he was childless, was called 'Absalom's hand'. The excavations at Hazor brought to light a sanctuary with steles symbolizing the members of the royal family.[a] It is a memorial of this nature that is here designated as 'hand'. 'Monument and name' is to be taken as hendiadys—the name of the person concerned is preserved for the generations to come in the monument erected to him within the precincts of the temple: it is continuously in the mind of the community that speaks of its ancestors and remembers them. The name which thus continues to live for the community is, v. 5b says, more valuable than sons and daughters, for it is an everlasting name, which shall not be cut off. The change in the community's structure is particularly evident here. In the case of the old Israelite, the one thing that made him one of the chosen people was the fact that he had been born into it. What gave him a past and a future were purely physical things—his parents, and the fact that he lived on in his children. To Abraham, the promise made in Isa. 56.5b would have been incomprehensible; it would have had no meaning. But here, with Trito-Isaiah, the physical and the spiritual have ceased to be necessarily united in this way. The name may live on without descendants born of one's body. There is the new possibility of living on in the community, even although one is a 'dry tree'. The new community is on the way to a new form of association which is no longer identical with the old concept of the chosen people. As early as here we find present important elements of the New Testament's concept of community.

[7] To counter the foreigner's lament the promise is made that 'I bring you to my holy mountain'. Here the metaphor applies to the realm of the cult—foreigners may have part in my worship. The words let us see how a piece of specifically Jerusalem theology had come to be part of the general language of worship. In the case of Deutero-Isaiah, the promise of return had been accompanied by a summons to rejoice. Now, a share in that joy is assigned to foreigners. But it is a joy completely divorced from the realm of history. It is 'joy in the wonderful worship of Yahweh'. Significantly, the temple is now

[a] K. Galling, *ZDPV* 75 (1959), pp. 1–13.

called 'house of prayer'. Because sacrifice had not been possible during the exile, the spoken element in worship had become the dominant one. Thus *tᵉpillā* lost its specific meaning of intercession, and became a general term for prayer. Before this there had been no such general and comprehensive term.

[7b] Foreigners are assured that the sacrifices which they bring will be wholly acceptable (*lᵉrāṣōn* is a sacrificial term). This makes them members of the community in full standing. In the time of Trito-Isaiah the offering of sacrifice had also a social and economic aspect. The sacrificial animals represent a proportion of the family property. By sacrifice the home has its part in worship. Sacrifice begets blessing and respect in the locality. The acceptance of foreigners' sacrifice means that, properly speaking, they cease to be foreigners.

[7c] What makes the temple a 'house of prayer for all peoples' is the fact that this present regulation now opens access to it and to its worship to members of other races.

[8] The apposition, 'who gathers the dispersed of Israel', takes up a promise well-known to those who listened to it (e.g. Isa. 11.12), one that was subsequently taken up as a divine predication into the language of prayer (Ps. 147.2 and the tenth prayer of the Eighteen Benedictions). In the post-exilic period this predication is so often met with, and has such an emphasis put upon it, that it may almost be said to replace the earlier 'who delivered you from Egypt'. This, too, can—in some measure at any rate—be due to Deutero-Isaiah and his proclamation of the new Exodus which was even to surpass the one at the beginning of the nation's history. But what Trito-Isaiah says is essentially different. The unique, world-shaking act is replaced by a continuous activity on the part of God. This is shown first by the verb *qibbeṣ* (gather), and then by the drafting of the two clauses v. 8a and b—God, who gathers the dispersed, is to go on to gather others besides. Instead of the expectation of the one great miracle that is to change everything, what we now have is the looking for a gradual bringing in of individuals, and this without change of the natural order. The opening of the community to eunuchs and foreigners, too, is made in the context of the promise that Yahweh is to gather the dispersed of Israel—he 'gathers' Israel also from those who hitherto have not been able to belong to her.

A final note on 56.1f. and 3–8. The commentary has shown that, as compared with chs. 40–55, 56.1f. and 3–8 introduce a new voice and a different state of affairs. The verses are programmatic, and therefore form a fitting introduction to a new body of material. Salvation is near (v. 1b). This is the reason why a new order of things is coming to birth. Participation in it depends on acting righteously and keeping the Sabbath (vv. 1f.). This enables two sets of people hitherto excluded from the community which worships Yahweh to be admitted to it. This means the inauguration of a new era in the saving history.

The passage is in the tradition of Deutero-Isaiah. That is to say, it is a specifically prophetic tradition that proclaims, and substantiates by means of an oracle, that the gates of the community which worships Yahweh are now open to the world. This is as opposed to a priestly and legal tradition which seeks to limit the community to those who are Jews by birth.

CHAPTER 56.9–12

His watchmen are blind

9　All you beasts of the field, come to devour—
　　all you beasts in the forest.
10　His watchmen are blind,　　　　　they are all without knowledge,
　　they are all dumb dogs,　　　　　they cannot bark.
　　They talk confusedly in their sleep,　they love to slumber;
11　they are also dogs with a mighty　they never have enough.
　　appetite,

　　The shepherds [also][a]　　　　　have no understanding,
　　they all turn to their own way,
　　each to his own gain, one and all;
12　'Come, I bring wine.
　　Let us fill ourselves with strong drink.
　　Tomorrow will be like this day,
　　great beyond measure.'

[9–12] Verses 9–12 form a unit apart, a proclamation of judgment

---

[a] Read *wᵉgam hārōʿîm*.

in the genuine prophetic style. Any difficulty that we may have had hitherto in defining the various passages and marking them off now ceases. Here, and in the passages which follow, we are furnished with criteria upon which we can rely. In v. 9 no more than a hint is given at the proclamation of judgment. The order to the beasts of the field and the forest to devour is the result of God's intervention. God is going to take measures against those charged in vv. 10ff. An enemy is to inflict so grievous a defeat upon them that the corpses lie around and are devoured by wild beasts. That this is what is meant here is proved by numerous parallels in the pre-exilic prophets. The remainder, vv. 10ff., substantiates the proclamation of which, up to now, only a hint has been given. Those charged are the watchmen (vv. 10–11a) and the shepherds (vv. 11b–12). Watchmen and shepherds are terms for leaders. The distinction seems to be no more than a matter of style. The same designations of the nation's leaders are also found in Ezek. 34.1–10; Jer. 6.17; and Ezek. 3.17. They, who as watchmen and shepherds of the nation and its ways, ought to have taken care, are reproached with two things: (1) they have no conception of what their office is, and (2) they act for their own advantage. Both charges are also found in the pre-exilic prophets. They are in conjunction in Ezek. 34.1–10, and there, too, although the context is slightly different, we find devouring by wild beasts (vv. 5 and 8). In point of content, then, Ezek. 34.1–10 is a close parallel to Isa. 56.9–12. But when form, style and diction are compared, Isa. 56.9–12 obviously represents the earlier form. In the Ezekiel passage the form, prophetic oracle of judgment, is very much broken down. There are repetitions and reflections, and the metaphor of the shepherd and the sheep is spun out. In contrast, in Isa. 56.9–12 the style is terse and extremely forceful. There are no repetitions, expansions or reflections whatever, and the passage is in harmony with the simple form of oracle of judgment as found in the prophets. While the two passages look very much alike, set them in parallel columns, and there can be no doubt that Isa. 56.9–12 is the older.

In addition, the diction of vv. 10ff. is quite clearly the diction of the prophetic charge as found in the pre-exilic prophets and these alone. The charge made against the leaders is that they, who ought to have been the 'watchmen', do not see the menace that is overtaking the nation. They are dumb, for they utter no warning in face of it. Both charges are couched in the extremely terse and vivid language of early prophecy. The noun clause uses only two words to point to a glaring contrast—'your watchmen . . . blind'. (The second half-verse should probably be expanded in the sense of 'they are without knowledge of how to take notice'.) The second part of v. 10 has a challenging metaphor—'all of them . . . dumb dogs'. Again, the second half-verse makes it explicit—'they cannot bark'. This is the impassioned scorn of prophetic accusation. The next verse suddenly goes over to a different metaphor designed to describe the same situation from a different angle: 'they talk confusedly in their sleep, they love to slumber'. This second metaphor enables the prophet to make a masterly transition from the first charge to the second, which here is no more than suggested, by means of the metaphor 'dogs with a mighty appetite, who never have enough', and is then developed in the second part of the section, vv. 11b–12.

[11b–12] In the case of the charges made against the shepherds, the first is quite brief, 'they have no understanding', but the second is developed, and this in two aspects. The first of these contains the charge, the two half-verses of v. 11c supplementing each other, 'they all turn to their own way', that is to say, they are only interested in what concerns their own selves (or, they look to their own advantage). The words are similar to Isa. 53.6, but here, spoken as they are with reference to the leaders, they have a rather different meaning. This is brought out more clearly in the second part of the verse, 'each to his own gain'.[a] Once again, this charge tallies with the one made against the leaders by the pre-exilic prophets, for example, Jeremiah's utterance against king Jehoiakim, Jer. 22.13–19. Here the form is, 'you have eyes and heart only for your gain', or again, Isa. 3.13f., where part of the charge made against the leaders runs, 'it is you who have devoured the vineyard.' With the pre-exilic prophets the charge is often expanded by quoting words spoken by the accused which both corroborate the charge from his own mouth and shed light upon it. This is also the case here, in v. 12. This is a little drinking-song, the rather silly motifs of which are the same all the world over. In just the same way Amos (4.1ff.) quotes the wealthy women, the 'cows of Bashan', who say to their husbands, 'Bring, that we may drink.' There is also a point of style which confirms what we have just been saying. In the pre-exilic prophets' pronouncements of doom, the proclamation and the substantiation (the charge) are often connected by means of a play on words. This also occurs here;

---

[a] I am not certain that *miqqaṣēhū* at the end of v. 11 can mean 'one and all', as Volz translates and Kessler adopts. It is absent in LXX.

'come' in v. 12 answers the same word in v. 9. The suggestion is this: now you summon the tipplers to drink, 'Come, I bring wine'; but the day is coming when the wild beasts will be summoned to 'come to devour'.

There can therefore be no shadow of doubt that 56.9–12 is an early, pre-exilic oracle of judgment. Long ago Ewald assumed this (for 56.12–57.13), as do, nearer our own time, Volz, Eissfeldt (in his *Introduction*), and others. In their case, the reasons are of a more general kind, but form-critical comparison makes it certain that here pre-exilic prophetic words of judgment have been taken up into Trito-Isaiah. How this came about can only be explained after the commentary on 57.1–13.

CHAPTER 57.1–2

The righteous man perishes

1   The righteous man perishes,
      and no one lays it to heart.
      And the faithful men are taken away
      [and]ᵃ no one gives heed.
      Is it from calamity that the righteous is taken,
      who goes on his upright way?ᵇ

2   They rest in their beds, [go]ᶜ about in peace.

[**1–2**] Verse 3 begins a fresh oracle of a different kind; therefore vv. 1f. are to be taken as an independent unit. The passage has a parallel in Ps. 12.2 (1) and Micah 7.2. In both places the words are a lament. It is the lament over the rapid growth of the transgressors who have spread to such an extent that, because of their power, the devout and upright have disappeared. The three lines in Isa. 57.1 correspond to the lament in Ps. 12 both in content and, to some extent, verbally as well, both being similarly introduced, 'the righteous man perishes'. But these same words also occur in Micah

---

ᵃ Read *weʾēn* instead of *beʾēn*.
ᵇ The second half-verses in 1c and 2 are to be transposed.
ᶜ Instead of *yābōʾ* read the plural.

7.2, where they have combined with them a description of the transgressors, 'the devout have disappeared from the land, there is none upright among men. They (the transgressors) all lie in wait for blood, and each lays a net for the other.' While the text of Micah 7.1ff. is difficult, the passage is also evidence of how a prophet can associate a charge with a lament. This is also the case here; vv. 3ff. append a charge to this lament. It is perfectly possible that this conjunction gives us the reason why pre-exilic prophetic oracles of judgment found entrance into the pages of Trito-Isaiah. The break-up into two different groups which began after the return, the one regarding itself as that of the devout and righteous as over against the transgressors, caused earlier prophetic oracles of judgment to be taken up and interpreted with reference to the new situation. In the present case, those addressed in vv. 3ff. were interpreted as the 'transgressors' of the day.

Verse 2 is hard to elucidate, and, in addition, there is disorder in the text. The transgressors are contrasted with the devout man 'who goes on his upright way'. It is said of him that 'he goes about in peace', and 'they rest in their beds'. The change from singular to plural is evidence of textual disturbance. Further, the juxtaposition of transgressors and devout, so frequent in the Psalms, is not perfectly clear. Here it is important to notice that the two pronouncements of judgment, 57.3–6 and 7–13, are set within a framework of words taken from the Psalms. That is to say, the words which introduce the lament over the increase of the transgressors have, in 57.13c, words corresponding to them, also taken from a psalm, but here applied to the devout: 'but he who takes refuge in me shall inherit the land, and shall possess my holy mountain.' In respect of their content, the fragments contained in 57.2 go along with this 'but' clause contrasting the devout and the transgressors. This placing of the pronouncements of judgment within a framework of words concerning the transgressors and the devout taken from the Psalms is certainly intentional. It shows what tradition did with the pre-exilic pronouncements of judgment in order to use them in collections of oracles of the post-exilic period.

CHAPTER 57.3–6

You Sons of the Sorceress

3 But you, draw near hither,   sons of the sorceress,
   offspring of the adulteress and [harlot].ᵃ
4 Of whom are you making sport?
   Against whom do you open your mouth wide
   and put out your tongue?
   Are you not children of transgression, offspring of deceit?

5 You who burn with lust among the oaks,
   under every green tree;
   who slay your children in the valleys,
   under the clefts of the rocks.

6 In the bed of the river-valley you will meet your destiny;ᵇ
   that, that is your lot.
   There you have poured out a drink offering,
   and brought cereal offerings. [   ]ᶜ

Again, 57.3–6 is a self-contained prophetic pronouncement of judgment, the particular form being that of a trial-speech. The accused are summoned (v. 3) to appear before the judge, and to some extent the change has the form of a question in an examination. The divisions are as follows: Verse 3 is the summons, the address of which itself contains accusations. Verses 4f. give the crimes, v. 6a pronounces sentence, and v. 6b adds a further charge. The style—short, terse phrases, impassioned charges, and the play upon words as between charge and pronouncement of sentence—is again unmistakably that of the pre-exilic prophets of doom.

[3–4] The address, which at the same time reprimands the accused, alleges charges well-known from the pages of pre-exilic prophecy: sorcery (so Isa. 2.6; Micah 5.11; Jer. 27.9; in all cases the

---

ᵃ Read *wᵉzōnā* with Vss.

ᵇ Literally, 'among the smooth stones of the valley is your portion'; the translation above is an attempt to reproduce the word-play in the Hebrew.

ᶜ Following the proposal in *BH*, the final words of v. 6 are transposed to the end of v. 7. On v. 5f., see M. Weise, 'Jesaja 57.5f.', *ZAW* 72/1 (1960), pp. 25–32.

same word is used) and whoredom (often in Hosea and Jeremiah), probably with the transferred meaning of idolatry. In so doing, v. 4 says, you have transgressed against Yahweh. Isaiah's question (37.23) has exactly the same drift; 'whom have you mocked and reviled? Against whom have you spoken haughtily . . . ? Against the Holy One of Israel.' Both places use the form, question in an examination, to raise the charge of blasphemy. It is to be noted that the verb *hit'annag* is used in a different sense here (to make sport of) from what it has in 58.14 and 66.11. The gestures—opening the mouth wide and putting out the tongue—otherwise used to show contempt for men (e.g. Ps. 35.21), are here deliberately rude gestures to show contempt for God, as in Isa. 37.23. These strong terms are perfectly possible for the prophets; the gestures of contempt show the real nature of the rebellion against God (? show that the rebellion against God is a real thing). The last question in v. 4 sums it all up. In the great majority of its occurrences in pre-exilic prophecy, *peša'* means transgression against God (Jer. 2.8). 'Offspring of deceit' is to be understood in the same sense. The term is often found in Jeremiah.

[5] A further charge is now made. It gives the typical and recurrent description of the worship at the high-places accompanied by child-sacrifice (Ezekiel, Jeremiah and the C strand in Jeremiah). The verse could be a later addition (so Duhm and Volz), but this is not certain.

[6] Now finally comes the pronouncement of sentence, 'among the smooth places of the valley is your portion'. The only thing obvious is that the accused hear the death-sentence passed upon them, but the picture is not clear. Does it mean that they are to be buried under the stones of the brook in the valley? Verse 6b resumes the charge. Israel offered sacrifice to the 'smooth places of the valley' which now turn into her doom. The reference is to idolatry of some sort, which we cannot determine very precisely. The correspondence between the transgression and its punishment is in keeping with pre-exilic prophetic discourse.

CHAPTER 57.7–13

You loved their bed

7 Upon a high and lofty mountain
  you set up your bed.
  Thither you also went up to offer sacrifice;
  shall I have compassion because of this?
8 And behind the door and the doorposts
  you set up your symbol.
  For, deserting me,[a] you uncovered your bed,
  you went up to it and made it wide.
  You made your [bargain] with them for [the wages of a paramour],[b]
  You loved their bed, you looked on the hand (their nakedness).[c]
9 You squander oil on the king (Melek)[d]
  and multiplied your perfumes.
  You sent your envoys far off,
  deep down even to Sheol.
10 You wearied yourself with many journeys,
  but you did not say, 'it is hopeless.'
  You found life for your hand,
  therefore you did not leave off.

11 But whom did you dread and fear, when you deceived?
  You did not remember me,
  did not give me a thought.
  Did I not hold my peace [and cover][e] (my eyes),
  and yet you did not fear me.

12 [Yet][f] I made manifest your righteousness,
  and your doings—they do not help you,
13a nor do [your abominations][g] help you when you cry out.
  The wind carries them all off, a breath takes them away.

---

[a] *mē'ittī* = 'away from me' is quite uncertain.

[b] For *wattikrāt* (?) read *wattikri* (BH: Duhm, Ginsberg, etc.). For the object, supply, following LXX, 'wages of a paramour'.

[c] *yād* = 'hand', probably as representing *membrum virile*. Perhaps also in v. 10.

[d] The translation of the first line of v. 9 follows P. Wernberg-Møller, *VT*, VIII, 3 (1958), p. 308.

[e] Read *ūma'lim*.

[f] Read *wa'ani* with LXX.

[g] Read *šiqqūṣayik*.

13b   But he who trusts in me shall inherit the land,
                         he shall have my holy mountain as his own.

57.7–13 are also a prophetic oracle of judgment. Israel is charged
with apostasy. The reference is obviously to the fertility cult of
Canaan. The charge is reminiscent of Hosea, and in many ways also
of Ezekiel. While it is detailed at considerable length in vv. 7–11, it
is, as the very first words make clear, the self-same charge throughout,
idolatry. It has a positive (vv. 7–10) and a negative (v. 11) side to it.
The latter corresponds to Isaiah's 'yet you did not look to the Holy
One of Israel' (31.1). The pronouncement of sentence (vv. 12f.) has
the normal divisions: God's intervention, consisting in his revealing
of Israel's doings (v. 12), and the consequences of this, irretrievable
destruction.

[7–10] The blunt way in which the idolatry at the high places is
described as adultery or whoredom is such that some connection
between idolatry and sexual excess, perhaps temple-prostitution,
must, as with Hosea, be included in the charge. It alleges sacrifice
on the high places (v. 7), and, in v. 8, the symbol behind the door
probably refers to the representation of a phallus as a symbol of
fertility. In v. 9 *melek* (king) is certainly the name of a god. Duhm
thinks that it refers to Milcom, the god of the Amorites, but it could
also be the Canaanite god Melek. At all events, in vv. 9b and 10 the
charge relates to resort to foreign deities (as, for example, in II Kings
1.2), which nevertheless, in spite of all the pains taken, is senseless,
the very same thing as Jeremiah says (2.25). The meaning of 'you
found life for your hand' is unknown. It could be an allusion corresponding to v. 8 (similarly Ginsberg). In any case *yād* cannot have
the meaning of 'strength' here (Volz, Kessler).

[11] Here we have a particularly good example of the language
used by the early prophets, which can say so much in so little compass. The prophet confronts Israel with the glaring contrast involved
in her conduct in the way that Jeremiah does in ch. 2, where he com-
pares the foreign gods with broken cisterns which, after all, fail to
supply water. Who then are the people, asks the prophet, whom you
then dreaded and feared? And then at the end of v. 11, 'but me you
did not fear. And he takes this still further: when you gave yourself
trouble with the other gods, you could forget me, 'you did not give
me a thought'. And in the process you failed to notice that, while you
were running after the other gods, I held my peace and refused to see

a thing—for your sake. 'And yet you did not fear me.' This verse (11) is thus a shining exemplification of the utterly personal relationship that subsisted between God and Israel and which we find stated with such ardour and passion everywhere in the early prophets—this wooing of his disobedient people, this pained astonishment at the way in which it runs away from its God, its helper and deliverer, to the 'wells that are full of holes'.

[12–13] As compared with the charge, the pronouncement of sentence is very brief, a mere suggestion. God's intervention in v. 12 contains scathing irony (is the reminiscence of the Psalms, 'I will tell of your righteousness', a deliberate one?): I will bring to light your 'righteousness' and your 'doings'. And then—there is nothing to save you, neither your 'doings', i.e. the great pains to which you put yourself to gain security from other gods (vv. 9f.), nor these gods themselves, abominations as they are.

Verse 13b forms part of the framework. Taken from a psalm, it is a promise made to the man who puts his trust in Yahweh.[a]

Summary. 56.9–57.13 represent a short, self-contained collection of prophetic oracles of doom dating from the pre-exilic era. Their setting, 51.1f. and 13b, verses taken from psalms, suggests the reason why they were added to the collected oracles of Trito-Isaiah (see above). We have here preserved three prophetic oracles from the days before the exile which are, both in form and content, perfectly on a par with the words of the writing prophets known to us. In my own view, it is not possible to attribute them to any of these. It is also uncertain whether the three oracles have one and the same prophet as their author. They do prove, however, that, in addition to the prophetic books which have come down to us, there were still isolated traditions (perhaps oral, perhaps written) of words of pre-exilic prophets which lasted on into the post-exilic era.

The fact that this little group of oracles found a place within Trito-Isaiah's collected oracles has a further important piece of information to give us about the way in which the books of the prophets were handed on. When the exile was over, the pre-exilic prophets' oracles of doom were given a fresh significance for the present. The charges were made to refer to the conduct of the transgressors, the 'godless', from whom the devout or righteous were increasingly obliged to sever themselves.

[a] Cf. the commentary on 57.1f.

CHAPTER 57.14–21

Peace, Peace to the Far and to the Near

14 And he says,
    'Build up, build up, prepare the way.
    Remove the obstruction from my people's way.'

15 For thus says the high and lofty One
    who is enthroned eternally and whose name is the Holy One:

    I dwell in the high and holy place,
    and [I look upon]ᵃ him who is of a contrite and humble spirit,
    to revive the spirit of him who is bowed down,
    and to revive the heart of him who has been smitten.

16 For I do not contend for ever,
    nor am I always angry;
    for [their]ᵇ spirit proceeds from me,
    and the breath of life, which I created.
17 Because of [his] sins I was angry [for a moment],ᶜ
    I smote him, hiding myself in wrath;
    he went backsliding on the way of his own will,ᵈ
18 I saw his ways.

    But I will heal him and [give him rest],ᵉ
    and will requite him with comfort.
19 For his mourners I create the fruit of the lips,
    peace, peace to the far and the near,
    says Yahweh—and I heal him (?)

20 But the wicked—like the tossing sea,
    when it cannot come to rest.
    Its waters toss up mire and dirt.ᶠ
21 No peace—says Yahweh—for the wicked.

ᵃ Add 'er'e.
ᵇ Read rūḥām.
ᶜ Read beᶜawōnō regaᶜ.
ᵈ A. Rubinstein, VT, IV, 2 (1954), p. 200.
ᵉ Read wa'aniḥēhū.
ᶠ J. A. Montgomery, 'Ras Shamra Notes IV', JAOS, 55, 3 (1935).

Bibliography: W. W. Cannon, *ZAW* 52/1, New Series 11, 1934.

This is the first occasion in Trito-Isaiah that we encounter an express oracle of salvation. It is in fact a proclamation of salvation, although this form is, like the rest, not so clearly contoured here as it is in Deutero-Isaiah. Two things are perfectly clear with regard to the utterance, its provenance from Deutero-Isaiah, and its difference from him. Hence it is a perfect instance of what was demonstrated by Zimmerli in his study, 'On the language of Trito-Isaiah',[a] namely, that in chs. 56–66 quotations from, or reminiscences of, Deutero-Isaiah consistently change the meaning of what they found on 57.14 in relation to 40.3ff. Zimmerli says:[b] 'the call to prepare the way, still understood in Deutero-Isaiah in its literal meaning, is here intended to be taken figuratively, it has become part of general devout parenesis'.

Structure

In vv. 15–19 the call to prepare the way (v. 14) is substantiated by means of an oracle (introduced as such in v. 15a). It is a proclamation of salvation. This does not properly start until v. 16; the introduction to the oracle given in v. 15a and expanded by means of divine predications, is followed, in v. 15b and c, by an expansion of these in terms taken from descriptive praise turned into the first person. The oracle of salvation in vv. 16–19 falls into two parts. Verses 16f. look back to the time when God was angry, a time that is now over, while vv. 18f. announce his new turning to save, as well as comfort for those who mourn, and peace. Verses 20f. add that this peace is not, however, for the transgressors.

[14] The words which introduce the utterance, 'and he says', are textually quite uncertain. The Vulgate has the first person, LXX the third person plural, and DSS Isa.[1], the third person imperfect (Muilenburg). In 62.10 practically the same imperatives are without introduction, and only in v. 15 is the oracle expressly introduced as such. The presumption is therefore that *we'āmar* at the beginning of v. 14 was prefixed here when Trito-Isaiah's utterances were in process of

---

[a] *Schweizer Theologische Umschau*, Nr. 3/4 (1959), pp. 1–13.
[b] *Op. cit.*, p. 6.

collection, in order to make a clear division between 57.14ff. and what precedes.

While there can be no doubt that the imperatives which introduce the oracle make a link with 40.3f., they also change the meaning of the imperatives in Deutero-Isaiah's prologue (see the quotation from Zimmerli above). 'Here, the way which is to be prepared is not the processional way home for Yahweh and the returning exiles, but purely metaphorically and spiritually the "road" for the salvation that is to come' (Volz). The word is used in the same transferred sense in Mark 1.3. The literal meaning of the word for 'obstruction' (*mikšōl*) is an obstacle on the road which can cause a man to fall (Lev. 19.14). The same word applied to the path of life occurs in Ps. 119.165. In Isa. 8.14; Jer. 6.21; and Ezek. 3.20 God himself puts the obstruction in the way of the nation. When it speaks of the removal of obstacles, the parallel passages in 62.10 clearly means preparation of a way for the advent of salvation. The same will also apply here. There may, however, be as well a suggestion of the sense in which Ezekiel uses the term. In Ezek. 7.19; 14.4, 7; 18.30; and 44.12 it means 'stumbling block leading to iniquity'. 'Obstruction, obstacle is everything that stands in the way of the advent of salvation' (Volz). The person who utters the cry and those to whom it is made are not more nearly defined.

[15] There is a further point of agreement with the prologue in Deutero-Isaiah. In vv. 18f. this preparation of a way leads to comfort received by the nation. Nevertheless, the word of salvation solemnly introduced in v. 15 is obviously different in kind as compared with the earlier prophet. In this connection particular attention has to be paid to the sequence of the words and the structure in detail.

The one who speaks the word of comfort and salvation is 'the high and lofty one', 'the Holy One', 'who is enthroned eternally'. These attributes are clearly reminiscent of Isa. 6; and if this utterance, the introduction to Trito-Isaiah's message of salvation, shows a combination of motifs taken from the prologue of Deutero-Isaiah and motifs taken from the vision received at his call by First Isaiah, then this is certainly no accident. We can discern the line of tradition revealed in the subsequent amalgamation of Isa. 1–39; 40–55 and 56–66. However, v. 15b and c add a different line of tradition. These two verses speak the language of the Psalms, being similar to Ps. 113. Verse 15b presents a difficulty. If *'et* in the second half-verse is taken as a preposition meaning 'with, at my side', the words must be translated 'by the side of the contrite and humble' (Kessler, others similarly). But it is very unlikely, and quite unparalled, for Yahweh to be spoken of as dwelling (in the sense of being enthroned) *at the side* of the stricken and humble. The parallel passage, Ps. 113, suggests that the verb *'er'e* should be supplied at the end of the second half-verse, 'and I look upon the contrite and humble'. Then the connection in v. 15c, the infinitive with *le*, is exactly the same as in Ps. 113.5, 6 and 8. And the connection requires the supplying of the verb if it is to make sense. In Ps. 113 the verb has the same object as here. There, too, it is the 'needy' upon whom God looks down in pity, in order to lift them up out of their need. If what has just been proposed is correct, v. 15b and c represent an expansion couched in the language of the psalms of praise. But there is a characteristic difference from Deutero-Isaiah. With the latter, praise of God is completely integrated into his proclamation. But here one feels that it is an addition, and that the connection is a merely superficial one. The purpose of this expansion of the divine predications is clearly that of preparing the way for the oracle of comfort and salvation which ensues. The one who now speaks to Israel is the God who, from his exaltation, condescends to the bowed down and the stricken.

[16] The oracle proper only begins at v. 16 (the resumption in v. 16a of the *ki* of v. 15a corresponds to the nature of the expansion contained in v. 15b, c). Once again, it takes up an utterance of Deutero-Isaiah, 54.7f. (the words which resemble it in Ps. 103.9 are also dependent on Isa. 54.7f.). But there is again a difference. 54.7f. achieve their end of showing the effect which the word of release has by way of making God's anger and his mercy alternate twice in the one verse. In 57.16–19, however, the negative part, v. 16a, does not come until v. 18; the 'for' in v. 16a is awkwardly followed in v. 16b by a 'for' with a different frame of reference. It is easy to see that 57.15–19 are a variation and expansion of the motif taken from Deutero-Isaiah, but the expansions are so numerous that the contrast suffers. Verse 16 refers to the charge brought against God, in which the question was put, 'how long wilt thou continue to be angry with us?' This is given its answer in the word of salvation, 'I will not be angry for ever', and in the lament in the first person ('my spirit faints' occurs in Ps. 77.4 [3]) united with the motif 'you let your creature, the work of your hands, dwindle away' (Job 10.3, 8ff., in particular v. 12). Here (v. 16) therefore Trito-Isaiah follows the

method of expansion which he used in v. 15. In both cases the motifs
are those of the psalms, in the one (v. 15) psalms of lamentation, in
the other psalms of praise.

[17–19] Verse 17a reverts to the basic motif found in Isa. 54.7f.
The text is not in order. The translation given follows LXX, and finds
support from its closeness to Isa. 54.7f. The words are all taken from
the lament, and are here used to look back on the time of God's anger.
The style used in a lament is also the source of the characteristic combination of God's anger and of his hiding himself. What causes God to
be hidden from the sufferer who makes entreaty to him is the fact that
the latter does not see God's 'face', and this means that his kindness,
his turning towards the sufferer in friendliness, is hidden from him.
Verse 17b follows badly on v. 17a; some editors have tried transpositions (v. 17b before 17a). Verse 17b gives a further reason for God's
anger. Israel became unfaithful and went the way of her own choice.
But God saw her ways. In any case, in respect of content, v. 18b links
with v. 17a; for a short time God was angry at Israel's unfaithfulness:
now, however, he purposes to heal her and give her rest (I follow
Köhler). This proclamation of salvation contained in vv. 18b and 19
shows the difference from Deutero-Isaiah. With the latter the salvation was a clearly contoured, once for all event, the release and
return. The utterance here swings indeterminately between the announcement of an event and the description of a state. This is typified
here in the metaphorical 'I will heal him', which, strictly speaking,
goes back to an individual lament, and in the reiterated 'peace';
šālōm cannot possibly describe salvation as event, but only as state.
'For' refers to the people still in exile. Another small but conspicuous
difference from Deutero-Isaiah is also typical. When the latter speaks
of comforting, the object is 'my people' (40.1). Trito-Isaiah, on the
other hand, speaks of 'comforting the mourners'. This is an indication
that, while the salvation which the prophet proclaims is destined for
everyone in the nation, it does not apply to all alike without further
reference. 'Fruit of the lips' means praise of God, God's saving act is
to turn lamentation into praise.

[20f.] Most editors regard the oracle addressed to the transgressors
(vv. 20f.) as an addition. The oracle of salvation ends with the words
'says Yahweh' at the end of v. 19 (the verb which follows, 'and I heal
him', is uncertain). The beginning of v. 20, 'but the transgressors',
has no equivalent in vv. 18b–20, while the words describing their
state in v. 20a have nothing corresponding to them in what precedes.

Verse 21 was obviously added as a counterweight to the proclamation of peace for the far and the near in v. 19.

This addition, which is also found in 48.22, is important for the question of the compilation of Isa. 56–66. The prophet Trito-Isaiah himself still promised salvation to the entire nation, thus agreeing with Deutero-Isaiah. Shortly after his time, however, there came about a cleavage which seemed to render such a word of salvation embracing all alike impossible. Now there had to be a proclamation of salvation to such as were loyal to Yahweh, but one of doom to the transgressors. This can be particularly clearly seen in 66.5. As a result of this new situation, the word of salvation composed of 57.14–19 was given the addition of the utterance concerning the transgressors, vv. 20f. Whereas v. 21 is a new coinage to oppose v. 19b, v. 20 has a well-defined form, that used to describe the wicked in individual laments.

CHAPTER 58.1–12

Fasting that is pleasing to God

1   Cry with all your might, spare not,
    lift up your voice like a trumpet,
    and declare to my people their transgression
    and to the house of Jacob their sins.

2   They seek me daily,
    and desire to know my ways;
    like a nation that does righteousness
    and does not forsake the ordinance of their God;
    they ask me what judgments are righteous,
    they wish to draw near to God.

3   'Why do we fast, and thou seest it not?
    we mortify our flesh, and thou takest no knowledge of it?'

    Behold, in the day of your fast you pursue your own business
    and urge on all your workers (?).

4   Behold you fast to quarrel and fight
    and lay about yourselves with wicked heels.

Fasting like yours is no fasting
to make your voice to be heard on high.
5 Would such be the fast that I would take pleasure in,
a day when a man mortifies his flesh,
bows down his head like a rush,
spreads sackcloth and ashes under him?
Do you call this a fast,
a day in which Yahweh takes pleasure?

6 Is not this the fast that I choose:
to loose the bonds of wickedness,
to undo the thongs of the yoke,
to let the enslaved go free,
that [you]ᵃ break every yoke.
7 Does it not mean sharing your bread with the hungry,
and bringing the homeless poor into [your] house,ᵇ
when you see someone naked, to cover him,
and not to withdraw yourself from your own flesh?

8 Then shall your light break forth like the dawn,
and your healing will spring up at once,
your salvation goes before you,
and the glory of Yahweh is your rear guard.
9 Then you shall call, and Yahweh answers,
you cry, and he says, Here I am.
If you take away from the midst of you oppression,
the pointing of the finger, and speaking wickedness,
10 and bestow your breadᶜ on the hungry,
and satisfy the desire of the afflicted,

then shall your light gleam in the darkness,
and your gloom be as the clear day.
11 Yahweh will guide you continually,
and satisfy your desire in the thirsty land.
And he will make your bones young again,ᵈ
you shall be like a watered garden,
and like a spring whose waters fail not.

12 Ancient ruins shallᵉ be rebuilt by you,
you raise up the foundations of many generations,
you shall be called the repairer of the breach,
the restorer of what was tornᶠ down to dwell in.

ᵃ With the Vss. read the last verb as a singular.
ᵇ Read *bēteᵏā*.
ᶜ Read *laḥmeᵏā*.
ᵈ Read *yahᵃlīp*.
ᵉ Read *weᵣnibnū*.
ᶠ Read *neᵗīṣōt*.

The central part of this chapter, vv. 5ff., takes the form of an admonition. Both what precedes and follows it are related to it. Therefore the whole is best taken as a speech of admonition (Haller). Initially, vv. 5ff. may be taken by themselves; they give an answer to the question, what constitutes proper fasting, or, as v. 3a puts it, effectual fasting. The question itself (v. 3a) is, 'why do we fast, and thou seest it not?', and the answer is, 'Is what you do fasting that pleases Yahweh?' (v. 5). No, fasting that pleases God is . . . (vv. 6f.). Several expansions have been made in order to build up this basis of the admonition or admonitory piece of instruction into a speech of admonition. Its introduction takes the form of a command to the prophet to declare her sin to Israel. This closely follows earlier prophetic words. Strictly speaking, however, it can only form the introduction to vv. 2ff., for vv. 3b–4 alone contain a prophetic accusation, which vv. 2–3a set against the background of an endeavour in other respects to be serious about God. In this connection it should be noted that ungenuine fasting is defined in different ways as between vv. 3b–4 and v. 5. Quite obviously, the speech has been put together from entirely disparate elements. The affirmatory answer to the question about proper fasting given in vv. 6f. is related in a different way to what follows—it serves as the condition of a conditional promise in vv. 8–9a. In the light of vv. 8–9a, v. 6 must originally have begun 'if you loose the bonds of wickedness'. The second part of the conditional promise (v. 9b), 'If you . . . then' (v. 10b), has precisely the same beginning as this. Verses 9b–12 thus constitute a conditional promise such as we find, above all, in the speeches of Job's friends, e.g. 11.13–19. This takes us very far away from prophetic discourse proper. And this comes out in the drafting as well—from v. 8 onwards God is spoken of only in the third person, whereas the beginning is in the shape of direct speech by him. The change also comes out in the fact that the promise of salvation contained in vv. 8–9a and 10b–11 only has an individual in mind and resembles the promise made to the devout in Job's friends' speeches. Strictly speaking, it is a promise of blessing. Verse 12, the promise of reconstruction, is the only one that is different. This is the one and only verse that refers to Israel, although strictly, according to v. 1, it is she who is to be addressed throughout. Thus, ch. 58 is a very complex entity. It contains many disparate elements, of which only a few are prophetic discourse. Beginning as it does with a command to a prophet to bring a charge and then passing over into a conditional promise of blessing, it is symptomatic of the coming together of prophetic and liturgical speech which is in harmony with the change which came over prophecy after the return.

[1] This command re-echoes two earlier prophetic utterances, Hos. 8.1 ('Set the trumpet to your lips, for') and Micah 3.8 ('to declare to Jacob his transgression and to Israel his sin'). This way of beginning also serves the same purpose as does Micah 3.8—it expresses the fact that the speaker here has full authorization to speak in God's name. Doing this in words which either take up earlier prophetic utterances or at least contain unmistakable echoes of them—an echo of Isa. 40.9 would also be possible—constitutes an important feature in post-exilic prophecy observable also in Zechariah and Malachi ('pre-exilic prophets . . . seldom if ever borrow in this way', Muilenburg). They regard themselves as successors of the earlier prophets whose tradition lay before them, a tradition with which they make a deliberate link. As many editors (e.g. Duhm) have observed, one consequence of this is that the introduction given in v. 1 does not in actual fact harmonize with all of the speech that follows. In respect of subject-matter, there is a point of contact between 58.1 and 61.1ff. where, too, the speaker of the words of salvation contained in chs. 60–62 shows himself to be commissioned so to do by God. Here, too, this is done in phraseology taken from tradition, and this raises the question whether the similarity in the opening in both places may not indicate the same author. At all events, both point to an activity by word of mouth on the part of the speaker here, even if in principle ch. 58 is to be thought of as a compilation in writing. 'Everything suggests that the prophetic leader was speaking in public, perhaps in the synagogue at an assembly for fasting' (Volz).

[2–3a] The beginning at once shows the difference from the pre-exilic proclamation of judgment, which is apparently what v. 1 introduces. In place of its abrupt, uncompromising charges from which nothing was safe, the present speaker brings in the word 'yet' which right away takes the sharp edge off the allegation. There is no denying, he says, that the accused put themselves to trouble in the matter of God. They seek Yahweh, and desire to know his ways: cf. Amos 5.4, 6, consult Yahweh, in order to be given direction and answers by him. Thus, 'to know my ways' signifies the ways which I have pointed out. As in 56.1, 'righteousness and judgment' refers to the dealings of men. The last line puts it in still another way. *šā'al* here is the equivalent of *dāraš* in v. 2a. 'They take pleasure in drawing near to God', cf. the people in Ps. 73.28. The whole of this relates to acts of worship, denoting a variety of attempts to hold fast to God. But these obviously represent only one aspect of worship. One and all have to do with its spoken element, the directions (and answers) which God issued for the life of the community and of the individual. There are only a few places where this is mentioned in such detail as here. The present paragraph shows the great importance it must have come to have for Israel. As in ch. 58 throughout, the passage before us has absolutely nothing to say about the sacrificial system or the temple. Presumably then, this utterance was made previous to the restoration of the temple. Basically, holding fast to God is enquiring about his will. In this case, the man-to-man direct communication of the latter by word of mouth must have been the thing of supreme importance. It could have been done either by prophets or priests. But, to judge it from Ezekiel, Haggai, Zechariah, Malachi and Trito-Isaiah, in the early post-exilic period as during the exile itself, the major role was apparently taken by the prophets. What the things enumerated in vv. 2–3a aim at is a specific question put to God—as the context shows, this was certainly put by the prophet—and this is cited: 'Why do we fast, and thou seest it not?'

As Zechariah tells us (7.3; 8.18), to the post-exilic community the fasts were a source of great perplexity. As attested in particular by Lamentations, the fast days, basically seasons of lamentation, came into being following upon the disasters of the year 586, and they became a customary observance prescribed for certain days (the four dates are given by Kissane as the day when the siege began, the day when the city was captured, the day when it, and the temple, were burnt, and the day of the murder of Gedaliah). In the course of time, people began to question such continuing occasions of lamentation. They had also led to abuses (vv. 3b–4). Zechariah was asked (obviously after the restoration of the temple) whether they ought still to go on. In all probability, the utterance of Trito-Isaiah which we are now to consider contributed towards their being given up.

[3b–4] But, even although the situation is very different from what it was in pre-exilic times, the prophet's answer—that is, God's answer as mediated by the prophet—speaks a genuine, living prophetic word. There is not the slightest feeling of mere imitation. Instead, it brings to life again all the edge, the clarity and the freedom of the old prophetic utterances. In respect of subject-matter the allegation made in vv. 3b–4 corresponds to utterances such as those of Amos (2.8), in which the allegation that unreality has made its way into worship is united with a charge concerned with social matters. What is censured is not observance of fasts as such. On the contrary, it is taken for granted that these can in fact 'make your voice to be heard on high'. What mars the fasts is the fact that, with those who observe them, their whole being is not involved in their supplication. They pursue their business on a fast day, and make their workers work for them then (or, they press their creditors, so Köhler and Kessler). Indeed, the fast day is an occasion for wrangling and quarrelling (this was presumably connected with business affairs). It even comes to deeds of violence. So far all is clear. The prophet raises a complaint about serious abuses which have gained ground on fast days. His concern is not with the days as an institution, but with the question whether the turning to God in prayer—and prayer is the central thing in them—is a genuine and complete one.

[5] Here we find a change that surprises us. Verse 5 starts an essentially different polemic against the fast days. After the attack on the desecration of the fast days contained in vv. 3b–4, one would expect approval of their rites in so far as they were holy. But in v. 5 the exact opposite is the case. No doubt here, too, the attack is not on the really central thing in the fast days, supplication to God by reason of the great calamities that befell Jerusalem. Instead, it is on the 'external rites' attached to their observance. And it must be admitted that these long-standing rites are here given a challenge in principle—this is not the observance of fasting that is pleasing to God. This is a different critique of the fast days from that found in vv. 3b and 4, and perhaps other than prophetic motifs have their part in it. The words, 'bows down his head like a rush', sound rather like the ridicule of a rationalist. A feature belonging to the wisdom literature may come in here, as in the polemic against sacrifice in Ps. 50. The divergence of v. 5 from v. 4 justifies what was said above about the chapter's structure.

[6] We are now told of the fasting that does please God. Action directed towards God is replaced by action directed towards human beings. Can this still bear the title of fasting? We must not be blind to the fact that the prophet's way of putting is not that 'you are to do something else in place of fasting'. His meaning can only be that the actions towards men and women now detailed have some connection with fasting, and that they may be designated as a mode of fasting. What makes the link is the factor of restricting oneself, doing without,

which enters into both fasting and the acts of helping which mean giving things up oneself, as in Matt. 6.16ff. The remarkable accummulation of different ways of expressing one single act of proper fasting (as against v. 7, where four clauses name four different acts) shows that, in the eyes of the speaker here, of all the conceivable acts of help, one, loosing from bonds and setting men free, was of supreme importance. There can be no doubt that this is to be understood as a direct repercussion of what the entire nation had had experience of, bondage in the exile (so also Kessler). In Deuteronomy, in the context of the laws relating to slavery, Israel is reminded, 'remember that you were a slave in Egypt'. Similarly here in Trito-Isaiah, in the context of acts of help, releasing from any sort of bondage is given pride of place; the nation remembers the bondage which it endured itself, and the release that followed.

It is also said in connection with the commissioning of the prophet in 61.1ff., 'to declare liberty to the captives, and the opening . . . to those who are bound'. There the words form part of the message of salvation to the nation. Here they are an admonition to the individual Israelite. Seen against this background, this exceptionally penetrating and emphatic admonition to help to set people free reveals something of the way in which Deutero-Isaiah's proclamation of the release worked out in history. What God promised to Israel, and she had experienced, resulted in a new value being attached to what we call freedom. Now, helping to restore a person's freedom is more pleasing to God than the practice of mortifying one's flesh. This is the beginning of that great change which declared, in God's name, that men and women are of greater importance than cultic rites directed towards himself.

[7] Verse 7 goes on to list the traditional acts of help to those in trouble. 'A pageant of people whose social standing is poor passes before the spectators' eyes—disfranchised, down and outs, slaves, prisoners, the hungry, the homeless, the cold. It is a similar picture to the one in Matt. 25.35f.' (Volz). The words at the end of v. 7, 'you are not to withdraw yourself', are found in identical terms in Deut. 22.1. The change from infinitives to the commandment form as generally employed in Deuteronomy is a very forcible indication of the change in style. A transition has been made from prophetic utterance to speech of admontion, the style found in the preaching (or parenesis) of the levites in Deuteronomy. The words 'who is your flesh' are like those of Job 31.15, in a similar context: the passages in

Job shows that the reference is to fellow-men and not to fellow-countrymen.

[8–9a] If you do all of this—what vv. 6f. designate as the fast that is pleasing to Yahweh—then . . . : on this ensues a promise of blessing, the closest parallel to which is to be found in the friends' speeches in the book of Job (cf. also Pss. 91; 121). This is addressed to individuals—just as, in fact, the admonitions contained in vv. 6ff. are really admonitions to individuals. As compared with v. 1, where the summons is said to be made to Israel, there is a clear change. In their content, too, the words which now follow are quite out of keeping with the task assigned in v. 1.

The breaking forth of the light of dawn is reminiscent of 60.1f. This again suggests that both passages may have been spoken by the same man (so Elliger). The words, 'and your healing will spring up at once', are characteristic in the highest degree. In Jer. 8.22; 30.17; 33.6, the word *'ᵃrūkā* means 'the new layer of skin that grows over a wound that is healing' (Duhm, following Levy). Like the verb 'to spring up', the term denotes a gradual process, not an instantaneous transformation of the whole scene. This continues in what comes next, of which Duhm says, 'v. 8b is another of those citations of Deutero-Isaiah (52.12) of which Trito-Isaiah could make use if he re-interpreted them.' Zimmerli[a] takes this further: 'the terms used (in 52.12) have turned into terms hallowed by religious usage, now to be taken in a transferred and metaphorical sense.' But the process of re-interpretation has caused a change. In 52.12b the two related concepts, 'Yahweh' and 'the God of Israel', expressed the fact that when the Lord led the caravan through the wilderness, he was himself present in person. But in 58.8b they have lost this vividness and stand for 'your salvation, the brightness of Yahweh'. This loss of vividness makes the expression better adapted to the change in the way in which it is now understood. Up to this point, and therefore inclusive of what is said in v. 8, the promise of blessing, a form meant to apply to an individual, has been related to the nation Israel. In the case of v. 9a, as is shown by the parallel in Job 14.15 (cf. 5.1), its wording applies to an individual. But here it is very ingeniously related to Israel and her supplication at the fasts (vv. 3a; 4c). This verse (9a, cf. Isa. 30.10; 65.24) is of particular importance for the understanding of what the Old Testament means by salvation. When Israel (or an individual) calls upon God and he hears, that is, lets it

[a] *op. cit.*, pp. 3f.

be known that he hears, answers, says, 'Here I am', this is being saved or salvation. This does not properly mean 'an unceasing hearing of prayer' (Volz). Instead, it is the being saved that consists in the inter-relation of word and answer. Salvation is not described as a state of bliss, but as the constancy of the dialogical relationship between man and God (Buber).

[9b–10a] From here onwards, the second point in the admonition connected with the promise of blessing, any idea of Israel's being addressed is completely abandoned. Only individuals are envisaged. And further, nothing more is said of the contrast between proper and improper fasting. In vv. 9b–10a the admonition contained in the conditional clause includes a good work of a representative kind, giving food to the hungry, and also a bad one, it, too, is representa-tive, 'pointing the finger and speaking wickedness', that is to say, the gesture of derision and the defamatory word. 'And satisfy the desire of the afflicted' again represents the voice of experience. Israel had not forgotten how abasing hunger can be. Lamentations speaks most movingly of this.

[10b–12] The terms and metaphors which it employs makes it quite plain that the promise contained in vv. 10f. relates to an indivi-dual. Verse 12 is quite different. It promises the rebuilding of a city or a country. Comparison with Job 11.13–19 shows that the back-ground of these verses is the pattern followed by a conditional promise of blessing to an individual. In the case of Isa. 58.9b the condition runs, 'if you take away from the midst of your oppression', and in Job 11.14, 'if iniquity is in your hand, put it far away'. In the promise, what is said in 58.10b is 'then shall your light shine in the darkness', and Job 11 'and your life will (then) be brighter than the noonday'. In connection with this metaphor of the arising of light, which also occurred earlier, in v. 8, we have once again to remember 60.1. The words that follow are reminiscent of Ps. 23. Their meta-phors of making the bones young again, of the watered garden, the spring of water, and waters that fail not, employ the language used in the blessing. In the case of Deutero-Isaiah, when he spoke of springs in the desert and the latter's transformation into a garden, this was all related to the all-transforming event of the return follow-ing upon the release. With Trito-Isaiah it is a state of bliss having no association with definite historical events, a state that is much more related to the life of the individual than to that of the nation. Only at the end, in v. 12, is there an additional promise relating to the

nation. The verse reminds one of 61.4. The promise is the same in
point of subject-matter, and some of the words are also the same.
This final verse, too, shows the closeness of the link between ch. 58
and chs. 60–62; as is often the case in chs. 60–62, the proof of the new
salvation is the bestowal of new names.

CHAPTER 58.13–14

Hallowing the Sabbath

13 If you turn back your foot from the Sabbath,
    from doing your business on my holy day,
    and call the Sabbath a delight,
    the honourable (day) holy to Yahweh,
    and honour it, not going your own ways,
    or pursuing your own business and trading,
14 then you shall take delight in Yahweh,
    I make you ride upon the heights of the earth,
    make you enjoy the heritage of Jacob your father,
    for the mouth of Yahweh has spoken.

These two verses form a distinctive and impressive example of
parenesis connected with the commandments. Unlike that part of the
chapter with the conditional clauses in it (vv. 6f. and 9b–10a), where
in each case the admonition formulated in the conditional clauses
gave a series of acts to describe a line of conduct, vv. 13f. are a commentary on a single commandment, the fourth. This itself shows that
vv. 13f. are an addition to vv. 1–12 dictated—just like 56.2—by zeal
for this one commandment which has particular stress put upon it.
Since a new section begins in ch. 59, one may surmise that the two
admonitions concerning the Sabbath, 56.1f. and 58.13f., were deliberately designed as a framework for the section composed of chs.
56–58. In subject-matter, too, there is a difference from the preceding parts with conditions in them, a difference in what each has
in view. In the latter, everything has to do with turning towards one's
fellow-men, whereas in v. 13 the interest is exclusively concentrated
on the holy day. In the conditional part, v. 13, the drafting is obviously that of the person who here gives the admonition to hallow the

Sabbath—his way of expressing himself is all his own; on the other hand, the part containing the promise, v. 14, consists almost entirely of phrases taken from tradition. Compare vv. 13f. with vv. 3f., where, too, the subject is a holy day, the day of fasting, and one feels the difference even more. Verses 3f. are a forthright allegation (v. 3b contains a few words the same as found in v. 13a), but v. 13 is mere admonition. In the earlier verse, the accent is upon relations with one's fellow-men (strife and wrangling, laying about oneself), while v. 13 speaks only of the desecration of the holy day.

[13] The verse affords us a vivid picture of the importance of the Sabbath in the post-exilic period. Obviously, it was open to people to do what they are here admonished to abstain from. The conditions presupposed are those of the city. After the return, when the economy was straightened and things were hard, business apparently went on on the Sabbath without regard to the commandment forbidding work on it. (It is very significant that nothing is said of either the farmer's or the craftsman's work, cf. to the contrary Ex. 20.12.) It is equally significant that the old apodictic commandment and the articles in the penal code relating to it (Ex. 31.15: whoever does any work on the Sabbath day shall be put to death) had now apparently become a dead letter. This is what rendered the parenesis with promises attached necessary. Holding out the prospect of such rewards for keeping the Sabbath would have been inconceivable in the older days. This background also explains a further feature in v. 13. Here the Sabbath has ceased to be understood as a day of rest (as, e.g. in Ex. 23.12; Volz drew attention to this). In Gen. 2.1ff. the two motifs are united; the seventh day is hallowed as a day of rest. Since, however, the reason for its being hallowed is that it was the day upon which God rested, the motif which predominates is that of the day hallowed by God. Here in Isa. 58.13 the motif of rest for men has completely disappeared. This makes the holiness attaching to the day all the more strongly emphasized; it is *the* 'holy day'. The name here given it is nothing short of 'the holy (day) of Yahweh', and as such it is honourable. We have to take it that, at the time, this was the only way in which Israel could have the Sabbath preserved for her in face of clearly observable signs of disintegration. But the Sabbath's character has suffered change. Now it is no longer an integral part of the national life, a day on which to draw one's breath (Ex. 23.12). It is a 'perpetual obligation' (Ex. 31.16), a confession of the divine holiness by way of making this day holy, a

confession which separates those who fear God from the transgressors.

[14] For the most part, the promise is made up of citations of stereotyped phrases. The opening words are found in one of the conditional promises of blessing in the friends' speeches in Job (22.26). The second line occurs in Deut. 32.13, 'a passage from which the third, too, is borrowed' (Duhm). Both here and in Deuteronomy 'riding upon the heights of the earth' is purely metaphorical: high over all depressions and obstacles. 'Enjoying the heritage of Jacob your father' means undisturbed possession of the land.

CHAPTER 59.1–21

Yahweh's hand is not shortened

1 Behold, Yahweh's hand is not shortened, that it cannot save,
    and his ear is not dull, that it cannot hear,
2 but it is your iniquities that make a separation
.   between you and your God.
    And your transgressions, they hide his face
    from you, so that he does not hear.
3 For your hands are defiled with blood
    and your fingers with iniquity;
    your lips speak lies, your tongue mutters transgression.

4 No one enters suit justly, no one goes to law honestly.
    They rely on empty pleas, speak vanity,
    conceive mischief and bring forth deceit.
5 They hatch adders' eggs, they weave the spider's web.
    He who eats their eggs dies,
    and from one which is crushed a viper is hatched.
6 Their webs do not serve as clothing,
    men do not cover themselves with what they make.
    Their works are works of iniquity,
    deeds of violence are in their hands.
7 Their feet hasten to evil,
    they run to shed innocent blood.
    Their thoughts are thoughts of iniquity,
    desolation and destruction are in their highways.
8 The way of peace they know not,
    there is no justice in their paths.

They make their roads crooked,
no one who goes in them knows peace.

9   Therefore justice is far from us,
    and salvation cannot reach us.
    We hope for light, and behold, darkness,
    and for brightness—and we walk in gloom.
10 We grope for the wall like the blind,
    we fumble about like those who have no eyes.
    We stumble at noon, as in the twilight,
    and [sit in darkness]ᵃ like the dead.
11 We all growl like the bears,
    and moan like the doves.
    We hoped for righteousness—it came not,
    for help, but it is far from us.

12 For our transgressions are multiplied before thee,
    and our sins testify against us;
    our transgression is with us,
    and we know our sins,
13 apostasy from Yahweh and denying him,
    we turn away from following our God,
    speaking falseness and revolt,
    [murmuring]ᵇ the words of deceit from the heart.
14 So justice is turned back
    and righteousness must stand far off.
    Truth stumbles in the market,
    and uprightness cannot enter.
15a Thus honesty was lacking,
    he who departs from evil makes himself a prey.

15b And Yahweh saw it, and it displeased him,
    that there was no longer any justice.
16 He saw that there was no man,
    and wondered that none intervened.
    Then his own arm helped him
    and his salvation upheld him.
17 He put on righteousness as a breastplate,
    set the helmet of salvation upon his head;
    he put on vengeance as a garment [   ],ᶜ
    wrapped himself in zeal as a garment.
18 [He requites his adversaries with anger,
    and pays his foes with vengeance.]ᵈ

ᵃ Read *wannēšēb baḥªšēkīm* (*BH, app. crit.*).
ᵇ Read *wᵉhāgō*.
ᶜ Delete *tilbōšet*.
ᵈ See the commentary.

19   So that men should fear the name of Yahweh from the west,
     and his majesty from the rising of the sun.

     For he comes like the rushing stream
     when the wind of Yahweh drives it.
20   Yet he comes for Zion as Redeemer
     and for those in Jacob who turn from apostasy, says Yahweh.

21   But as for me, this is my covenant [with them],ᵃ says Yahweh:
     my spirit, which is (put) upon you
     and my words which I have put in your mouth,
     shall not depart out of your mouth,
     or out of the mouth of your children,
     or out of the mouth of your children's children,
     says Yahweh, from this time forth and for evermore.

Chapter 59 is a most curious and odd creation. It is plainly a unity.
But with what does it present us? A token of the difficulty can be seen
in the fact that a large number of editors (Haller, Procksch, Muilenburg, etc.) describe the chapter as a liturgy, while some (Kessler)
call it a sermon. But surely there must be a difference between a
sermon and a liturgy! What certainties do we have? As all editors
remark, the chapter contains elements taken from a lament, a
community lament. This is the first point for investigation. Verses
1f. relate to the charge brought against God in the body of the community lament; why, Yahweh, is your hand too shortened to help?
Why do you hide your face? Verses 1f. challenge this. This means
that, right at the beginning, vv. 1f. contain the two elements which
lay down the lines for the whole chapter—the community lament to
which v. 1 relates carries on, but so also does the prophetic voice
raised in v. 1 to counter the unjustified charge brought against God.
This is the explanation of the curious interweaving of words taken
from a lament and words spoken by a prophet (and this interweaving
is the reason why some designate the whole thing as a liturgy, while
others call it a sermon). The chapter's skeleton is that of a community
lament. But it is a lament that has had an answer given it. What is
responsible for the change is the fact that the voice of a prophet
rebuts the charge brought against God, the lament addressed to him
(v. 1). He for his part brings charges against the nation (vv. 2f.) and
develops them (v. 4; expanded in vv. 5–8). This makes a change on
the lament in the first personal plural which comes next (vv. 9ff.); it

ᵃ Read *'ittām*.

is now substantiated ('therefore' in v. 9) by means of the charge just made against the nation. The confession of sin which ensues in v. 12, being a part of the community lament, remains unaltered. In its present context, however, it also serves as an answer to the charge made by the prophet—the nation admits the sins of which it was accused. The expansion represented by vv. 13–15a carries that of vv. 5–8 further. After the confession of sin God turns again to his people who cry to him in their extremity (vv. 1f.), and intervenes as redeemer against their enemies and for Zion (vv. 15b–20).

Verse 21 forms no part of what precedes it. It has a different context. The difficulties still remaining in connection with the structure of the chapter must be kept for the commentary.

[1] The disputation with which the chapter begins corresponds to 58.3b and 4a. In both places the word *hēn* forms the introduction. The charge brought against God, merely implied in 59.1, is cited in 58.3a. One is reminded of the community laments cited in Deutero-Isaiah, such as 40.27; 50.2, etc. But 59.1ff. were spoken after the return had taken place. Then, as here revealed, the acuteness of the state of affairs which the chapter was designed to meet is disturbing in the extreme. Such things could still be said even after the great change, salvation, had come about, even after the edict of liberation and the return! This means that, even after the change to salvation proclaimed by Deutero-Isaiah, the lamentation which he had been sent to silence or to turn into praise had not been, or was only partially and temporarily, hushed. There can be no clearer proof of the need to renew or carry on Deutero-Isaiah's proclamation even after the exile was a thing of the past.

The two parts of v. 1 correspond to the two component parts of the petition in psalms of lamentation—the prayer for God's turning towards the suppliant (hear), and that for his intervention (help). Like his arm, Yahweh's hand signifies his power, exactly as in 50.2, 'is my hand shortened, that it cannot redeem?'; cf. Num. 11.23 'that it cannot hear', as in Isa. 6.10 and Zech. 7.11.

[2–3] The prophet challenges the lament which is also the charge brought against God. The reason for the straitened circumstances is not that God is withholding. The thing responsible is 'your sins'. This new section reveals the change which the exile wrought upon prophecy. The words here used could be those of a charge made by a prophet of pre-exilic days (to some extent they are this, word for word). Here, nevertheless, what the charge gives the reason for is not a divine judgment which is proclaimed along with it, but the present condition of things. What it wishes to bring about is that the people whom it addresses should appreciate the transgressions they have committed. It is not designed at the eleventh hour to avert the judgment threatening, but to help the present state of affairs to mend. This means that the 'prophetic' charge loses the strictly prophetic character, its reference to the future which gave such a charge the edge and tension associated with it in the pre-exilic period. The present passage makes it quite clear that the vital thing in the charges which the prophets made was the reference to the future. Let this drop out, and they also lose their immediacy as a message from God. This is the reason why the direct address in the charge (vv. 2f. use the second person) imperceptibly goes over into a description (v. 4a, b onwards), a general description of the condition of things which ceases to be a direct and specific charge.

This is the only occurrence of *hibdīl* meaning 'to separate' in such a context. And here, as in many other parts of ch. 59, there are signs that the language belongs to a late period (Odeberg). 'Your transgressions, they hide the face': the versions have 'his face', which would be better. But possibly even now *pānīm* is a technical term for God's presence (Odeberg). Verse 3: 'your hands are defiled with blood' is almost word for word identical with Isa. 1.15. Comparison of the two passages shows that in Isa. 1.15 their context gives the words the precise and forceful meaning which they have. Here they are words taken from tradition, any trace of a specific allegation being now lost. The same thing can also be seen in the words designed as a parallel to Isa. 1.15, 'and your fingers with iniquity'. In v. 3b—apart from the fact that a different word is used for 'sin'—the same phrase is expanded to take in the lips and the tongue. This is the expansion of rhetoric. The present passage makes it perfectly plain that, while such 'preaching of sin' taken from the tradition of the prophetic charge persisted, it turned into something else. The style itself reveals the transition to the way in which the transgressors are described in the Psalms. There it is said of them that they talk deceit (Pss. 101.7; 109.2; 120.2). 'The tongue mutters transgression'—just as in Job 27.4.

[4–8] Verse 4a is again the language of the prophets. Even although the words of the pre-exilic prophecy have not come down to us, this could be a verbal citation of them. 'Call' has the meaning of 'enter suit' or 'cite' as in Job 5.1; 9.16; 13.22. The same expression, *qārā' bᵉṣedeq*, is used in 42.6, but with an entirely different meaning. *niṣpat* with the meaning of 'going to law' is also found in 43.26; 66.16, etc. From v. 4b onwards there are further traces of the language of the Psalms; 'speak vanity', Pss. 12.3 (4); 41.7; 144.8, 11; it also occurs with late prophets in a prophetic charge, Ezek. 13.8; Zech. 10.2. The words 'conceive mischief and bring forth deceit' come from Job 15.35, also a description of the transgressors (similarly in Ps. 7.15 [14]). Verses 5–8 are generally regarded as an addition, both on grounds of form (transition from direct address to the third person: but since the transition is already made in v. 4, Volz regards the addition as vv. 4–8), and on grounds of subject-matter (those charged in v. 3 are the whole nation, but vv. 5–8 picture a section of it, the transgressors). But important considerations of style and subject-matter challenge the view that vv. 4 (5)–8 are an addition. To take style first: the very thing that gives the poem the odd character which it has are the expansions. But these comprise not only vv. 3ff., but as well vv. 10f. and vv. 13–15a. They are all of the same type. They extend the description and enlarge upon it. And their style is perfectly familiar. Many of the Psalms employ it to describe the transgressors (e.g., Pss. 58.3–6 [2–5]; 55.10ff., 21f. [9ff., 20f.], etc.), and it is used in the friends' speeches in the book of Job. Then, to take the reasons suggested by the subject-matter: ch. 59 is a very impressive exemplification of the way in which the prophetic change broke down. Its form, and words taken from it, are still present in vv. 2f., but its subject-matter is no longer the same because of the dropping of the unconditional proclamation of judgment. This is replaced either by the conditional proclamation and, associated with it, either the conditional accusation or the lament over the goings-on of the transgressors. But this is the very transition which we see in ch. 59. And it is to be seen not only in vv. 5–8, but throughout the entire chapter. As early as v. 3b we found the language in which the Psalms speak of the transgressors. This explains a further breakdown in point of style. The parts taken from the community lament are expanded by means of a motif taken from the individual lament, the description of the transgressors. We also find the same thing in some of the psalms, e.g. Ps. 83. This breakdown in style shows that the old antithesis, Israel and her foes, has had superimposed upon it the new one, the righteous and the transgressors.

There is no progress from part to part in the description of the transgressors given in vv. 5–8. It represents an accumulation. The various verses and phrases bear hardly any relationship to one another; and for this reason they also occur in many other passages (v. 7a resembles Prov. 1.16; v. 8 is reminiscent of Prov. 10.9; Ps. 1 speaks of the ways of the devout and the godless; in LXX the description of the transgressors in Ps. 14.3f. is added to vv. 7f., and in this form the latter were taken up into the description of the godless in Rom. 3.10–18). Precise interpretation of the various parts in this description is scarcely possible or worth-while. They are not intended to indicate specific characteristics of the transgressors, but with as great a variety of words and phrases as possible to give a picture of their flagrant wickedness.

[9–11] The second part of the lament, the lament in the first person plural, carries on the first, the charge made against God implied in vv. 1f. The 'therefore' at the beginning of v. 9 connects this verse with what precedes it: because of all this transgression the nation must now suffer. The lament begins (v. 9) by saying that the state of affairs is one into which salvation does not enter; as in 56.1 *mišpāt* and *ṣedāqā* are parallel, although their sense is different in the two places. Verse 9b describes the disillusionment in terms almost identical with the community lament in Jer. 14.19c; cf. also Lam. 4.17. Verses 10f. expand the lament in the first person plural by means of phrases and similes taken from tradition. With v. 10a cf. Lam. 4.14, 'they wander through the streets like blind men.' The next two sentences put the same thing in different words. The meaning of the final half-verse cannot be gathered from the text itself, and the translation given is a mere conjecture. The comparison of the sounds of mourning with those made by animals is found in Babylonian psalms. Zimmerli[a] adduces words from a hymn to Ishtar: 'I sigh like a dove day and night'; in the Old Testament itself cf. Isa. 38.14 and Nahum 2.8. There is no known parallel to the growling of the bear as a sound of mourning. Verse 11b reverts to v. 9. Reading this lament (vv. 9f.) with an eye to the state of affairs which it describes and attending to the emphasis put on vv. 9b and 11b—which of course also form the background of the charge against God contained in vv. 1f.—one is given a moving testimony to a mood of bitter disenchantment and despondency as over against the lofty and brilliant prophecies which had proclaimed that the exile was at its end. In all probability we today just cannot conceive how deep

[a] *Op. cit.*, p. 186.

the disillusionment went then, or what it meant, in this state of affairs, to continue to hold fast to God's promises. The fact that Trito-Isaiah's proclamation does this is what gives it its categorical importance in the history of prophecy.

[12] The lament in the first person plural is followed by the confession of sin. In v. 2 the prophet brought the charge against the nation. But here, as is usual in laments in the first person plural, he includes himself in the confession, a sign that the harsh confrontation between prophet and nation of the earlier period no longer obtained. Verse 12 alone is confession of sin in the strict sense of the term, vv. 13–15a being an expansion of the description of the transgression. Their style is that of vv. 5–8, and they could equally well have been their continuation. The accumulation of words for 'sin' is very noticeable: 'few chapters in the Bible are so rich and diverse in their vocabulary of sin (cf. Ps. 51)' (Muilenburg). Taken by itself, v. 12 confesses sin with a directness and seriousness such as we find in Ps. 51 or Ps. 90, of which there are even reminiscences in various words and phrases used. There can be no doubt that v. 12 represents words used in the worship of the time. The two verses 12a and 12b are co-ordinated as follows: v. 12a depicts the grievousness or actual presence of the sin, while 12b expresses the consciousness of it, the sinners' admission of guilt.

[13–15a] In the final verse of the section (v. 15a), the words, 'and . . . was' or 'so . . . was', reveal that it has now stopped being a confession of sin. The description of the transgressors or their transgression given in vv. 5–8 is now carried further. Verse 13a shows the sin in the relationship with God, the latter being represented as 'following God'. This is reminiscent of the phraseology of Deuteronomy. Apostasy and unfruitfulness result in ceasing to follow God. Verse 13b adds the sin as displayed in the life of society. This is typified as 'deceitful words'. In v. 14a *mišpāt* and *ṣedāqā* have a different frame of reference from what they had in v. 9. Here they refer to the dealings of men one with another. The judicature may be intended, since v. 14b speaks of public life, probably business life in particular. Verse 15a rounds off this description. It has absolutely no connection with the confession of sin contained in v. 12. Instead, the last half-verse, 'he who departs from evil makes himself a prey', sound more like a description taken from a lament, or a description bewailing the existent state of affairs such as v. 4 above.

[15b–20] The entire passage (15b–20) is a part of the community lament. The divine intervention for which supplication was there made is pictured as an epiphany. The same combination, community lament (of which only the suggestion is here given) and description of an epiphany, is also found in Ps. 60; and supplication is made for such an epiphany in the community lament contained in Isa. 64.1ff. The one thing involved in an epiphany is God's advent to destroy Israel's foes and save her herself (as e.g. in Judg. 5 or Ps. 18). Everything said in vv. 16–20 points to an intervention of this kind against foes from without, which means the international sphere. But as against this ch. 59 has never even mentioned foes from without. According to vv. 3–8 and 13–15a the threat comes from the transgression or the actions of the transgressors within Israel. Once more the reason for this is the charge made by the prophet, which vv. 2f. combine with the community lament. This is what causes the difficulty in vv. 15b–20. The section can only be taken as using language that is not appropriate. In speaking of God's advent to deliver his chosen people, it uses the language of the past. But in the present state of affairs this is obsolete.

The structure of vv. 15–21 is as follows: God sees (vv. 15b and 16a) and intervenes (vv. 16b–20), corresponding to the two parts of the prayer. The structure of vv. 16b–20 is this: God puts on his armour (vv. 16b–17) in order to intervene against the foes (v. 18) and on behalf of chosen people (v. 20). The world trembles at his advent (v. 19).

[15b] Verse 15b makes the transition. In the earlier epiphanies what God sees is the oppression of his people. Here he sees that 'there was no justice (well-being)'. This relates to the description of the transgression and the transgressors in the preceding verses, and makes a connection between this and the epiphany. As stated in the charge made by the prophet at the start (vv. 2f.), God's intervention can only consist in judgment upon the transgressors. But there are two aspects of God's action in an epiphany—the destruction of Israel's foes, which is here equated with the destruction of the transgressors, and a release for Israel, which is restricted to the devout in her midst.

[16] God saw that there was no man. The meaning is, no one to help (as 63.5a). This corresponds to the words of the lament, 'and there is no one to help'. The one thing that v. 16b wants to bring out is that, as he intervenes, God is quite alone. The same words are also found in 63.5. Duhm is correct in his belief that they are original in 63.5 and secondary here. 63.1–6 make it particularly clear that

the words can only be used of an intervention against foes from without.

[17] The above is the only way of giving any meaning to the description, which now comes, of Yahweh as a warrior. He is also designated warrior in Isa. 42.13 and 52.10. Apart from the present verse we have no detailed description of his equipment, and the colouring in which the warrior is here depicted verges on the allegorical—the terms which state the divine warrior's arms anticipate the battle's outcome, an event with two aspects of it, salvation for the devout (v. 17a), and retribution upon the transgressors (foes) (v. 17b).

[18] The two aspects of the arming, which were only suggested in v. 17, are now developed. Yahweh comes to exact retribution on his foes (the text is so corrupt that the content can only be conjectured).

[19a] Words with a pattern like these consistently form part of the description of an epiphany—God's advent to punish his foes takes place before the eyes of the whole world, which is terrified at his sovereign power, e.g. Isa. 33.3. Very probably a change has come over the original order of vv. 18ff.; v. 19a has the appearance of forming the end of a passage. The reason for the transposition was no doubt to make Yahweh's advent to redeem Israel come at the end. Verse 19 is in entire accord with the old descriptions of an epiphany in that Yahweh's advent is described as an elemental action that shakes the cosmos, e.g. Ps. 18.8–16 (7–15).

[20] In the first half of the verse LXX reads 'from Zion', and this is what we also find in Paul, Rom. 11.26 (Paul treats the passage messianically, 'the redeemer' being in his view Christ). Duhm adopts this reading as being the more original, but in order to correspond with v. 18 the context demands MT's reading, 'for Zion'. The variant in LXX finds its explanation in the history of the description of the epiphany.[a] The early descriptions picture the advent as Yahweh's coming from afar, either from a place on the earth's surface (Hab. 3.3, from Teman; Judg. 5.4, from Seir), or from heaven (Ps. 18.10 [9]), and in later texts from Zion (Ps. 50.2). It is this late form that is represented in the LXX's variant. The LXX also has a different text in the second half of the verse: 'to put away the transgression from Jacob' (thus Duhm, who adopts this version). Here, again, MT's text is to be preferred. However, MT and LXX agree that

[a] On the epiphany, see Westermann, *The Praise of God*, pp. 93ff.

God's redemptive act effects a separation. The first half-verse in v. 20 signifies, taken strictly, that God's advent means redemption, deliverance, for Israel in her entirety. But according to the second half-verse, this is only the destiny of those who turn away from transgression, or, as LXX puts it, it consists in Israel's being purged of the transgressors. Astonishingly enough, the places where the epiphany is brought into connection with the allegation that precedes it and with the description of the transgressors are the two half-verses v. 15bβ (see above) and v. 20b. Apart from them, the entire description of the epiphany is left in its traditional form, God's coming to free Israel from her foes (without).

We may once again notice how the speaker here strives with all his might to give present-day relevance to the old traditions in which the nation made lamentation before God as a unit and, in the charge brought by the prophet, was arraigned as a unit. But the actual state of affairs which he addresses forces a breakdown on the traditions. The words of the accusation have to be directed against a section of the nation, and they thus pass over into the description of the transgressors, and the confession of sin into a description, as in a lament, of the state of affairs due to them. Further, the promise made in the description of the epiphany, that God will intervene, is given two sides to it—against the transgressors and 'for those in Jacob who turn from apostasy'.

[21] Verse 21 diverges so much in both style and subject-matter from 59.1–20 that this cannot have been its original placing. Practically all editors agree in this. On the other hand, it is so similar to the final verses in the book, 66.22ff., that it can be taken along with them (see the commentary there).

CHAPTERS 60–62

Following the lead of not a few recent editors we may regard these three chapters as the basic nucleus of the matter gathered together in chs. 56–66. They form the corpus of a self-contained message of salvation quite distinct from that of Deutero-Isaiah, yet having at the same time, in many ways, a clear connection with it. If we may speak

at all of a prophet called Trito-Isaiah, the chief support comes from
the corpus contained in these three chapters. They lead us to presume
that they are the legacy of a definite person, a prophet active in
Jerusalem and Judah not long after the return. This is given support
by the proclamation of the messenger who in 61.1ff., which is the
central point of the corpus, says of himself that Yahweh sent him to
proclaim salvation to Zion. This self-introduction is repeated in 62.1.

From first to last, the three chapters are a proclamation of salvation,
containing as they do—apart from 60.12, which is an addition—
neither the announcement of judgment upon the nations nor judgment for a section of Israel (the transgressors). Basically they are
proclamation, proclamation of the salvation soon to come, although
one or two parts of them do pass over into description of this same
subject. In essence, the salvation consists in a change, a turning
towards salvation, within the historical realm itself. Here, however,
this is not expected, as in Deutero-Isaiah, to be inaugurated by a
definite historical event, but by the divine, miraculous transformation of a condition, the nation's oppression and its impoverishment,
into its opposite. The three chapters reveal no progression of thought.
The picture of the change towards salvation resembles a stream that
keeps pouring and breaks its banks, the connection between the one
trait and the next being associating of ideas. All that can be said is
that, in correspondence with the three members of a lament, ch. 60
stresses the change vis-à-vis the lament about foes (the movement of
the nations to Zion), ch. 61 the lament in the first person plural
(the more strongly personal tone which Köhler brings out), and ch.
62 the change on Yahweh himself. But this is not exclusively true.

CHAPTER 60.1–22

Arise, shine!

1   Arise, shine, for your light comes,
        and the glory of Yahweh rises upon you!
2   For behold, [darkness]ᵃ covers the earth,
        and thick darkness the peoples;

   ᵃ Delete the article in *hošek* (dittography).

but upon you Yahweh arises,
and upon you is his glory seen.
3 And peoples come to your light
and kings to the brightness of your rising.

4 Lift up your eyes round about, and see;
they all gather together, they come to you!
[they bring]ᵃ your sons from afar,
and your daughters shall be carried in the arms.
5 Then you shall see and be radiant,
your heart shall be thrilled and be enlarged;
because the abundance of the sea shall be turned to you,
the wealth of the nations come to you.
6 A multitude of camels shall cover you,
dromedaries from Midian and Ephah;
all those from Sheba come.
They bring gold and frankincense,
and proclaim the glorious deeds of Yahweh.
7 All the flocks of Kedar gather to you,
the rams of Nebaioth minister to you,
they come [up] with acceptance [on] my altarᵇ
and I glorify the house of my honour.

8 Who are those that fly like clouds,
like doves to their windows?
9 For me [the ships assemble]ᶜ
the ships of Tarshish leading,
to bring your sons from afar,
their silver and gold with them,
for the praise of Yahweh, your God,
the Holy One of Israel, because he makes you glorious.

10 And foreigners build up your walls,
and their kings minister to you;
for in my wrath I smote you,
but in my favour I have had mercy on you.
11 Your doors [remain]ᵈ open continually,
not shut day and night,
that men may bring to you the wealth of the nations,
their kings [led in procession].ᵉ
12   For the nation and kingdom that does not serve you
shall perish. and the nations shall be destroyed.

ᵃ Read *yabī'u.*
ᵇ Read (with Vss.) *lᵉrāṣōn ʿal.*
ᶜ Read *ṣiyyīm yiqqāwū.*
ᵈ Read (with the Vss.) *wᵉniptᵉḥū.*
ᵉ Read *nōhᵃgīm.*

13 The glory of Lebanon shall come to you,
   cypresses, spruces, and elm-trees together,
   to beautify my holy sanctuary,
   that I may make the place of my feet glorious.
14 And there come to you bending low
   the sons of those who oppressed and despised you [ ],ᵃ
   and they call you the city of Yahweh,
   the Zion of the Holy One of Israel.

15 Whereas you were forsaken,
   hated, and without one [to help],ᵇ
   I make you majestic forever,
   a joy from age to age.
16 You shall suck the milk of the nations,
   suck the [breast]ᶜ of kings,
   and shall know that I, Yahweh, am your helper,
   and your redeemer is the mighty one of Jacob.
17 Instead of bronze I bring gold,
   and instead of iron I bring silver,
   and instead of wood, bronze,
   and instead of stones, iron.
   I make your overseers peace,
   and those that drive you righteousness.
18 Violence shall no more be heard in your land,
   devastation or destruction within your borders.
   You shall call your walls salvation,
   and your gates praise.

19 The sun shall no more be your light by day,
   nor for brightness shall the moon give light to you [by night];ᵈ
   but Yahweh will be your everlasting light,
   and your God your glorious brightness.
20 Your sun shall no more go down,
   nor your moon withdraw itself;
   for Yahweh will be everlasting light for you,
   and your days of mourning are at an end.

21 As for your people, they are all righteous (partners in the salvation),
   for ever shall they possess the land,
   a shoot of [Yahweh's]ᵉ planting,
   the work of [his]ᶠ hands, that he may be glorified.

ᵃ With LXXʰ delete 'they throw themselves down at the soles of your feet'.
ᵇ Read ʿōzēr (LXX).
ᶜ Read wešad.
ᵈ Supply hallaylā with Vss. and DSS.
ᵉ Read mattaʿ yhwh.
ᶠ Read yādāyw (with Vss.).

22 The least one shall become a clan,
and the smallest one a mighty nation.
I, Yahweh, [have spoken it],[a]
in its time I will hasten it.

Bibliography: G. von Rad, 'The City on the Hill', *The Problem of the Hexateuch and other Essays*, trans. E. W. Trueman Dicken, Edinburgh 1966, pp. 232–42; P. Grelot, 'Un parallèle babylonien . . .', *VT*, VII, 3 (1957), pp. 319–21.

Chapter 60 is homogenous and is a unity. Chapter 61, where someone speaks of himself as commissioned by God, begins a fresh unit. From the first verse to the last, proclamation is made to Zion that her salvation is at hand. The first section, 60.1–9, is arranged round the imperatives at the beginning of vv. 1 and 4, and the question in v. 8. Imperatives at the start of a sentence are themselves recognizable as a stylistic device borrowed from Deutero-Isaiah, and in addition, the beginning of the second part of the section (v. 4) is actually taken over word for word from him (49.18). In this first section, the leading feature is movement—first in vv. 1ff., the arising of the light through Yahweh's coming to Israel, and then, in vv. 4–7 and 8f., the coming of the nations to Israel or to Zion. While traces of it still remain in the second section, vv. 10–22, the most prominent thing there is the description of the new state of salvation. This section is not so clear in its arrangement as the first. Verses 10–14 tell of the rebuilding of Jerusalem, and vv. 15–18 of the change to be wrought on Zion: in vv. 19–22 this takes in the cosmos as well. Taken altogether the chapter combines proclamation of salvation and description of the same. These run through one another, the former being predominant in the first section, and the latter in the second.

[1–3] This fine utterance, with its mastery in painting a picture, is a very impressive example of the biblical promise, and the fact that it takes pride of place in worship at Advent means that some part of the dynamic that attached to the Jewish community's worship after the exile, when the utterance was first made, lasts on down to the present day. As their background the verses have the old motif of Yahweh's ephiphany (e.g. Judg. 5. 4f.; Ps. 18.8–16 [7–15], and see commentary on 59.15b–20). But great changes have come over it. The element of war is completely lacking, and of the natural pheno-

[a] Supply *dibbarti*.

mena which formed the accompaniment of God's advent there remains only the shining of the light. The old concept is thus very
greatly spiritualized, and the words bear more resemblance to the
way in which the New Testament (particularly the Gospel of John)
speaks of light and darkness. The reason for this divorce from the
concrete and from history is the fact that, unlike Deutero-Isaiah,
Trito-Isaiah does not link Yahweh's coming to Israel with a definite
historical event. Nevertheless, the advent and the era of salvation
which it inaugurates still lie in the future, for, in his view, this all-
transforming era which all men were to see was not initiated by the
first return from Babylon. But just because, in his republication of
Deutero-Isaiah's message of salvation, Trito-Isaiah finds himself
unable to point in advance to a definite historical event, the divine
advent is now considerably more dissociated from history. For this
reason he does not, like 40.9ff., identify God's advent with the return
of those still living in foreign lands. Instead, the latter is included in
the counter-move of the nations to Zion which ensues on God's
coming in salvation. A description of this is given in v. 3, and v. 4
develops it.

The introductory section, vv. 1ff., is not strictly announcement,
but a summons to Zion (Zion alone can be meant; the versions
add 'Jerusalem') substantiated by the announcement of salvation.
It is similar to the many other urgent summonses found in Deutero-
Isaiah which, too, often serve the same purpose of summoning men
joyfully to accept the message of salvation. In just the same way as
does 51.17, the first call, 'Arise', bids the mourners cease to be weary.
And the tones of this—'be joyful'—carry over into the second call,
'shine'. What the prophet has in mind is a beaming look on the face.
Although this imperative of the verb 'to shine' has no parallels, it
does correspond to the prayer in the Psalms, e.g. Ps. 13.4 (3); 27.1.
In summonses such as this Deutero-Isaiah always uses the double
imperative of the same verb, but Trito-Isaiah uses two different verbs.
Light and glory as parallels are also found in 58.8. There is something
odd about the way in which the verbs denoting coming and appearing
(equivalent to the rising of a star) in vv. 1 and 2b pass over into one
another—'your light comes', 'Yahweh's glory rises upon you',
'Yahweh goes up' (the only instance in the Old Testament), 'his glory
rises upon you'. The old concept of the epiphany, which presupposes
that Yahweh does actually draw near, is almost entirely obliterated
by that of a star's rising. This is typical of Trito-Isaiah's way of

expressing himself, equating God's advent with the advent of salvation (56.1; 59.11; 60.1; 62.11; 63.4; 66.15; cf. in Deutero-Isaiah, 40.10 and 50.2), but leaving it in the air without firmly fixing it in history; and this is reinforced by the metaphor of the rising of the light. These opening verses of ch. 60 are similar to Isa. 9.1ff., where, too, the people in darkness are promised the beaming of a light upon them.

The coming of the light upon Zion leaves the rest of the world in darkness (v. 2). In consequence, nations and kings (often mentioned side by side in the Psalms, e.g. 102.16 [15]) have recourse to 'the brightness of your rising (v. 3). This connects the move described in vv. 1f. with the other for which it was responsible, and which is now developed in detail in vv. 4–9.

[4–9] The summons in v. 4a, 'lift up your eyes, they come', is followed by a description of the train of people on the move to Zion. They come with 'your children' (vv. 4b–5a), bring the wealth of the nations (vv. 5b–6), bring animals for sacrifice (v. 7), and come with ships and bring 'your children' and their treasures (vv. 8f.). The special character of this chapter which occupies the central place in Trito-Isaiah's message of salvation is brought out in the way in which the one move follows the other and in their inter-relationship. (These are, of course, the advent of God or of salvation, and the streaming of the nations towards Zion [v. 3], which at the same time puts the salvation that rises upon Israel into operation.) This twofold move shows the distinctive character of Trito-Isaiah's message of salvation. Behind him lay an era which was under the aegis of a contrary move—the withdrawal of salvation (the topic of the laments in chs. 59 and 63, the framework within which the present message of salvation is set) and the many people who were taken into exile, resulting in depopulation, impoverishment, bloodshed and deportation. And, in his view, the return of the first exiles after the edict of Cyrus had not brought about any real change. The move towards Zion had been a merest trickle. What still needed to come and bring salvation was a mighty stream, the streaming of the nations to Jerusalem.

[4–5a] What is it to bring? Zion is amazed and deeply stirred as she sees the train of people approaching (v. 4a = 49.18a; this, too, is followed by the children approaching). Thrilled and trembling with joy, what she sees first of all are the strangers bringing Zion's sons and daughters. This stands at the head of the description and reappears at the end in v. 9b. Thus, in Trito-Isaiah's time the return of the exiles was still a matter of expectation. By far the greatest number, then, must not have come back. The return envisaged by the prophet was to be a new miracle. No intervention by force of arms is needed. The nations are to come to Jerusalem of their own free will, bringing with them from afar Israel's sons and daughters.

[5b–6] But these are not all that they bring. Trito-Isaiah also expands the scope of Deutero-Isaiah's miracle, or surpasses it, by making the nations bring their treasures along with them. The picture of this aspect of their advance is fuller, and its colours gayer, than that of the bringing back of Zion's children. It is a move towards Zion both on land and sea. Huge caravans come (v. 6a), and whole fleets (v. 9a). And they come from many different lands, from Midian and Ephah (a clan of the Midianites), from the sea-peoples (in Zech. 9.3, Tyre), from Sheba (cf. I Kings 10), and herds are driven from Kedar and Nebaioth (cf. Gen. 25.13), 'districts famous for the abundance of their sheep and rams' (Volz.) Verse 7, a bold picture, says that the train of animals destined for sacrifice goes up on the altars of their own free will, and this glorifies the temple erected in God's honour. Then after vv. 8–9a have added to the train of caravans that of the ships (ships of Tarshish, Isa. 2.16; Ps. 48.8 [7]; I Kings 10.22; 22.49; Tarshish was a Phoenician colony in the south of Spain), v. 9b at the end of the section uses the same verb 'to glorify'. But here the meaning is that Yahweh uses these miraculous events as a means of glorifying his chosen people. Thus in one and the same event glory accrues both to God and his people. Each is involved in the other. The whole thing thus serves the renown (*šēm*, name in the sense of God's praise or honour is also found in Trito-Isaiah in 56.6; 59.19; 60.9, but it never occurs in Deutero-Isaiah) or the glorifying of God. The verb 'to glorify' (*qal* and *hitpā'el*) is particularly characteristic of Trito-Isaiah (60.7, 9, 13, 21; 61.3; the noun *pe'er*, 60.3.10; *tip'eret*, 60.7, 19; 62.3; 63.12, 14f.; 64, 10). God's glorifying of himself in and through the glorification of Zion is a topic which runs through his entire proclamation of salvation. The great importance which John's Gospel attaches to glorifying and glorifying oneself is comparable, though not very closely so.

This concept also furnishes the best angle of approach to the procession of the nations to Zion which is the subject of vv. 4–9. Some editors connect this with the pilgrimage of the nations to Zion in Isa. 2 and Micah 4. Muilenburg, however, rightly points out that the end which this pilgrimage is meant to serve is basically different. Here in Isa. 60 the nations are merely bearers and bringers of all that is to glorify Zion in the new age; they are the ministers of this glorification. This is in line with the statements made in the Psalter about the nations' astonished and reverential recognition of the mighty acts of God (126.2b), in consequence of which 'all kings must fall down before him, all nations serve him' (Ps. 72.11; similarly Pss. 22.28 [27]: 66.4; 86.9; 102.22f. [21f.]).

[10–16] Verses 4–9 depicted the nations' move towards Zion. The subject of vv. 10–16 is the renewal of, and the new state of salvation for, the city (vv. 10f.) and the temple (vv. 13f.). Verses 15f. gather up and round off. Verses 10f.: the words are the fruit of long and bitter servitude to people of another race (cf. also 62.8); this was the experience in which the promise was given that someday there was to be a change of roles. Then the aliens will rebuild the walls of Zion and their kings be obliged to serve Israel! The way in which v. 10b follows upon v. 10a is very characteristic of Trito-Isaiah—this precisely, precisely this change, is to make it apparent that God has turned again towards his chosen people in grace. There is a quotation from Deutero-Isaiah here (54.8). But it almost feels like a set form of words, and it comes as a parenthesis between v. 10a and v. 11a, the latter being the real continuation of v. 10a. If v. 10b were not there, it would never be missed. From the walls (v. 10a) v. 11a goes on to speak of the gates. They are to be open continually. Properly, this is a sign of security. But the *leitmotif* in vv. 4–9 makes a change. The reason why the gates stay open is to allow the nations which, with their riches, stream towards Zion to pass through them unceasingly.

[12] Verse 12 announces the destruction of such nations as do not serve Israel. But both in its subject-matter and its form—it is in prose —it so little suits its context that it must be regarded as most, editors take it, a later expansion of the text. As Muilenburg says, it is very probably a marginal gloss intended to elucidate the final words of v. 11. As these stand in MT, they should be translated as 'with their kings led'. Duhm and others think that the participle should be active, 'their kings leading them'. MT's vocalization could be taken in the sense of 'the kings are to be led into captivity', and, because this does not suit the context, it was elucidated in the marginal gloss.

[13] Verses 13f. continue vv. 10f. The renewal of the city is followed by the renewal of the temple. Here, too, the *leitmotif*, the move in the direction of Zion, is taken up and carried on with great poetic force, 'the glory of Lebanon' joining the great train—the magnificent and costly trees of the far-away forests come to Zion for the building of

the new temple. In point of subject-matter, the coming of the animals for sacrifice, v. 13 goes along with v. 7. This proclamation that, in the days to come, the worship in the temple in Jerusalem was to be glorified is odd. This is the only place in Trito-Isaiah where this is spoken of in these terms. It reveals a continuous and continuing approbation of the sacrificial system (not so 66.1–4). This is in line with the pre-exilic prophets of salvation, and it is found, differently expressed, in Haggai and Zechariah as well. Even although what Trito-Isaiah proclaimed was not an intrinsic change in the worship to be, but only an embellishment and enrichment of it, there is no mistaking the difference between him and Deutero-Isaiah whose utterance in 43.22–28, reviewing the earlier sacrificial system, is entirely at one with that of the pre-exilic prophets of doom.

[14] Another part of the future glorifying of worship in Jerusalem is the fact that the sons of those who once oppressed Israel now come thither bending low and acknowledging it as a holy place, 'the Zion of the Holy One of Israel'. The announcement of the train of nations coming to Zion made in v. 3 is developed in two directions. That is to say, in the salvation that is breaking over Zion, the nations have a twofold function. First, they themselves take part in the renewal of Jerusalem by bringing and serving (vv. 4–9; 10a, 11b). At the same time, by acknowledging that Zion is a holy place from which go forth light and blessing, and by confessing that the God there worshipped is true and mighty God, they renew Zion's honour. A lament bewails not only suffering, but the shame that goes with it. Similarly, one part of the renewal of the city's honour is the restoration of material things. It is particularly to be noticed that there is no talk of punishment of the nations or of taking vengeance upon them.

[15–16] While the two verses round off the section composed of vv. 10–16, v. 15 already includes the motif of transformation which is thereafter developed in vv. 17–22. While the four half-verses, 15a, b, 16a, b form a connected unit, the first and last of them are not in perfect keeping with what comes between. Verses 15a and 16b come from Deutero-Isaiah (with v. 15a cf. 54.1ff., especially v. 6; with v. 16b cf. 49.26b). The thing proclaimed in both is an act, a deliverance to be wrought by Yahweh. But the middle two half-verses picture a condition, a state of salvation. Since Trito-Isaiah does not connect Yahweh's help and redemption with an act on God's part, but with a changed condition, the terms lose their directness and force. 'In Isa. 60 the statements made about glorifying are built into the description.

This one makes a reference to the divine honour, and then ingenuously reverts to the statements about the glorification of Zion. The statements fall to a lower level than they had had originally, and begin to become more conventional statements in use among the devout'.[a] And on v. 14 Zimmerli remarks, 'the second statement made in 49.23 is turned to account in 60.14 by being slightly altered. . . The picture of the wet-nurse which Deutero-Isaiah used in its literal meaning is here emptied of that to become a non-literal figure of speech and is made to apply—not happily—to the kings as well'.

[17–22] The great change. The dominant thing in this final section is the description of a condition, and not of an act, of salvation. The nations streaming towards Jerusalem fall out of the picture. The description makes a flat contrast between the present state of affairs and one that is to be. With quite exceptional conciseness it gives a mirror-like reflection of the conditions obtaining when Trito-Isaiah made this utterance. The times in which the prophet lived and spoke were sorry times. Only people who have lived through a similar period, for example, the years after the second world war, can understand the implications of v. 17—the base being turned into the noble, the crude into the refined. Sorry times are kept sorry because of the sorry stuff that men are obliged to make use of if they want to stay alive. It must be substitutes all along the line, a life vexatious, constricted and wretched, when the finer stuffs, which are not to be had, take on an importance that is more than material because they become symbols of a freer and fairer life. These verses shed light on the very remarkable way in which vv. 4–9 stress the riches and abundance that the nations bring to Jerusalem—this is due to the shortage of so many things that made the pinch felt in the years after the first return. This is also the angle of approach to the remarkable prominence given in Trito-Isaiah's picture of the future salvation to the economic and the material. In the present passage, a place where one would certainly not expect it, the prophetic proclamation contains a considerable element of acceptance of the refinements of civilization. God's turning towards his people goes so far as to change stuff that is base, mean, and crude into what is noble and fine.

[17c] Even the administration is to be involved in the change. Here Trito-Isaiah's imprecision about the actual facts of the new state of affairs becomes particularly noticeable. All he says is that foreign

[a] Zimmerli, *op. cit.*, pp. 5f.

overseers and 'drivers' are to be replaced by peace and righteousness, without, however, giving any hint about the kind of direction that there is to be. However, as little as his master Deutero-Isaiah does he cherish any messianic expectation; the era of salvation has no king. 'Peace and righteousness' are explained in v. 18. The unending succession of deeds of violence and disasters, the broken walls and the gates that give no security—all this is to end. Verse 18b does not mean that 'salvation' and 'praise' are to take the place of walls and gates (so Muilenburg etc., following Zech. 2.4f.), but that the renewed walls and gates mean salvation and praise for Zion.

[21–22] Verse 17c spoke of the change in the authorities. Linked with this, in vv. 21f., is the change in the nation itself. Much depends on the meaning of *ṣaddīqīm*. Taking it as Duhm does, 'then moral and religious imperfection, too, has disappeared, and the community consists exclusively of zealous adherents of the law', one can only concur in the verdict which he himself passes: 'in all this long poem (there is) only the one word on this subject . . . what a difference as compared with the earlier prophets!' Volz takes the word in the sense of 'partaking in salvation'. This has in its favour both the parallelism and the whole context in vv. 21f., which are the equivalent of a proclamation of blessing. Nothing in the whole chapter envisages a spiritual change in the nation. The thing stressed is that the coming salvation is destined for all alike. This is notoriously different from other places in Trito-Isaiah where salvation can no longer be proclaimed to all alike, but only to a section of the nation, a group within it (so, for example, 59.20). Trito-Isaiah expands the old promise of the land by adding the word *'ōlām*; they are to possess the land for ever, never again to be driven forth from it. God's power in blessing makes it a 'shoot of his planting': by its increase and its prosperity it will show itself to be a work in which he is glorified. Verse 22a is reminiscent of the old blessings of the clans—the generations now diminished and decimated are to grow into mighty clans. The final verse (v. 22b) is made clearer and given a better sense if we may add *dibbarti* to the first half-verse, as proposed in *BH app. crit.* Read thus, this closing verse takes up a motif frequent in Deutero-Isaiah (e.g. 46.10; 48.3), the reliable connection between what God says and what he does. The hearers may rest assured that what is here proclaimed will come to pass.

[19–20] These verses go far beyond the changing of a sorry, restricted and vexatious present into the freedom of a fair and prosperous future for Zion. Here the change towers up to assume cosmic proportions. Kessler well describes ch. 60 as 'a view of salvation as it forces itself on the people observing it at close quarters, people encompassed every day by a sorry state of things, darkness and oppression'. Verses 19f. do not fit in with this view, for in it the things to be changed do not fall within the categories of shortage or restriction. In all the rest of ch. 60 the salvation proclaimed never transcends the confines of this world and of history. As opposed to this vv. 19f. are an apocalyptic picture presupposing that 'while the earth remains . . . day and night shall not cease' (Gen. 8.22) has come to an end. This is also the sense in which the utterance was taken up into Revelation (21.23). In addition, when 60.1ff. speak of God's being a light, the way they do so is completely different. We may assume, then, that this apocalyptic description of how, in the era of salvation, sun and moon will be deprived of their functions and be replaced by God himself, is a later addition. It forms part of the strand in which Trito-Isaiah's promise of salvation goes over into the realm of apocalyptic.

CHAPTER 61.1–3

The Spirit of the Lord is upon me

1 The spirit of the Lord Yahweh is upon me,
because Yahweh has anointed me.
He has sent me to bring good tidings to the poor,
to bind up the broken hearted;
to declare liberty to the captives,
and the opening . . . to those who are bound;
2 to declare a year of Yahweh's favour,
a day of vengeance of our God,
to comfort all who mourn,
to give [joy]ᵃ to those who mourn in Zion;
3 to give them ornament instead of ashes,
oil of gladness instead of mourning,
a song of praise instead of a faint spirit;
that they may be called trees of salvation,
a planting of Yahweh's, that he may be glorified.

ᵃ With Duhm and Volz read *lᵉsammaḥ*.

We are at once aware of the way in which these three verses stand out in relief from their context, the message of salvation as given in chs. 60–62. They are differentiated as being a proclamation made by a man who was aware that God had sent and equipped him to proclaim the message of salvation. It is not an account of a call such as Isa. 6 or Jer. 1, nor is it like the account of the same suggested in 40.6ff. On the other hand, this utterance is reminiscent of 42.1–4 and 49.1–6. Several of the expressions and concepts found in 61.1–ff. derive from these two passages. A leading feature in this proclamation made by the messenger of salvation is the accumulation of mediatorial functions, and of the qualities for it, that are here heaped upon one person. This makes it very apparent that, at the time when these words were spoken, they had lost the clear co-ordination with definite functions which they once had, and in the process had also ceased to be precise.

[1] The opening words should be compared with 42.1b, where God says of the Servant, 'I have put my spirit upon him.' At the same time, there is a closer parallel in Micah 3.8 where the speaker, again a prophet, and speaking in the first person, says of himself, 'But as for me, I am filled with the spirit of Yahweh . . . to declare to Jacob his transgression.' Since this is the final utterance of an oracle against false prophets, Micah may possibly have taken up, with modification, a stereotyped form current in prophecy of salvation. One reason which suggests this is the fact that the pre-exilic prophets of doom normally avoid appeal to endowment with the spirit (so, for example, Volz and Muilenburg *ad loc.*), most probably in opposition to a kind of *nebî'îm* from whom they regarded themselves as different. We may thus assume that these words which open the chapter represent the taking-over of a statement made in pre-exilic prophecy of salvation in connection with a call. It may go back to that old body, the seers—the seer's endowment with the spirit is attested in Num. 24.2 and II Sam. 23.2. The second line uses the word 'to anoint' in a non-literal and transferred sense, something like 'to give full authorization'. In any event, the prophet was not thinking of any anointing of the body. Anointing and endowment with the spirit occur together in II Sam. 23.1–7 (see above), and in I Sam. 16–13 anointing is the means by which a man is given the spirit. Apart from the present passage—and as in those just mentioned—the Old Testament almost exclusively reserves anointing for kings, who may be designated as 'Yahweh's anointed'. The anointing of priests as well came later. The verb in the prophet's commissioning proper, 'he

has sent me', fits in very badly with what precedes it, for (despite the one place, I Kings 19.19, Elisha's anointing at the hands of Elijah) anointing is to an office that continues, this being what consecrates its holder. This lets us see how refined these concepts have become—to such an extent that 'anointing is no more than a rather loftier expression for sending' (Duhm). The series of infinitives which, down to the end of v. 3, set forth the purpose for which the messenger was sent are dependent on that verb (to send). Somewhat oddly, they combine thep rophet's task with its purpose or results—'to proclaim . . . to declare . . . to declare . . . to bind up . . . to comfort. . . to give'. All that he has to do is speak. Nevertheless, in and through this proclaiming he is to effect a change on those to whom he is sent. 'Thus to proclaim salvation is almost as much as to summon it into existence or bring it about'.[a] These words show that Trito-Isaiah was very much aware that he had received a call. Right away they make clear that, after the end of the exile, prophecy, vigorous prophecy, made a fresh start in his hands. Two things are revealed in the utterance before us. Trito-Isaiah knows that his task takes up that of Deutero-Isaiah. On the other hand, the way in which he describes this shows the difference between him and his master, a difference which comes to light both in the general drift of the utterance (cf. Isa. 40.6ff.) and in the slight difference in the way in which he uses the same words as his master did. For example, Trito-Isaiah knows that he has been sent 'to bring good tidings to the poor'. The verb *bissēr* occurs in 40.9 and 52.7. But there it is used as strictly as it ought to be, as the proclamation of an event that has already come about. And the people who bring the good tidings are not the prophet, but the watchers. Duhm is correct; 'Trito-Isaiah mistakes the bringers of good tidings for the prophet.' The prophet's proclamation is destined to heal wounds and bring liberty to the captives. 'To bind up the broken hearted'—a striking, perhaps even absurd, figure of speech. Was Trito-Isaiah thinking of 42.3? The liberation of the captives does not mean the exiles, but, as in 58.6, people put in prison for debt and the like. The dawning of the age of salvation proclaimed by the prophet, the great transformation (ch. 60), is also destined to work a change on the personal suffering of the large number of people who were actually in suffering at the time. This enables Trito-Isaiah to compare his own proclamation with the

---

[a] T. H. Robinson on prophecy of salvation in Micah 3.5–8, *Die zwölf kleinen Propheten*, HAT.

crying of a herald announcing release to people in slavery because of debts (Jer. 34.8ff.; Ezek. 46.17; Lev. 25.10). In v. 2a the juxtaposition of 'year' and 'day' shows that no particular event is in mind, but a new era. 'To proclaim a year acceptable to God' shows another divergence from what Deutero-Isaiah had proclaimed. His promise of blessing, which looks on the change as already brought about as far as God is concerned, is replaced by the turning in grace which God is to make reality in an indeterminate, although near, future. 'The day of vengeance of our God' takes up the old concept of the 'Day of Yahweh', Isa. 2.12; 13.6; Joel 2.1ff. It is also called the 'day of vengeance' in Isa. 34.8; 63.4; Jer. 46.10. Here there is no idea of God's taking vengeance on Israel's foes. As the parallel shows, the word is to be taken in the sense of 'for' and not 'against'—restoration; as is also true of the original meaning of 'revenge' in the days before Israel became a state: 'the restoration of wholeness'.[a] Similarly also Mendenhall, followed by Muilenburg, in the light of Ugaritic usage. The prophet's task is, finally, 'to comfort all who mourn'. The way in which the verb 'to comfort' is used shows a difference from Deutero-Isaiah characteristic of his successor. The phrase 'to comfort mourners', frequent in Trito-Isaiah, is never found in Deutero-Isaiah. With the latter, the object of the verb is invariably particularized, as in 40.1. This is a further example of the way in which Trito-Isaiah alters words of his predecessor to make them indeterminate and general. Another characteristic of his way of speaking about salvation is the manner in which he illuminates the change to salvation by the use of contrasts which (in the Hebrew) are reinforced by paronomasia, 'ornament instead of ashes, oil of gladness instead of mourning'. Here it should be noticed that God could be the subject of the verb 'to give them' equally with the prophet. The smooth transition from the messenger's proclamation to the description of salvation—it is made in v. 3 and continues in vv. 4ff.—lets us see that the prophet had meditated upon his task and upon how he should describe it before setting it down as he does here. To the best of our knowledge, this was the last occasion in the history of Israel on which a prophet expressed his certainty of having been sent by God with a message to his nation with such freedom and conviction.

[a] See *The Interpreter's Dictionary of the Bible*, ad loc.

Chapter 61.4–11

The seed that Yahweh blesses

4 They build the ancient ruins,
raise up what was destroyed aforetime;
repair ruined cities,
what many generation held in honour [arises].[a]

5 Aliens shall feed your flocks,
foreigners shall be your ploughmen and vine dressers;
6 but you shall be called the priests of Yahweh,
men shall call you servants of our God.
You shall enjoy the wealth of the nations,
and with their riches shall they [adorn][b] you.
7 Because [your][c] shame was double
and disgrace and [spitting][d] was your portion,
therefore in your land you will inherit double,
you shall have everlasting joy.
8 For I, Yahweh, love justice,
I hate robbery with transgression.
I faithfully give you your recompense,
and make an everlasting covenant with you.
9 Your descendants shall be known among the peoples,
and your offspring in the midst of the nations.
All who see you shall acknowledge you,
that you are the seed which Yahweh has blessed.
11 For as the earth brings forth its shoots,
and as a garden causes what is sown in it to spring up,
so the Lord Yahweh causes salvation to spring up
and praise before all the nations.

10 I will rejoice in Yahweh,
my soul shall exult in my God;
because he clothed me with the garments of salvation,
and covered me with the robe of righteousness;

---

[a] As Köhler suggests, the first verb in v. 5, *ʿāmᵉdū* (omitting *wᵉ*) is to be brought into v. 5.

[b] Read *tithaddārū* (Köhler, Kissane).

[c] Read the third person.

[d] Read *dāroq* instead of *yārōnnū*.

like the bridegroom who [decks]ᵃ himself with the turban
and the bride, who adorns herself with her jewels.ᵇ

If we are to understand this section in Trito-Isaiah's proclamation
of salvation, we must remember that it connects directly with the
messenger's proclamation contained in 61.1ff. As we have already
seen, the transition between the two is a smooth one. Trito-Isaiah was
aware that he had been sent 'to comfort all who mourn', and what
gave these their comfort was the great change described in the 'in-
steads' of v. 3b. Verses 4–11 go on to say how, and in what, this
change in Zion's favour is brought about. It is brought about by the
re-building of the city (v. 4) and the restoration of her honour (v. 7).
Both of these things God accomplishes on her behalf (v. 8), and the
whole world must acknowledge it (v. 9). Finally, in v. 11, the whole
change is once more represented as due to God's saving work. This
is done by means of the simile of growth, which connects directly
with the final line of vv. 1–3, 3c. This saving action of God's is
answered by the song of praise sung by those to whom the salvation
accrued (v. 10).

This closely-knit and clearly arranged proclamation of salvation
pre-supposes a community lament, one in the first person plural. This
bewails the destruction of the cities of Judah and of Jerusalem, which
for so long have been lying devastated (v. 4). It also bewails the shame
involved in being thus laid low before the eyes of the world and
particularly before those of the neighbouring nations (v. 7). In this
respect v. 4 and v. 7 go closely together. But the verses between them,
vv. 5 and 6, are different both in subject-matter and drafting. They
are an address, in the second person, their drafting being that of the
promise of blessing, whereas vv. 4 and 7ff. are proclamation in the
third person. As regards subject-matter, they diverge from their
context in that vv. 4, 7–11 merely depict the change in Judah's
fortunes in broad outline, but vv. 5f., speaking of a state of things, are
a description in detail. The particularly remarkable thing is that
what is said of foreigners in 61.5ff. sounds very different indeed from
what was proclaimed in 60.4ff. There the nations and kings contribute
towards the renewal of Zion, but here in 61.5f. the intention is to
give the reason for a continuing state of things in which aliens do the
menial work while the Israelites all belong to the class of the spiritual

ᵃ For *yᵉkahēn* read *yākin*.
ᵇ Take v. 10 after v. 11 (so Köhler and Kessler).

leaders, the priestly class. Probably therefore vv. 5f. represent a late addition (so Volz). If we are not inclined to accept this, we must at all events realize that vv. 4 and 7 give the basic description of the change proclaimed in v. 3, and that what vv. 5f. do is expand and illuminate this.

In their description of the restoration, the four lines of v. 4 look back to the lament. The word 'to build' is often found in Trito-Isaiah ('more frequent, by proportion, than in any other part of the OT', Odeberg), 58.12; 60.10; 61.4; 65.21, 23; 66.1—a trivial but undoubted sign that Trito-Isaiah's main theme is the rebuilding while Deutero-Isaiah's was the return.

[5–6] While the motif of the train of the nations coming to Zion (60.4ff.) is here presupposed, an alteration has been made on it. This is purely description of a state of things—Israel may dispose over the aliens' treasures; the latter are obliged to do the hard manual labour and to support Israel, while as priests the Judeans form the spiritual leaders. What a vast difference between this and the joy that the Israelite farmer once took in his land, and from the way in which Deuteronomy, for instance, speaks of the blessing that accrues from work in the fields!

[7–9] Israel had bewailed, as well as the suffering due to the destruction of the cities (v. 4), the shame which this suffering had brought upon her. This (the 'double' is reminiscent of 40.2) is now to be removed; she is to have possession of the land and joy in this restored to her. This change is the work of the God who loves righteousness and hates violence—this one allusion to 'robbery with transgression' is all that recalls the violence of the capture of Jerusalem. Now, however, as is her due, Israel is compensated for her long years of suffering, and the new salvation is destined to be permanent, assured by a covenant in perpetuity (as 55.3). Verse 9 gives the positive complement to v. 7—the effect of God's saving work is to be manifest to the whole world; among the other nations Israel is to be known as the nation which God has blessed. In vv. 7ff. the background is obviously Deutero-Isaiah's proclamation.

[11] Verse 11 develops the final words of v. 9, 'the seed which Yahweh has blessed'. Trito-Isaiah likens salvation's springing up to the growth of the plants in the garden, that is to say, the place that is cultivated and tended. As thus described, God's saving work for Israel's sake is very different from a once-for-all act of deliverance. Instead, what is here described is the steady and uneventful effecting

of blessing, as at the end of v. 3, with which v. 11 obviously connects back, 'trees of salvation, a planting of Yahweh's'.

[10] The verse is a unit in itself, corresponding entirely to the hymns of praise which form the end-pieces in Deutero-Isaiah's larger complexes (as e.g. 44.23). It is the community's responsory of acceptance of the message of salvation, 'a hymn of praise sung by the generation which Yahweh blessed' (Kessler). Once more, the difference between Deutero-Isaiah and Trito-Isaiah is characteristic. The former's hymns are hymns sung by the community (call to praise in the imperative), the call to praise being given its substantiation in the destined saving act on God's part. The hymn in Isa. 61.10 is introduced as a psalm sung by an individual, and its substantion is described generally as saving action on God's part towards the individual. The really important thing, however, is that here Trito-Isaiah continues the connection made by Deutero-Isaiah between the proclamation of salvation and the community's hymn in answer to it.

CHAPTER 62.1–12

I cannot keep silent

1 For Zion's sake I cannot keep silent,
   for Jerusalem's sake not restrain myself,
   until her salvation goes forth as brightness,
   and her help as a burning torch.
2 And the nations shall see your salvation,
   and all kings your glory.
   And you shall be called by a new name
   which the mouth of Yahweh will give.
3 You shall be a crown of beauty in the hand of Yahweh,
   a royal diadem in the hand of your God.
4 You shall no more be termed Forsaken,
   and your land (can) no longer (be termed) [Desolate],[a]
   but you shall be called My delight,
   and your land Married.
   For Yahweh delights in you,
   and your land shall be married.

[a] Following 54.1 read *šōmēmā*.

5 For [as]^a a young man marries a virgin,
   so do your [builders]^b marry you,
   and as the bridegroom rejoices over the bride,
   so does your God rejoice over you.

6 Upon your walls, O Jerusalem,
   I have set watchmen;
   all the day and all the night
   they shall never be silent.
   You who put Yahweh in remembrance,
   you have no rest,
7 and give him no rest,
   until he establishes and makes
   Jerusalem a praise in the earth.

8 Yahweh has sworn by his right hand
   and by his mighty arm:
   'I will not again give your grain
   to be food for your enemies,
   foreigners shall not again drink your wine
   for which you have laboured.
9 But those who garner it shall eat it
   and praise Yahweh,
   and those who gather it shall drink it
   in my holy forecourts.'
10 Go out, go out through the gates,
   prepare the way for the people!
   Build up, build up the highway,
   clear it of stones!
   Lift up an ensign over the peoples.
11 Behold, Yahweh has proclaimed to the ends of the earth;
   Say to the daughter of Zion,
   'Behold, your salvation comes;
   behold, his reward is with him,
   and his recompense before him'.
12 And they shall be called the holy people,
   the redeemed of Yahweh;
   and you shall be called sought out,
   a city that does not stay forsaken.

Bibliography: S. Mowinckel, 'Der metrische Aufbau von Jes. 62.1–12', *ZAW* 65 (1953), pp. 167–87.

This chapter is probably the clearest exemplification of the

^a Read *kī kibʿōl*.
^b Read *bōnāyik*.

special features in the prophecy of Trito-Isaiah. But up to now neither its structure nor the purpose which it was designed to serve have ever been satisfactorily explained. The key is supplied, however, when we recognize that the three chapters, 60–62, are based on the three component parts of a lament—ch. 60 is the lament because of enemies (countered by the train of nations coming to Zion), ch. 61 the lament in the first person plural (countered by the building of Zion and the restoration of her honour), and ch. 62 the charge made against God. It is countered, in the middle of the chapter, by the proclamation that God has turned back again towards his chosen people (vv. 4b–5 and vv. 11f.) The charge is also the background which explains the odd way in which the chapter begins, vv. 1–2a, which are resumed in vv. 6f. The structure of these two parts shows that they go together:

| 1a I cannot keep silent | 6 I have set watchmen . . . they shall not be silent . . . |
| 1b until . . . (the coming of the salvation for Jerusalem) | 7 until . . . (the coming of the salvation for Jerusalem). |

The word until ('ad), which is so strongly emphasized in both places and is the thing that gives the chapter its tense and vivid bearing upon the future, can easily be understood when it is seen as the 'how long'? ('ad mātay) of the community lament converted. The timid and despairing question, 'how long, O Lord, dost thou continue to be angry with thy people?', is replaced by the watching, mentioned in the promise, that keeps importuning God, the putting him in remembrance of his promise that gives him no rest (v. 7). It is possible to point to further parallels between the two sections of ch. 62. After vv. 1–2a comes the new name to be given to Jerusalem (v. 2b–4a), the substantiation of which is God's turning back towards his people (vv. 4b–5). In reverse order, vv. 6f. are followed, at the end of the passage, by God's turning back towards his people—this is done by means of a quotation from Deutero-Isaiah (v. 11)—and at the very end there is the new name (v. 12). If in both sections we were to scrutinize the names which express God's fresh turning towards Israel, we should find that the ones which come first, the Forsaken, the Desolate, and the city that did not remain Forsaken, are obviously reminiscences of the lament, first and foremost of the charge made against God contained in it. In Deutero-Isaiah, of whom there are echoes here almost sentence by sentence, the final promise is introduced by the summons to go forth (52.11f.). The same thing is done here. The final promise, given in vv. 11f., is introduced by a summons to go forth, this being expanded (v. 10) by means of imperatives taken from Deutero-Isaiah's prologue. Thus, the only end served by the verse is that of emphasizing and underlining the final promise. Verses 8–9 alone do not fit into the parallelism between the two sections of ch. 62, vv. 1–5 and vv. 6–12. They re-occur in almost identical terms in 65.21f., and in their present context they feel abrupt, and foreign to it.

[1] 'For Zion's sake': 'Just as the singer in Ps. 137 cannot forget Jerusalem, so he (the prophet) cannot keep silent for Jerusalem's sake' (Volz). Most present-day editors believe that the speaker here is the prophet. But what he means by the words 'I cannot keep silent' can only be understood in the light of the provenance of the two verbs which he employs. The verb for 'to be silent' (ḥāšā'h) is found in the very next chapter in the community lament(64.11): 'Canst thou restrain thyself at these things, Yahweh? Dost thou keep silent, and afflict us sorely?' And the other verb (šāqaṭ) occurs in the community lament in Ps. 83.2 (1): 'O God, do not keep silence (as 64.11); do not hold thy peace or restrain thyself, O God' (cf. also Isa. 42.14). We may take it as quite certain that Trito-Isaiah was making a link between this introduction to his prophecy of salvation and the words of the community lament. There were familiar to his hearers from lines like those just quoted. But he uses them in quite a different sense; and the alteration corresponds to his strong conviction, expressed in 61.1ff., that he had been sent. Now that the exile was over, the charge brought against God, of which the words properly form part, fell very much into the background, and is practically never found thereafter.[a] In the present utterance it is replaced by the urgent, impassioned clinging on to the promise, this clinging being described in greater detail in v. 7 which follows. We have in 67.1, 7 quite the clearest statement of the purpose of Trito-Isaiah's prophecy. He was aware that he had been sent to counter God's silence and restraining of himself of which the state of things gave evidence—although this is not spoken of so openly as was done in the old community laments— by loud proclamation of his promises. He himself, therefore, was sent not to keep silent or restrain himself. Instead he was to 'put God in remembrance'—and give him no rest (v. 6c), until finally salvation came. This course of action was the very one for the situation obtaining at the time, as we see from a similar utterance of Zechariah's

[a] Westermann, 'Struktur und Geschichte der Klage im Alten Testament', *Forschung am Alten Testament*, Munich, 1964, pp. 266–305.

(1.12): ' "O Lord of hosts, how long will thou have no mercy on Jerusalem and the cities of Judah, against which thou has had indignation these seventy years?" '. Verse 1b has clear echoes of 60.1b; this utterance, too, has to be set against the background of an epiphany. In terms of this, the subject of the verb 'to go forth' (*yāṣāh*) ought to be God. This is one of the numerous passages in Trito-Isaiah where he speaks of the coming of salvation in words which properly refer to God's coming. Verse 2 as well has a reminiscence of 60.1ff. It corresponds to 60.3—salvation comes about before the eyes of the whole world (Deutero-Isaiah's prologue (40.3) speaks of 'nations and kings'): so also 60.3 and 61.11. In contrast to ch. 60, this is all that is said of the nations, the reason being that each of the three chapters stresses a different thing (see above). The only purpose of v. 2 is that of indicating one aspect of the salvation accruing to Zion (v. 1b)—it is to become known to the whole world. The third aspect attaching to it, the fact that Jerusalem's new glory is based on the grace of God, comes next, in v. 3. 'Verse 3 describes the very close relationship in which the glorified Jerusalem stands to Yahweh, how precious she is to him' (Volz). Stummer[a] draws attention to a Babylonian inscription referring to Bel: 'Borsippa is your tiara.' Jerusalem is therefore described as a magnificent ornament in which God takes pleasure, indeed which serves to adorn him, even if the prophet shrinks from saying so. This is another occurrence of *tip'eret*, ornament or adornment, a word so characteristic of Trito-Isaiah. And this comparison in v. 3 shows how, from Trito-Isaiah's time onwards (Deutero-Isaiah reveals only a few traces of this), terms taken from aesthetics made their way into the language of theology.

[2b, 4] In subject-matter v. 3 goes with vv. 1b and 2a (see above), whereas vv. 2b and 4 speak of the changing of Jerusalem's name and the new name. This has led a large number of editors to rearrange and read v. 2b after v. 3. But Duhm was right in seeing that this does not do away with the difficulty. Jerusalem's new name is not told us in v. 2b. God keeps it to himself. In contrast, v. 4 does tell us the new names. Duhm (and others) therefore assumed that v. 2b was added to v. 4 by a reader who wanted to guard against the renaming's being taken literally. Actually, v. 2b has a rather different ring about it as compared with v. 4. The names in the latter are not intended as names in the true sense of the word, but as predications, whereas v. 2b apparently means a renaming, a thing which Trito-Isaiah certainly

[a] *Op. cit.*, p. 186.

never had in mind. Verse 2b is therefore quite possibly an addition. Also, it sounds like prose.

[4–5] The contrast evidenced by the old and the new names is due to God's having once turned away from Jerusalem and his turning towards her now. Until now it might have been said of Zion that she had been forsaken by her God, and that in consequence her land had been laid waste and made desolate. The land's lying waste indicated that God had forsaken it. Now, however, Zion is called 'My delight' or, to be more precise, 'my delight is in her'. (In this connection we must bear in mind that the Old Testament uses both *'azūbā* and *hepṣibā* as names of persons [I Kings 22.42: II Kings 21.1]. In such a personal way as this—we might almost say in such an ingenuously personal way as this—can Trito-Isaiah speak of the salvation for Jerusalem for which he longs! Verse 4c explains the two new names— not that there was any necessity for this, for they are perfectly clear; both v. 4c and the substantiation given in v. 5, which gathers the whole thing up, simply underline what is the topic of the entire chapter, the fact that God has now turned towards his people. As used in the name in v. 4b and in the explanation of this in v. 4c, the word *hēpeṣ* is given a different meaning from what it has in Deutero-Isaiah. In 44.28; 46.10 and 48.14 it signifies God's will or intention. Yahweh as Israel's bridegroom or wedded lord occurs particularly in Hosea, Jeremiah and Ezekiel. Elliger draws attention to the carefully thought-out arrangement of vv. 4f.: 'the construction should be noticed. Verse 4aβ is the promise of the new name: (a) negatively and (b) positively. Verse 4c is the substantiation of b. Verse 5 is the completion of 4b, 5a that of 4bβ and 5b that of 4bα (chiasmus).' The finest expression of the utterly personal nature of the promise comes in v. 5b: 'as the bridegroom rejoices over the bride, so does your God rejoice over you.' In the quite large number of Old Testament passages which use the metaphor of marriage to describe relationship with God, God's partner is always a community and never an individual. This means that the relationship is invariably expressed from the divine point of view, as in the words mentioned above, 'so does your God rejoice over you', and never from the human. The subject is always God. This is the reason for saying that married love as metaphor for, or the expression of, the subjective attitude of man to God, an attitude which the mystics imported into Christianity, is fundamentally unbiblical.

[6–7] These two verses are hard to understand; hence the many different interpretations of them in the various commentaries. Yet they are extremely material for the understanding of Trito-Isaiah. The first question is the identity of the speaker who speaks in the first person singular. The parallels both in form and subject-matter as between vv. 1 and 6f. (see above) leave us in no doubt that in both places he is the prophet (so Volz, etc.). We may go a step further and say that the watchmen of v. 6a are the same people as v. 6c designates as *mazkīrīm*, those who put in remembrance. Both parties are told that they are not to be silent until . . . This very well suits the 'remembrancers', but less so the watchmen. Trito-Isaiah's meaning is therefore best grasped by starting out from the metaphor of the *mazkīrīm*. The *mazkīr* is a royal official: 'who calls to remembrance', II Sam. 8.16; Isa. 36.3. This suggests that the watchmen and the remembrancers are to be conceived as heavenly beings. Duhm says that 'they are officials in heaven who do the same thing as the angel of Yahweh in Zech. 1.12'. This presupposes that the speaker of v. 6 is God. But the idea of God himself appointing and setting on Jerusalem's walls heavenly beings who are to give him no rest until he effects salvation is an improbable one. Because of this the majority of editors now try to find a different interpretation. Muilenburg suggests prophets, and Kessler men at prayer. But it was the prophet himself, Trito-Isaiah, who set up these watchmen or remembrancers —whatever can this mean? The parallels in v. 1f. furnish the solution. It is given still more emphasis by the fact that the two terms connected with one another in v. 1, 'keep silent' and 'restrain oneself', are here in v. 6 balanced by the other pair, 'keep silent' and 'rest'. The contexts are the same. Both verbs of v. 6 occur in Ps. 83.2 (1); these are the only two passages with the term *dǒmī*. Thus here, too, in v. 6 the reference is to countering God's silence by insistently putting him in remembrance of his promise. Here, in v. 6 the prophet sets the watchmen who are not to keep silent until . . . In v. 1 he said of himself that he could not keep silent until . . .Thus, vv. 6f. must refer to the people to whom he addresses his proclamation, in so far as they accept this, hold now to the word of salvation, and always hold it up before God. In this passage, too, then, Trito-Isaiah is the successor of Deutero-Isaiah; the watchmen here correspond to those of 40.9ff. Further, this part of the prologue (see above) has correspond-ing to it the hymns of praise which accompany Deutero-Isaiah's proclamation, and in which those to whom his proclamation is made speak their Amen to it. But a similar hymn of praise is actually found in Trito-Isaiah as well, 61.10. Here, however, we once more discover a change from Deutero-Isaiah. Verses 6f. cannot strictly have been designed as a hymn in response to the proclamation and anticipating the fulfilment of this. It is rather continuous prayer for the arrival of salvation. The verses show how at this point the prayer made by the community takes over something of the prophet's function of intercession.

The final words of v. 1, 'until her salvation goes forth as brightness', are matched in v. 7b by 'until he establishes Jerusalem a praise in the earth'. The same end is envisaged in both cases. And it is to be assumed that the final part of the poem, vv. 10ff., follow directly on vv. 6f.

[8–9] While all the rest of ch. 62 is a proclamation of salvation, these two verses describe the state of things in the era of salvation, and are found almost word for word with the same frame of reference in 65.21f. Here, then, in all probability they represent a later addition. (In DSS, v. 9 ends with 'says Yahweh', which underlines the apartness of vv. 8f.). On the other hand, the verses fit into the new state of things as described in ch. 60, and there can be no doubt that Trito-Isaiah is their author. They also reflect, like much of ch. 60, the bitter experience of long ago, army occupation of the land and its effects on the economy. What painstaking hard labour won from the fields and the vineyards had to be handed over. Thus, there was no more joy in work, and there began to be constant shortage of things and depressing, sorry times, of which ch. 60 revealed so much. Verse 9 brings a fresh point of view to bear. The sorry state of the economy inevitably affected the nation's worship—this, too, is clearly pictured in ch. 60. In the same way the turn towards salvation is reflected in worship. 'The verse speaks of the three great festivals which from the time of Deuteronomy onwards (ch. 16) were celebrated at the temple, and at which men gave thanks to God for the new harvest of grain and for the vintage, struck up the note of festal joy, and "rejoiced before God" as they enjoyed the new gifts' (Duhm).

[10–12] 'The strophe is almost a catena of quotations from Second Isaiah' (Muilenburg; similarly all editors). The best explanation of the three verses is that they form an end-piece to the message of Trito-Isaiah. They strengthen the grounds for assuming chs. 60–62 to be a complex by itself. These final verses give us our clearest picture of Trito-Isaiah as his master's disciple. They also show that it was impossible, even when the thing initiated was a message of salvation, to return to the words used in the original. The situation as between God, the prophet and the nation was a different one from Deutero-Isaiah's, and for that reason the same words no longer said the same thing. Verse 10 takes words from the beginning of the prologue (40.3) and v. 11 from its end (40.9ff.), while v. 10 also has reminiscences of 52.11. But all this fits in exactly with the final gathering up which Deutero-Isaiah wanted to make in 52.10ff. Thus, the quotations here were not made at random. Both in subject-matter and style they entirely correspond. The change in the quotations' frame of reference is at its strongest in two places. Firstly, the people summoned to go forth are not the Israelites in exile. Instead, those then dwelling in Jerusalem are summoned to go out through the city's gates in order to prepare the way for the 'people', that is, for the exiles whose return was still being awaited. Here the building of the highway and the clearing it of stones are meant metaphorically, the removal of the obstacles which prevent the many Israelites still living abroad from returning to Jerusalem. The lifting of the ensign simply means showing the way home from abroad.

As for the second change in the frame of reference: the proclamation of God's advent, concrete (40.10), is replaced in v. 11 by the proclamation of the advent of salvation, abstract (LXX changes to 'your saviour'). This it is that is to be said to the daughter of Zion (v. 11a); this it is that Yahweh causes to be proclaimed (*hišmia‘*, equivalent to 'cause to hear', is here used as a technical term for proclamation of the message of salvation). The last clause of v. 11 is 40.10b word for word. The latter states that God brings the returning exiles along with him as his reward. But here the words have no specific reference, and can only have the general sense of 'reward' and 'recompense' for Israel. In v. 12 Trito-Isaiah leaves off quoting and goes back to the change in the name of v. 4b, and so to the central statement made in ch. 62—God has now taken his chosen people back.

CHAPTER 63.1–6

Who comes here from Edom?

1 Who comes here from Edom,
in crimsoned garments from Bozrah?
He, glorious in his apparel,
[striding]ᵃ with mighty power?
It is I, speaking in righteousness,
I, mighty [in power]ᵇ to help.

2 Why is thy [apparel]ᶜ red
and thy garments like his that treads in the wine-press?

3 I trod a wine press alone,
and from the peoples no one was with me.
I trod them in my anger,
and trampled them in my wrath.
Their lifeblood spurted on my clothes,
I have stained all my raiment.

4 For the day of vengeance was in my heart,
and my year of requital had come.
5 When I looked and no one helped,
I was amazed that no one upheld me,
then came my arm to my help
and my wrath, that gave me support.
6 So I trod down the people in my anger,
and [dashed them to pieces]ᵈ in my wrath.
And I poured out their lifeblood on the earth.

The poem is based upon a form that is not hard to recognize, the enquiry made by the watchman or the question put by the sentry. The form consists of a twofold question and answer. The first of these is put by the watchman or sentry at the gate to someone whom he sees approaching. 'Who goes there?' 'What do you look like?' The answer is, 'It is I, so and so. I look as I do because I have done

ᵃ Read ṣōʿēd.
ᵇ Read ʾᵃni rab kōaḥ.
ᶜ Delete the first l.
ᵈ Read wāʾᵃšabbᵉrēm.

such and such a thing.' The dialogue with its twofold question and answer therefore depicts a situation well known to everyone who listened to the poem; they were at once surrounded by an atmosphere with definite associations. Even though this form, 'the sentry's question', is found nowhere else, this simply proves conclusively that a large number of similar forms were extant which never attained to fixed form in writing. Even here the sentry's question is not designed as such, but as a means of describing something entirely different.

[1] A difference. Consummate artistry is shown in the way in which quite a simple thing, the sentinel's question, is 'transcended' by giving to the first answer, the answer to the question, 'Who goes there?', the form of a divine self-predication. This editors have failed to notice, the result being attempts to change the text. But, realize the self-predication, and further explanation is quite unnecessary— the one who comes from Edom is God. But if we do take the answer in v. 1b in this way, we have no right to regard it as the obverse, otherwise absent in the chapter, of God's judgment on the nations. That is, we may not say that this is judgment in order to effect salvation for Israel. This is not the meaning. The verses' purpose is merely that of identifying the one who comes.

De Lagarde suggested a brilliant emendation on the song's opening lines. With a very slight change in the text (*mē'oddām* and *mibbōṣēr*) he read, 'who is he that comes stained with red, his garments redder than a vinedresser?' The change has been widely accepted (e.g. Duhm and Köhler), and deserves careful consideration. In my own view, however, there are no compelling or sufficient reasons for altering. Duhm objected that the question in v. 1a anticipated a part of the answer. But this loses its force if we say that, showing a considerable degree of artistry, the poet inserted 'from Edom' and 'from Bozrah' in order to indicate the scene of events, cf. Isa. 34.6.

[2–3] The second question brings the dialogue to its climax. If we are to realize how much is packed into the drama of these two questions and answers, we must keep our eyes firmly fixed on the quite simple point of departure, the question put by the sentry, and the particular atmosphere surrounding it. The poem has something of the ballad about it. The Scottish ballad 'Edward' starts in a similar way to this.[a] The mother asks her son who comes with his sword spattered with blood, 'Why is your sword with blood so red, Edward, Edward?'

[a] Herder, *Stimmen der Völker in Liedern.*

The simile of the treader of the wine press in the question put by the watchmen brings in the second viewpoint for the interpretation of the event; 'and thy garments like his that treads the wine-press?' For this comparison points to a traditional simile for God's action in judgment. And it can even be used with reference to God's judgment on his own chosen people, 'Yahweh has trodden as in a wine press the virgin, the daughter of Judah' (Lam. 1.15). This passage was presumably the place where the simile originated (although it may go further back than Lamentations to a prophetic proclamation of judgment unknown to us). Used of the judgment of the nations, it occurs, as well as in the present passage, in Joel 4.13 (3.13) in a similar context, and it was later taken up by Revelation, again with reference to the judgment of the nations (14.19; 19.15). But none of these passages achieves to the extent that Isa. 60.3 does the realism and dramatic power in depicting the horror of it all. Isa. 34.1–6 is parallel in respect of subject-matter. The word for wine press (*pūrā*) in v. 3 is not the same as in v. 2. Its only other occurrence is in Hag. 2.16. The emphasis on 'alone' both here and again in v. 5 is odd; cf. 59.16. The explanation, 'and from the peoples no one was with me', is also curious. Is it a taking over of the motif of 44.24, that Yahweh performed the creation alone? Or is this said, as Duhm believes, in opposition to Deutero-Isaiah, where Yahweh makes Cyrus the instrument of his victory over the nations, the implication being that the present poem looks for God to intervene anew against the nations in a way that has no need of such tools? In my own view, the poem more probably has no reference either one way or the other to Deutero-Isaiah, and the words, 'alone, no one with me' represent a feature taken from the realm of myth, the force of which has disappeared. It corresponds to the struggle with chaos as reflected in Ps. 74.13f. and Isa. 51.9. In the past, as I see it, comment on Isa. 63.1–6 has paid too little attention to what is the really characteristic feature here, the change made in the description of the divine judgment on the nations so that it becomes a battle engaged in by a single person, a description which, strictly and in respect of its origin, only suits a battle between two parties, a battle such as that of Marduk against Tiamat and those who came to her aid in *Enuma elish*. This is the only way of seeing the point in picturing the event here in the form of a sentry's question—the one who comes is a single person. And this, too, is the one satisfactory explanation of the emphasis laid on the words 'alone, no one with me'. In the case of the picture here then, the basis is one of the standard correlatives, 'in the beginning . . . at the end' (Gunkel). A battle fought by a single person is also indicated by the parallel verbs in v. 3b, 'trod, trampled'. Their suffixes, 'I trod *them*, I trampled *them*', cannot possibly refer to the peoples of v. 3a. They can only mean the foes, but since these are not specified, the suffixes are left unrelated. Leaving 'them' obscure may be intentional. As shown by the repetition in v. 6, the object must be 'the peoples' who are mentioned in v. 3, although the meaning there is different (possible helpers). The word *neṣaḥ* meaning juice (of life) occurs only here, Isa. 63.3 and 6.

Verse 3 rounds off the answer to the question put in v. 2. The events described in vv. 1ff. are at an end. What comes next, in vv. 4ff., is explanatory. Yet, to some extent these verses merely repeat rather than explain. Verse 6a is almost identical with v. 3b. Verse 6b is a half-verse standing alone, and something is probably missing after it (so Duhm and many others). Verse 5 is similar to v. 3a, and it also occurs in almost identical terms in 59.16 (although here the words are different). The parallelism represented by 'day' and 'year' suits a proclamation which specifies no definite time, but not the event just described. As a result, the connection between incident (vv. 1ff.) and explanation (vv. 4ff.) is at best loose. Verses 1ff. form the essence of the poem. They are the part which must be allowed to determine exegesis.

In v. 4, *kī* cannot possibly connect up with the sentence immediately preceding, but must relate to the passage (vv. 1ff.) in its entirety. This, too, witnesses to the looseness of the connection between vv. 4ff. and what goes before them. 'Year of my requital' follows Köhler's rendering; the noun *geʾūlīm*, from *gāʾal*, to redeem, occurs only here: 'time, state of the *gōʾēl*=avenger of bloodshed' (Köhler, *Lexikon*). The verse speaks of the awaited day on which God intervenes to take vengeance on his people's foes for the ignominy they had inflicted on her. In v. 5, too, as can be seen from the parallel passage 59.16, the thing envisaged is basically an intervention on the part of God on behalf of his people. In 59.16 the parallel to 'my arm' of v. 5b is my (there 'his') righteousness, which some manuscripts also read in 63.5. 'My wrath' may have come in from v. 3b, for it is not suitable to the verb and it is repeated in v. 6a. Whereas the diction in vv. 1ff. is succinct, concrete and forceful in the extreme, much in vv. 4ff. is obscure and uncertain.

Finally, we must again ask, what is the poem driving at, and why was it inserted in Trito-Isaiah? We have found that what supremely marks off 63.1–6 from the rest of the book is the fact that it depicts the battle which annihilates the nations as one waged by a single person, and that in the course of it he is bespattered all over with blood. There can be no doubt that this points to the combat between two parties or combat at hand to hand as found in myth. Realistic and concrete as is the beginning of the incident, the sequel to which it is intended to relate, the annihilation of nations by a single person in single combat with them, is entirely unrealistic and unhistorical. What we here meet is a description such as is found in apocalyptic and couched in terms taken from myth. 'The nations' form a single entity, the eschatological 'foe'. This is also the reason why they can be lumped together and designated by a singular, 'Edom'. This foe's annihiliation has ceased to be an act within history, in the same way as the nations are now not historical quantities. The whole thing is apocalpytic. Furthermore, in Isa. 60.1–6 the one at whose hands the annihilation comes about is never given the name Yahweh or God. The might as such that does this is set forth in the one who treads the wine press.

Glancing back from here to chs. 60–62, we see that the terms in which these chapters speak of the nations and the lot that awaits them are entirely different. There, when God's salvation comes, they are given their part in it as Israel's servants. The chapters also say that they come to the light which rises over Israel. This and their annihilation are quite incompatible.

Isa. 63.1–6 cannot possibly, then, have been uttered either at the same time or by the same man as chs. 60–62. Because of its apocalpytic nature, Isa. 63.1–6 is presumably later than chs. 60–62, and therefore must be a later addition. Apocalyptic texts thus appended to collections of prophetic utterances, or inserted within their body, are found more than once, e.g., the insertion of chs. 24–27 into Isa. 1–38.

CHAPTERS 63.7–64.11

O that thou wouldst rend the heavens!

63.7–14   I will sing of the gracious deeds of Yahweh . . .

7   I will remember the gracious deeds of Yahweh,
   the praiseworthy deeds of Yahweh,
   according to all that he has done for us,
   Yahweh, rich in goodness to the house of Israel,
   which he has granted them according to his mercy
   and the abundant granting of his faithfulness.
8   For he said to them, they are my people,
   sons who will not deal falsely.
   And he became their saviour in all their afflictions.
9   Neither envoy nor messenger—he himself saved them
   in his love and in his pity—he redeemed them,
   and he delivered and carried them   all the long while.[a]

10   But they rebelled
   and grieved his holy spirit.
   Therefore he turned to be their enemy,
   and himself fought against them.

11   And [they][b] remembered the days of old,
   of Moses, [his servant].[c]
   Where is he who [   ][d] brought up out of the sea
   the shepherd of his flock?
   Where is he who put in the midst of them
   his holy Spirit,
12   who caused his glorious arm
   to go at the right hand of Moses,
   who divided the waters before them
   to make for himself an everlasting name?
13   Who led them through the depths,
   as horses in the desert do not stumble,

  [a] P. Winter, 'Is. LXIII. 9 and the Passover-Haggadah', *VT*, IV, 4 (1954),
pp. 439ff.
   [b] Read *wayizkᵉrū*.
   [c] Read *ᶜabdō*.
   [d] Read *hammaᶜᵃle*.

14   as cattle go down into the valley,
      the spirit of Yahweh brought them to rest.
      So thou didst lead thy people,
      to make for thyself a glorious name.

Isaiah 63.7–64.11 is a community lament in psalm form. It could easily have found a place in the Psalter. And in many respects it is also reminiscent of Lamentations. It is a hymn to be used by the community in worship. While all that it says is laid down by the form traditional to psalms of communal lamentation, nevertheless as compared with these it has not a few special features of its own. The most important is the way in which it expands one part of the community lament, the survey of God's earlier saving acts, into what is almost an independent historical psalm (63.7–14). God is not directly addressed until 63.15: thus, the psalm of lamentation really only begins there. But from there onwards it follows the normal pattern. The introduction, 63.7a, can only be regarded as due to the expansion at the start of God's earlier saving deeds. The same introduction is to be found in Ps. 89.2 (1). There the opening section, again a community lament, is expanded even more (vv. 2–38 [1–37]; v. 39 [38] corresponds to Isa. 63.15). Psalm 44 is similar. The introductory retrospect stretches from v. 2 to v. 9. In all probability, these three psalms all came into being about the same time, not long after the fall of Jerusalem in 587. One can perfectly well understand why this was the time when, above all, so much importance was attached to surveys of history. It was surveys of this kind, summing the whole thing up with a confession of guilt sub-joined, that contemporaneously called the Deuteronomic history into being. Another sign of the way in which the introductory part tended to be elaborated for its own sake is the fact that it has its own rise and fall, its own dramatic portrayal.

Following upon v. 7 and strictly speaking, the introduction to a piece of descriptive praise, vv. 8f. give a summary of God's gracious acts on his chosen people's behalf. But then comes the reception with which they met—the nation's rebellion against him, and, as the result, his turning against his people (v. 10). Verses 11–14 join directly on to v. 9 and tell of that saving deed at the start of the nation's history which brought her into being. But both the diction of the verses and the stamp which they bear are odd. Nothing like them is found elsewhere. Verse 11 may well have begun the psalm in its older form (this would to some extent correspond with Ps. 44). Verse 11—the words, 'where is he'—also makes the first reference to the lament absent in vv. 7–10. We thus find that the introductory section has a structure very reminiscent of the Deuteronomic history:

7a   Introduction: I will remember the gracious deeds of Yahweh . . .

7b–9   God, deliverer and preserver of his chosen people.

10b   Israel turns against God, whereupon God turns against Israel.

11–14   In their extremity they thought about God's deeds in the past.

[7] The speaker here wants to quicken remembrance of God's deeds in the past. This is much more than just a recalling to mind, a merely mental process. Actualization of God's gracious deeds is the equivalent to an appeal to that gracious will which once upon a time wrought these deeds, and is now entreated to perform them afresh. In the Hebrew, grace and praise, the two grammatical objects of this calling to memory, are in the plural, a thing impossible in German. In Hebrew the first word may also stand for the granting of grace, and the second for that which is praiseworthy, that is to say, God's praiseworthy deed. God's grace and his action in grace, says the present passage, and the praise of the community and that which it praises, can be as little separated as this. To as limited a degree as this can God's deeds as experienced in history be separated on the one hand from his own being, and on the other from the response of the people by whom their effects are felt. The next line uses the verb *gāmal* to render these activities on God's part. The meaning which it would convey at the time can be learned from the brief closing words of Ps. 13, which express the breath of relief now that lament has been turned into joy: 'because he has dealt bountifully with me'. This marks the transition from the introduction to praise of God; the speakers extol him who 'is rich in goodness to the house of Israel' and praise him for 'the abundant granting of his faithfulness'.

[8–9] He set his seal on this by making Israel his chosen people through the covenant into which he entered with them. Implicit in this, however, was an expectation—that as his sons they would be loyal and true to him. During the course of the history which the covenant inaugurated God himself undoubtedly proved to be 'saviour in all their afflictions', to be redeemer, and their deliverer and preserver. One cannot help noticing the piling up of words that might describe his acts in grace towards his people and the fact that these were dictated by goodness, mercy, faithfulness, love and pity (the only other occurrence of the last word is in Gen. 19.16; it appears in a different form in Ezek. 16.5). This was the way in which Israel thought of her God, and these are the words in which she preserved the memory of her encounter with him—not with an intermediary being, but with him himself (cf. Ex. 34). We must wait for the other sections of the psalm to see the point of accumulating these words here at its beginning.

[10] All of God's acts toward his people expect an answer, a reaction to them, a response. The normal and obvious answer to his action as stated in vv. 8f. would be to follow, praise and serve him. Thus, the answer actually forthcoming, 'but they were rebellious and grieved his holy spirit'—was not the obvious or natural one. 'To be rebellious' with the same meaning as it has here is found elsewhere, e.g. Num. 20.10, and Ezekiel calls Israel 'the rebellious house' (2.8, etc.). In the *qal* the second verb means 'to afflict' and in the *pi'ēl* 'to grieve'. The phrase 'his holy spirit' is very odd. In the Old Testament the concept 'holy spirit' occurs only here and in Ps. 51, and is undoubtedly a late expression. The sole reference of all these many words in vv. 8f. was to God's grace in turning towards Israel. Yet here in v. 10 the thing put to grief is not his goodness, but his holiness. This is very characteristic of Old Testament thought. To grieve God's goodness is to assail his holiness. And this causes God himself to change: he changes into his chosen people's enemy. The reason for this is his wounded holiness. The nerve-centre of all that happens in history consists in the fact that, when God's holiness has been wounded, things cannot go on as they are. This is the very same thing as was central in the message of the prophets, the overtones of which are heard in the sharp antithesis in the present verse.

[11–14] We now come to the actual survey of God's previous saving acts, a regular component part of psalms of communal lamentation (see above). In the Old Testament such surveys are one of the most important occasions of actualizing history. Words such as these allow us to see how at that time, despite terrible breaks in Israel's history, it was nevertheless felt to have continuity. Her history had a coherence about it. The surveys also show the way by which men reached this view. For the very reason that the only present manifestation of God's action was action against his people, hostile action, the community clung passionately to this same God who in their own past had manifested himself in such an entirely different way. This resurrecting of the past is a moving 'conjuring up' of what is over and done with. At present the only thing which the past still 'has' for the community is the fact that the same God as is now their enemy was once upon a time their friend. To this sameness it holds fast with all its might, 'remembering'.

This impassioned harking back to long ago finds its voice in the twofold 'where is?' at the beginning of the second and third lines of v. 11. Verses 11–14 preserve an odd and unique tradition about the Exodus. Unlike the versions of it elsewhere, this one mentions the name given to Moses; he is called 'shepherd of his flock'. Moses' significance for his nation on this occasion is attributed to God's 'glorious arm', that is, to his power which works glorious things, and to his holy Spirit. 'Spirit' here has its old meaning of power that works miracles. The same meaning attaches to 'Spirit of Yahweh' (without 'holy') in v. 14, but in v. 11 it is wider and more general. Taking the three occurrences together and noticing how often the term comes, we realize that this is the first step towards the employment of 'Spirit' in relation to God in which each and all of his acts can be attributed to his Spirit or to God's holy Spirit. This contrasts with the earlier usage in which only a few, and they quite specific, modes of activity, as, for example, the endowment of charismatic leaders with the Spirit, could be described as the operation of God's Spirit. This later usage comes near to the *pneuma* of the New Testament, but is differentiated from it by the fact that in the Old Testament the action of God's Spirit is restricted to action in history. Volz calls it 'the power that operates in Israel's history'.[a]

[11b] Duhm's comment on the verse is: 'it is not perfectly clear whether the words "the shepherd of his flock brought up out of the sea" refer to the rescue of Moses from the Nile (*yām* for the Nile as in 18.2 and 19.5), or to Israel's deliverance at the Red Sea.' Of the alternatives he prefers the first, and late traditions suggest that this is perfectly possible.

In vv. 11b–12a the subject is what God did to, and by means of, his servant Moses. But in vv. 12b–14 God himself, he alone, leads and delivers his chosen people. He was the one who 'divided the waters' before Israel—this may be the last echo of the cleaving of the chaos dragon of mythology. By reason of this 'he made for himself an everlasting name' (cf. the praise given him in vv. 7ff.). He was the one

[a] Excursus on 'Geist', pp. 270f.

who, in so doing, led them by a safe and firm way, which kept their pursuers apart from them, into 'rest', into security. The road made through the divided waters was as safe and firm as the ground on which cavalcades of horses course over the desert. The way is as peaceful as that on which, in the evening, cattle are driven into the valley to drink.

This section, vv. 13f., is a particularly fine example of the significance which Israel's early history had for her. The place where she met with her God was her history. History, its ebbs and flows, its ups and downs, testified to the vital power of her God, and to his incomprehensible goodness and terrifying holiness. But history itself was not the revelation. He had actually spoken to them, that is to say, he had revealed himself in his word. And this and his action in history went together. There were no exceptions; God said something: it was invariably followed up. Never could the speaking be divorced from history. Never could men be given his word in dissociation from history, its miracles and its abysses.

63.15–64.11   O that thou wouldst rend the heavens!

63.15   Look down from heaven and see,
     from thy holy and glorious habitation.
     Where are thy zeal and thy might,
     the yearning of thy heart and thy compassion?[a]
16   [Withhold not thyself][b] for thou art our Father;
     for Abraham does not know us,
     and Israel does not acknowledge us.
     Thou, O Yahweh, art our Father,
     our Redeemer from of old is thy name.

17   Why, O Yahweh, doest thou make us err
     from thy ways
     and harden our heart,
     so that we fear thee not?
     Return for the sake of thy servants,
     the tribes of thy heritage.
18   [Why] may [transgressors] [slight] thy sanctuary,[c]
     our adversaries tread down thy holy places?

[a] On v. 15, see W. F. Albright, 'Zabul Sea', *YPOS* 16 (1936).
[b] Transfer v. 15b to v. 16a and read *'al⁻nā' tit'abbāq.*
[c] Read *lāmmā ṣiᶜᵃrū reˢāᶜīm.*

19   We are as thou hadst not been our lord from of old,
      like those who are not called by thy name.

(64.1) O that thou wouldst rend the heavens and come down,
      that the mountains might quake at thy presence—
64.1 (2) as when fire kindles brushwood
      and the fire causes water to boil—
      to let thy name be known to thy adversaries,
      and that the nations might tremble at thy presence!
2 (3) Because thou doest terrible things which we looked not for [ ]ᵃ
3 (4) and from of old have not perceived;
      for no [ear]ᵇ has heard, no eye has seen
      a God besides thee,
      who works for those who wait for him.
4 (5)   [O]ᶜ that thou [ ]ᵈ wouldst meet such as work righteousness,
      who remember thy ways.

      Yet thou wast angry, we sinned,
      [because of our unfaithfulness we transgressed].ᵉ
5 (6) We have all become as unclean,
      and all our righteousnessᶠ like a polluted garment.
      We all fade like a leaf,
      our sins take us away like the wind.
6 (7) And no one calls upon thy name,
      bestirs himself to take hold of thee.
      For thou hast hid thy face from us,
      abandoned us because ofᵍ our iniquity.

7 (8) Yet, O Yahweh, thou art our father,
      we are the clay and thou our potter,
      and we are all the work of thy hands.

8 (9) Be not exceedingly angry, O Yahweh,
      remember not our iniquity for ever.
      Behold, consider, we are all thy people.
9 (10) Thy holy cities have become a wilderness,
      Zion has become a desert, Jerusalem a desolation.

ᵃ The last four words in MT are a repetition of 63.19.
ᵇ Read *he'ᵉzīnā 'ozen*.
ᶜ Add *lū* at the beginning.
ᵈ With Vss. read *'ose* for *sās wᵉ'ōséh*.
ᵉ In place of the last four words of v. 4 read (with Köhler) *wᵉnipšā' bᵉma'ᵃlēnū*.
ᶠ On 64. 4b–5a (5b–6a) see S. H. Blank, 'And All Our Virtues', *JBL*, 71, 3 (1952), pp. 149–54.
ᵍ On *bᵉyād* with the meaning 'because of', see Dahood, *Bibl.*, 44 (1963), pp. 289–303.

10 (11) Our holy and beautiful house,
where our fathers praised thee,
has been burned by fire,
and all our pleasant places lie in ruin.

11 (12) Canst thou restrain thyself at these things, O Yahweh,
Dost thou keep silent, and afflict us sorely?

This psalm is probably the most powerful psalm of communal lamentation in the Bible, but it is hard to see its structure. The usual sections in a lament do not simply follow upon one another, but are very freely interwoven. The broad outlines of the structure are best taken as follows. The psalm begins with the prayer that God should turn towards Israel (63.15). To this is clearly related the prayer that God should intervene which comes in the middle (63.19b); and at the end (64.11 [12]) an anxious question which had earlier been joined to the introductory prayer (v. 15b) is urged upon God.

63.15a	Look down from heaven and see.
15b	Where are thy zeal . . . and thy compassion?
19b (64.1)	O that thou wouldst rend the heavens.
64.11 (12)	Doest thou keep silent and afflict us sorely?

The disposition in detail is therefore as follows:

63.	15f.	Introductory prayer that God should turn to Israel and a confession of confidence.
	17–19a	Lament with the usual three parts, 17b prayer with a reason annexed.
63.	19b–64.4a (5a)	Prayer that God should intervene by an epiphany.
	4b–6 (5b–7)	Confession of sin inserted into the charge brought against God.
	7 (8)	Confession of confidence.
	8ff. (9ff.)	Prayer that God should turn with a reason annexed, and a lament for Zion.
	11 (12)	Concluding question, 'canst thou restrain thyself?'

[15–16] To understand the introductory prayer, 'look down from heaven and see', it is important to remember a characteristic which attaches to supplication in the Old Testament; the prayer that God should intervene and give help is invariably preceded by one asking that he should turn towards the suppliant. Only as we realize this can we see how vv. 15f. and 19b–64.1 (2) go together. The background of the way in which v. 15a is put is praise of the God 'who is seated on high, who looks far down' (Ps. 113). His 'holy and beautiful house' does not imply that he has a habitation such as we find in myth. It means the far-off sovereign realm of God on high, into which the suppliant's prayer that God should turn to him has to make its way. The question 'where is thy zeal?' and the charge which it contains express the feeling of the lostness of those who make the lament. Their whole existence is so dependent upon God's mercy that, when this is lost, they regard themselves as lost. This is the very thing substantiated in the confession of confidence which comes next. The Psalter has practically no limit to the ways by which it can express the idea of taking refuge with God. Nevertheless, the words, 'for thou art our Father' (again in 64.7 [8]), are only found in this one psalm. The reason why the designation of God as father is so rare in the Old Testament is that, in the world in which Israel was set, the physical fatherhood of the gods was a basic feature of thinking in terms of myth. The Old Testament will have none of this. Man is not God's child, but his creature. God is never designated as father before the post-exilic period, and even then it is only on the odd occasion. By this time the danger of the term's being misunderstood, in the sense which it had in myth, had dropped into the background. We can therefore very well understand why, unusual as it is, it is given an unusual explanation. Isaiah 63.16 is poles apart from John 8.33. There, the men with whom Jesus engaged in conversation had every confidence—and they were proud to be able so to do—in taking their stand on the fact that they were the descendants of Abraham. Here, however, as the community makes its supplication to God, it says that it cannot put its trust in Abraham or Jacob: they do not know it. The way in which God is the father of Israel is entirely different from that in which Abraham and Jacob are the nation's fathers. God is a living and present father. He knows. He acknowledges. He sees. What makes him Israel's father is the fact that men may call upon him, and that he can turn in grace towards his chosen people. God's fatherhood is thus in marked distinction to any merely romantic or traditional designation as father. For the chosen people there is only one vital father: 'our redeemer from of old is thy name'. Tradition—this is implied rather than said outright—is of importance. But at the same time it has its limitations. Positively, it makes the God who had dealings with the ancestors of the race a present reality. Negatively, if, as

'that which has always been', it becomes the thing on which the community relies, it can be a source of perversion.

[17–19a] After the introductory prayer, here changed because of
the confession of confidence, comes the lament proper. Its three component parts are the charge brought against God (v. 17a), the complaint regarding enemies (v. 18), and the lament in the first person
plural (v. 19). In between (v. 17b) comes once again the prayer that
God should turn towards Israel, with a reason annexed. The question
put to God in v. 17 is an odd variation of the simple charge brought
against him: There are already suggestions of the confession of sin in
it (64.4b–6 [5b–7]). God is reproached by being asked, why did he
make Israel turn aside from obeying him? Such language is only
possible where men who believe that all things come from God choose
one or other of two things. However much it perplexes them and
challenges their faith, they believe that God can harden his chosen
people's heart. Or else they regard this hardening as due to the work
of some other force antagonistic to him. What brought Israel up
against these insoluble problems was her firm belief, admitting of no
qualification, that God is one (Deut. 6.4). A second question beginning with the word 'why' looks at the foes, the foreign armies, which
desecrate God's sanctuary. 'How canst thou allow this, O God?' asks
the community as it makes its lament, again a constant question
whenever men believe that God is one but at the same time cannot
see any way of reconciling his workings with the facts as they are.
Here—and this is the only difference—the question is not put *about*
him, but *to* him. The third part of the lament, v. 19a, is not a question, but a statement. If that is possible, that it goes even beyond the
questions; 'we are'—it is bold enough to say—'as if thou hadst not
been our Lord'. Taken in sober earnest, this lament in the first person
plural expresses something of actual 'darkness as regards God'
(Buber). When they speak about God and make supplication to him,
men can come to an abyss. They are impassioned and devoted in their
adherence to him. But they make shipwreck. The hard facts against
him are too strong and convincing: 'we are as though thou hadst not
been our lord.' In the Old Testament's psalms of lament one of the
most material things for the present day is the fact that they anticipate the forceful and cogent arguments brought by atheism. To be
sure, the psalms put them in a different way. The suppliants themselves put these arguments before God in the lament.

[19b–64.4a (4b)] This prayer for God's intervention, which corresponds to the one that he should turn towards Israel (63.15), forms the central part of the psalm. It takes the form of a wish that God might appear with power and in sovereign majesty to bring Israel help. These words grandly span millennia of tradition. The epiphanies[a] were the forms which ancient Israel used to describe God's miraculous appearing (coming) to deliver his people from some kind of extremity, as in the Song of Deborah (Judg. 5.4f.), Ps. 18.8–16 (7–15), etc. The epiphany always has (descriptive) praise allied with it: a description is given of how, when the extremity was at its worst, God appeared in order to intervene and help. In the present psalm, on the other hand, while the old words of the epiphany are used to make supplication for God's intervention, the descriptive part is turned into the form of a wish, although clear traces of the basic elements of the old description of the epiphany still remain. We must assume that the present verses are based on a very ancient epiphany tradition corresponding to the passages mentioned above. There is a Christian hymn which imitates our passage and relates it to the advent (appearing) of Jesus Christ, 'O Heiland, reiss die Himmel auf'.

[19b (64.1)] With the beginning we may compare Ps. 18.10 (9), 'he bowed the heavens and came down'. There, too, we find the quaking of the mountains (v. 8 [7]). 64.1a (2a) is quite uncertain. Many (e.g. Köhler, Elliger) regard the verse as untranslatable, and many (e.g. Kessler, Abramowski) take it to be a gloss. Surprisingly enough, Duhm makes no objection to it, and relates the two comparisons to the two parts of 63.19b. Since v. 9 (8) of the description of the epiphany in Ps. 18.8ff. (7ff.), the one closest to the present passage, speaks of devouring fire, 64.1a (2a) should not be struck out, even if we grant that the text may not be the original one. At all events, it is connected with the manifestations of fire which form part of the description of an epiphany. The trembling of the nations in the face of God's awful drawing near is also a regular feature in epiphanies, cf. Hab. 3.6.

[64.2–4a (3–5a)] 'The terrible acts of God are the overthrow of adversaries and the establishment of the ascendancy of Yahweh's people' (Duhm); cf. Deut. 10.21 and Ps. 106.22. Verse 2b (3b), a repetition from 63.19b (64.1), is to be deleted (so all editors). Volz gives a good explanation of how the words came to be put here. The words, 'what we looked not for, and from of old have not perceived', give a very clear picture of the situation in which this psalm was

a Westermann, Praise of God . . . , pp. 64–81.

composed. The miracles experienced by Israel which form the background of the epiphany are now far back in the past, and we can never hope that they will come back again!

The prayer for God's intervention couched as a wish for a new epiphany comes to its end here. Verse 3b (4b) is a final piece of praise suggestive of standing in awed silence at the mighty miracles recounted in the epiphanies. On this supervenes a wish (v. 4a [5a]). The verse is very corrupt. Volz saw that it does not suit the context and therefore translates, 'O that thou wouldst afflict'. But Duhm and others rightly object that this would be an *ad hoc* meaning not found elsewhere. It should be translated, 'O that thou wouldst meet such . . . !' The verse is entirely out of place in a community lament. But it makes sense when taken as the devout addition on the part of a reader who had been shocked at the boldness of the prayer, 'O that thou wouldst rend the heavens', and countered it with his devout wish that among his people God may meet with such as work righteousness and remember his ways.

[4b–6 (5b–7)] Removal of the above words also better brings out the contrast between v. 4b (5b), 'yet thou wast angry', and v. 3b (4b), with which to begin with it was directly linked. Next, in vv. 4b–6 (5b–7), comes the confession of sin. At this point we should remember that this had already been suggested, or involved, in the charge brought against God (63.17). Here in 64.4b–6 (5b–7) the confession is placed in the body of the charge, 'thou art angry . . .' (v. 4b [5b]), 'thou has hid thy face from us' (v. 6b [7b]). Looking at the history of psalms of lamentation, we notice that from the exile onward the charge brought against God falls more and more into the background until in the end it completely disappears from the prayer. As a result, greater and greater importance is given to the confession of sin. Isaiah 63f. are a good illustration of this transition. What kindled God's wrath which vented itself so terribly on Israel were her unfaithfulness and transgression. Now, after the downfall of the state, this is admitted, and the admission is brought before God. Its transgression made the entire nation unclean and polluted (v. 5a [6a]). It cut the connection with the fountain of living waters (Jer. 2.13), so that the nation withered like leaves (Deutero-Isaiah, in 40.7, takes exactly the same view). When it can be said, 'our sins take us away like the wind', the sin and its consequences are viewed as one and the same thing. What is responsible for it all is the destruction of the vital link with God made by calling upon him and trusting in him (v. 6a [7a]). This brings the confession back to the thing that had in fact called it forth and been its origin, God's wrath, the hiding of his face, which, however, came about 'because of our iniquity'. Thus, the affirmation of their own iniquity gives the charge brought against God its quietus.

[7–8 (8–9)] There is a feature here which is particularly subtle, as well as profound, in its theological implications. In v. 7 (8) with its *waw* adversative which, in psalms of lamentation, often marks the transition from lamentation to confidence, the same words, 'thou art our Father', are used to testify to confidence in God after confession of sin as had been used at the beginning (v. 16) in face of the simple lament at their sufferings. It is to her Father that Israel turns in straits. It is to her Father that she turns when burdened with iniquity. We can see that there has been some deliberate structuring here; while the two confessions of confidence are apparently the same, in 63.16 the accent falls on God's being a Father, but here in 64.7 (8) it is on the fact that the speakers are children. Very significantly, in order to rule out any idea of physical fatherhood, v. 7b (8b) goes on to describe this condition as the status of a creature. As in Ps. 139, being a creature ('the work of your hands') signifies belonging, trusting, taking refuge. The prayer which now ensues in v. 8 (9) is derived from the confession of sin. It takes for granted that God cannot simply overlook his people's sin, and that this is bound to arouse his anger. Thus, the line taken in asking for forgiveness is not that God should simply cancel this sin; it has been committed, and it has its inevitable consequences. Instead, supplication is made that, in spite of it, it should still be possible to go on living. This possibility is created if God only looks, if he only turns again towards sinful Israel. The prayer is reinforced by an annexed reason designed to move God: 'we are after all thy people'. We should expect a parallel verse here. The prayer breaks off with an odd abruptness. In point of subject-matter, this is the place for 63.17b, which is not in context where it stands at present. In this case, the cry, 'O look here', and the cry, 'turn', are parallel, as are 'we are all thy people' and 'for the sake of thy servants'.

[9–10 (10–11)] The reason why the lament is here resumed is that as against 63.17ff., vv. 9f. (10f.) bewail one specific thing, the sanctuary (cf. Ps. 79.1). Certain striking expressions such as 'our beautiful house' and 'thy holy cities' are probably due to the tradition of the lament for the sanctuary. Bewailing the destruction of the sanctuary, which we also find in Mesopotamia, presupposes that the sanctuary is the middle-point of the land, the place from which issue blessing and prosperity for the whole of the land. However, in keeping with the present passage, mention is made of another function served by the temple: 'our . . . house, where our fathers praised thee'. These words incidentally reveal the centrality and importance of praise in Israel's worship. 'Our fathers' means all the generations of ancestors up to the time of the destruction of the temple. While this is a witness to Israel's tradition of praise of God's mighty acts as handed on from father to son, it also witnesses to the fact that the strains of the Psalter's hymns of praise were in fact raised in the temple at Jerusalem. There can be no doubt that in the present context 'our valuables' or 'our pleasant place' refer to the decorations of the temple and its vessels.

[11 (12)] The fact that a psalm of lamentation like this ends with an anxious question put to God (so also Lam. 5) shows how genuine the language of these psalms is, and how it chimes in with the facts of the case. The final words make it apparent that the entire psalm is designed as a question put to God by men who waited anxiously for him. It also shows that men who spoke in this way looked to God and to his turning again towards them as the sole source of a change in their lot. A psalm like this enables us to see why it was precisely with this anxious question that Trito-Isaiah's proclamation made the link. And this was the question to which it proclaimed the saving answer.

CHAPTER 65.1–16a

The Faithless and the Obedient

65.1–7   It is written before me

1   I am ready to be sought by those who did not ask for me;
    I am ready to be found by those who did not seek me.
    I say, 'Here am I, here am I,'
    to a nation that did not call upon my name.

2 I spread out my hands all the day
    to a faithless [and rebellious]ᵃ people,
    who walk in a way that is not good,
    following their own thoughts,
3 to people who provoke me
    to my face continually.

    Who sacrifice in gardens
    and burn incense upon bricks (?),
4 who crouch in tombs,
    and spend the night in caverns;
    who eat swine's flesh,
    and broth of unclean things is in their vessels;ᵇ
5 who say, 'Stay where you are,
    do not come near me, for I make you unclean.'
    They are a smoke in my nostrils,
    a fire that burns all the day.
6 Behold, it is written before me:
    'I will not keep silent, until I have requited it,
    I repay into their bosom [their iniquities],ᶜ
7 and [their]ᵈ fathers' iniquity together', says Yahweh.
    Those who burn incense upon the mountains
    and blaspheme me upon the hills,
    to them I will measure the recompense [upon their head]ᵉ
    [and repay] into their bosom.

65.1–16a form a unity. Yet vv. 1–7 can be taken as a section complete in itself. At first sight it looks like a prophetic announcement of judgment such as the pre-exilic prophets of judgment have made us familiar with, but close inspection reveals considerable divergencies from this. This is due to a considerable change in situation as between the two. Verse 8 furnishes the key to the poem. From v. 8 onwards— and v. 8 also substantiates what follows—the prophetic announcement divides into an announcement of salvation and an announcement of doom, the one applying to the devout in the nation and the other to the transgressors. The section preceding, vv. 1–7, is purely an announcement of doom. It is substantiated by means of the allegation of idolatry (vv. 3b–5, 7a). Before the exile this would have led

  ᵃ Supply *ūmōre* with Vss.
  ᵇ On vv. 3–4, see M. J. Dahood, 'Textual Problems in Isaiah', *CBQ* 22 (1960), pp. 400–9.
  ᶜ The first word of v. 7 has been drawn into v. 6.
  ᵈ Read the third person instead of the second.
  ᵉ With Volz and Kessler read *bᵉrō'šām* and then supply *wᵉšillāmtī*.

on to an announcement of judgment against the nation in its entirety, because by tolerating this they all become partners in its guilt. This is where the difference comes in. The nation has ceased to be a single entity in the sense that the transgression of a small number, or even of a large, has its effects on the whole body. As a result, the announcement of judgment contained in vv. 1–7 applies only to the transgressors themselves and, correspondingly, the announcement of salvation comes in alongside it in vv. 8–16a. Chapter 65 is a perfect illustration of the change which came over the prophetic announcement of judgment because of the new state of things created by the downfall of the year 587. For this state of affairs the characteristic form of announcement is that of salvation for the one body of people and of doom for the other.

The structure of vv. 1–7 is clear. Verses 1f.: God's turning again to his people: vv. 3ff., to the rebellious nation who provoke God (v. 3) and practise all kinds of idolatry (vv. 4f.); vv. 6f.: announcement of their punishment.

[1–2] The punishment of the faithless announced in vv. 6f. is substantiated in two stages. The actual allegation of idolatry is preceded (vv. 1f.) by a statement of the efforts which God had made to win the faithless back. This corresponds to the motif of contrast in pre-exilic prophecy (e.g. Amos 2.9ff). The verses are a particularly fine example of the divine *gratia praeveniens*, which, however, is bitterly disappointed in its efforts to forestall. To catch the overtones of the verses one has to remember the particular state of affairs which obtained after the exile. In the sufferings of the period it was a subject of loud and continual lament that God did not allow himself to found, that he kept silent and gave no answer (e.g. 64.11). Then, however, had come his superabundant offer of grace as we see it in the proclamation of Deutero-Isaiah and its revival, after the exile was over, by Trito-Isaiah. This is the superabundant offer referred to in the opening verses of ch. 65, and this, our passage can only say, was rejected. There, absolutely close by them, God has it proclaimed, 'Here am I, here am I', but they follow their own thoughts.

[3a] One can see only too well that, when such a statement falls to be made, God must start to punish afresh, and that there must be renewed proclamation of this: they provoke God to his face continually. This is what makes it impossible for the proclamation to be solely one of salvation, as in chs. 60–62; there has to be a renewal of the message of judgment. These three verses of ch. 65 give a telling

explanation of how and why, after the return, there came to be a revival of prophetic oracles of judgment. Indeed, the prefacing of the actual allegation and the pronouncement of sentence with vv. 1–3a (or 2) can only mean that the reason for such oracles had to be made clear. The process reminds us of words in the Deuteronomic strand in Jeremiah such as 25.1–11, where, too, the allegation made against the nation is introduced by a reference to the way in which God had gone to endless trouble with it. There are reminiscences of the language there used in the expressions 'to a faithless and rebellious nation', 'following their own thoughts' (Jer. 18.12) and 'to provoke God' (Deut. 4.25; Jer. 7.18; 11.17 etc.). 'To my face continually' is a term used in worship: in a good sense of the shewbread, Ex. 28.29f.; cf. Ex. 30.8; Lev. 24.3, 4, 8; in a bad sense Jer. 6.7, cf. 52.2.

[3b–5] Now comes the description of the apostates in a long series of participial clauses. In style they resemble not the charge made by the prophets, but rather the description of the transgressors in the psalms of lamentation. The offences are all of a cultic kind. First comes the matter of places where worship is offered; v. 7, whose subject-matter ranges it with vv. 3b–5, has to be taken along with v. 3b, for the words, 'who burn incense upon the mountains and blaspheme me upon the hills', can only refer to worship at the high places. Apparently, there had been a reveival of this in some places either during the exile or soon after the return. Verse 3b, 'who sacrifice in gardens', also refers to this. The meaning of the second half-verse, 'and burn incense upon bricks', is uncertain. Köhler takes lᵉbēnā as meaning 'pavement of place of offerings'; it could also be a derogatory description of an altar of earth (so Duhm). At all events it refers, as do all four lines, to sacrifice at the high places. Verse 4 goes on to add further cultic malpractices. 'Crouching in tombs' was for the purpose of obtaining oracles from the dead, and 'spending the night in caverns' signifies incubation rites. This is also said in the explanatory addition found in LXX, διὰ ἐνύπνια, for the sake of oracles received in dreams. Eating of swine's flesh was expressly forbidden the Israelites by cultic law (Lev. 17.11), as was also use of unclean meats ('broth of unclean things') for sacrifice. This verse expresses abhorrence of all that is cultically unclean. Verse 5, too, refers to an idea that was alien to the worship of Yahweh—that of contagious 'holiness' due to the cult, which is thus equivalent to cultic impurity. Verse 5b is similar to Jer. 17.4, and also to Deut. 32.22.

[6–7] The pronouncement of sentence. What now comes only remotely resembles the pre-exilic announcement of judgment; vv. 6f. merely give an assurance that God will yet requite the faithless for their sins. Since the people affected are a group living among others to whom the oracle of judgment does not apply, it is difficult to picture the way in which the judgment is to be meted out to them. This is the reason for emphasizing that these sins are written before God (v. 6a). The meaning is that God's intervention to punish their offences is not to take place at once. But punishment will certainly yet ensue (v. 6b). The reference to the sins of the fathers (v. 7a) probably means no more than that this generation's transgression has a connection with the sins committed by their fathers (worship at the high places, v. 7b). Verse 7c repeats v. 6b in order to emphasize it. The text is not in order, and should probably be supplemented to be like v. 6b. 'Into their bosom': 'to measure what someone has earned, e.g., a quantity of grain, Ruth 3.15; Jer. 32.18' (Duhm).

Three aspects are of importance for an answer to the question whether 65.1–7 go along with chs. 60–62. (1) The sins of the 'faithless' are exclusively cultic. There is no suggestion of apostasy to other gods, but only of illicit cultic practices. This presupposes that the speaker's standpoint is wholly cultic. But such emphasis on the ritual side of worship never appeared in chs. 60–62. (2) Whereas in chs. 60–62 the prophet constantly relates himself to Deutero-Isaiah, and traces of the latter's diction, in quotations or allusions, are to be found throughout, this is not the case in 65.1–7; in some places here the diction is reminiscent rather of the Deuteronomic school. (3) The third aspect only appears more clearly in vv. 8ff. In chs. 60–62 Trito-Isaiah's announcement of salvation is addressed to the whole body of the nation, but here we find the beginning of a division into two sections. When these three aspects are put together, the probability is that the speakers in ch. 65 and chs. 60–62 are different people. However, we must first see what the second section, vv. 8–16, has to tell us.

65.8–16a My Servants—but You

8 Thus hath Yahweh said:
    'As juice is found in the cluster, and they say,
    "Do not destroy it, for there is a blessing in it",

so I will do for my servants' sake,
so that I do not destroy them all.
9   I bring forth descendants from Jacob,
from Judah inheritors of my mountains.
My chosen shall inherit it,
and my servants shall dwell there.
10   Sharon shall become a pasture for flocks,
the Valley of Achor a place for herds to lie down,
for my people, for those who seek me.
11   But you who forsake Yahweh,
who forget my holy mountain,
who set a table for Gad
and pour out the wine for Meni;
12   you do I destine to the sword,
you must all bow down to the slaughter.
Because, when I called, you did not answer,
when I spoke, you did not listen.
You did what was evil in my eyes
and chose what I did not delight in.'
13   Therefore the Lord Yahweh has said thus:
'Behold, my servants shall eat,   but you shall be hungry;
behold, my servants shall drink,   but you shall be thirsty;
behold, my servants shall rejoice,   but you shall [weep],[a]
14   behold, my servants shall sing for gladness of heart,
but you shall cry out for pain of heart,
and shall wail for anguish of spirit.
15   You must leave your name
for a curse to my chosen [   ][b].
But [my] servants [will be called][c]
by a different name.[d]
16   He who blesses himself in the land, let him bless himself in the true
God,
and he who takes an oath in the land, let him swear it in the true God.

[8] In the next few verses the announcement divides up. Judgment
is restricted to one section of the nation, while the other, God's
servants, has salvation announced to it. Since the transition in v. 8,
'so that I do not destroy them all', obviously bears upon the preceding
announcement of judgment, and since v. 12b relates to the faithless of
vv. 1–7 and v. 10b alludes to vv. 1f., vv. 8ff. must go along with the
opening section of the chapter. The section which begins with v. 8

[a] Read *tibkū*.

[b] With Marti and Köhler delete, as a gloss, 'and the Lord Yahweh slays you'.

[c] Read *wᵉlaᶜᵃbāday yiqqārē'*.

[d] On v. 15 see E. Pfeiffer, 'Der altestamentliche Hintergrund der liturgischen
Formel "Amen" *KuD*4, 1948, pp. 129–41.

carries on until v. 16a (not, as editors often suppose, only until v. 12). The structure is clear. After the verse which makes the transition (v. 8) comes the announcement of salvation for those who seek Yahweh (vv. 9–10); then that of judgment upon the faithless (vv. 11f.). Then, summarizing both of these (the reason why the introduction is repeated at this point), vv. 13–16a gives the announcement as it applies to each of the parties concerned. Verse 8a explains what follows it by means of a proverb-like figure of speech (in prose) about the vintager at the vintage. In the same way as Isaiah (28.23–28) likens God's action to that of the farmer, the phrase 'do not destroy it, for there is a blessing in it' suggests that there is an idea of throwing the grapes away, but someone objects to it, saying 'there is blessing in it'—some of the fruit is still good, that is to say, there is still juice in the grapes. This proverb-like turn of phrase retains the oldest meaning of $b^e r \bar{a} k \bar{a}$, blessing = power of giving increase.[a] Since all such power is God-given, it would be transgression to destroy it. In just the same way, the nation in which the transgressions described in vv. 3b–5 are committed nevertheless still contains a remnant for whose sake God forbears to destroy the entire nation (v. 8). This verse shows how ch. 65 effects the transition from the earlier prophecy of doom to a new form of the announcement of God's action, one which at one and the same time announces salvation to some and judgment to others. This was an extremely momentous change, because a divine intervention at once bringing ruin upon one section of the nation and salvation upon the other cannot possibly be conceived in terms of history. In this chapter the change is apparently made with full consciousness of what is being done; its whole way of speaking gives the impression that this division which made the divine action have two modes to it was felt to be something new, and required explanation (v. 8). If this is so, ch. 65 comes at the beginning of this development, in the early post-exilic period.

[9–10] A remnant from Jacob and from Judah are promised possession of the land. The breadth of the latter is indicated by means of two valleys, one (Sharon) in the west, and the other (Achor, near Jericho) in the east; these verge on the hill-country of Judah and Israel. Throughout this area they are to dwell in peace. Some editors feel something odd about the half-verse (10b) with nothing to balance it: 'for my people, those who seek me', and Duhm and others

[a] Cf. J. Pedersen, *Israel, Its Life and Culture*, London and Copenhagen, 1926 and 1946, I, pp. 182–212.

omit it as breaking the rhythm. But, as Volz rightly sees, it is this very
half-verse that links the prophecy contained in vv. 9f. with v. 11f.
('there is a reference back to v. 1 and a clear contrast with it').
Closer examination shows that the entire prophecy (vv. 9f. with the
omission of v. 10b) does not really fit into the state of affairs as
envisaged in the chapter. For, taken strictly, v. 9 says that the people
who are to possess Palestine are not the people to whom this oracle is
spoken, but their descendants. Further, nowhere do vv. 9f. (omitting
10b) make the slightest suggestion that this is a prophecy applying to
the devout who hold fast to God. Rather, what is here taken up is a
prophecy spoken during the exile, promising the descendants of those
then living in foreign countries that they will eventually re-possess
the land. It is thus a prophecy that runs parallel to those of Deutero-
Isaiah ('chosen' and 'servants' are also parallels with him). The
author of ch. 65 had to have v. 10b to allow him to put this prophecy
which he took over into its present context.

[11–12] Whereas the prophecy contained in vv. 9f. was couched in
the third person, vv. 11f. address the faithless in direct speech. This
makes it still more apparent that they are different both in style and
content. The faithless have destruction announced them. 'Sword' and
'slaughter' must mean destruction in war. But how? Here, too, it is
evident that the author has taken up stock-terms used in the announcements of judgment of older days. Joined to the prophecy is a substantiation (v. 11) which alleges two things. 'You who forget my holy
mountain' can only mean ceasing to attend the services of worship
on Mount Zion or else contempt for them. The other thing looks like
open idolatry. Gad and Meni are gods of fortune, Gad being a
Syrian deity, preserved in personal names such as Baal-Gad (Josh.
11.17) and Migdal-Gad (Josh. 15.37). The name is also attested in
inscriptions in Phoenicia and at Palmyra (Muilenburg). 'Meni is
probably identical with the deity Manat, one of the three principal
deities venerated by the Arabs before the time of Mohammed'
(Volz, who gives further references). This charge is surprisingly
different from the one made in vv. 3b–5. A charge of open idolatry is
surprising in the post-exilic period. It might hint that both the oracle
of salvation contained in vv. 9f. and the oracle of judgment contained
in vv. 11–12a were simply taken over from tradition. As in vv. 9f, the
oracle of judgment is adapted to its context by means of an addition
(v. 12b) which shows clear traces of the language of Deuteronomy.

[13–16a] The juxtaposition of 'my servants' and 'but you' refers back to the same words in v. 9b and 11a. It is therefore deliberate, in order to join together vv. 9f. and vv. 11f. As a result, vv. 13–16a also go with what comes before them (as opposed to Elliger and others). The fact that the words of the introduction, 'therefore the Lord Yahweh has said thus', are here repeated is now more fully explained. In vv. 9f. and 11f. what effects the separation between the two groups are words of salvation and of judgment, taken respectively from tradition. But v. 13 represents the newly-spoken oracle which takes in both groups together. This is the reason why the things announced in vv. 9–12 and vv. 13–16a do not exactly square. As has often been pointed out, this is particularly evident with the oracles of judgment on the faithless. In v. 12 they are to be destroyed in war. But in vv. 13f. they are to be hungry and thirsty, and to weep and cry out. For the announcement of a salvation or a destruction to which effect is given in the realm of history, vv. 13–16a substitute an announcement of blessing and curse (cf. Deut. 27f.). Part of the responsibility for this change is borne by the fact that the announcement has at one and the same time two different frames of reference (see above)—from of old blessing and cursing spoken simultaneously could at once apply to two different persons or sets of persons.

This new form of simultaneous announcement of salvation and its opposite with its basis in blessing and cursing became very important in the post-exilic period. It continued on into Jesus' proclamation, as we see from Matt. 25. It was also the source from which the twofold judgment of the day of judgment derived.

Chapter 65.16b–25

The former troubles are forgotten

16b Because the former troubles are forgotten
   and have vanished from my eyes.
17 For behold: I create new heavens and a new earth.
   The former things shall not be remembered
   or come into mind.
18 But be glad and rejoice for ever
   [over]ᵃ that which I create.
      ᵃ Supply ʿal before ʾᵃšer.

For behold, I create Jerusalem a rejoicing,
and her people a joy;
19 I rejoice in Jerusalem,
and am glad in my people.
No more is heard in it
the sound of weeping and the sound of a cry.
20 No more is there [there]ᵃ an infant that lives but a few days
or an old man who does not fill out his days,
but the youngest shall die a hundred years old,
and he who does not attain to this is held accursed.
21 They build houses and inhabit them;
they plant vineyards and enjoy their fruit.
They do not build and another inhabit,
do not plant and another enjoy.
For like the days of a tree shall the days of my people be,
and my chosen shall long eat the work of their hands.
23 They labour not in vain,
or bear children for sudden terror;
for they are the offspring of the blessed of Yahweh,
and their children live with them.
24 Before they call I answer,
while they are yet speaking I hear.
25 Wolf and lamb shall feed together,
and the lion eat straw like the ox [   ]ᵇ.
They do not hurt or destroy
in all my holy mountain, says Yahweh'.

The part of the chapter at which we have already looked, vv. 1–16a, had its lines laid down by the contrast between the faithless and God's servants, and the future awaiting both. The subject in vv. 16b–25 is another contrast, that of the troubles of the past (v. 16b) and the salvation to come (vv. 17–25). Verses 17–19a announce the latter and vv. 19b–25 give a description of it.

[16b] The word 'because' at the beginning cannot possibly connect with what goes before it. Had it been causal, it would have had a summons to rejoice, etc. coming before it. In that case, the structure would be the same as in 60.1 and 2. Such a summons to rejoice does in fact ensue, in v. 18a. The text there is generally changed, the imperfect being read instead of the imperative. There is no need for this. Transfer the summons to rejoice to the beginning, and this right away makes sense of 'because' in v. 16b. A summons to rejoice would also be very much in keeping with the whole idea contained in vv.

ᵃ Read *šām*.
ᵇ 'And dust shall be the serpent's food' is a gloss.

16b–25. The words, 'the former troubles are forgotten', echo 43.18f. There, too, God's new creation also follows on, although the frame of reference is somewhat different. Here, the former troubles have vanished from God's eyes, meaning that God, who was their author, now wills that they should come to an end.

[17–18] In Deutero-Isaiah the verb *bārā'* was used in the sense of the new creation (cf. 41.20). Here, too, 'new' means the miraculous transformation, as again in Deutero-Isaiah (42.9; 43.19; 48.6). The words, 'I create anew the heavens and the earth', do not imply that heaven and earth are to be destroyed and in their place a new heaven and a new earth created—this is apocalyptic, Rev. 21.1; II Peter 3.13, and the addition in Isa. 66.22. Instead, the world, designated as 'heaven and earth', is to be miraculously renewed.

Verse 17b means the same thing as v. 16b; people are no longer to think of the troubles of the past. Here, too, the background of 'the former things shall not be remembered' is 43.18a. In 43.18, however, the meaning is that the former saving acts of God will be forgotten in view of the tremendous new saving act. This taking over of words of Deutero-Isaiah, while giving them a different sense because the context is different, is exactly the same as what is done in chs. 60–62.

[18] When the summons to rejoice (v. 18a) is transferred to the beginning, before v. 16b, v. 18b follows directly on v. 17, and this makes it clearer that the reference in v. 17a is to the change to be wrought on Jerusalem and its population. Jerusalem and Judah are the only subjects concerned in the renewal of the world. We today of course feel that the gulf is too great—announcing a new heaven and a new earth, and then representing the new salvation as for Jerusalem alone. The commentaries draw attention to this odd inconsistency. Either v. 17a is the language of exaggeration and the speaker was not conscious of the inconsistency, or else we have to reckon with another possibility, namely, that through the placing of v. 17a at the beginning and v. 25 at the end, an announcement of salvation for Jerusalem and Judah has been made into a description such as we find in apocalyptic. For these two verses, at the beginning and at the end, are the only two which do not suit the description of a new salvation for Jerusalem.

At all events, the announcement of the fresh creation of heaven and earth—a basic idea in later apocalyptic—is oddly isolated here. Either the author of vv. 16b–25 only meant it to be taken figuratively, as the language of exaggeration, or else at some later date it was taken from a context unknown to ourselves and added to the present section along with v. 25.

The joy which the new Jerusalem is designed to have is a reciprocal one. It is not just that the inhabitants of Jerusalem are summoned to rejoice: God, too, can take joy in his new creation; cf. 62.5, 'so your God rejoices over you'. There can be no doubt that Deutero-Isaiah is also the origin of the accumulation of words for joy.

[19b–24] Verse 19b marks the transition from the announcement to the description. In the new Jerusalem transformed by God's new creation and among its inhabitants there is to be no more making lament or weeping (v. 19b). There is also no more premature death (v. 20), because they are the blessed of Yahweh (v. 23b), and the link with God never again breaks (v. 24). Verse 25 adds that even the animals are to live in peace.

[19b] The statement that weeping and crying are no more to be heard in the Jerusalem which God miraculously transforms may be a deliberate contradiction of Jeremiah's announcement of judgment which said that the sounds of joy would cease in Jerusalem (7.34; 16.9; 25.10). Something of the same is said—although this goes much further—in the Isaiah apocalypse, 25.8: 'God will wipe away tears from all faces'; cf. Rev. 21.4. 51.11 (= 35.10) is a direct prototype of our passage. There the thing described is the return, here a permanent condition.

[20] In the Old Testament life is fulfilled life. But only if it is not cut off prematurely is it such. Thus long life, life lived to the end, is to be everyone's in the era of salvation. In this respect there is an even clearer difference from the Isaiah apocalypse. Unlike Isa. 25.8, even in the era of salvation death still remains. It is only premature death, death that cuts off in the midst of the years or at the beginning, that is no more. Duhm tripped over the last words in v. 20, 'and the sinner a hundred years old shall be accursed', and he wondered what they meant. Köhler found that (according to Buhl) here the participle *haḥōṭē*' can only mean 'the one who does not reach (it)'. The words thus mean that if a person happens not to attain to a hundred years, there must be some exceptional reason for this.

[21–22] There is to be no more work that is vain and pointless. We have already met with verses like these in 62.8f. They did not fit into their context there, but here they do. This is undoubtedly where they stood to begin with. They make it perfectly clear that the era of salvation as here envisaged is in no sense thought of as lying beyond

space and time. It remains within the limitations imposed by existence in history, part of which is work. This work was just of the kind
with which the speaker's own circumstances had made him familiar,
building houses, sowing fields and planting vineyards, and tending
these. The only difference now is that the worker is assured of the
fruits of his labour. This is the voice of experience, of the ordinary
man living in a land constantly overrun by enemies, the bitter
experience of men living under enemy occupation. We can see that a
very special stress is laid on this element in the picture; v. 21 is
repeated in the negative in v. 22a, v. 22b gathers up v. 20 and vv.
21f., and then v. 23 again repeats, 'they labour not in vain.' Compare what Jeremiah says in his letter to the exiles, 29.5. A few brief
words give a touching filling out of the picture: the same thing holds
true for the women's 'labour': 'they do not bear children for sudden
terror.' The meaning is perfectly clear. It is what many a mother
today thinks of as she wonders about what the future has in store for
the child whom she has borne.

[23b–24] In this era of salvation men and women are 'the blessed
of Yahweh'. In v. 22 they are called 'my people' and 'my chosen'
(cf. 61.9). And the length of their life is likened to that of a tree (cf.
Job 14). The thing thus announced is simply a blessed existence round
which God has set peace as a fence. Yet part of this, indeed the most
important part of it, consists in the fact that the footing on which
men stand with God is a sound one. And this is not here expressed in
any terms that denote a state of 'blessedness', but by saying that the
dialogical relationship is a sound one. When men call upon God, they
are given an answer, cf. 58.9 and Job 14.15. With this access to God
via word and answer, there is free access to the wellspring of life.

[25] The passage might well have ended with v. 24. Verse 25
follows on somewhat abruptly and does not entirely suit what
precedes it. In vv. 19b–24 the conditions of life are those of present
historical existence, and they are only transcended in v. 17a and v.
25. These verses alone speak of a transformation of conditions in the
present world, whereas in vv. 19b–24 the transformation is from
trouble to salvation for Judah and Jerusalem. In addition, v. 25 also
occurs in Isa. 11.6–9. There, the peace among the animal-world is
depicted with broader strokes of the brush and in greater detail; it is
generally assumed that 65.25 is a quotation from Isa. 11. If both v.
17b and v. 25 represent later additions to this oracle of salvation, this
lets us see an important step in the transition from prophecy of

salvation addressed to Judah and Israel to the description of a transformed world such as we find in apocalyptic.

In conclusion, what is the relationship between vv. 16b–25 and
65.1–16a and also to Trito-Isaiah in general? As opposed to 65.1–16a,
the verses have this in common with chs. 60–62—they proclaim
salvation to the whole of the nation; vv. 16b–25 make not the slightest
suggestion of any cleavage. Another indication that vv. 16b–25 go
along with chs. 60–62 are the striking links with Deutero-Isaiah's
proclamation (vv. 16b and 17b with 43.18a; v. 19b with 51.11),
with the concepts and terms which he employs (new creation, the
former things, summonses to joy, designations for the chosen people),
and with the whole feel of his style of writing. None of these characteristics applies to 65.1–16a. There can be no doubt that 65.16b–25
forms part of the nucleus of Trito-Isaiah's proclamation (57.14–21;
60–62). And, as the doublet to 62.8f. (65.21ff.) still shows, 65.16b–25
may once have formed the direct continuation of chs. 60–62.

Chapter 66.1–4

Heaven is my throne

Thus says Yahweh:
1 Heaven is my throne,
   and the earth my footstool;
   where then is the house which you might build for me,
   where is the place where I might rest?
2 All these things my hand has made,
   and all these things are [mine]ᵃ,   says Yahweh.

But this is the man to whom I look, he that is humble and contrite in
      heart,
and trembles at my word.

3 He who slaughters the ox—kills a man;
   he who sacrifices a sheep—breaks a dog's neck;
   he who presents a cereal offering—it is swine's blood;
   he who offers incense—he blesses the idol.

ᵃ With Vss. read *wᵉlī hāyū.*

As they choose their own ways
and take pleasure in their abominations,
4 so I choose affliction for them
and bring their fears upon them.

Because, when I called, no one answered,
when I spoke, they did not listen;
they did what is evil in my eyes, ·
they chose that in which I do not delight.

Verses 1–4 go together, without, however, being a closely-knit
unit. Verses 1–2 form a complete and rounded-off utterance, with the
building of the temple as their subject. Next comes, in vv. 3–4a, an
utterance concerning sacrifice, which resembles a prophetic word of
doom. Verse 4b and c are an addition, the words being the same as
65.12b and c.

[1–2] There has been great debate about the meaning of this
utterance. But we arrive on firm ground once we recognize that vv.
1a, 2a and 2b are verses such as can be found in the Psalter. They are
praise put into the first person (frequent in Deutero-Isaiah). More
closely defined, they represent the motif found in descriptive psalms
of praise: God is seated on high—and looks far down (Ps. 113.5f.)
This explains first of all how v. 2b, which at first sight seems abrupt,
does in fact go with v. 1a. It is its necessary supplement, 'the heaven
is my throne—and I look down upon him that is humble.' Secondly,
this removes any doubt that the words 'all these things' at the
beginning of v. 2 refer to heaven and earth in v. 1. Thirdly, it
establishes the fact that 66.1f. are an example of the same combination
of the language of the psalms with that of the prophets as we find in a
number of psalms, in particular Ps. 50, whose subject-matter, too, is
parallel to that of the present verses.

But if this is so, it rules out any idea that the verses represent
polemic against the building of a particular temple, whether that of
the Samaritans or of some other schismatics. Instead, they are as
general as the normal language used in the Psalms. Muilenburg
offers an extremely good conspectus of the interpretations hitherto
suggested, and the reader is referred to this. He comes to the same
conclusion as I do. For heaven as God's throne, see Pss. 11.4; 103.19;
Isa. 40.22. Elsewhere God's footstool is the ark (Ps. 132.7, etc.): this is
the only passage where it is the earth. A temple cannot contain God's
majesty: this is also said in I Kings 8.27: 'Behold, heaven and the

highest heavens cannot contain thee; how much less this house that I have built!' These words from the Deuteronomic account of the prayer at the consecration of the temple may come from about the same time as Isa. 66.1f. Compare also II Sam. 7.5f. These passages are sufficient to show that Isa. 66.1–2 are not entirely solitary in the Old Testament. Volz is correct in saying that this utterance was made shortly after the return in order to oppose a way of thinking which believed that salvation was entirely dependent on the building of the new temple (Hag. 2.19). It is important that we should be aware that Haggai's proclamation that the completion of the building of the temple would usher in the era of salvation here had a voice raised against it, one that found itself unable to approve of the idea that salvation should be so exclusively tied to the rebuilding. But the numerous commentaries which say that the verses represent the contrast of spiritual worship and formal worship do not, in my view, reflect what the man who spoke them was trying to say, since v. 2b, the verse taken from the psalm, is expanded in by 'and trembles at my word' (so also in 66.5 and Ezra 9.4; 10.3). The fact that the passage is set within a frame of words taken from the Psalter (vv. 1a and 2b), as well as the strong emphasis which v. 2b puts on God's word, are suggestive of the new form of worship which had grown up during the exile, a prototype of worship by means of the spoken word which was the origin of the synagogue. Where the essential things in worship are God's word and the response of the community that gives him praise, the holy place, God's house, loses its status as worship's indispensible precondition.

[3] The problem here is, how are we to conceive the relationship between the two unconnected, juxtaposed participles in the four lines of v. 3? The formulation is odd, and its background may possibly be the language of a *tōrā* on sacrifice (Elliger). There are two possible ways of taking the relationship: (1) 'he who sacrifices a sheep is *as* one who breaks a dog's neck', and (2) 'he who sacrifices a sheep is *also* one who breaks a dog's neck'. If the first is what is meant, it is a condemnation of the legitimate sacrificial procedures by putting them on a par with the worst sort of anal cult; the one is as loathsome as the other. Such a condemnation of legitimate sacrifice goes far beyond any other critical statements about it in the whole Old Testament (Muilenburg). But to adopt the alternative explanation is to make an odd divorce between v. 3 and vv. 1f. In this the subject is something entirely different. This is polemic against a form of

syncretism. The regular sacrifices to Yahweh are still offered (the four participles at the beginning of each line), but loathsome anal cults are practised along with them. There was the offering of human sacrifice (Jer. 7.31; 19.2–6; Ezek. 23.39) and of dogs. On this Muilenburg comments: 'According to Justin (*History of the World*, XIX, 1, 10) Darius forbade the Carthaginians to offer human victims in sacrifice or to eat the flesh of dogs.' The fact that the present enumeration resembles 65.3b–5 (and v. 7) in mentioning the offering of swine suggests that both passages have the same class of cultic malpractices in mind. *Mazkīr* in the last line of v. 3 is an abbreviation; properly, 'he who makes a memorial offering of incense'. The second part of the line means literally, 'blesses the evil power'. In 65.1ff., the 'unfaithful' are the people who go in for such cultic malpractices; those condemned here are 'those who take pleasure in such abominations', and they have God's judgment announced them. The announcement, vv. 3b and 4a, is in the regular form and is very different in style from the series of participles contained in v. 3a. One has the impression that, protracting as their every word does—'as they . . . so I'—the inter-relationship between guilt and punishment, vv. 3b and 4a represent a later addition to the extremely terse series of participles. The motive would be a desire to give v. 3a the form of a prophetic oracle of doom. Verses 4b and c agree almost word for word with 65.12b and c. The language is manifestly Deuteronomic, and the allegation a perfectly general one. 65.12, too, has the feel of an addition. In both places rehearsals during worship of such words as these against cultic malpractices may have been responsible for their addition. They are stereotyped, and represent something like a refrain in them. This would also show that we are now not dealing with prophecy of doom in its old sense. This is polemic in worship against cultic abuses dressed up as the old announcement of doom.

CHAPTER 66.5

Your brethren who hate you

5   Hear the word of Yahweh,
    you who tremble at his word:

    'Your brethren who hate you
    and thrust you out for my name's sake,
    say, "[Let Yahweh be glorified],[a]
    that we may see your joy." '

    'But it is they who shall be put to shame.'

This fifth verse of the final chapter forms a unit in itself. Quite
obviously, the summons to hear in v. 5a marks the beginning of a
fresh utterance. But at the same time, as is made plain by the many
similar opening words in prophetic oracles, there can be no mistake
that v. 6a, too, starts another fresh utterance. If we are to understand
v. 5, we have to take it entirely by itself. It will shed light on an entire
strand of oracles in Trito-Isaiah.

While v. 5 is modelled on a prophetic announcement of doom, this
is very much transformed. The announcement comes in the closing
words, 'but it is they who shall be put to shame'. It is intended as an
announcement of salvation for the people addressed in v. 5a, 'who
tremble at his word'. This means the devout or those who are faithful
to Yahweh, and they are told that their opponents, 'your brethren
who hate you', who at present mock them and 'thrust them out', will
inevitably be put to shame. Nowhere else is the state of affairs between the two parties so clearly brought out.

The people addressed are those 'who tremble at his word'. We have
met with this designation already, at the end of 66.2. Since its only
other occurrence is in Ezra 9.4 and 10.3, it must be a designation
of the devout used in worship, but current only for a short time after
the return and thereafter completely ousted by the term 'those who
fear God'. The emphasis put upon God's word is important. Since the

---

[a] Read *yikkābēd* for *yikbad*.

others' mockery relates to a specific word, the proclamation of salvation, the reference is presumably to such as still believed in this.

'Your brethren who hate you say': this states quite clearly that the two parties are still members of the same community. Glahn is right when he says that 'the "hated" and "persecuted" are fellow-countrymen opposed by fellow-countrymen . . . They are next-door neighbours, in the same towns and villages'. The very fact that the devout still call their opponents brothers shows that the cleavage in the nation which eventually had such tragic results was only at its start. So far they are not designated in terms implying condemnation, such as transgressors, godless, etc. Further, there is no suggestion here that they are transgressors or godless. Thus we cannot be sure whether 66.5 refers to the same people as those accused in 65.1ff. and 66.3 of cultic malpractices. It may be so. But we cannot presume it offhand. One thing only is said of them here—they hate and thrust out those who in piety hold to the word of God. The oracle itself does not state the reason for their hatred. In all probability it reflects only the first stages of the growing tension between the devout and the transgressors. The thing that particularly suggests this is the forceful way in which the opponents of the devout display their superiority—'they thrust you out'. In the Talmud this word is the technical term for excommunication, exclusion from the synagogue. In the present passage it is not yet so; no more is said than that they are 'thrust out' or 'thrust forth'. The substantiation, 'for my name's sake', can only mean that, unlike their opponents, the devout range themselves on the side of God and his word. Connect this with the quotation which follows, and the reference may be to continuing belief in the prophecies. The clearest statement of the situation comes in the quotation which follows, spoken in mockery. It is in full accord with the way in which his opponents mocked Isaiah: 'Let him make haste, let him speed his work, that we may see it' (5.19), the only difference being that Isaiah's announcement is one of doom, and here it is of salvation. The words, 'let Yahweh be glorified', may have a connection with 60.1ff., and 'that we may see your joy' one with 61.10. Why is the object of mockery and hatred the holding fast to the prophecies? This is hard to say. Maybe the pious who awaited the time when salvation should come refused demands which their opponents deemed to be more urgent.

A final note on v. 5. The utterance presumes that signs of a cleavage were beginning to appear in Judah in the early post-exilic period. It is a word of salvation designed to give support and encouragement to the people who held fast to Yahweh's words and, in particular, to the announcements previously made that God was to intervene and bring in the era of salvation. So far, however, the cleavage had not led to the formation of different parties. This utterance cannot be contemporaneous with chs. 60–62. These show no trace of such a cleavage. But v. 5 does presume the publication, and acceptance, of a prophecy of salvation, and in all probability this was Trito-Isaiah's (chs. 60–62). In this case, 66.5 represents a stage which came sometime after the publication of Trito-Isaiah's announcement of salvation, but before the parting of the ways between the two groups within the nation.

CHAPTER 66.6–16

Rejoice with Jerusalem

6 Loud uproar from the city,
  a loud voice from the temple,
  the voice of Yahweh,
  bringing retribution to his enemies

7 Before she who was in labour gave birth,
  before her pain came upon her, she was delivered of a son.
8 Who has heard such a thing? Who has seen a thing of the kind?
  Shall a land be brought forth in one day?
  Shall a nation be born in a moment?
  For as soon as Zion was in labour
  she brought forth sons.

9 Shall I bring to the birth and not cause to bring forth?, says Yahweh,
  Shall I cause to bring forth and shut the womb?, says your God.[a]

10 Rejoice with Jerusalem
  and be glad for her, all you who love her.
  Exult with her in joy,
  all you who mourn over her.

[a] On vv. 7ff. see C. M. Edsman, 'The Body and Eternal Life (Isa. 66, 7–8)', *Horae Soederblomianae* (1946), pp. 33–104.

11   That you may suck and be satisfied
     with her consoling [breast],[a]
     that you may drink deeply and refresh yourselves
     from the abundance of her glory.

12   For thus says Yahweh:
     Behold, I extend prosperity to her like a river,
     and the splendour of the nations like an overflowing stream.
     Your infants shall be carried upon her hip,
     dandled upon her knees.
13   As one whom his mother comforts,
     so I will comfort you.
     And you shall be comforted in Jerusalem.
14   You shall see, and your heart shall rejoice,
     your bones shall flourish like the grass,
     Yahweh's hand shall be known upon his servants,
     and [his][b] wrath upon his enemies.

15   For behold, Yahweh comes [like][c] fire,
     his chariots like the storm wind,
     to render his anger in fury,
     his rebuke with flames of fire.

16   For by fire Yahweh judges [the whole earth][d]
     and by his sword all flesh,
     and those slain by Yahweh shall be many.

The difficulty here is due to two transitions which are hard to explain, that from v. 6 to v. 7 and that from v. 14 to vv. 15f. It is reflected in the numerous attempts that have been made to smooth them out or elucidate them. But the difficulty can be very simply resolved. Verses 7–14, which form a unit and are obviously part of the nucleus of Trito-Isaiah, have been set within the framework (vv. 6 and 15f.) of an epiphany in which God comes to judge the world. This has a parallel in Deut. 33, where the 'Blessing of Moses' is also set within the framework of an epiphany (vv. 2 and 26f.). The reason for giving the same treatment to one of Trito-Isaiah's utterances of salvation can be easily seen if it is remembered that the same thing was done with chs. 60–62; they had the judgment of the nations appended to them (63.1–6). Such framing gives us a clear view of the

---

[a] Read *miššad*.
[b] Read *wᵉzaʿmō*.
[c] Read *kāʾēš*.
[d] With LXX supply *ʾēt-kol-hāʾāreṣ*.

first step from Trito-Isaiah's post-exilic prophecy of salvation to apocalyptic which was just entering the lists. While this apocalyptic links on to Trito-Isaiah's proclamation of salvation, it interprets the latter as signifying a final large-scale divine intervention in which the other nations are destroyed, and which, for Israel, creates salvation in perpetuity.

[6] The verse depicts the uproar of a battle in which Yahweh brings retribution to his enemies, the speaker being a spectator at some distance off. The same word for 'uproar' (*šā'ōn*) is found in the same context in Isa. 13.4; 'Hark! a tumult on the mountains as of a great multitude doing battle!' Here, too, the verse introduces God's judgment upon the nations. The same expression for 'to bring retribution' occurs in 59.18 in the context of a community lament; 'he repays wrath to his adversaries and bring retribution to his enemies' (cf. also Jer. 51.6). These two parallels make it clear that the subject here is a divine judgment on foreign enemies of Israel. So also Muilenburg, who also refers to Joel 3.9–17, especially v. 16: 'the great theophany of the day of the Lord is implied'. In v. 6 the mention of the temple only makes sense on the presumption that it had already been rebuilt (see also Duhm).

[7–9] As in Isa. 49.20–23 and John 16.20ff., birth is here used as imagery for the advent of the era of salvation. But here the imagery is not simply set alongside the thing to which it is likened. It has been pondered upon, and as a result considerably altered. Once again we see that, while the basis is the proclamation of Deutero-Isaiah, the way in which it differs from this is perfectly plain. This simple imagery is developed along two lines. First, this is miraculous birth: the birth and the beginnings of the birth-pangs are simultaneous (v. 7). Secondly, this is unprecedented—'who had heard such a thing?' (v. 8a); what this means is explained in v. 8b: 'for as soon as Zion was in labour she brought forth sons.'

Verses 7–8 bear the stamp of pure announcement of salvation— the land of Judah has her exiled children all of a sudden restored to her, and this by a miracle, with no birth-pangs at all, that is to say, without wars or other dire events. But v. 9 appends a kind of disputation, a disputation of the scepticism that has ceased to think that the salvation will be a complete one. The idea that things would never come to actual birth has a question mark put on it. God has already begun his fresh saving work on Israel's behalf (the first return of 538): shall he not bring it to its completion? This tells us perhaps better than anything else of the conditions in which Trito-Isaiah delivered his message. The imagery shows that Deutero-Isaiah's salvation had come to a stop half-way along the road. But now at this point begins Trito-Isaiah's proclamation, that the salvation is bound to come to birth, for it is the work of God.

[10–11] As a response to the message there is a summons to rejoice, one very closely dependent on Deutero-Isaiah. In the case of Trito-Isaiah we have already found such summonses to rejoice in 61.10 and 65.18 (cf. also 62.5b). But in both instances there was a slight change from Deutero-Isaiah. The same thing is to be found here in 66.10f. With Deutero-Isaiah Zion and his people are one. But here they are separate entities. Characteristically, Trito-Isaiah's summons to rejoice is made to 'all you who mourn over her', cf. 61.2 etc. The over-drawing of the imagery in v. 11 is also typical. As is so often the case with Trito-Isaiah, the turn towards salvation is reinforced by imagery suggestive of abundance. It means no more than 'that in order that you may share in the consolations which she is to experience'. Here, too, cf. 61.2. The word for 'to refresh oneself' occurs also in 55.2 and 58.14. *ziz* for udder or breast is only found here.

[12–14] We can now see the way in which vv. 7–14 are built up. The utterance begins with the message of salvation, vv. 7ff., verses 10f. summon people to rejoice in it, while vv. 12ff. merely give a fuller description of what this breakthrough to salvation will mean for Zion.

The likening of the salvation to a river is similar to 48.18. Gen. 39.21 uses the verb 'to extend' in exactly the same way of the extending of favour. The bringing of the riches of the nations to Zion is as in 60.5: 'the wealth of the nations shall come to you' (cf. 60.13; 61.6), the careful carrying of the children is like 60.4, cf. 49.22. Verse 13, in which the oracle of salvation attains its climax, is of particular importance for Old Testament discourse on the subject of God. 'This is the first time in the Old Testament that the witness borne to Yahweh breaks through the reserve which elsewhere it observes so strictly and associates feminine predications with him. This lends all the greater conviction to what is here said of the passionateness of God's love for those who in sorrow and with humility wait for his salvation' (Kessler). The words, 'and you shall be comforted in Jerusalem', are an explanatory addition. Verse 14a corresponds to 60.5a. The likening of the revival to the springing up of the grass is to be understood against the background of a lament. In anguish the bones waste away (Ps. 31.11 [10]). Similarly, in joy they become green.

[14b] '. . . and his wrath upon his enemies': Duhm takes this to refer to 'punishment of the Samaritans', others to that of the faithless. But throughout there is never any suggestion that the promise applies to only one set of people or one part of the nation. It applies to the entire chosen people, as always in Trito-Isaiah. Once it is recognized that the subject of vv. 15f. is God's judgment on the nations, then the last line of v. 14 can only have been meant as transition to this.

[15–16] The words 'for behold' at the beginning of v. 15 link on to v. 6 (see above). Details about God's judgment on the nations there announced (v. 6) are now given here. The key-words are, 'Yahweh comes'. What is described is God's drawing near to execute judgment on the nations. Among its concomitants are 'his chariots', which sweep on like the storm wind. His drawing near has its power given it by the power of his anger (v. 15b), and its goal is a combat to annihilate 'all flesh', 'the whole earth'.

The basis of these verses is the old description of an epiphany. It depicts God's drawing near to bring his chosen people help and to smite the enemies who oppress it (see above, p. 104). Here the emphasis is put on the annihilation of the enemies. Unlike what we find in the old epiphanies, these are not the various specific enemies who oppressed Israel at different times. They are the sum-total of the other nations, whose combined might is the last enemy, and God is to destroy them. The old epiphany whose purpose was to deliver Israel has been transformed into one whose import is the judgment of the world. There is a close similarity between the present description of God's advent to judge the nations and the one given in Isa. 30.27ff., and it is akin to the introductions to the oracles against the nations in Jer. 25 and Isa. 13. The various features in the description occur frequently. For the 'storm wind' in a similar context, see Isa. 29.6, for 'his chariots', Hab. 3.8; Ps. 68.18 (17); cf. Jer. 4.13; Isa. 17.12ff. Several of the concepts are found in Isa. 30.27ff.; in the old epiphanies Yahweh is the one who rides upon the clouds (Pss. 18.10 [9]; 68.34 [33]). God's judgment is upon 'all flesh' as in Jer. 25.21. Since there these words introduce the oracles against the foreign nations, there can be no doubt that here it also refers to God's judgment upon them. The final words are reminiscent of 63.1–6.

CHAPTER 66.17

(going together with 65.3b–5, 7b)

17　those who sanctify and purify themselves to go into the garden
　　behind one in the midst (?),
　　eating swine's flesh and [reptiles]ᵃ and mice,
　　[their thoughts and their deeds]ᵇ shall come to an end together,
　　　　says Yahweh.

Although vv. 17–24 are frequently called an appendix due to a
redactor, this is not accurate. The passage is a compilation of various
units, each of which has to be evaluated in isolation from the rest.
Verse 17 is an independent unit. It has no natural connection with
what comes before and after it. On the other hand, it so obviously
goes along with 65.3b–5 and 7 that it should be taken as a later
expansion of the latter verses' description of cultic malpractices.
Kessler made a plausible conjecture; 'should it not be put in after
65.5a?'.

As in 65.3b, the case is one of a cult practised in the 'gardens'.
66.5 also speaks of particular consecratory rites for this cult, and also
of the sacrifice of unclean animals. In addition to swine's flesh
(65.4b) we here have reptiles and mice. But we also find an essentially
new feature: the sanctifying and purifying is undertaken 'behind one
in the midst'. Unfortunately, the text is uncertain. 'One' could also
be read as a feminine, which would imply a priestess. Verse 17 is the
main plank of Volz's thesis that mystery cults are here described.
'This recalls the mystagogue of the Eleusinian mysteries or the *pater
patrum* of the worshippers of Mithras who initiated the members of the
community into all the secrets.' He is therefore forced to make the
verse very late. This is improbable, since a similar description in
Ezek. 8.7ff. also has the words 'one in the midst'. Ezekiel describes
cultic malpractices in use directly before the fall of Jerusalem.
Therefore, both here and in Isa. 65, we should think of a revival of
such cults in the early post-exilic period. For other possibilities, see
Muilenburg *ad loc.*

ᵃ For *šeqeṣ* read *šereṣ*.
ᵇ 'Their thoughts and their deeds' should be transferred from v. 18 to v. 17.

CHAPTER 66.18–24

The final portion of the chapter, vv. 18–24, presents yet another great difficulty. Editors are in the main unanimous that the passage does not come from the author of chs. 60–62, but is a late addition. But, is it a unity? Verse 21 is the place where the difficulty is clearest. Who are the people meant by 'and some of them also I take?' Taking the words by themselves, there seems to be no way of getting round interpreting them in the sense of 'not only from the Israelites, but from the Gentiles as well'. In spite of this the majority of editors have referred them to the Israelites. Their reason for so doing is the verse which comes before them (v. 20), whose subject is the Israelites. In this case, the meaning would be that 'also from those brought back by the heathen as an offering I take some and make them priests and levites'. An objection to this is that some of those brought back might well be priests and levites already, but they could not now for the first time be assumed as such. But if it is impossible to relate v. 21 to v. 20, it can only be related to vv. 18f. In this case, vv. 18f. and 21 form one independent unit, and vv. 20, 22ff. another, the latter being a deliberate correction of the unprecedent statement made in the former. One can very well understand that to orthodox circles in the post-exilic period the announcement made in vv. 18f. and 21 would sound intolerable and therefore in need of amending! Thus, right at the end of the utterances collected in Trito-Isaiah, we are given testimony, both striking and moving, to the fact that, after the return, Israel had no one voice about the fate to overtake the Gentiles on the last day.

Verses 18f. and 21 are governed by the idea of the move out to the Gentiles throughout the world, a missionary move which is destined to reach them all. But vv. 20, 22ff. are governed by the idea of the move towards Zion and Judah, which are to be the scene where the division is made as between eternal adoration and eternal annihilation. The final section of Trito-Isaiah gives an abrupt confrontation between universalism and particularism. The Old Testament never again brings them into harmony.

66.18, 19, 21.   My Glory among the Nations

18   But I am coming [   ]ᵃ
to gather all nations and tongues;
and they come and see my glory.

19   And I set up a sign among them,
and from them I will send survivors to the nations,
to Tarshish, [Put]ᵇ and Lud,
[Mesech and Rosh],ᶜ Tubal and Javan,
to the islands afar off,
that have not heard tidings of me
or seen my glory;
and they declare my glory among the nations.

21   And some of them also I take
as priests [and]ᵈ levities, says Yahweh.

Bibliography: G. Rinaldi, 'Gli "scampati" di Is. 66.18–22', *Memorial A Gelin*, Éditions Xavier Mappus, Le Puy, 1961, pp. 109–18.

---

[18] The opening words, 'but I am coming', relate directly to the words 'he comes' in v. 15 of the epiphany. The present speaker means that God's advent to judge the world is far from being the final act. It is followed by something else, a gathering for which there is no precedent. God's action in gathering, which elsewhere refers exclusively to the dispersed of Israel, is here extended to include all nations and tongues. This utterance makes God's salvation truly universal. The expression, 'all nations and tongues', is characteristic 'of later apocalypse and the New Testament, Zech. 8.23; Dan. 3.4, 7, 29; 6.25' (Muilenburg). The purpose of their being gathered is that they should come and see God's glory. It is hardly possible to pinpoint the meaning of *kābōd* here: it is God's proof of his sovereign

---

ᵃ See p. 422, n. 2.
ᵇ Read *pūt*.
ᶜ Read *mešek weroš* with LXX.
ᵈ Supply *we*.

power as attested by all that he does. It may perhaps mean the same thing as what was said in the trial-speeches of Deutero-Isaiah—God proves himself to be the one and only God as over against the gods of the nations.

[19] God sets up a sign (DSS plural) among the nations. It could mean a signpost showing those whom God sends the way. But the sign could also be the sending of the messengers itself. The 'survivors' are those preserved from the judgment of the nations. This links the passage with one of Deutero-Isaiah's (45.20–25), where the 'survivors of the nations' (v. 22) are invited to participate in salvation. The author of the present passage knew what that one implied (see *ad loc.*) And here he takes the earlier announcement a step further. The 'survivors of the nations', there invited to be participants in the salvation and to realize that Yahweh, the God of Israel, is the only true God, are here made into his ambassadors, missionaries sent to the far islands in order to proclaim God's glory among the other nations. This is the first sure and certain mention of mission as we today employ the term—the sending of individuals to distant peoples in order to proclaim God's glory among them. This completely corresponds to the mission of the apostles when the church first began. One is amazed at it: here, just as the Old Testament is coming to its end, God's way is already seen as leading from the narrow confines of the chosen people out into the wide, whole world. The annihilation of all the other nations in a great world-judgment—no, this is not the final word. But equally, it is not that they all journey to Zion and are absorbed into the community there. The final thing is the way taken by the word, borne by the messengers of his glory, to the peoples who are not Israel, all the nations in the world. This not only agrees with what Deutero-Isaiah said in 45.20–25. It also agrees with the places in the servant songs where the Servant is appointed to be a light to the Gentiles, and is destined to bring God's justice to them. There can be no doubt about it: the people who tell the tidings of God's glory are also characterized as witnesses. As those saved from a catastrophe (the 'survivors') and, as saved, having experienced that Yahweh is God, they go to those who have not seen or heard. As his witnesses they can be made into people who proclaim his glory among the nations.

Something still falls to be said about the various nations mentioned in v. 19b. Duhm deletes it, giving this as his reason: 'if the author of this passage is Trito-Isaiah himself, the names of the nations in v. 19

must be regarded as a later addition.' Köhler agrees with him. But if, as we have already seen, this utterance presupposes what is said about the judgment of the nations and represents a strand later than the nucleus of Trito-Isaiah, there is no reason for deleting the list. Duhm draws attention to a similar list in 11.11. The two may be contemporaneous. In its present context it makes the general terms, 'nations' and 'islands', refer to particular places. It has been composed on the basis of Ezekiel, and this is characteristic of the later period. Tarshish (Tartessus) was a Phoenician trading city in Spain, cf. 60.9, and Javan stood for the Ionians of Asia Minor or Greece (Joel 4.6, *BH*). Both are found associated in Ezek. 27.12f. The same is true of Tubal and Mesech (again in Ezek. 38.2 and 39.1). They are probably the same as the Moshi and Tiberani of whom Herodotus speaks, in Assyrian inscriptions Muski and Tabal. They are to the south or south-east of the Black Sea. Put (emendation for Pul) and Lud are peoples in Africa (Gen. 10.6, 13; Ezek. 27.10; 30.5). In place of *qešet* Duhm suggested reading *rōš*, since it stands alongside Mesech and Tubal in Ezek. 38.2 and 39.1. This shows that Trito-Isaiah had no special purpose to serve in giving the list as he did. It simply represents a collocation taken from Ezekiel.

[21] This final verse in the passage is designed to say that the witnesses and messengers from the nations are really just as much a part of the chosen people as those whom they won over by their witness. They are therefore qualified for service in the holy place. Here 'priests and levites' is simply a term equivalent to servants at the holy place.

This is a thing the orthodox never dreamed of—the admission to the innermost circles of priesthood, the prerogative of descent, of heathen! We can well understand why something was added to this. The nations and their future needed to be seen in their proper perspective!

66.20, 22–24 Eternal Worship and Eternal Destruction

20 And they bring all your brethren from all the nations
   as an offering for Yahweh,
   upon horses and chariots and in litters,
   and upon mules and upon dromedaries
   to my holy mountain, to Jerusalem, says Yahweh,

just as the children of Israel bring their cereal offering
in clean vessels to the house of Yahweh.ᵃ

22 For as the new heavens and the new earth,
which I make, shall remain before me, says Yahweh,
so shall your descendants and your name remain.
23 And new moon by new moon, sabbath by sabbath,
all flesh shall come,
to fall down before me, says Yahweh.
24 And as they go forth,
they look on the dead bodies of the men
who rebelled against me.
For their worm shall not die,
their fire shall not be quenched,
and they shall be an abomination for all flesh.

Here the move out to the nations in all remote regions to win them
to the faith has a move in the other direction as its counterpart; all
the nations come to Zion. While there can be no doubt that v. 20
takes up the promise contained in ch. 60 (particularly vv. 4–9) and
reiterates it, still, coming as it now does after v. 19, the promise has a
very different ring about it. Its purpose is to amend an aberration.
God's work upon the distant peoples by the hand of his messengers is
cut down to what it signifies for Israel. One end alone is to be served
by the great move out to the nations of v. 19—the nations are to
bring back all| the Israelites still dwelling in distant places. This
is likened to the Israelites' bringing of offerings in clean vessels to the
temple, a small yet not inconsiderable change as compared with the
same procedure in ch. 60. The term 'offering' at the beginning and
end of v. 20 represents the bringing back of the Israelites as a sacral
procedure: God's holy mountain in Jerusalem and the sacrificial
worship in Yahweh's house upon it are the middle-point of the world;
absolutely everything moves round this middle-point. The thinking
in terms of mission of vv. 18, 19 and 21 is sharply confronted in vv. 20,
22–24 by a sacral mode of thought that is conservative and absolutely

---

ᵃ Perhaps 59.21 should be inserted between v.20 and v.22:

And as for me: this is my covenant with them, says Yahweh:
my spirit which is (laid) upon you.
and my words which I have laid in your mouth,
shall not depart out of your mouth,
or out of the mouth of your children,
or out of the mouth of your children's children,
says Yahweh, from this time forth and for evermore.

static. Verse 22 promises the final, absolute and uninterrupted continuance of the Jewish cultic community ('your descendants and
your name'). Here interest is so closely tied to this community that
the 'new heavens and the new earth' (taken from 65.16) only serve as
an illustrance of its continuance—it is to be as enduring as they.

Verses 23 and 24 develop aspects of this final, everlasting persistence, everlasting worship (v. 23) and everlasting judgment (v. 24).
Exactly the same thing is found at the end of Trito-Zechariah (14.
16ff.), which is closely parallel to the end of Trito-Isaiah. It looks as if
the intention in v. 23 had been to go even further than Zechariah.
With the latter the survivors of the judgment of the nations come up
to Jerusalem year by year for the feast of Tabernacles. But according
to the present passage 'all flesh' (the meaning is as general as in e.g.
Ps. 65.3 [2]) is to worship before Yahweh every new moon and
sabbath. The absolute, uninterrupted continuance of the temple
worship, in which 'all flesh' takes part, is the goal of history. Volz is
right when he speaks of a 'cultic universalism'. But absolute, uninterrupted continuance also holds for the other aspect of it. Here
for the first time, right at the end of the Old Testament, an addition
made to another addition to Trito-Isaiah no longer represents God's
punishment by way of annihilation as a once for all act, but as an
eternal state, perdition. This is the earliest idea of hell as the state of
perdition. It is destined 'for all who have rebelled against me'. This,
too, is to be taken as of universal application, for all of God's enemies
both within Judah, and beyond it. It should be noticed in this
connection that the origin of this idea of everlasting annihilation was
a counterpart to the everlasting worship in the temple on Mount
Zion. It is a perpetuating of something within the temple and something outside of it in which all the movement of history is rigid. The
world and the briskly moving course of history are radically reduced
to the two localities, the mountain and the valley. The latter is the
valley of Hinnom at the foot of Mount Zion, *gēhinnom*, which became
Gehenna, hell, the place of torment. The people who worship before
Yahweh in the temple thereafter go forth and look at the dead bodies
of men whose annihilation is for ever; here this means seeing confirmation of God's victory over all his enemies. These are an 'abomination for all flesh'. The word for 'abomination', *dērā'ôn*, only occurs
again in Dan. 12.2, which suggests that the addition is very late.

The Masora directs that, when this passage is read in the synagogue, v. 23 is to be re-read after v. 24. Many manuscripts also

repeat v. 23 after v. 24, 'in order that the reading in the synagogue should not end with the awful oracle of doom, but with a promise' (Volz).

This shows that, even in the synagogue, and even if they express themselves with reserve, there were people who were critical of this utterance. This is not the only place where the idea is found. It appears in similar terms in Zechariah 14, and then recurs in the apocalypses (e.g., Enoch 27.2f.); Mark 9.43–48 has a number of citations of Is. 66.24. Thus, the idea of eternal destruction must have made a deep impression.

At the end of his book Kessler says of the verse: 'this is a witness to the way in which Yahweh's holiness that judged all men was becoming more rigid in the form of the cultic and legal piety of later days.' One cannot but go a little further than the synagogue's reserved, almost unvoiced, criticism of this addition. The fact that vv. 18f. and 21 and vv. 20, 22ff. stand side by side make it terribly clear that in the post-exilic period what people had to say about the way in which God was going to act upon Israel and upon the other nations lost all unanimity and took two different roads. These two passages show both of them, the second being obviously designed to amend the first. In the light of the New Testament our only course is to agree with the first, the one which proclaims the great missionary move out to the nations. This means, then, that we must be critical of vv. 20, 22ff. But over and above this, an Old Testament critic is bound to say that a theology which ordains one place of eternal annihilation for all God's enemies along with the perpetuation of a worship restricted to one place is alien to the central core of the Old Testament. Here, in the interests of rendering absolute a worship that is tied to a place and in the counterpart which the verses give this, the avowal of God's action in history and towards the people who are travelling onwards, the avowal which was Israel's very foundation, is abandoned.